NATIVE AMERICAN LANDSCAPES

NATIVE AMERICAN LANDSCAPES

An Engendered Perspective

Edited by Cheryl Claassen

The University of Tennessee Press / Knoxville

The paper in this book meets the requirements of American National Standards
Institute / National Information Standards Organization specification Z39.48–1992
(Permanence of Paper). It contains 30 percent post-consumer waste and is certified
by the Forest Stewardship Council.

Library of Congress Cataloging-in-Publication Data

Names: Claassen, Cheryl, 1953- editor of compilation.
Title: Native American landscapes : an engendered perspective /
edited by Cheryl Claassen.
Description: First edition. | Knoxville, TN : University of Tennessee Press, [2016] |
Includes bibliographical references and index.
Identifiers: LCCN 2016004226 | ISBN 9781621902539 (hardcover : alk. paper)
Subjects: LCSH: Feminist archaeology. | Social archaeology. | Indian women—
History—To 500. | Sex role—History—To 1500. | Women, Prehistoric.
Classification: LCC CC72.4 .N37 2016 | DDC 930.1—dc23
LC record available at https://lccn.loc.gov/2016004226

CONTENTS

ILLUSTRATIONS

Figures

Tables

ACKNOWLEDGMENTS

Thanks to the University of Tennessee Press personnel for crafting this book. Thanks also to William Ringle, Thomas White, and Alice Wright for help with the figures in Chapter 9.

NATIVE WOMEN, MEN, AND AMERICAN LANDSCAPES
The Gendered Gaze

Cheryl Claassen

The origin of "landscape" in Western thought and thus archaeology and anthropology is traceable to the appearance of countryside paintings beginning in the early 16th-century canvases of Albrecht Altdorfer (Wood 2014) discussed herein by Jessica Christie (Chapter 8) and Shankari Patel (Chapter 9). The feminist exposé of the mindset behind landscape paintings, is one that renders the land passive, docile, and subjective, the same attitude projected by men onto women. This feminization of country, countryside, and sea was in fact deeply rooted in ancient European beliefs that associated the earth and the sea with female deities and spirits. Ironically, at least from the perspective of Native Americans, the Westerners' feminization of the land and sea signals the (illusory) mental triumph of men over the elements of nature through the use of machines and the concept of capital.

Even a cursory read of American ethnographies indicates that Native peoples unmistakably saw "landscapes" and even gendered elements of landscape. But rather than viewed as passive, rather than subdued by Native men, these landscapes were filled with very active spirits and deities that demanded continual human attention. This mindset forged an unending interaction between spirits and humans that often was one of reciprocity involving gifts. Similar to Europeans, Natives saw many aspects of the landscape to be filled with female spirits, particularly springs, caves, waterfalls, the earth, and the night sky (and in ancient Europe as well). Other topographic and geological features were residences of male spirits. Opportunities to study a gendered or sexed landscape that was not pacified or "conquered" by humans should be valuable to modern ecofeminists and environmentalists who seek to understand both the current Western condition and alternatives to it.

The current Western analysis of landscapes admits a gendered gaze across them—that of men exclusively. It is the thesis of this volume that Native men *and* Native women of the Americas also recognized landscapes as gendered but somewhat differently from each other. Women and men gazed across the landscapes they chose to inhabit with tasks in mind, with rituals in mind, with stories in mind. There were as many places known as there were yet to be discovered. There were places of personal importance and places of family, clan, and tribal importance. This multivocal landscape—the idea that individuals and groups could look at the same landscape but perceive differences in it—is well documented and now established in archaeological thought (e.g., various papers in Ashmore and Knapp 1999, Christie 2009, Rodman 1992, Staller 2008).

The present collection of papers uses exclusively Native American case studies to address multivocality of landscape, particularly those views rendered through *gendered* gazes upon landscapes and gendered activities. This social dimension has rarely been isolated in landscape studies even though the people moving through, using, and imbuing the landscape with definitions, meanings, and places are women and men, girls and boys. (Differently gendered people, although difficult to pinpoint with references, would likewise have a different perspective than either men or women and a case of the heyokas' gaze is given below.)

The one author to attend to gendered landscape discusses a particular Aboriginal case. Kearney (2008:250) learned from participating in women's rituals that while they know of "men's Business and Law, song, and ceremony" and men of women's, neither practices the other's laws. Gendered knowledge and practice are embodied by Australian individuals and the cultural knowledge that women inscribe upon the land through ceremonies that extend "existing and new meanings on the physical places and objects with which they engage in ceremony." Fundamental to the project at hand are these claims, that girls and boys learn about gendered landscapes and embody that learning, that women and men have distinctive realms of knowledge and practice, and that embodiment of knowledge and practice of ritual cause men and women to imagine slightly, and in some cases, even significantly different landscapes in their minds.

The evidence of a gendered gaze across Native North American topography is presented by nine authors in this collection ordered by region to emphasize the different research perspectives on similar landscapes offered by the concepts of taskscape, ritescape, and storyscape. Each author chose to address taskscape, storyscape, or ritescape from a gendered perspective, usually that of women.

We begin with explorations in the eastern United States. Two papers address the Cumberland Plateau. The rock shelters and bedrock mortars of the Cumberland Plateau as viewed in a taskscape are the subject of a paper by Jay Franklin, Lucinda Langston, and Meagan Dennison (Chapter 2), and the role of rock shelters in the ritescape as fertility shrines is explored by Cheryl Claassen (Chapter 1). The idea of fertility shrines is demonstrated with mortars, the crevice shape, deep ash deposits, and footwear offerings. Bleeding places, caused by several geological processes, and vulvar markings are also discussed. The ancient Ozarks are explored with two papers on Dhegihan storyscape by James Duncan and Carol Diaz-Granados and by Natalie Mueller and Gayle Fritz (and somewhat in Chapter 1). The former paper (Chapter 3) focuses on rock markings in southeastern Missouri and the latter (Chapter 4) examines the female stone statuary of the American Bottom region.

Chapters by Mavis Greer and John Greer and Alice Beck Kehoe look at historic and contemporary northwestern plains groups' storyscape and ritescape respectively. The Greers (Chapter 5) are the first of several authors in this volume to point out how rites of fertility were place-based rites. They examine the historic use of the Indian Lake Medicine Boulder by women who married non-Indian men and kept alive the knowledge of the whereabouts and efficacy of this fertility shrine. Alice Beck Kehoe (Chapter 6) drives home the point that gender, as used by anthropologists, is a foreign concept. Nevertheless, she provides numerous examples of how male and female deities and cultural heroes marked the landscape—forming a storyscape—for the Blackfoot.

Western U.S. chapters by Barbara Roth and Jessica Christie examine the ancient taskscape of the Mojave desert (Chapter 7), and the current storyscape of the Kwakwaka'wakw and Hawai'ians (Chapter 8). Roth examines the Mojave Desert where gendered tasks were important in structuring the use of that environment as well as gendered ceremonies. Christie asks the question "why do two Pacific chiefdoms have such different storyscapes" and concludes that the answer lies in the different topography and biological communities present in each.

Finally, movement through a ritescape of the Mexican Gulf Coast by pilgrims is presented by Shankari Patel (Chapter 9). Many of the shrines identified along contact routes actually had shrines to female deities. Landscape is truly multivocal—for people of the past and for today's researchers.

For the rest of this chapter, I will revisit the male gaze of archaeologists and then present the case of a gendered gaze in the past. Here we confront two frequently held assumptions about women's limited mobility. The concept of a gendered gaze in the past while implicitly extended to men during hunting and women during gathering has been underappreciated and underutilized by archaeologists. Ethnographic references to women's mobility during various activities and the concept of storyscapes together create what constituted and continues to constitute gendered gazes when viewing space and landscapes.

Archaeological Perceptions of Women in Landscape

Landscape studies have embraced the idea that landscapes are perceived and created by social groups. Yet with but one exception, none of the studied groups have been gender based, the most fundamental of human social groupings. Add to this vacuum a long history of a male gaze upon the past, well documented by feminist archaeologists who show how the past has been stripped of women by archaeologists, and we have created old landscapes perceived, created, and used only by men.

I ask first-year students "when was being alone on the landscape more dangerous for women—now or 2000 years ago?" For at least fifteen years their answers have been strikingly consistent—the majority of women students vote "now," the majority of men students vote "then." Perhaps this is why male archaeologists have envisioned women at home (Gero 1985) while men trade, raid, and explore far and wide. Surely it is the assumption that women moved about the land only in the company of men, which made an interpretation of a women's nutting camp so radical an idea (Sweely 1994), made all shell-bearing sites—an activity usually attributed to women—*family* encampments rather than women's extractive camps (but see Claassen 1991, 2010) and women's pilgrimage shrines non-existent (see Chapter 9). The presence of women's tools (spoons, pottery) casts all rock shelters as *family* camping shelters (but see Claassen 2011a). Rock art, typically in remote locations or in high places, is nearly always presented as the product of men (for a different interpretation, see Chapter 5 and Ison 2004). Perhaps because we archaeologists understand something of the profession of "shamans," that they seek visions and medicines in the surrounding countryside, we, and most of the public, assume ritual specialists are men (Prentice 1986). And surely it is our assumptions about women's (in)mobility and consequent ignorance of the landscape that removes them from the role of hunters (reinforced by Christie in Chapter 8 for the Kwakwaka'wakw but contradicted by Brumbach and Jarvenpa 1997 for the Chippewa), map makers, and traders and even allows us to forget about the Native women guides for European men as they explored the New World wilderness. How many European men survived life in the wilderness only because of a Native wife or servant girl?

Restrictive Assumptions

Two assumptions can encapsulate the information above and explain why gendered gazes across landscapes—other than men's, of course—have not been the focus of research in archaeology. These two assumptions are 1) that women stayed at home and 2) the notion of the dangerous landscape. The woman-at-home was discussed in detail by Joan Gero (1985) and ancient women have been set free somewhat since that publication by research on women in the past, such as the implications of trade in pottery (Rautman 1997), the making of rock art (Ison 2004), and retreating practices to distant rock shelters (Claassen 2011a). Patel (Chapter 9) critiques the continued use of the Western idea of a public/private divide by Mesoamerican archaeologists who consequently remain ignorant of the role of pilgrimage in ancient Maya women's lives, the consultation of goddesses at pilgrimage shrines, and the travels of pregnant elite women to oracle shrines. I will return to this assumption shortly.

The dangerous landscape idea begs some exploration. Just how dangerous was the ancient landscape of the Americas? The documented violent deaths in the eastern U.S. 8,000 to 4,000 years ago (e.g., Mensforth 2007, Smith 1995) indicate that men were much more often killed than were women. Only men's bodies were mutilated although both men and women were scalped and beheaded (Mensforth 2007). The statistics also indicate that a much stronger case could be made for men staying at home in that era. In several studies of late prehispanic warfare (e.g., Milner et al. 2013), it seems that warfare had increased over earlier periods (for an exception, see Smith 2003) posing what may have been greater danger to women than was the case during the prior 11,000 years. In the Historic period, Swanton mentions that Chickasaw women were vulnerable to enemy warriors when going to and while staying in retreat locations (1928a:358–359, Galloway 1997:49).

There were also dangers for women posed by men in the early Hispanic period in California. Rape and abduction were the precipitating cause of 47 of 83 (European) explanations for Indian wars, but the extent to which Europeans were involved is not mentioned (Whelan et al. 2013:674). Whelan et al. do say that kidnapping by enemy men for wives occurred between tribes although specific accounts of captures are rare. The Lemni Shoshone teenager Sacajawea was captured by Hidatsa men in 1800, when she was about twelve years old, along with several other girls. All were taken from their Idaho homes to a Hidatsa village near present-day Washburn, North Dakota.

Other dangers were equally anticipated by both women and men when out— poisonous snakes, passing too close to a spirit's home, hunger, thirst, etc. But these dangers did not deter women from exploring hunting, gathering plants, fibers, or firewood; visiting; escaping captors; trading; farming; participating in ritual treks; riding in raiding parties; or leading expeditions. Nevertheless, there simply are not enough cases to support a too dangerous landscape perspective for women prior to the late prehispanic period without building yet a stronger case for men to have stayed home.

Indeed, several Native women are known to non-Native peoples for their great landscape and linguistic knowledge. These are Sacajawea, without whom the Lewis and Clark expedition would have been unsuccessful, the woman chief of the South Carolina province of Cofitachequi who led the Spanish through uninhabited territory from central South Carolina to the southern Appalachians (Waddell 2005:345), and the teenager Malinche who led Cortez from Veracruz to the Aztec king himself (Karttunen 1997). Seemingly lost to history are the Ojibwa women chiefs who were called to treaty meetings by U.S. government officials that required multiple days of traveling (Buffalohead 1983).

Sacajawea, a Lemhi Shoshone girl aged between sixteen and eighteen, guided Lewis and Clark thousands of miles from her home in North Dakota to the Pacific Ocean between 1804 and 1806. "On the return trip, they approached the Rocky Mountains in July 1806. On July 6, Clark recorded 'The Indian woman informed me that she had been in this plain frequently and knew it well. . . . She said we would discover a gap in the mountains in our direction' which is now Gibbons Pass. A week later, on July 13, Sacagawea advised Clark to cross into the Yellowstone River basin at what is now known as Bozeman Pass. This was later chosen as the optimal route for the Northern Pacific Railway to cross the continental divide" (Wikipedia).

The activities that required girls and women to learn the details of the land they moved within included: gathering firewood, clay, edible plants, and medicinal plants; fetching meat killed by men; delivering meat and medicine to distant families and trading partners; attending distant ceremonies; retreating during menstruation; questing for visions; disposing of certain animals' bones; tending to field crops; walking into trading posts, forts, and missions; and going on pilgrimages. The movement of women across landscapes through marriage arrangements was crucial for the transfer of ceremonial names and privileges among the Kwakwaka'wakw, and multiple marriages for a woman greatly increased her social status according to Christie (Chapter 8) while surely enlarging her mental map of terrain. Duncan and Diaz-Granados (Chapter 3) talk about how high- ranking women were crucial gifts in ritual exchanges between high-ranking men and a case of such an exchange between two men living several hundred miles apart is presented. Both the woman and her new husband would know the terrain from the Ohio River, through the Ozarks, and into Kansas by the time they returned to his home. It would be worthwhile to investigate whether women came to know more terrain living in patrilineal societies or in matrilineal societies. Native women married to Anglo men in the upper Missouri River region knew far more about the landscape than did their husbands, even remembering and maintaining distant boulder shrines (Chapter 5).

Women's knowledge of the terrain and distant landscapes also may have been acquired while hunting. Chippewa women, today and in the past, hunt. When two anthropologists arrived at a camp near Knee Lake in June 1992, "an elderly couple in their eighties and a middle-aged female resident were away moose hunting. A second elderly couple in their seventies and their forty-year-old daughter had recently returned from an extended moose hunting trip" (Brumbach and Jarvenpa 1997:21). Life cycle related obligations greatly condition women's availability for hunting such that

> Adolescent and younger women are quite active, often as apprentices or partners to older relatives. It is within these mother-daughter or, more commonly, grandmother-granddaughter partnerships that many Chipewyan women learn necessary hunting and food-processing skills ... most women reported a decline in long-distance travel for purposes of pursuing large mammals, when faced with advanced pregnancy or faced with increased family responsibilities although some women continued managing snarelines or fish nets closer to home.

Once beyond those family responsibilities, many Chipewyan women resume their prior involvement in hunting large game and long-distance treks (Brumbach and Jarvenpa 1997:22).

The accounts by women of their hunting experiences that Brumbach and Jarvenpa collected clearly demonstrate that Chipewyan women hunt and trap alone, with other women their own age, with grandmothers/ granddaughters, and with husbands and fathers. Many women started hunting and trapping at the age of eight or nine walking or canoeing for several days distance away from their camp. Their knowledge of the landscape and resource patches was as sophisticated as many men by the time they were adults.

Granting now that women did not stay at home but moved about the landscape well beyond what they could see from a camp or village and while negotiating whatever dangers that arose, let us explore how women might have viewed the landscapes they moved within. What is the basis for a claim of a "gendered" gaze? In light of the paper included herein by Alice Kehoe (Chapter 6) that argues against this very notion in some languages, a word of explanation about the use of "gender" in this volume is in order.

Gender is a term used by linguists, not by Natives. It is, however, a useful heuristic device for the task at hand. All societies recognized male and female beings and many accommodated, even reified, their separation in some arenas, often involving separate knowledges and practices as discovered by Kearney (2008). For example, "Ojibway oral tradition emphasized the distinctiveness of the sexes, and child-rearing practices stressed sex separation in work roles, dress, and mannerisms" (Buffalohead 1983:244). Scholars have even documented languages created by and for women among some southeastern United States Native groups. Readers of this volume are probably quite familiar with academic studies of gender and sex and will understand the use of "gender" in this context to mean men and women and to move us beyond images of sex and the use of the dehumanizing terms "male" and "female." The phenomena to be discussed—women, men, landscape, rituals, tasks, stories, cosmology—are profound cultural constructs. Thus, "gender" is a more appropriate term than "sex" even where "gender" is a foreign overlay on the bodies being discussed.

Kehoe also points out that for individual First Nations People there is the potential for and actual occasions to perform other than one's sex category. Nevertheless, there are bodily presentation norms practiced by the vast majority of people that we readers and the community members can recognize as overwhelmingly one of only two genders.

Sexed Landscape Features—
The Building Blocks of a Gendered Gaze

It is perhaps a universal occurrence that landscapes for Native peoples are filled with the homes of sexed (as well as sexless) personages. Furthermore, all cultures have stories of how the world and their group in particular began and how they acquired the landscape in which they live and the traditions that they practice. Origin stories further contradict the assumptions by archaeologists of women at home and the dangerous landscape by featuring women figures who create and explore the landscape, negotiate its dangers, and roam their environs. Sometimes female deities even create the dangers. Stories of Historic times do the same showing us traveling women who deliver foundational rites to their communities. In this section I will further strengthen the case that women have always had a broad geographical knowledge and created gendered perceptions of the landscape around them through my analysis of several ethnographic examples. It should go without saying that many male figures are cited in Beginning time accounts as well as in historic accounts and their movement through the landscape is implied or specified as well. Male characters in storyscapes are presented in papers by Duncan and Diaz-Granados (Chapter 3), Kehoe (Chapter 6), and Christie (Chapter 8) and in every case serve to underscore the point of a gendered gaze.

Beginning Time Stories

Several stories of beginning times tell of a female body—human or animal—whose bodily features become terrestrial elements: the springs, rivers, mountains, and plants of this world. The body of the Aztec deity Tlaltecuhtli, the earth monster goddess (Miller and Taube 1993:167) was torn apart by Queztalcoatl and Tezcatlipoca and half of her used to form the surface of the earth. Her hair became the trees, flowers, and grasses; her skin other flowers; her eyes wells, fountains and rock shelters; her nose the valleys and mountains; and her shoulders other mountains (Miller and Taube 1993:168). Less violent is the Lakota belief that the earth is a female spirit named Earth that Moves (LeBeau 2009:82). A significant male spirit is Rock who Moves and who dwells in rocks, each rock having a piece of him and capable of communicating with Lakota through dreams or apparitions (LeBeau 2009:84).

Papers in this volume by Duncan and Diaz-Granados, Mueller and Fritz, and Kehoe also introduce storyscapes with the actions and places of significant female beings. First Woman/Old Woman/ Grandmother travels many places, for long periods of time and finally, as a spider, weaves the Middle World of humans (Duncan and Diaz-Granados, Chapter 3). Her vagina (cave) was the entrance to the Below World where the dead were kept (Duncan and Diaz-Granados 2004). In narratives about the Corn Mother, she dies and her body produces corn annually (Mueller and Fritz, Chapter 4).

Other stories show us that women were the first explorers of the land. Mature Flowers or Woman who Fell from the Sky (Seneca) was the first to enter (albeit involuntarily) the world below by falling through the hole in the Upper World created when her husband uprooted a great tree. She fell into this world with dirt in hand which became the earth. While lying under a new great tree, she birthed a daughter. This daughter explored the island daily causing it to increase in size and her trips away to grow increasingly long (Tooker 1979:35–47).

The Wixarika origin story (north central Mexico) includes the tale of the search for the land of the Beginning Time called Wirikuta, located in the modern state of San Luis Potosi, Mexico (Schaefer 2002:186–188). A goddess first sought it out, then several other women on separate occasions also tried to reach Wirikuta. All were unsuccessful and one was turned into a mountain—another set of beliefs that saw the origin of mountains in the body of women. Still later three goddesses wanted to go to Wirikuta but did not know the way so they wove a belt on the top of another mountain to learn the path. One goddess did not have a vagina so she could not continue on and she became a mountain. The other two goddesses entered Wirikuta with the deer messenger and became pregnant. One stayed and became Mother Peyote, and the other brought peyote back to the people.

Once the earth was created and the work of humans begun, historic women continued to figure prominently in landscape use. It was the determination of an "old woman" to find a healing herb during a vision quest (accompanied by her granddaughter) that led to the discovery of peyote, which she carried back to the Comanche. The Blackfoot story that the buffalo calling stone, the original iniskim (fossil), sang out to Mink Woman while she was gathering firewood and it gave itself to her so she could bring it to the people so that they could call bison into their corrals (Kehoe, Chapter 6). "Shappa, head chief of the Yankton Dakota, sent his Ojibway wife . . . with his 'peace pipe' to arrange a peace between his people and the Ojibway of the Pembina band" (Buffalohead 1983:243). Ojibwa Hanging Cloud Woman accompanied her father and brother on a hunting expedition and when they were attacked and her father killed, she pursued the murderers (Buffalohead 1983:243).

The emplacing of stories of the Beginning times onto the landscape creates the inscription of aspects of ancestral founders or actual events onto topographical features. These storied places form part of the embodied self. Rajnovich (1994) gives ample evidence of gendered places in Algonkian speakers' landscape perception, such as crevices that are female (even being incorporated into a human figural image as the vaginal area [Peterborough Petroglyph Site, Ottawa]) and the arrows shot into crevices by men as penises. Far away in southern California, the exact same association of crevices with vulvas and their incorporation into human figural images is evident (McGowan 1978). In between these two areas lies the Ozark Plateau where beliefs about Old Woman or First Woman, (who populated the earth with her children) were inscribed into hundreds of rocky features, including boulder crevices and fissure "caves" (rock shelters at best) usually as oval shapes with line motifs (Duncan and Diaz-Granados 2004 and Chapter 3). Some crevices (called "rock shelters") served women as menstrual and birthing retreats (Claassen, Chapter 1) and served men as hunting shrines where bones of killed animals were placed to petition their rebirth (Claassen 2010).

The northern and central Mexican landscapes of Nahuatl, Otomi, and Purepecha speakers are explicitly gendered and replete with examples of gendered topographical elements. Springs, caves, sinkholes, and cavities of all sorts are feminine. Even winds are gendered with age and personality attributes. Winds have homes in named caves (Furst 1995). Several U.S. Puebloan groups, as well as Uto-Aztecan speakers, see celestial water—rain, hail, frost, and snow—as male and terrestrial water—springs, pools, and lakes—as female. Among many Plains and Great Lakes groups, bluffs are likely homes of spirits often described with the "he" pronoun (Irwin 1994).

Other aspects of landscape that carry gendered connotations based on cosmology are places and destinations "west" and places and destinations "east." Both the Pawnee earth lodge (Chamberlain 1982:97) and the Osage cosmogram equate west with female and east with male. With west are other concepts including moon, dark, conception, wet, left, down, shell. While no rock art sites are known for ancient Cahokia, to the west of Cahokia and to the south are vulva glyphs evoking Old Woman (Duncan and Diaz-Granados, Chapter 3). With east are other concepts including masculine, sun, light, birth, right, up, eagle (López Austin 1988:I:272).

South is also associated strongly with women and north with men in many cultures, including the Osage (DeBoer 2005). In keeping with these associations, it is perhaps not surprising that in a modern rain-calling ceremony of San Andres de la Cal, near Cuernavaca, Mexico, a woman specialist led processions to the southern springs and caves and a man specialist lead processions to northern caves (Peralta 2010). Colors, numbers, specific tree and animal species, and stages of human life are also partitioned into these associative sets (DeBoer 2005) although the members of the set vary somewhat between cultures.

As makers and shapers of the earth, it would seem that there is no question about women's mobility and familiarity with landscape features. In the next section, it will be argued that one's identity as woman or man was partially formed by the landscape.

Identity Formation and the Gendered Gaze across Landscape

The question before us is whether Native women and men responded and continue to respond to landscape features differently? Or put another way, did Native people perceive differences in the natural world around them as a result of their socialization as women or as men? There are at least two closely related ways that we can expect a female gaze and a male gaze to develop when considering the landscape. The first of these ways is encapsulated in the anthropological concept of locality, be it matrilocality, patrilocality, or virilocality, a social aspect that is slowly gaining interest among archaeologists. Tomszak and Powell (2003) have observed that patrilocality characterizes most hunter/gatherer groups particularly when fishing is important in subsistence. Fishing in particular seems to be a multi-male activity. Matrilocality is more common among agricultural groups. Nevertheless it is in patrilocal societies that the breadth of women's geographical knowledge might be the greatest—knowing both their natal territory and that of their husband's territory. Conversely, these residence practices surely predestined a dominant female or male gaze upon the landscape for both extractive purposes and spirit-filled places depending on who was the longer gender in residence, as well as a more nuanced knowledge for that gender.

The second way a gendered gaze is created is through the process of identity formation encouraged by the storyscape. The landscape is infused with place-specific ties to the stories (e.g. Basso 1996, Christie 2009, Scully 1989, and Staller 2008) often encapsulated in place names. On one level, for some groups the stories indicate that from a feminine body all terrestrial waters—springs, creeks, rivers, and waterfalls—and the soil were generated by women and are then likely abodes of feminine earth spirits. For other groups, the origins of the familiar derive from the actions of one or more spirits or deities referred to with a male name. On another level, the events described in origin stories are located at specific landscape features that are named by the community. "Place names may be used to summon forth an enormous range of mental and emotional associations, associations of time and space, of history and events, of person and social activities, of oneself and stages in one's life" (Basso 1996:76). Thus we get storyscapes, such as that of the eastern Cherokee for the Asheville-Sylvia area of western North Carolina (Ashcraft and Hansen 2009), the Keres for New Mexico and Arizona (Scully 1989, Snead and Preucel 1999), and the songscapes covering California and Nevada of the Nuwuvi (Klasky 2009/10).

The Keres world "is divided in half along gender lines with the deities of the northwest and southwest being female, and those of the northeast and southeast, male. The female deities are frequently mentioned in oral narratives, and Thought Woman . . . is regarded as the creator who 'thought people into being'" (Snead and Preucel 1999:176). The Keres worldview consists of three nested squares with the farthest outside northwestern corner being the home of Thought Woman. The farthest southwestern corner is the location of the home of Spider Grandmother. The homes of several male deities, associated with the sun, predictably, are located in the eastern sector corners. At the midpoints of the outer square, in the zenith and in the nadir, are the mountain homes of pairs of male and female deities "who bear special responsibility for the weather and the seasons" (Snead and Preucel 1999:177).

Even more specifically:

> Every ceremony and ritual act possessed by the Lakota has an origin story . . . the name of the spirit being that brought the ceremony or the practice is almost always named. Furthermore origin stories reveal the purpose of the ceremonies and ritual acts, how these things are per-formed, where they are most commonly performed at, and when they are most commonly performed . . . the origin stories always describe in vary-ing amounts of detail an associated spiritual altar and a specific type of

medicine bundle (LeBeau 2009:76). Is it any surprise then that the oldest tradition among the Lakota—the fasting vision quest—which is explained through a long genealogy of men receiving and passing on the rite, is so strongly associated with Lakota men (LeBeau 2009:146–147)?

The Lakota in the northern Plains of the U.S., as described in a recent dissertation by LeBeau (2009:36, 116–120), provide the first set of examples of gendered perceptions of the landscape and identity formation with respect to places. It is typical for traditional Lakota people to seek visions, make offerings, make prayer places, and gather ceremonially important resources in natural settings as instructed by the old stories. For the vision quests of most men, isolated, treeless hills in the shapes of saddles or buffalo humps or mesas are chosen as their destination. Women and winjkte (men living as women) most often choose a hill that rises to a promontory and then has a ridgeline sloping away from it in a hill system (LeBeau 2009:120). These women's places also typically overlook waterways and natural dams, or grassy, treeless prairies and have a pine or cedar tree near the top, or have rock outcrops. Flat top hills or mesas, the exclusive fasting vision places for male heyoka [clowns] are commonly associated with natural rock images (LeBeau 2009:142). Finally, some men, guided by stinging man or spider man spirits, seek fasting places near caves, swamps, fossil beds, snake dens, and burial grounds in order to receive 'witch medicine' (LeBeau 2009:144).

Even new stories can facilitate a gendered gaze upon the landscape. Consider the following story of Sebastian LeBeau's own vision quest in 1989 during which a sacred place revealed itself to him. A dream instructed him to seek a vision on a hill that was not customarily used (LeBeau 2009:22):

> My vision directing me to fast there, my going there with my brother and witnessing the impression of a bear's paw print on the side of the hill; those two things have completely changed my family's and many of my people's perception about this location. In the succeeding years after 1989 more members of my family, and then other tribal members, began using the hill as a place to fast and pray. Between 1990 and 1995 the area below the butte became the location of a Sun Dance ceremony held there because this butte had become an *ohé okítaninn* "manifesting special place," a place spirits visited, where young men could go to pray.

Obviously these differences in fasting places indicate that men and women view the landscape with gender specific criteria. The more frequently used prayer sites and altar sites, too, reflect gendered perceptions of the landscape. The stone ring lodge altar, which is exclusively built by men, consists of one to four rings of stones often perceived in a natural scatter and then highlighted with additional rock. Menstrual retreat places also required a gendered gaze: "A woman's menses bundle is set out inside stands of plum trees or thorny stands of wild rose or gold buffalo current and is called a 'woman's little place.'" It is "a gender specific site and is strictly avoided by men. The site is commonly spatially associated with . . . 'dwelling alone' sites and the ritual rite of passage is a . . . 'sing of isolation.'" When a productive stand is used for this purpose the site is no longer considered a gathering place. "Only when the menses bundle is gone do women re-enter the location to collect a resource and thus cause the site . . . 'to live again'" (LeBeau 2009:240).

Dwelling alone sites, such as the menstrual retreat location, always require a consideration of landscape, of setting. These retreats are placed near plum tree stands that serve as the offering place. The structure should face west or east and be located well outside the main village to the south in a secluded area (LeBeau 2009:148). In the case of these little places, all women living a traditional lifeway, every month, continue to perceive the landscape with a woman's gaze.

The excellent ethnography about Wixarika women weavers (Schaefer 2002) provides numerous examples of gendered elements in the surroundings in north central Mexico with which women surely come to identify. Important places for offerings before a baby's naming ceremony are various caves and shelters known as 1) the house of children, 2) the home of Niweit+ka, goddess of birth, 3) the god house of Ut+anaka, the earth goddess, 4) and the cave of Takutsi Nakawe Grandmother Growth. Each of these deity homes is visited before a baby is named to leave offerings and fill bottles with sacred water. Women who make a five year pledge to "complete" in a craft or other skill

> make special pilgrimages to the xirikite [temples/shrines] of the more traditional gods . . . undertaken at any time of the year, and usually occur after a ceremony in which an animal has been sacrificed, so that the offering can be anointed with its blood. Miniature woven offerings for Takutsi Nakawe were left in her stone xiriki in the center of San Andrés, where a carved representation of the goddess resides (Schaefer 2002:163).

The ethnographer herself left offerings during a pilgrimage with a woman and her family to Lake Chapala where the goddess of the lake was addressed. Another pilgrimage went to the sea.

In 1987, "I accompanied Yolanda, her young son, and her mother Andrea on their pilgrimage [from San Andres in north Jalisco] to Haramaratsie on the San Blas coast [of Nayarit], where Haramara, the goddess of the Pacific Ocean, lives. The Carrillo family had sacrificed a pregnant cow in the church during the Semana Santa ceremony, and now Andrea had journeyed from the sierra with all the family's offerings for the sea goddess (Schaefer 2002:155).

While we learn how youths might come to identify with physical places according to their gender, the specifics of how this occurs were provided by Schaefer (2002:101). When boys and girls reach five years of age, they are gathered together before a ritual specialist who takes them on a spiritual, not actual, peyote pilgrimage. The ritual specialist, "by his special magical powers and the assistance of Kauyumari [the deer] succeeds in lifting himself and the children out of the everyday context into a non-ordinary, magio-mythical temporal and spatial environment . . . what every peyote hunt is supposed to re-enact . . . and *from which is drawn the cognitive map of the sacred geography the child is expected to assimilate* on his magical flights" (emphasis added).

A similar rite is held for adolescent boys by the Kumeyaay:

The Kumeyaay representatives told me that the ground painting in Waterman was used in a puberty rite to represent all that for which the young men would be held responsible as adults. Presumably both of these ground paintings represents a geographical area with which both the initiates and initiators identify. This geographical area defines the geographical boundaries of the initiates' responsibilities; the mountains define the specific group territory associated with an adult member's role (Wilson 2002:15)

In both cases cited above, children or adolescents hear and see, perhaps for the first time, topographic features for which they personally will be responsible, which impart community history and identity. These are powerful moments of personal identity formation.

In old age, a lifetime of exploring the spiritual and physical landscape earns women great respect from younger Wixarika, documented in the following quote.

Women who have completed themselves many times over in the arts and other spiritual pursuits, as well as numerous religious cargos, are looked to as the wise women in the community. As Eger Valadez (Eger 1978:53) writes, "These women are familiar and have communicated with the deities and visited the landmarks which figure in the Wixarika cosmology.

They have educated themselves about the supernatural powers of the plants and the animals in their environment and have developed their mental powers through the use of peyote, from which they have received insight. . . . They have attained the highest level of cultural knowledge available to women (Schaefer 2002:128).

The stories explain even why women collected some, but not other, resources and men some, but not other, resources. Basso's (1996) observations about the Western Apache are the foundational observations for this argument and similar observations have been offered by others.

Basso (1996) points out that Western Apache of Cibecue, Arizona, believe that an individual is molded by the "landscape," and in some cases of errant behavior, molded by named places, having been "shot with a story" that took place at that named location. And while the examples cited by Basso (1996) make it seem that the maleness or femaleness of the person described in the story is actually irrelevant, they do, and his discussion does, show us how an individual's identity—boy or girl—is shaped by places.

Another way of approaching this identity-formed-by-places idea is expressed by LeBeau (2009:45): "there are processes people go through to make place and imbue place with meaningfulness because we invest ourselves emotionally in them." When such a place "is viewed by a Lakota it functions as a symbolic trigger causing the individual viewing it to 'remember all things well' as 'tradition manifests itself'" thus evoking powerful 'memories' of 'custom' and 'practices,' things which reinforce one's own sense and awareness of his or her cultural and ethnic identity," forming examples of Basso's mnemonic devices for moral learning. "We create and name significant places based on the kind of activity we conduct there" (LeBeau 2009:55). The Lakota traditional cultural properties are examples of "places that live in your emotions, hence the forming of an attachment." Most significantly, these attachments are conceptualized by the Lakota as *younger relatives* [humans, emphasis added] engaging in an important way with an *elder* [land] (LeBeau 2009:86). Social rules for the interaction of elders and youths, relatives in general, are replete with gendered considerations, protocol, behavior, and names. Chief Seattle said something similar, in fact: "every part of this country is sacred to my people. Every hillside, every valley, every plain and grove has been hallowed by some fond memory or some sad experience of my tribe "(from his 1854 speech to the territorial governor, cited in National Museum of the American Indian 2005:27), creating personal, gendered memories.

Writing about the vision quest among Plains and Prairies people, anthropologist Lee Irwin had these pertinent things to say about the formation of self, embodiment of place, and gendered perceptions of landscape (1994:27): "These topological features . . . communicate varying degrees of signification. . . . Those seeking wealth and leadership in war will see certain features as more or less significant than do those who become healers or who excel in conjuring. Men will tend to see or interpret aspects of the dreaming topology in ways distinct from those of women."

As a final offering in building the case of a gender infused landscape, I offer the Virgin Mary in Mesoamerican experience. The numbers of virgin manifestations in Mesoamerica and the U.S. Southwest are many. The most visible and celebrated of these versions of the Virgin Mary is that of the Virgin of Guadalupe. She first appeared in 1531 on the top of a hill now incorporated into Mexico City, in fact the very hill/cave complex of the Aztec earth goddess, Tonantzin. Thousand of people subsequently have spied her countenance in rock faces, bark, and other natural substances, and they have built thousands of roadside shrines (as well as indoor adorations to her in their homes, bus stations, and churches) to her out of adoration and thanks in places where her miracles were experienced. Mary can be encountered anywhere in the boundless universe but nearly always this is out-of-doors. These Virgin manifestations offer a startling contradiction to the feminist observation that in Western society women have been relegated to the home and are found inside while men experience life "outside." Instead, in Mesoamerica, Jesus is a markedly indoor personage whose image is rarely found in roadside shrines and who is rarely experienced as a vision. The Virgin Mary, in fact, has appeared in dozens of natural places in Mexico manifesting through trees (Virgin of Ocotlan), rock outcrops (Virgin of Guadalupe on Ixcoteopan road—Claassen 2011b), above caves (Virgin of Guadalupe at Tepeyac), on grazing land (Virgin of Guadalupe-Ocotan—Coyle 1998), and even arising from the green water of a cenote (Virgin of Tabí). Although not virgins other feminine *fantasmas* are expected outdoors, particularly at crossroads.

Conclusions

Because of tasks, stories, and rituals, "women's lives are predicated on different principles than are men's" (Sharp 1995:73, cited in Kehoe, Chapter 6). It is a thesis of this chapter and this book that women and men see, use, and memorialize different perceptions of landscapes, and this argument is supported by the observations of Roth (Chapter 7) for taskscape and Greer and Greer (Chapter 5), LeBeau, Irwin, Basso, and Schaefer for storyscapes and ritescapes. The same could be said for other gendered people as well.

I am aware that the "women" and "men" discussed in these chapters were/are not simple sets of identical people but were/are subdivided at least by family social positions. Greer and Greer (Chapter 5), Christie (Chapter 8), and Patel (Chapter 9) discuss distinctions among women and among men that clearly indicate differences in knowledge of landscape, as well as rituals appropriate to different places. I can predict that for cultures with pronounced family ranking where rank is linked to access to resources, such as several of the cultures of the Pacific coast, that women (more so than men) of different family ranks would come to know different landscapes. Slave women may have done the harvesting of molluscs from intertidal plots owned by noble families for instance among Northwest Coast groups.

One example of differences in the Lakota gaze by life course can be seen in the selection of topographic features upon which to seek a vision. Men who are clowns and contraries use different criteria for fasting vision places, including isolated conical hills for clowns and low, rather than elevated, fasting places for some clowns and contraries (LeBeau 2009:116, 141). Winjkti and those whose guiding spirits are Thunder Being, pray near fossil beds, snake dens, swamps, caves, and burial grounds.

My particular research agenda has focused on hunting-gathering peoples of the distant past so that my perception of the Native gendered gaze is probably most relevant to gathering, gardening, fishing, and hunting based cultures. Within these groups there surely were at least age differences in the gaze of males and females. All babies were born into a storyscape whose meaning and significant places would be revealed over a lifetime. The child—and then the adult—would discover nuances of the sacred in the surrounding landscape, thus developing both an individualized gaze as well as a gendered one. For example, a Kumeyaay woman might discover a vulva form split rock in southeastern California one day while searching for pickleweed seed. She recognizes its meaning—that in this rock the earth goddess is present—because of her enculturation but this locale was unknown to her before now. It might become her particular place to solicit favors from the earth goddess. From her base camp, she looks out in the direction of her discovery knowing that the earth goddess has manifested to her, that She is approachable "over there."

Eliade (1958:369) commented that sacred places reveal themselves to people, and I would add, are revealed in gendered patterns. Depending upon gendered expectations and experiences, different kinds of places can be understood. An old woman blessed by the spirits would know many such places. The female gaze and the male gaze were both taught and learned over a lifetime.

Excellent support for the proposal of a gendered gaze when people look at the landscape comes from Herr (2013:693) talking about the Western Apache, who live their lives at the scale of landscape Herr (2013:696) reminds us: "During the tour of the SR260 project area in 2000, Apache consultants quickly divided into *two groups, one of men and another of women* (emphasis added). Plants were of particular interest to both. Small weed-looking plants were evaluated by the men who looked for medicines. The women identified inconspicuous shrubs and trees along the side of the highway as food." These ecologically stratified surveys are evidence of the point of this volume that women and men learn to expect different things from the landscape and even see different landscapes.

REFERENCES CITED

Ashcraft, Scott, and Lorie Hansen
2009   The Cherokee's Tsul kalu and the Judaculi Rock Petroglyphs of Western North Carolina. Paper presented at the Annual Meeting of the Society for American Archaeology, Atlanta.

Ashmore, Wendy, and Bernard Knapp (editors)
1999   *Archaeologies of Landscape: Contemporary Perspectives.* Blackwell, NY.

Basso, Keith
1996   *Wisdom Sits in Places: Landscape and Language Among the Western Apache.* University of New Mexico Press, Albuquerque.

Brumbach, Hetty Jo, and Robert Jarvenpa
1997   Woman the Hunter: Ethnoarchaeological Lessons from Chipewyan Life-Cycle Dynamics. In *Women in Prehistory: North America and Mesoamerica,* Cheryl Claassen and Rosemary Joyce, editors, pp. 17–32. University of Pennsylvania Press, Philadelphia.

Buffalohead, Priscilla
1983   Farmers, Warriors, Traders: A Fresh Look at Ojibway Women. *Minnesota History* 48(6):236–244.

Christie, Jessica (editor)
2009   *Landscapes of Origin in the Americas: Narratives Linking Ancient Places and Present Communities.* University of Alabama Press, Tuscaloosa.

Claassen, Cheryl
1991   Gender, Shellfishing, and the Shell Mound Archaic. In *Engendering Prehistory: Women and Production,* Joan Gero and Margaret Conkey, editors, pp. 276–290. Basil Blackwell, Oxford.

2010   *Feasting with Shellfish in the Southern Ohio Valley: Archaic Ritual and Sites.* University of Tennessee Press, Knoxville.

2011a   Rock Shelters as Women's Retreat Places: Understanding Newt Kash. *American Antiquity* 76(4):628–641.

2011b   Waning Pilgrimage Paths and Modern Roadscapes: Moving through Landscape in Northern Guerrero, Mexico. *World Archaeology* 43(3):493–504.

Coyle, Philip E.

1998   The Customs of Our Ancestors: Cora Religious Conversion and Millennialism, 2000–1722. *Ethnohistory* 45(3):509–542.

DeBoer, Warren

2005   Colours for a North American Past. *World Archaeology* 37(1):66–91.

Duncan, James, and Carol Diaz-Granados

2004   Empowering the SECC: The "Old Woman" and Oral Tradition. In *Rock-Art of Eastern North America*, Carol Diaz-Granados and James Duncan, editors, pp. 190–218. University of Alabama Press, Tuscaloosa.

Eger, Susan

1978   Huichol Women's Art. In *Art of the Huichol Indians*, Kathleen Berrin, editor, pp. 35–53. Fine Arts Museums of San Francisco/Harry Abrams, New York.

Eliade, Mircea

1958   *Patterns in Comparative Religion.* World Publishing Co., New York.

Furst, Jill

1995   *The Natural History of the Soul in Ancient Mexico.* Yale University Press, New Haven, CT.

Galloway, Patricia

1997   Where Have All the Menstrual Huts Gone? The Invisibility of Menstrual Seclusion in the Late Prehistoric Southeast. In *Women in Prehistory: North America and Mesoamerica*, Cheryl Claassen and Rosemary Joyce, editors, pp. 47–64. University of Pennsylvania Press, Philadelphia.

Gero, Joan

1985   Socio-Politics and the Woman-at-Home Ideology. *American Antiquity* 50(2):342–350.

Herr, Sarah

2013   In Search of Lost Landscapes: The Pre-Reservation Western Apache Archaeology of Central Arizona. *American Antiquity* 78(4):679–701.

Irwin, Lee

1994   *The Dream Seekers: Native American Visionary Traditions of the Great Plains.* University of Oklahoma Press, Norman.

Ison, Cecil

2004   Farming, Gender, and Shifting Social Organization. In *Rock Art of Eastern North America*, Carol Diaz-Granados and James Duncan, editors, pp. 177–189. University of Alabama Press, Tuscaloosa.

Karttunen, Frances

1997   Rethinking Malinche. In *Indian Women in Early Mexico*, Susan Schroeder, Stephanie Wood, and Robert Haskett, editors, pp. 291–312. University of Oklahoma Press, Norman.

Kearney, Amanda

2008   Gender in Australian Landscape Archaeology. In *Handbook of Landscape Archaeology*, Bruno David and Julian Thomas, editors, pp. 247–255. World

Archaeological Congress Research Handbooks in Archaeology. Left Coast Press, Walnut Creek, CA.

Klasky, Philip

2009/10 The Salt Song Trail Map: The Sacred Landscape of the Nuwuvi People. *News from Native California* 23(2):9–12.

LeBeau, Sebastian

2009 Reconstructing Lakota Ritual in the Landscape: Identification and Typing System for Traditional Cultural Property. Doctoral dissertation, Department of Anthropology, University of Minnesota.

López Austin, Alfredo

1988 *Human Body and Ideology Concepts of the Ancient Nahuas.* University of Utah Press, Salt Lake City.

McGowan, Charlotte

1978 Female Fertility Themes in Rock Art. *Journal of New World Archaeology* 2(4):15–27.

Mensforth, Robert

2007 Human Trophy Taking in Eastern North American During the Archaic Period: Its Relationship to Warfare and Social Complexity. In *The Taking and Displaying of Human Body Parts as Trophies by Amerindians,* R. Chacon and D. Dye, editors, pp. 218–273. Springer Verlag, New York.

Miller, Mary, and Karl Taube

1993 *An Illustrated Dictionary of The Gods and Symbols of Ancient Mexico and the Maya.* Thames and Hudson, London.

Milner, George, George Chaplin, and Emily Zavody

2013 Conflict and Societal Change in Late Prehistoric Eastern North America. *Evolutionary Anthropology* 22:96–102.

National Museum of the American Indian

2005 *Listening to Our Ancestors: The Art of Native Life Along the Pacific Northwest Coast.* Museum of the American Indian, Smithsonian Press.

Peralta, Anna

2010 Authority and Ritual in the Caves of Tepoztlan, Mexico: Women Priestesses in Popular Religion. In *Women and Indigenous Religions,* Sylvia Marcos, editor, pp. 69–90. Praeger, Santa Barbara, CA.

Prentice, Guy

1986 An Analysis of the Symbolism Expressed by the Birger Figurine. *American Antiquity* 51(2):239–266.

Rajnovich, Grace

1994 *Reading Rock Art: Interpreting the Indian Rock Paintings of the Canadian Shield.* Natural Heritage/Natural History Inc., Toronto.

Rautman, Alison

1997 Changes in Regional Exchange Relationships During the Pithouse-to-Pueblo Transition in the American Southwest: Implications for Gender Roles. In *Women in Prehistory: North America and Mesoamerica,* Cheryl Claassen and Rosemary Joyce, editors, pp. 100–118. Philadelphia, University of Pennsylvania Press.

Rodman, Amy

1992 Textiles and Ethnicity: Tiwanaku in San Pedro de Atacama, North Chile. *Latin American Antiquity* 3(4):316–340.

Schaeffer, Stacy

2002   *To Think with a Good Heart: Wixárika Women, Weavers, and Shamans.* University of Utah Press, Salt Lake City.

Scully, Vincent

1989   *Pueblo: Mountain, Village, Dance.* University of Chicago Press, Chicago.

Smith, Maria

1995   Scalping in the Archaic Period: Evidence from the Western Tennessee Valley. *Southeastern Archaeology* 14:60–68.

2003   Beyond Palisades: The Nature and Frequency of Late Prehistoric Deliberate Violent Trauma in the Chickamauga Reservoir of East Tennessee. *American Journal of Physical Anthropology* 121:303–318.

Snead, James, and Robert Preucel

1999   The Ideology of Settlement: Ancestral Keres Landscapes in the Northern Rio Grande. In *Archaeologies of Landscape: Contemporary Perspectives,* Wendy Ashmore and A. Bernard Knapp, editors, pp. 169–197. Blackwell, Malden, MA.

Staller, John (editor)

2008   *Pre-Columbian Landscapes of Creation and Origin.* Springer Science, New York.

Swanton, John

1928   *Social Organization and Social Usages of the Indians of the Creek Confederacy.* Bureau of American Ethnology 42nd annual report (1925):43–427. Washington DC.

Sweely, Tracy

1994   Male Hunting Camp or Female Processing Station? An Evolution within a Discipline. In *Women in Archaeology,* Cheryl Claassen, editor, pp. 173–181. University of Pennsylvania Press, Philadelphia.

Tomczak, Paula, and Joseph Powell

2003   Postmarital Residence Practices in the Windover Population: Sex Based Dental Variation as an Indicator of Patrilocality. *American Antiquity* 68:93–108.

Tooker, Elizabeth

1979   *Native North American Spirituality of the Eastern Woodlands.* Paulist Press, New York.

Waddell, Gene

2005   Cofitachequi: A Distinctive Culture, Its Identity, and Its Location. *Ethnohistory* 52(2):333–369.

Whelan, Carly, Adrian Whitaker, Jeffrey Rosenthal, and Eric Wohlegemuth

2013   Hunter-Gatherer Storage, Settlement, and the Opportunity Costs of Women's Foraging. *American Antiquity* 78(4):662–678.

Wilson, Diana

2002   Response to comments on UCLA report on Kumeyaay affiliation. http://www.learningace.com/.

Wood, Christopher

2014   *Albrecht Altdorfer and the Origins of Landscape: Revised and Expanded.* 2nd edition. Reaktion Books, London.

NATIVE AMERICAN LANDSCAPES

PART ONE
THE CUMBERLAND AND OZARK PLATEAUS

1
ROCK SHELTERS, BOULDERS, AND BLEEDING ROCKS
Uncovering Elements of Women's Ritual Landscape in the Midcontinent

Cheryl Claassen

I propose that women and men surveyed and assayed the landscape differently from one another, both when contemplating places for products and when contemplating auspicious places for wealth/health. This usually implicit concept has long been held by archaeologists when discussing extractive activities for hunter-gatherer groups. Envisioned as hunters and tool makers, men have often been depicted as searching the landscape for telltale signs of game, hunting stands, and toolstone as well as forming logistically organized gathering/hunting trips to exploit those resources. In doing so, men have been implicitly cast as the makers of trails. Women, too, are seen as ever vigilant for patches of vegetative edibles from spring greens to mid-summer berries to fall nuts. Both men and women are allowed, although seldom explicitly so, to scan the landscape/taskscape with different criteria in mind, exercising separate economic gazes. Roth and Franklin et al. explore the taskscape of women in their respective chapters in this volume. In this chapter, I am concerned with identifying a woman's gaze across the landscape when she looked for ritual locations.

Both men and women probably equally acknowledged topographic points on the horizon, such as high peaks, horned peaks (Scully 1975), caves, notches, and stony projections (e.g., Milne 1994, Scully 1975), to be significant elements in group origin and continuity. It was in the details of topography, however, that gendered perceptions about the spirituality inherent in the landscape occurred. A stretch of river bank (Smith 2005), a rock slab (Franklin 2002), a vertical cliff face at the edge of a lake (Norder 2003), a thicket of bois d'arc or royal ferns (Stelle 2012), a spring head, a vein of toolstone, an erosional exposure of medicinal or potting clay, a cave behind a waterfall, a vulvar split in rock (McGowan 1978, 1982), or a rock profile of a being are examples of the sexed details in the ritual landscape. The role of boulders in both subsistence pursuits and for ritual is one of the pervasive themes in this collection of papers. Some of these details are recorded in ethnographies invoked in these other chapters and a few details are found in the introductory chapter.

Here, I will explore a probable women's ritual landscape created and maintained on the Cumberland and Ozark escarpments that employed some rock shelters and boulders. I believe that these places were situated within and drew reference from a larger storyscape whose elements we can predict and can read about in Duncan and Diaz-Granados's Chapter 3. Some of those places were associated with a female spirit that surely resonated with women more deeply than with men. In proposing female or male landscape perspectives, gendered gazes, it need not be that these places were exclusively visited by women, for example, or unknown to men but just that they were most often the destinations for women. It has been said about Arnheim Land Aboriginal peoples that while women know of "men's Business and Law, song, and ceremony" and men of women's, neither practices the other's Law (Kearney 2008:250).

The segments of storyscapes that were the most ubiquitous within human groups and probably the most fundamental were the birth of this world and then the creation of humankind or the "tribe." Such are the story segments presented by Christie for Kwakwaka'wakw and Hawai'ians (Chapter 8) and by Duncan and Diaz-Granados for Dhegihans in Chapter 3, and chapters in the book *Landscapes of Origin* edited by Christie (2009). Rituals for continuance of humankind then are often undertaken at the homes of those spirits. These rituals may be performed by individuals or groups of single or mixed genders, young and old (Claassen 2013). Significantly, fertility—immediate and long term—was understood to reside in natural places where earth deities could be approached, such as caves, mountaintops, sinkholes, vulvar-shaped crevices, rock shelters, and springs, and, beginning in late Early Archaic times, in created places such as burial grounds with a matrix of freshwater shells (Claassen 2010) or in dirt mounds. Seeking fertility also required offerings, an observation echoed by Duncan and Diaz-Granados (Chapter 3), Greer and Greer (Chapter 5), Patel (Chapter 9), and Claassen (2013). Fertility petitioning then, involving places and gifts, is an excellent entry point into the investigation of gendered landscapes, which ironically, might be more easily done by archaeologists than by other type of researchers since sites and artifacts are the stuff of our research.

Nut processing occurred in rock shelters along the Tennessee River in the Early Archaic and then greatly intensified during the Middle Archaic in Dust Cave, Stanfield-Worley, and Russell "Cave" (actually a rock shelter) (Homsey et al. 2010). In this valley then, it is apparent that women had moved to a pattern of logistical processing within rock shelter locations (as well as other upland locations). Stafford (1991) annotates some upland open air nut processing camps in Illinois, and Versaggi et al. (2001) argues for basketry stave gathering camps in Pennsylvania during the Late Archaic—both authors presuming these camps to be women's camps. The most distinctive places in terms of landscape, and archaeology, however, are the natural sandstone and limestone shelters.

Given the rather frequent choice of rock shelters for nut processing, it should be no surprise that by late Late Archaic times (3,500 years ago) rock shelters, such as Newt Kash in eastern Kentucky, were also being selected by women for medicinal and birthing retreats. This function is detectible in the pattern of remains—cradleboards, mortars and nutting stones, cordage and fabrics, remarkable quantities of nutshells, and Native domesticates, although not all shelters have all of these elements. In as much as these shelters were visited numerous times for specific ritualized purposes, they constitute shrines, specifically fertility shrines.

Fertility Shelter Shrines of the Eastern United States

It is common among American matrilineal societies for women to retreat from their communities during menstruation and birth (Galloway 1997). It has only recently become evident that sometimes these retreat places were rock shelters. Using as evidence of a menstrual retreat location the bedrock mortars, medicinal plants, cradleboards, plant fibers in bast, string, rope, and textile form, as well as shell spoons and copious nutshells, I have argued that Newt Kash Hollow Shelter in eastern Kentucky's Cumberland Plateau was a women's retreat used from the late Late Archaic through the Woodland periods (Claassen 2011).

Newt Kash is not the only identifiable medicine/birthing shelter. Other shelters can be found on the Ohio and Kentucky segments of the Cumberland Plateau. The history of archaeology on this section of the Cumberland Plateau is ably covered in the chapter by Franklin et al. (Chapter 2) and need not be repeated here. A larger set of Ohio and Kentucky Cumberland Plateau shelters—to be considered in this report—warrant several additions to the materials pattern extracted from the Newt Kash report and specified in Claassen (2011). Underappreciated in that exposé was the ash accumulation, the bedding, and the footwear. Considering particularly the ash deposits, many more shelters in the Wolfe, Lee, Powell, and Menifee county area of eastern Kentucky (Figure 1.1) should be pinpointed for this interpretation. It is also possible to provide more discussion about the mortar holes than was originally presented. In the following section, mortar holes, ashes, bedding, and rock shelter form are explored for their relevance to a retreat function and will result in a collection of specific shelters that can be used

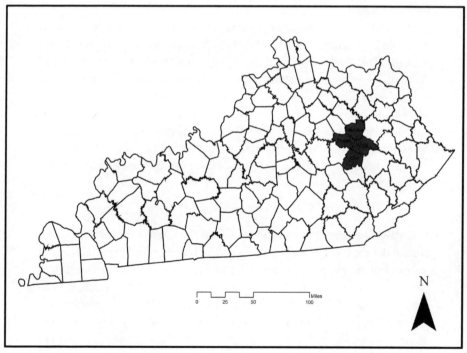

Figure 1.1. Map of eastern Kentucky counties referred to in text. Drawn by Joshua Pierce, Appalachian State University.

to explore the elements of landscape that women were attuned to when selecting a shelter. The selection criteria they used for locating bedrock mortars in the Tennessee section of the Cumberland Plateau has been detailed by Franklin et al. in Chapter 2. Curiously, those authors report no evidence of retreat shelters nor rock art or cultigens associated with shelters in the northern Tennessee section of the Cumberland Plateau.

The Mortar Hole

Mortar holes, typically one or two, in sandstone slabs outside of or inside of a shelter on the Cumberland Plateau of eastern Ohio, Kentucky, and Tennessee are common attributes of those shelters I think were fertility shrines. Ostensibly used for pounding nuts, mortar holes show a curious variation in diameter and in depth for a processing *technology* that presumably would have rather uniform equipment. Often there are no more than two of these holes in one or two slabs. One wonders how someone would extract the nutmeat from the bottom of a 15 in. deep hole and how one or two holes could be sufficient for the quantity of nut remains recovered in several shelters. Although the number of bedrock mortars for processing a known quantity of acorns is not recorded, for the Mono of California the depths of processing mortars are 9.5 cm (3.54 in.) at a maximum (Jackson 1991:305), and they occur in clusters of numerous holes. Only one hole recorded in Table 1.1 is that shallow and no rock surface contains more than two holes on a single slab. In other cases of Kentucky shelters, rocks with mortar holes are at the base of the fill inside of the shelter, therefore being buried and of no utility to other than the first visitors. Contrasting with the Kentucky situation where single holes, rock shelters, and rock art are often co-occurring, there is no such co-occurrence in the north central Tennessee segment of the Cumberland Plateau. There are, however, in Tennessee numerous boulders with as many as 25 holes, similar to those facilities in California (Franklin et al. Chapter 2). Given the use of pecked boulders in the Mojave Sink, central California, by the Hopi in Arizona, people in the northern Plains, and even the lower Ohio River in fertility rituals, these Tennessee bedrock mortar sites with dozens of holes may prove to be yet another type of fertility shrine in the Midcontinent.

What are we to make of these isolated mortar holes then? The mortar and pestle invoke images of intercourse reflecting a widespread American association of cupules and pestles with the uterus and penis (Parkman 1992:366). In the process of pounding rock with a pestle, rock powder

Table 1.1. Mortar Hole Dimensions in Some Cumberland Plateau Shelter Shrines

SITE	DEPTH	DIA.	SHARED ROCK	ROCK POSITION
Red Eye	15″	6″	2, 12″ apart	inside, surface
Red Eye	24″	6″	2, 12″ apart	inside, surface
Red Eye	9″	5″	no	inside, surface
Red Eye	6″	5″	no	outside, 15′ away, surface
Little Ash Cave	20″	5″	2, 6″ apart	inside, north end
Little Ash Cave	5″	?	2, 6″ apart	inside, north end
Glencairn	?	5″		in rock floor of shelter
S. Dehart	16″+	7″		
Newt Kash	6″	7″	yes	inside, east end
Newt Kash	3″	3″	yes	inside, east end
Benson	7″	5″	no	inside, north end
Benson	7″	5″	no	outside, north end
Jim Alexander	27	4″	no	inside
Rogers Upper		3–4 cm	yes, 4 on one	inside upper shelter

GREEN RIVER MORTAR HOLES (BUTLER CT. MARQUARDT AND WATSON 2005:43–52)

Blakenship	15″ (37cm)	9″	no	inside, shelter faces East
Curtis Lax	18″ (46 cm)	6″	no	inside, north end, shelter faces E
Peter Cave	16″ (41 cm)	5″	no	inside, w end, shelter faces S
Glen. Johnson	(few cm) 6″	no	inside, e side, shelters faces S	

is produced as well as is the sound of thunder, associated with rain and rain-calling. Rock powder derived while creating mortars is explicitly used in fertility rites by several California groups. Also, powder production is the explanation behind the Blood Run cupule boulder in Iowa (Callahan 2004) and is used to treat sterility in California.

Four other papers in this collection document or mention ritual use of boulders for fertility petitioning (Roth, Kehoe, Greer and Greer, and Duncan and Diaz-Granados). Three types of pitted boulders in the western U.S. are identified by Parkman (1992) all of which could be considered fertility shrines. The oldest of these may be the "work rocks" pounded by girls undergoing initiation and observed in historic times (Jackson 1991). "Rain rocks" were used by the Klamath and Shasta people who pounded boulders, making pits in the process, to call rain. "In fact, among the Kashaya Pomo, women grinding acorns in their mortars took special precautions to prevent unwanted rain" doing "their grinding beneath specially-prepared shelters ... and the Shasta covered their rain rocks" (Parkman 1992:367). (Most of the bedrock mortars in the rock shelters of the Cumberland Plateau were located inside and thus were covered. Was shelter sought for the same reason?) "Baby rocks" were boulders pounded specifically to produce rock powder and refer specifically to Pomo and Zuni practices. The known rocks "are covered with incised lines, cupules, and vulva-forms (Parkman 1992:364–365). Like I am suggesting here—that bedrock mortars served as a fertility referent—Parkman (1992:367) said "if the early pitted boulders were originally used to bring rain, there would have been an implicit reference to general fertility inherent in the practice ... at some point along the way, the implied reference to human fertility was made explicit as exemplified by the Pomo baby rocks and the Mother Rock at Zuni."

Bedrock mortars occurred not only in two clusters in the state of Kentucky but also in 18 sites in southern Illinois (Carey et al. 2010), three sites in Indiana, 12 in Alabama, and 20 in Tennessee (Franklin 2002:171–172). A boulder "cup stone" from the north side of the Ohio River in Ohio has been recorded (Callahan 2004:68). Mortar holes are also found concentrated in the northern Plains and the Far West, from the Columbia Plateau through Oregon and Nevada, and in California (Parkman 1992). Less numerous are the mortar holes found on the NW Coast and in the Southwest and in northern Mexico, possibly dating to late Paleoindian times (Parkman 2007:2–3, 10). Those people responsible for the oldest pitted boulders were proto-Hokans in the vicinity of Fort Rock Cave and Lovelock Cave along the edge of the Great Basin (Parkman 2007:7), where the oldest sandals also were deposited, possible fertility referents themselves (see below).

"Nutting" stones, a subclass of bedrock mortars, have an assigned function long debated (e.g., Spears 1975). Instead of anvil stones for cracking nuts or cracking stones in bi-polar flaking, some portable "nutting stones" may have been a product of rock powder production, particularly in cases of multiple holes. Unusual numbers of nutting stones have been found at a few eastern sites, such as those on the slope above Austin Cave, TN (Barker 1997) and in Dillard Stamper Shelter No. 1 of eastern Kentucky (Funkhouser and Webb 1930:269).

The Ashes

Yet another characteristic of several of the potential retreat shelters on the Cumberland Plateau is the substantial quantity of ash in them.

They are all characterized by the large accumulation of wood ashes on the floors of the shelters that must represent fires burned over a long period or by a large number of inhabitants. These beds of ashes are often twelve to fifteen *feet* thick and buried in the ashes are to be found skeletons, artifacts, and the usual camp debris. The ash beds show rather definite stratification and indicate that the ashes have formed, at varying intervals, the floors of the shelters. Apparently while the shelters were inhabited, if the ashes became too deep for comfort, a layer of sand, grass and leaves was spread over them, thus forming a new surface and making it unnecessary to clean out the ashes. In many places these definite floor coverings are so perfect and have been so little disturbed that there can be no doubt as to their purpose (Funkhouser and Webb 1929:41).

Instead of cleaning the site by removing the ashes, some material, usually clay but often sand, was carried in and spread over the ashes. New fires were then started, and later, when the ash layer grew to be three to five inches thick the process would be repeated (Funkhouser and Webb 1929:64).

Why is there so much ash in a minority of shelters—those that for other reasons appear to be retreat shelters—and no ash in most shelters? Possibly, ashes are related to renewal and medicine rites.

The Cherokees ceremonially connected women with medicine. Several situations are given in Hill (1997:13–14) where seven Cherokee women danced or women danced seven times around the fire to heal. "Women, wood, medicine, and healing all interwove in ritual to express and implore power." And wood was burned.

Burning, too, may be associated with renewal. It was customary for women upon conclusion of their menses, birthing, and even initiations into adulthood or to sodalities, to bathe and shed soiled clothing replacing it with new clothing. Contemporary Lakota women deposit menstrual bundles in wild plum groves planted next to their retreats, called "living alone" structures (LeBeau 2009). Plums are not taken from these trees until all of the bundles have been *eliminated*. Could it be that the frequent moss and vegetal mats (called "quids") found in some shelters are menstrual pads and baby diapers? Perhaps periodically, these blood offerings were burned and the shelter renewed. Such a practice is logically consistent with practices elsewhere where blood offerings are made and burned (e.g., Maya blood let onto paper that was burned). The so-called "ash caves" of the Cumberland Plateau may constitute our best examples of menstrual and birthing retreats.

The Beds

Funkhouser and Webb (1929, 1930, Webb and Funkhouser 1936) often refer to dense mats of leaves, bark, and reeds as "beds" and "bedding." Beds would of course have been needed for the retreating woman and possibly for initiates into adulthood or a medicine society and for sick individuals. Beds may not have been used for birthing as standing or squatting are the positions reported. "On these floors (of alternating sand and ash] were evidences of numerous beds of grass and leaves" (Funkhouser and Webb 1930:249) and again in their description of Buckner Hollow (Funkhouser and Webb 1929:85): "Beds of leaves and moss intentionally constructed were evident in two places under the ledge. In these beds were found scraps of textiles, fragments of leather and bits of plaited and twisted rope." In the Newt Kash Hollow, large pieces of folded fabric were also referred to as "beds" (Webb and Funkhouser 1936). Beyond a derivation from "cleaning" or renewing a surface, the occasionally thick strata of sand—typical of the ash caves of Kentucky—may have constituted beds as well.

The Rock Shelter Form

The most striking characteristic of retreat locations is the rock shelter form (Figure 1.2). "The sites are all much alike in general appearance and structure. Although they are called 'ash caves' by natives of the region, they are not caves at all but merely huge rock shelters formed by enormous overhangings in the cliff walls" (Funkhouser and Webb 1929:41). In spite of the name "cave" for many of the archaeological places of interest, 99.9% of them are actually rock shelters due to the absence of dark zones.

Beyond the obvious shelter provided by rock shelters, this geological phenomenon often takes the shape of a crevice, an opening in walls of rock. Crevices large and small are identified by many groups as the vulva of an earth deity. Rajnovich (1994) documents this for Algonquian speakers, Duncan and Diaz-Granados (2004) for Dhegihan Siouan speakers, and McGowan (1978, 1982) for people in southern California. Shooting arrows (male referent) into crevices (female referent) was also a game of Northwest coast deities (Macnair et al. 2005:129) and a form of offering made around the Great Lakes (Rajnovich 1994) and in northern Mexico (Schaefer 2002). Some crevices in cliffs along the Mississippi

Table 1.2. Characteristics of Possible Cumberland Plateau Retreat Shelters Sites

	LOCATION	AREA SQ FT	CHAMBERS	FACING	ASH DEPTH	FOOT-WEAR/ CORDAGE	BEDS	MORTAR HOLE
Steven DeHart	Powell Ct, KY		yes f-b	SW	36''	F, C	x	1
RogersShelter	Powell Ct, KY		2 stacked	S		C		4
Haystack	Powell Ct, KY		2 stacked	SW		C		
Cloudsplitter	Menifee Ct, KY	2,153		SW	x			
Newt Kash	Menifee Ct, KY	12,375		S	48''	F, C	x	2
Hootan Hollow	MenifeeCt, KY							2
Edwards Branch	MenifeeCt, KY	2,100		E	x			2
Brier Branch	MenifeeCt, KY	1,375		?	"considerable"			
Bensen	MenifeeCt, KY	1,000		E	12''			
Hog Cr	MenifeeCt, KY				x			
LittleAsh	Lee Ct, KY			E?	x			
Big Ash	Lee Ct, KY			E	X			
Red Eye	Lee Ct, KY	2,580		S	46–60''	F	x	4
Buckner Hollow	Lee C, KY	1,800		E	<12''	F, C	x	
Worth Creech	Wolfe Ct ,KY	1,044		E	x		x	
SampsonSp	Wolfe Ct, KY	2,774	4	S	18''			
JimAlexander	Wolfe Ct, KY	975		E	24''			1
RhodaSmith	Wolfe Ct, KY	1,875	5 shelters	S	24''			
GeoSpencer	Wolfe Ct, KY	2,700	arc	E	x			1
James Spencer	Wolfe Ct, KY	2,625		S	x			1
NaomaSpencer	Wolfe Ct, KY	2,000		E	x			4
Glencairn	Wolfe Ct, KY			S	x			1
Dillard Stamper 1	Wolfe Ct, KY	6,000		S	x			
GreenGentry	Wolfe Ct, KY	2,280		SE	36''		x	
PeteCable	Wolfe Ct, KY		3 stacked	S	24''			
Two Sandal	Carter Ct, KY					F, C		
Mammoth	Barren Ct, KY		cave		no ash	F, C		
Ash Cave, OH	Hocking Ct, OH	3,000	arc	E	2'–3.5'	F, C		
KettleHill, OH	Fairfield Ct, OH					F, C	?	
Other								
Arnold RC, MO	Callaway Ct, MO					F		

River in Iowa were marked with images (Orr 1949). Bushberg-Meisner Cave, a fissure cave in the Ozarks, has an entrance that is a vulva crevice marked with a vulva sign (Duncan and Diaz-Granados 2004:200). Natural and enhanced slit rock shrines in southeastern California are well documented (McGowan 1978, 1982).

That rock shelters were often chosen for ritual purposes in the Midcontinent is implied by the high correlation between shelters and rock markings recorded in Kentucky (see Coy et al. 1997, Ison 2005) and the use of some shelters throughout the region for human and dog burial. Shelters chosen for retreat would constitute another type of ritual use, one that clearly implicates fertility concerns. What do the characteristics discussed above show us about women's criteria for retreat shelters?

Beyond the idea of the crevice, shelters also have dimensions and directional aspects (Table 2.2). Most of the possible retreat shelters for which I have information are small. They also have southern or eastern exposures (which may prove in the future to reflect two distinctive types of shelter use) and most are at the head of ravines or hollows and were difficult for archaeologists to access.

Other characteristics of some of the shelter/shrines are frequent enough to garner further consideration. The double shelter, often two cavities either side by side or a front and back room (Little Ash Cave, KY) or stacked shelters one above the other (e.g., Haystack and Rogers shelters, KY) and groupings of three and four adjacent shelters (e.g., Rhoda Smith shelter) frequently show evidence of retreat use (Table 1.2).

Elevation above the ravine floor seems relevant. Little Ash shelter's floor is 80 ft. above the stream, and Newt Kash shelter is some 40 ft. up the rock wall face.

It may or may not prove relevant in future study of the fertility shrines that many of the faunal remains are that of deer and the awls made from deer bones. Awls in Little Ash shelter were exclusively made from deer cannon bones. Many cultures in North America tell of deer/women (e.g., Mandan deer woman and the Wixarika 5 deer women) and associate cervid foot prints and hooves with fertility and women (Sundstrom 2004). Employing deer bone for awls may be more than an expedient choice—the animal and the activity requiring these awls may be a conceptual pair and grouped with women and fertility petitioning in these situations. The physiographic criteria and the material remains itemized here in some combination should alert archaeologists to the possibility of a fertility shelter, retreat, or shrine.

Other Types of Fertility Shrines in the Eastern U.S.

Apart from the retreat shelters just presented, there are a few examples of other types of women's fertility shrines in the Midcontinent that I shall call footwear shrines, vulvar and foot print glyph rocks, and bleeding rocks. The footwear shrines and marked rocks are most typically found in association with retreat/medicine shelters, but there are exceptions, such as Arnold Research Cave and Mammoth Cave.

Footwear Shrines

The introduction of a footwear shrine concept requires elaboration of the symbolism of footwear (sandals, slippers, and moccasins) and feet. Numerous references record that the crescent foot prints of herbivores are interchangeable symbols for the crescent moon, for vulvas, and ultimately with the meaning of fertility (e.g., Hall 1997, Moore 1974:152–153, Nagy 1994:27, and Sundstrom 2004). In some settings foot print marks may represent the Little People but that would not negate the possibility of a fertility referent for Little People also associated with the keeping and releasing of rain and game.

Going further afield, the Aztecs, and probably the 1300 year older Teotihuacanos who the Aztecs copied on many accounts, used foot prints in codices and murals to show both past and future time. In modern central Mexico, a found baby shoe is collected and displayed as a fertility charm, and baby socks and shoes are hung in fertility trees and rock shelter shrines along with umbilical cords to solicit pregnancy (Figure 1.3). Given that Native Americans saw a rabbit in the moon, and the goddess of the moon is depicted holding a rabbit while sitting in a crescent moon (Miller and Taube 1993:119), it is highly likely that the luck of the rabbit's foot is that of pregnancy. Indigenous people living today in central Mexico locate feet in the underworld as did the Inca (Classen 1993). "One shaman told me that the hills are the earth's head and face, the ground its body, and the underworld its feet" (Sandstrom 1992:241). A quote from Chief Seattle brings us back to northern North America: "the very dust under your feet responds more lovingly to our footsteps than to yours, because it is the ashes of our ancestors, and our bare feet are conscious of the sympathetic touch, for the soil is rich with the life of our kindred" (Chief Seattle from his speech to the territorial governor, 1854, quoted in MacNair 2005:27). Sassaman (2005:359) has also invoked a symbolic link between feet and immaturity when talking

Figure 1.2. Chalma Rockshelter fertility shrine. Photo by Cheryl Claassen.

about the possible body symbolism of the nested rings of Poverty Point: "(head to outside, feet to inside, with head symbolic of maturity, feet symbolic of immaturity)." The use of foot bones in divination games (cup-in-pin, astragalus dice) strengthens the association of future/fertility with feet.

Also supporting this association of feet, foot prints, sandals, and rock shelters with fertility is evidence from the probable Mississippian site near the East St. Louis mounds, taken from Duncan and Diaz-Granados in Chapter 3:

> For the Dhegihan peoples, the direction west also was associated with female elements in the cosmology. In the first half of the 19th century *this very important ledge [west of the East St. Louis Mounds] bore a realistic pair of human footprints* [emphasis added]. (Figure 3.17) . . . The footprints were associated with a cave, an entrance to the beneath world (the vulva of the First Woman). The modern Osage West Moon peyote church at Hominy, Oklahoma has a similar pair of footprints at the opening of

a west facing vulvar shaped altar (Mathews 1961:747, 753). This altar represents the vulva of First Woman where the Sun and his son, Morning Star, will enter at sunset.

Constantly in contact with the underworld, the source of new life, the human feet and cloven hooves were seen as fertility organs. Bird tracks in the Ozarks indirectly imply fertility as those birds were the helpers of Old Woman Who Never Dies, the progenitor of this Middle World (Duncan and Diaz-Granados, Chapter 3).

Beliefs that connect feet with fertility and span 5,500 miles are probably ones with great time depth. Given the relationship of feet and shoes to fertility, I think that the footwear found in some dry shelters were not merely accidental preservations but were offerings placed inside the entrance to the home of an earth deity responsible for pregnancy. Rock shelter homes of major and minor deities are still visited by Wixarika (Huichol) women and men for different ritual purposes, and textile offerings are often prescribed for the female pilgrim to deposit in these places (Schaefer 2002). Puebloan groups also deposit offerings to various beings in rock shelters (e.g., Feather Cave [see Ellis and Hammack 1968]) and footwear is found in approximately fourteen shelters on the northwestern Colorado Plateau (Gieb 2000). It is quite possible then that textiles, sandals, cordage, deer bone awls, stone projectile points, and other items often found in eastern shelters (and the western shelters around the shores of ancient Lake Bonneville) were deposited as *offerings*, petitioning for fertility. Footwear is not encountered commonly in eastern shelters, even in those dry shelters of the Cumberland Plateau, so this type of shrine seems to be unusual in the eastern U.S. while prolific in the Great Basin and Colorado Plateau.

Sandal offerings in rock shelters may mark the oldest fertility rites detectable by archaeologists in both the western United States and the eastern United States. Arnold Research "Cave" is the best example of a sandal shrine in the East and is the oldest, of an age on par with the oldest footwear found in Ft. Rock Cave, Oregon. Thirty-five specimens of fiber and leather footwear were recovered. Thirteen of them were at least 50% complete although all specimens had frayed or broken elements and dirt encrustation. The one sandal with published context came from the upper half of a pit (Shippee 1966:23). Foot sizes indicated that the *footwear of many children* and small adults had been left in the shelter. Today, in Mexico, baby shoes and socks are hung in fertility shrines (tress and rock shelters) by adults.

Footwear has been recovered in nine other shelters in the Ozarks that appear to be much more recent. One sandal comes from Kerr Canyon, IL (Koldehoff et al. 2008). Six shelters in the southern Ozarks yielded one sandal each (Indian Bluff, Elk Spring, Cob Cave, Ash Cave, Green Bluff, and Allred), one (Spiker Shelter) contained four sandals and Eden Bluff harbored three sandals (Scholtz 1975). Many of these same shelters produced baby cradles (Dellinger 1936), cordage, and textiles (e.g., Scholtz 1975). The recovery of odd numbers of footwear is reason enough to suspect that the footwear was an offering.

Differing from deposition in the shallow rock shelters mentioned above is the deposition of footwear in the deep passages of true caves. Slippers and sandals found in passageways within the Mammoth-Salts cave system amount to approximately 64 from Mammoth and 16 from Salts (Watson 1969:38, studied by Orchard [1920], Schwartz [1958], and King [1974]). Like the shelter examples, all slippers are well worn. Footwear in Mammoth and Salts are examples of close twining and represent "the most innovative article of clothing . . . unique in North American footgear" (King 1974:35). Those slippers and sandals intact enough to measure "were about 8 in. long" while the barefoot prints observed by Patty Jo Watson in two passageways in Salts Cave ranged in length from 7½ to 10¼ in. (Watson 1969:41). Bennett Young remarked that the slippers "range from child size to a number seven shoe'" (Young cited in Watson 1969:41), and Nelson said that two sandals measured 8 ½ in. long and one 6 in. long, the latter probably once belonging to a child (Nelson cited in Watson 1969:41). Rather than picturing children in the depths of Salts Cave, and in spite of a single child-sized foot print in Mammoth Cave (George Crothers Nov. 2013, pers. comm.) I imagine that adults were responsible for depositing the child-size slippers. Supportive of this assumption are more than 200 foot prints in the older Jaguar Cave of Tennessee made only by adults and one adolescent in the dark zone passageways (Watson et al. 2005:38). Crothers (2012) and I (2001) would have exclusively male priests performing rituals deep inside this cave system. It seems that they brought footwear into the cave as a part of a rite, perhaps a rite similar to that of the Winnebago clan ceremonies where presents of footwear were presented to 11 different deities including Disease-Giver (Tooker 1979:235).

Red Eye Shelter in eastern Kentucky's Cumberland Plateau is a good example of the rock shelter footwear offering place. Included in the ashes at Red Eye were burials, mussel shells, unburned wood, and areas of charcoal. Large matted areas of sand, grass, and leaves appeared to have been laid down on top of lens of ash "to form bedding or floor covering" (Funkhouser and Webb 1929:46). Protruding into the ash were occasional bark-lined pits containing sandals, as well as other fabrics, nuts, and naiads. "The position and arrangement of the floors [alternating layers of ash and of clay or sand], beds and the caches showed a distinct stratification representing at least four different periods of occupancy" (Funkhouser and Webb 1929:47).

One cache encountered was "well made and lined with leaves and grass and contained in the center three well made moccasins. This was near the center of the shelter" (Funkhouser and Webb 1929:47). Another pit contained one moccasin and several pieces of wood and a third pit was 8 ft. from the back wall, 2 ft. in diameter and 2 ft. deep, lined with fitted pieces of pine bark. It contained two moccasins. A fourth pit contained a small fiber bag 6 in. long and 3 in." in diameter filled with chinquapin meats (Funkhouser and Webb 1929:49), reminiscent of the miniature weavings produced by modern Wixarika women for offerings left at the cave home of one or another deity (Schaefer 2002).

Beside the shoes, the bag, and many fragments of fabric and string, there were only 40 other artifacts encountered (4 pestles, 1 hammer, 1 ax, 1 grooved stone, 1 whetstone, 1 net sinker, 5 pieces of worked mussel shell, 14 awls, and 12 arrowheads). The 14 burials in the shelter in many cases seemed to have been among the last activities conducted in the shelter (Funkhouser and Webb 1929:54).

Four other shelters in eastern Kentucky have provided footwear: Buckner Hollow, Steven DeHart, Newt Kash, and Two Sandal Shelter. At Buckner Hollow, in Lee Ct. KY, at least two moccasins were recovered (Funkhouser and Webb 1929:82). Fiber-filled beds in Steven DeHart shelter yielded at least three leather moccasins. Two of the three moccasins depicted were quite small, one with a hole in the sole (Funkhouser and Webb 1929:288–291), and the two at at Two Sandal shelter was well worn also (Applegate 2008:522). Child- and adult-sized slippers and sandals also have been found in Ash Cave and Kettle Hill Cave in southeastern Ohio (Murphy 1975:310–311).

The reader is probably aware that hundreds of rock shelters have been tested in the eastern Woodlands including many *dry* shelters, yet fewer than 25 have yielded textiles or footwear. I propose that these shelters do not contain unusual preservation conditions but instead were destination places for the deposition of textiles or sandals. Only some shelters were recognized in the past as auspicious places for fertility petitioning.

Vulvar Glyph Rocks

This type of glyph, the U or O with an interior line, is found on both the Ozark escarpment and on the Cumberland Plateau of Kentucky. "There are at least 18 sites on the west side of the Mississippi River in Missouri that have one or more vulvar motifs" (Duncan and Diaz-Granada 2004:191).

Vulvar motifs are present in two sites in eastern Kentucky: Sparks Indian Rock House in a county contiguous with those containing the retreat shelters and Trinity Shelter in Wolfe County, home to several of the retreat shelters. Sparks Indian Rock house faces northeast and contains five boulders marked with skeletal faces, rayed circles, and a human hand and one with foot prints and vulva forms in 1,845 m² of sheltered area (Coy et al. 1997:49–57). Another boulder in the shelter is marked with a pecked human foot and five shallow "pits" in a quincunx that may have been created during powder production.

Trinity Shelter is one of three connected shelters and has 2,529 m² of covered area. "Identifiable petroglyphs include a foot print near the northern arc of the boulder, a possible vulva form just to the south of the foot print, a possible human stick figure touching the vulva form on the west, and a series of V-shaped elements that may be animal tracks, possibly deer" (Coy et al. 1997:133). The association of vulvas with human feet and even deer foot prints supports the supposition that feet were fertility symbols and that this shelter served as a fertility shrine.

Blood of the Ancestors Grotto (BAG) in southern Illinois gives us evidence of women's use through the rock markings. Stelle (2012) points out that circles are the dominant design on the BAG walls in and around a slit rock and explains how they constitute an image of a medicine woman. He also mentions other circular motifs that seem to constitute medicine women, such as those at Reedyville in Kentucky and Leo Petroglyph rock in the Hocking Valley of Ohio, home to several fertility shrines. There a human has a circle between the legs and is near a vulvar image.

Vulvar motifs are also in focus in several publications by James Duncan and Carol Diaz-Granados (e.g., 2004). Old Woman seems to be the referent and specifically the vulva of Old Woman wherein can be found the dead. Two of these Missouri Ozarks rock mark sites are discussed by Duncan and Diaz-Granados in Chapter 3.

Bleeding Places

Stelle (2012) has coined the very apt term for the Blood of the Ancestors Grotto in southern Illinois as a "bleeding place," highlighting what may very well be the least ambiguous places for women in the past. Several natural phenomena create "bleeding rocks," which in a few cases have attracted Native attention. One of these places is a cupule rock of unknown age found along Blood Run Creek in Iowa (Callahan 2004). The name "Blood Run Creek" refers to a locale upriver that runs red (Rapid City Journal, January 13, 2013), probably the product of chemo-lithotropia.

A slightly different chemical process can be seen at BAG where the water occasionally runs red. Here a combination of "a permanent source of groundwater with the distinctive chemical properties of being (1) anoxic, (2) neutral to slightly acid, and (3) rich in dissolved iron" and several iron-eating bacteria including *Gallionella ferruginea* oxidizes iron dissolved in groundwater (Stelle 2009:209). "The iron is transformed into the insoluble precipitate ferric hydroxide [$Fe(OH)_3$], or the pigment in the thick, reddish-orange slurry. The 'pool' is actually a mound of living bacteria and decayed organic residues" (Figure 1.4; Stelle 2012:7).

BAG has several landscape features of note giving us a much richer view into the criteria women were looking for when selecting a ritual place: a 60 m stretch of bubbling springs whose anoxic water flows to a two–tiered waterfall falling into a stream in a natural rock walled basin, a shallow rock shelter inside that basin, and a bleeding rock in the resulting pool of water. "While the pool of 'blood' seems always present, it is only during the season of the winter solstice that the springs flow and the stream 'turns to blood'" (Stelle 2012:8). All of these landscape elements have fertility and female referents, some of which have been elucidated above.

Surely there a numerous other bleeding rocks awaiting our recognition. There is a bleeding rock on a cliff face in Franklin County, southern Tennessee, noted by Sarah Sherwood and shown to the author. The same cliff face has possible salamander pictographs and evidence of occupation.

Stelle also makes much of the presence of the royal fern *Osmunda regalis* at BAG, "a regionally uncommon plant that is commonly en-

Figure 1.3. Bleeding rock at Blood of the Ancestors' Grotto. Photo by Linville Stelle.

countered growing from and in association with the pool and springs of 11SA557" (Stelle 2012:12). This fern is persistently linked to "women's problems" in the literature, and Maidenhair and Lady ferns were used for breast diseases, acrid humors, and irregular menses (Stelle 2012:12). Royal fern parts were also found in both shelters of Rogers shelters in Kentucky (Cowan 1979b:213).

A public park has been established at another bleeding rock, Yellow Springs in western Ohio. With only vague references to Yellow Springs as an important religious place for the Shawnee, I propose that it was of particular importance as a fertility shrine.

Bleeding also is the phenomenon evoked by reddish iron streaks on cliff faces. Figure 1.4 offers a view of the streaked rock at BAG. Iron oxide streaking also occurs in association with Newt Kash. With a cliff face so streaked and a rock shelter of unusually large size, Newt Kash must have seemed quite portentous to the women who saw it 4,000 years ago. The prevalence of this feature is unknown for the set of shelters in Table 2.2 but may prove to be a predictive sign of a utilized shelter.

Figure 1.4. Iron streaking at Blood of the Ancestors' Grotto. Photo by Linville Stelle.

Discussion of the Female Gaze and Use of Shelters

There are several questions that these examples and interpretations raise, some of which can be dealt with at this time. Among these issues are: 1) the claim that women rather than men used them, 2) the evidence for year round use given monthly menses, 3) activities undertaken while in retreat (were they after all, simply nut processing locations given the abundant nut remains and mortar holes?), and 4) what history can be deduced for these various types of shrines.

Men or Women Users

Men, too, selected and used rock shelters for ritual reasons, such as to appeal to the keepers of game (the Little People):

> The Cherokee, for instance, believed that spiritual beings from the under-
> world [source of fertility] such as the little people favored rock shelters
> in river bluffs (Witthoft and Hadlock 1946). . . . Mooney's informants
> told him that hunters often went to such isolated locations, where they

appealed to the Little People in order to gain close proximity to deer and other game (1900b:334). This belief has also been documented among various Creek groups (Gatschet 1888), the Catawba of the Carolinas (Speck 1907), and even the Natchez of Louisiana (Loendorf et al. 2005:152).

The idea of Little People living in rock shelters along rivers is also a belief of the Iroquois (Harper 1999:159) and Algonquian speakers (Rajnovich 1994:67fn11). Other uses of shelters by men included retreat when seeking a vision or recuperation when wounded. "Wounded hunters were also taken to a secluded location near a river where they could heal" (Loendorf et al. 2005:151).

The high number of points in some shelters recommend the hunting shrine/petition use and this idea is developed further in other publications by the author (Claassen 2014, 2015). The presence of medicinal plants could support the healing use. The distinction between hunters' medicine and pregnant or menstruating women's medicine can be made by reference to different plant species. Abortatives were found in Newt Kash Hollow and the royal fern has been recorded in two other shelter shrines. Cradleboards and rattlesnake rattles are also particularly associated with women and their infants, and both were found in Ozark and Cumberland retreat shelters. And plums, whose pits were found in Rogers shelters and Newt Kash, have a widespread association with women—in women's gambling, plum trees for menstrual retreats (LeBeau 2009), and fruits for offerings (LeBeau 2009:158, Sundstrom 2004). The rock markings relating to vulvas and female spirits at BAG and elsewhere also allow us to assume women users as do the mortar holes on the Cumberland Plateau. But the selection criteria for shelters by men also need elucidating. Male shelter use furthers the claim of a gendered landscape gaze.

Year-round Use of Retreat Shelters

Both birthing and menstruation occurred year round so use as retreat shelters should give more than the fall use evidence supplied by the nuts. Fortunately there have been modern botanical analyses of six of these shelters: Rogers, Newt Kash, Haystack, Hootan, Red Oak, and Two Sandal (e.g., Cowan 1979a, b; Gremillion et al. 2000).

Funkhouser and Webb (1929) thought that the ash caves were not used during the colder months because no large hearths were encountered. Subsequent work supports this idea (e.g., Cowan 1979b:161). Plums ripen in June. A fecal specimen at Newt Kash contained a strawberry seed as well as crop seeds indicating a meal in June using fresh fruit but stored seeds (Gremillion 1996:530). A Haystack rock shelter fecal specimen contained spring pollen. The maygrass found there and at other shelters suggest late spring. There was "heavy spring-summer consumption of stored crop seeds . . . amply documented for the Mammoth Cave area of west central Kentucky" (Gremillion 1996:532). However, the edible plants recovered in Rogers shelters spanned the seasons of April through December (Cowan 1979b:161). In addition to the nuts present, pawpaws were found at Newt Kash, Haystack, Cloudsplitter, and Rogers that ripen in October and November and do not store well so they indicate the actual presence of women in those months, not just stored food. Honey locust pods and sumac seeds would have been available into December. Therefore, floral remains indicate use of the shelters from May to December, enough time to support the retreat shelter or fertility shelter functions.

Activities during Retreat

Nut harvesting and processing have been activities assumed for these shelter users. However, a closer look casts some doubt. Black walnuts were the dominant nut at the two Rogers shelters yet the trees were said to grow at a "considerable distance" from this shelter (Cowan 1979b:120). The same situation was specified for shellbark hickory nuts. According to Cowan, neither type of nut was actually processed at either of the stacked Rogers shelters because none of their thick husks were found. They were not nut processing places. Instead the nut parts found were being used in these shelters either for dying, oil production, or as a stored food. In fact, the nuts that would have been at hand around several of these shelters—hickories, chestnuts, and acorns—were significantly underrepresented (Cowan 1979b:167).

The remains from Newt Kash indicated abundant evidence of cordage production activities (Claassen 2011, Webb and Funkhouser 1936). Cordage production was documented at the Rogers shelters and Haystack rock shelter as well.

Rogers shelters and Haystack rock shelter also give us evidence of another activity conducted in these shelters—basket splint production and basket making (Cowan1979a, 1979b). Ninety-seven percent of the cane splint and strips recovered in the stacked Rogers shelters came from the lower shelter (Cowan 1979b:175, 178). These canes too were said to have been gathered at a considerable distance from the shelters.

Flakes and exhausted cores increase fivefold in the Early Woodland period, the same time as the ash accumulation in Cloudsplitter rock shelter (Cowen et al. 1981:74). It may well be that these flakes were employed in cane, bast, and bark processing dating the onset of these specific retreat activities.

There also may have been gambling or divination acts occurring in these shelters as suggested by the presence of 63 wild plum pits at the Rogers shelters (Cowan 1979b:132). Plums were used in association with fertility petitioning on the Plains (Sundstrom 2004) and plum stones were used as gambling die by women. "The greater plum stone game was found across the Northeast and Plains" and is the type of dice most frequently recorded by DeBoer and most frequently found among Native women (39 cases versus 3 of men) (DeBoer 2001:218).

Perhaps it is relevant that many of these shelters are in drainages known to have yielded salt in historic times. There is debate about whether salt was *produced* in prehistory (it was in historic times) or simply was known to attract wildlife. There is evidence, however, that women in particular worked salt sources in historic times, including the Omaha women who lived in the Ozarks (Thomas 2001) and Native women in Jackson County, Kentucky, who guided Daniel Boone. Further downstream in the Kentucky River watershed are the shelters of the Red River Gorge and salt licks on tributaries, such as Paint Lick Creek. Salt was processed also in historic times along the Salt River in Ohio in whose watershed are found the Ohio rock shelters listed in Table 1.2. Salt was likewise extracted from the soils and rivers of southern Illinois in the region of a sandal shrine there and BAG. "Intertwined with a discussion of 11SA557's [BAG] physical environment must be recognition that significant salt springs are to be found within its larger catchment. At a distance of approximately 10 km is found Half Moon Lick and, at 13 km, the Great Salt Spring of the Saline River" (Stelle 2012:10). The Great Salt Spring has a lengthy prehistoric record and in historic times was used by tribes from Michigan, Wisconsin, Indiana, Illinois, and Ohio (Stelle 2012:10). We can deduce then the retreat activities of nut oil production or dying, fiber/cordage production, basket split production, and possibly salt collecting.

Dating Fertility Shrines

The footwear offerings in Missouri's Arnold Research Cave date as early as 8325 cal B.P. to 7675 cal B.P. as well as to a later period (Kuttruff et al. 1998:72). Given the equally old practice of footwear offerings in shelters of the Great Basin, it may be that Sassaman's (2010) proposed Ancestry II migration from the eastern Oregon area into Missouri in the late Pleistocene is supported by the Arnold Research Cave footwear and the cultural practice of footwear offerings. Rock shelters in the Great Basin and Colorado Plateau, many of them important archaeological sites and misnamed "caves," often yield sandals as well as possible menstrual pads (so named by Aiken 1970), clothing, bedding, and evidence of women's labor, such as dehairing antelope hides and gathering pickleweed stems by the hundreds of bushels. We would have then a western cultural practice that seems to have diffused eastward but then died out in the East between 7675 cal B.P. and 5500 cal B.P. to be revived in that cave after about 4985 cal B.P.

Vulvar and foot print images, painted or pecked, would seem to be no older than Late Archaic. However, most of the cases cited here of rock markings are dated to the late pre-European era. Ash beds and mortar holes have an older history than vulvar and foot print glyphs. Where bedrock mortars are found in single component sites, those sites are Late Archaic (see Franklin et al. Chapter 2). Late Archaic dates also accompany the oldest cultigens in Cloudsplitter and Cold Oak shelters of eastern Kentucky (Gremillion 1996:522) at 1500 B.C.

Actual dated elements of the proposed fertility shelter shrines come from Cloudsplitter in Menifee County, Kentucky (Cowan et al. 1981). There the package of ritual features consisted of a shelter, interior small structure (sweat lodge? screen?), ash layers, and cultivars and was dated at 1,000 B.C. and later. The ashy layer itself, Zone 11b, returned a date of 2060 ± 60 B.P. (Gremillion et al. 2000:4). Much later refinements of dates brought about the comment "patterns of deposition changed significantly after about 800 cal B.P." (Gremillion 1998:8). The earlier change is also marked by cultivated weedy annuals that "make a sudden, and dramatic appearance" as well as "spatially isolated posts and postmolds and other features within" (Cowan et al. 1981:75), possibly a sweat hut. It is possible then, that ash layers in Cumberland Plateau fertility shrines occurred after 1000 B.C. and may indicate a new ritual practice in older retreat shelters. Four other Kentucky shelters with dates—Newt Kash, Hooton Hollow, Two Sandal, and Cold Oak—bracket the period 1975 B.C. to 53 B.C. for ash, beds and sandals (Applegate 2008:516). Five dates from Rogers shelters that contained cordage and basket staves fell between A.D. 465 and A.D. 705—a span of years that probably includes activities at many of the Cumberland shelters (Cowan 1979b:247).

The Ozark evidence offers an actual sequence of shrine types and landscape considerations. After the very early deposits of footwear in Arnold Research Cave, footwear offerings resume in small numbers in a few Woodland era retreat shelters. Retreat shelter shrines are followed by vulvar glyph rocks—those at Miller Cave date to Late Woodland— but they are primarily associated with Mississippian sites (Duncan and Diaz-Granados 2004:196). Finally, bleeding places appear. Both bleeding places and vulvar glyph rocks seem to reflect very late Dhegihan Siouan ritual practices (see Chapters 3, 4, and 5). Does this sequence reflect developments of Siouan women's ritual practices specifically and a long history of matrilineality in that group?

Conclusion

The archaeological record contains documentation of several different types of natural places chosen by women and then enhanced by them in ways to maximize fertility benefits. I have reviewed retreat/medicine shelters, sandal shrines, bleeding rocks, and vulvar rocks located in the Ozarks and the Cumberland Plateau. A surprising outcome of the papers assembled in this volume is the frequency of boulder-focused rites and their widespread geographical occurrence.

Several of the retreat shelters seem to have been places for group rites, such as Newt Kash (Claassen 2013). Many of them were also probably used by individual women, or a sick woman and a medicine specialist. In the case of retreat shelters, women seem to have spent much of their time working: making cordage, baskets, textiles, nut oil, and dyes. Possibly they collected medicinal plants and food while occupying the shelters, but they seem to have come to the shelters with dried food supplies or to have stashed dried foodstuffs for future use. The boulder shrines discussed by Duncan and Diaz-Granados (Chapter 3) and Greer and Greer (Chapter 5) also may have been visited by individuals more frequently than by groups. The Blood of the Ancestors' Grotto stands out as a place for group rites. I presume group use also occurred at Yellow Springs and the cliff face bleeding rock in southern Tennessee. The reuse of all of these places allows them to be called fertility *shrines,* shrines for addressing deities thought to be responsible for fertility.

I believe that in the case of the Cumberland and Ozarks plateau shelters we are looking at fertility shrines where it was appropriate to make sandal and textile offerings, much as is still done today in the Mexican state of Jalisco by Wixarika women. Typically these textiles are miniatures and are accompanied by miniature looms. Numerous small remnants of twined textile have been recovered in a handful of Midcontinent shelters such as the four pieces from Haystack that averaged 28.7 mm × 3 to 5 mm in diameter (Cowan 1979a:14). In places with such good preservation, should small remnants be considered the insignificant portion of a nearly completely decayed large piece of textile or a significant portion of a small textile? I think it is the latter—that the extremely small pieces of fabrics should be taken to reflect an extremely small parent source—in short, examples of miniature weavings or offerings.

The fertility shrines of the midcontinental U.S. provide an excellent inroad to explore women's gaze upon the landscape of the Cumberland Plateau and the Ozarks. They also suggest ancient groups who were matrilocal. Various chapters in Carr and Chase (2005) have argued that the southeastern Ohio Hopewell were matrilineal. Retreating was a trait associated with matrilineal societies, most often (Galloway 1997) allowing for the projection that much of the Cumberland Plateau and the Ozarks were occupied by matrilineal groups at least by late Late Archaic times.

These midcontinental fertility shrines can now be considered in tandem with the abundant examples of similar shrines in the western United States. Many more examples of sandal shrines can be found around the shores of ancient Lake Bonneville in the Great Basin (e.g., Hogup Cave) as can vulvar rocks in California, and in the Southwestern U.S. (e.g., McGowan 1982). Greer and Greer (Chapter 5) offer details of northern Plains vulva rocks. Details of these western places make an even better case for a woman's gaze across the landscape but lie outside the scope of this paper.

Whether hunter-gatherers, gardeners, or farmers, fertility for individuals and for groups—in the form of babies, descendants, and food—was a major concern. Far from being outside the capabilities of archaeologists, fertility is easily addressed with our techniques and place-based focus. While we now realize that hunter-gatherers spent far less time in the pursuit of food for physical survival than anthropologists once thought, I would assert that far more of their ritual, their artifact production, and their site-making was concerned with continuation than we currently realize.

REFERENCES CITED

Aiken, Melvin
1970   *Hogup Cave*. University of Utah, Anthropology Papers 93. Salt Lake City.

Applegate, Darlene

2008 Woodland. In *Archaeology of Kentucky: An Update*, Vol. 1, David Pollack, editor, pp. 339–604. Kentucky Heritage Council, Historic Preservation Comprehensive Plan Report No. 3. Lexington, KY.

Barker, Gary

1997 Upland Middle Archaic Adaptation in Tennessee's Western Highland Rim, a View from the Austin Cave Site. *Tennessee Anthropologist* 22(2):177–223.

Callahan, Kevin

2004 Pica, Geophagy, and Rock-Art in the Eastern United States. In *The Rock-Art of Eastern North America: Capturing Images and Insight*, Carol Diaz-Granados and James Duncan, editors, pp. 65–76. University of Alabama Press, Tuscaloosa.

Carey, Heather, Mary McCorvie, and Mark Wagner

2010 "A Peculiar Method" of Grinding: Examples of Indian Kettles and Hominy Holes from Southern Illinois. Paper presented at the Southeastern Archaeological Conference, Lexington, KY.

Carr, Christopher, and D. Troy Case (editors)

2005 *Gathering Hopewell: Society, Ritual and Ritual Interaction*. Springer, New York.

Christie, Jessica (editor)

2009 *Landscapes of Origin in the Americas: Creation Narratives Linking Ancient Places and Present Communities*. University of Alabama Press, Tuscaloosa.

Claassen, Cheryl

2001 Engendering Appalachian Archaeology. In *Archaeology of the Appalachian Highlands*, Lynne Sullivan and Susan Prezzano, editors, pp. 300–305. University of Tennessee Press, Knoxville.

2010 *Feasting with Shellfish: Archaic Ritual and Landscape in the Southern Ohio Valley*. University of Tennessee Press, Knoxville.

2011 Rock Shelters as Women's Retreats: Understanding Newt Kash. *American Antiquity* 76(4):628–641.

2013 Fertility, A Place-based Gift to Groups. In *Género y Arqueología en Mesoamérica. Homenaje a Rosemary A. Joyce*, María J. Rodríguez-Shadow and Susan Kellogg, coordinators, pp. 198–225. Centro de Estudios de Antropología de la Mujer, Las Cruces, NM.

2014 Offerings of Abundance. Paper presented at the Annual Meeting of the Society for American Archaeology, Austin, TX.

2015 *Rituals and Beliefs in Archaic Eastern North America: A Guide*. University of Alabama Press, Tuscaloosa.

Classen, Constance

1993 *Inca Cosmology and the Human Body*. University of Utah Press, Salt Lake City.

Cowan, Wesley

1979a Excavation at the Haystack Rockshelters, Powell County, Kentucky. *Midcontinental Journal of Archaeology* 4(1):3–33.

1979b Prehistoric Plant Utilization at the Rogers Rockshelter Powell County, Kentucky. Master's thesis, Department of Anthropology, University of Kentucky, Lexington.

Cowan, Wesley, Edwin Jackson, Katherine Moore, Andrew Nickelhoff,
and Tristine Smart
1981   The Cloudsplitter Rockshelter, Menifee County, Kentucky: A Preliminary
          Report. *Southeastern Archaeological Conference Bulletin* 24:60–76.
Coy, Fred, Thomas Fuller, Larry Meadows, and James Swauger
1997   *Rock Art of Kentucky*. University Press of Kentucky, Lexington.
Crothers, George
2012   Early Woodland Ritual Use of Caves in Eastern North America. *American
          Antiquity* 77(3):524–542.
DeBoer, Warren
2001   Of Dice and Women: Gambling and Exchange in Native North America.
          Journal of Archaeological Method and Theory 8(3):215–268.
Dellinger, Sam
1936   Baby Cradles of the Ozark Bluff Shelters. *American Antiquity* 1(3):197–214.
Duncan, James, and Carol Diaz-Granados
2004   Empowering the SECC: The "Old Woman" and Oral Tradition. In *Rock-Art
          of Eastern North America*, Carol Diaz-Granados and James Duncan, editors,
          pp. 190–218. University of Alabama Press, Tuscaloosa.
Ellis, Florence, and Laurens Hammack
1968   The Inner Sanctum of Feather Cave, a Mogollon Sun and Earth Shrine
          Linking Mexico and the Southeast. *American Antiquity* 33(1):25–44.
Franklin, Jay
2002   The Prehistory of Fentress County, Tennessee: An Archaeological Survey.
          Doctoral Dissertation, Department of Anthropology, University of Tennessee,
          Knoxville.
Funkhouser, William, and William Webb
1929   *The So-Called Ash Caves in Lee County Kentucky*, Vol. 1, No. 2.
          Department of Anthropology and Archaeology, University of Kentucky,
          Lexington.
1930   Rockshelters of Wolfe and Powell Counties, Kentucky. Vol. 1, No. 4.
          Department of Anthropology and Archaeology, University of Kentucky,
          Lexington.
Galloway, Patricia
1997   Where Have All the Menstrual Huts Gone? In *Women in Prehistory: North
          America and Mesoamerica*, Cheryl Claassen and Rosemary Joyce, editors,
          pp. 47–64. University of Pennsylvania Press, Philadelphia.
Gatschet, Albert
1884   *A Migration Legend of the Creek Indians*. Brinton's Library of Aboriginal
          American Literature, No. 4. D. G. Brinton, Philadelphia.
Geib, Phil
2000   Sandal Types and Archaic Prehistory on the Colorado Plateau. *American
          Antiquity* 65(3):509–524.
Gremillion, Kristen
1996   Early Agricultural Diet in Eastern North America: Evidence from Two
          Kentucky Rockshelters. *American Antiquity* 61(3):520–536.
1998   3000 Years of Human Activity at the Cold Oak Shelter. In *Current
          Archaeological Research in Kentucky*, Vol. 5, Charles Hockensmith,

K. Carstens, C. Stout, and S. Rivers, editors, pp. 1–14. Kentucky Heritage Council, Frankfurt.

Gremillion, Kristen, Kathryn Jakes, and Virginia Wimberley

2000   The Research Potential of Textile Artifacts: An Example from Carter County. In *Current Archaeological Research in Kentucky*, Vol. 6, David Pollack and Kristen Gremillion, editors, pp. 47–58. Kentucky Heritage Council, Frankfort.

Hall, Robert

1997   *An Archaeology of the Soul: North American Indian Belief and Ritual.* University of Illinois Press, Urbana.

Harper, Ross

1999   To Render the God of the Waters Propitious: Hunting and Human-Animal Relations in the Northeast Woodlands. Doctoral Dissertation, Department of Anthropology, University of Connecticut, Storrs.

Hill, Sarah

1997   *Weaving New Worlds: Southeastern Cherokee Women and Their Basketry.* University of North Carolina Press, Chapel Hill.

Homsey, Lara, Renee Walker, and Kandace Hollenbach

2010   What's for Dinner? Investigating Food Processing Technologies at Dust Cave, Alabama. *Southeastern Archaeology* 29:182–196.

Ison, Cecil

2004   Farming, Gender, and Shifting Social Organization. In *Rock Art of Eastern North America*, Carol Diaz-Granados and James Duncan, editors, pp. 177–189. University of Alabama Press, Tuscaloosa.

Jackson, Thomas

1991   Pounding Acorn: Women's Production as Social and Economic Focus. In *Engendering Archaeology*, Margaret Conkey and Joan Gero, editors, pp. 301–327. Routledge, London.

Kearney, Amanda

2008   Gender in Australian Landscape Archaeology. In *Handbook of Landscape Archaeology*, Bruno David and Julian Thomas, editors, pp. 247–255. World Archaeological Congress Research Handbooks in Archaeology. Left Coast Press, Walnut Creek, CA.

King, Mary

1974   Salts Cave Textiles: A Preliminary Account. In *Archaeology of the Mammoth Cave Area*, Patty Jo Watson, editor, pp. 31–40. Academic Press, New York.

Koldehoff, Brad, Jenna Kuttruff, Brian Butler, and Marie Standifer

2008   Kerr Canyon Textile and the Importance of Packrats (*Neotoma floridana*) in the Eastern United States. *Midcontinental Journal of Archaeology* 33(2):183–195.

Kuttruff, Jenna, Gail DeHart, and Michael O'Brien

1998   7500 Years of Prehistoric Footwear from Arnold Research Cave, Missouri. *Science* 281(5373):72–75.

LeBeau, Sebastian

2009   Reconstructing Lakota Ritual in the Landscape: The Identification and Typing System for Traditional Cultural Property Sites. Doctoral dissertation, Department of Anthropology, University of Minnesota, Minneapolis.

Loendorf, Lawrence, Christopher Chippindale, and David Whitley (editors)
2005   *Discovering North America Rock Art*. University of Arizona Press, Tucson.
Marquardt, William, and Patty Jo Watson
2005   Regional Survey and Testing. In *Archaeology of the Middle Green River Region, Kentucky*, William Marquardt and Patty Jo Watson, editors, pp. 41–70. Institute of Archaeology and Paleoenvironmental Studies, Monograph No. 5. Florida Museum of Natural History, University of Florida, Gainesville.
McGowan, Charlotte
1978   Female Fertility Themes in Rock Art. *Journal of New World Archaeology* 2(4):15–27.
1982   *Ceremonial Fertility Sites in Southern California*. San Diego Museum Papers No. 14. San Diego Museum of Man, San Diego.
Miller, Mary, and Karl Taube
1993   *An Illustrated Dictionary of The Gods and Symbols of Ancient Mexico and the Maya*. Thames and Hudson, NY.
Milne, Courtney
1994   *Sacred Places in North America: A Journey into the Medicine Wheel*. Stewart, Tabori and Chang, NY.
Moore, John
1974   A Study of Religious Symbolism Among the Cheyenne Indians. Doctoral dissertation, New York University.
Murphy, James
1975   *An Archaeology of the Hocking Valley*. Ohio University Press, Athens.
Nagy, Imre
1994   A Typology of Cheyenne Shield Designs. *Plains Anthropologist* 39 (147):5–36.
National Museum of the American Indian
2005   *Listening to Our Ancestors: The Art of Native Life Along the Pacific Northwest Coast*. Museum of the American Indian, Smithsonian Press, Washington DC.
Norder, John
2003   Marking Place and Creating Space in Northern Algonquian Landscapes: The Rock-art of the Lake of the Woods Region, Ontario. Doctoral dissertation, Department of Anthropology, University of Michigan, Ann Arbor.
Orchard, William
1920   *Sandals and Other Fabrics from Kentucky Caves*. Museum of the American Indian, Heye Foundation, New York.
Orr, Ellison
1949   The Enlarged Crevices of Iowa. *Minnesota Archaeologist* 15:7–23.
Parkman, Breck
1992   Toward a Proto-Hokan Ideology. In *Ancient Images, Ancient Thought: The Archaeology of Ideology*, Sean Goldsmith, Sandra Garvie, David Selin, and Jeannette Smith, editors, pp.365–370. Proceedings of the 23rd Annual Conference of the Archaeological Association of the University of Calgary.
2007   Pit-and-Groove Antiquity in New World Prehistory. *California State Parks Science Notes 89*. California Department of Parks and Recreation, Sacramento

Rajnovich, Grace
1994   *Reading Rock Art: Interpreting the Indian Rock Paintings of the Canadian Shield*. Natural Heritage/Natural History Inc., Toronto.

Rapid City Journal
2013   Blood Run on verge of becoming SD state park. 13 January 2013.

Sandstrom, Alan
1992   *Corn Is Our Blood*. University of Oklahoma Press, Norman.

Sassaman, Ken
2010   *The Eastern Archaic Historicized*. Altamira Press, Walnut Creek, CA.

Schaefer, Stacy
2002   *To Think with a Good Heart: Wixárika Women, Weavers, and Shamans*. University of Utah Press, Salt Lake City.

Scholtz, Sandra
1975   *Prehistoric Plies*. Arkansas Archaeological Survey, Fayetteville.

Schwartz, Doug
1958   Sandals and textiles from Mammoth Cave National Park. Manuscript, Mammoth Cave National Park Library, Mammoth Cave, Kentucky.

Scully, Vincent
1975   *Pueblo: Mountain, Village, Dance*. University of Chicago Press, Chicago.

Shippee, J.
1966   The Archaeology of Arnold Research Cave, Callaway County, Missouri. *Missouri Archaeologist* 28:1–107.

Smith, Donald
2005   Carpenter Brook Revisited: Social Context and Early Late Woodland Ceramic Variation in Central New York State. Doctoral Dissertation, Department of Anthropology, SUNY Buffalo.

Spears, Carol
1975   Hammers, Nuts and Jolts, Cobbles, Cobbles, Cobbles: Experiments in Cobble Technologies in Search of Correlates. In *Arkansas Eastman Archeological Project* Charles Baker, editor, pp. 83–116. Arkansas Archeological Survey Research Report No. 6, Fayetteville.

Stafford, Russell
1991   Archaic Period Logistical Foraging Strategies in West-Central Illinois. *Midcontinental Journal of Archaeology* 16:212–245.

Stelle, Lenville
2009   The Rock Art of the Blood of the Ancestors Grotto (11SA557): A Natural History of the Imaging Methodology. *Illinois Archaeology* 21:191–212.
2012   The Rock Art of the Blood of the Ancestors Grotto: The Archaeology of Religious Theater. *Illinois Archaeology* 24:1–70.

Sundstrom, Linea
2004   *Storied Stone: Indian Rock Art of the Black Hills Country*. University of Oklahoma Press, Norman.

Thomas, Larissa
2001   The Gender Division of Labor in Mississippian Households: Its Role in Shaping Production for Exchange. In *Archaeological Studies of Gender in the Southeastern United States*, Jane Eastman and Christopher Rodning, editors, pp. 27–56. University of Florida Press, Gainesville.

Tooker, Elizabeth

1979　　*Native North American Spirituality of the Eastern Woodlands*. Paulist Press, New York.

Versaggi, Nina, LouAnn Wurst, Cregg Madrigal, and Andrea Lain

2001　　Adding Complexity to Late Archaic Research in the Northeastern Appalachians. In *Archaeology of the Appalachian Highlands*, Lynne Sullivan and Susan Prezzano, editors, pp. 121–136. University of Tennessee Press, Knoxville.

Watson, Patty Jo

1969　　*The Prehistory of Salts Cave, Kentucky.* Reports of Investigations, No. 16. Illinois State Museum, Springfield.

Watson, Patty Jo, Mary Kennedy, P. Willey, Louise Robbins, and Ronald Wilson

2005　　Prehistoric Footprints in Jaguar Cave, Tennessee. *Journal of Field Archaeology* 30(1):25–43.

Webb, William, and William Funkhouser

1936　　*Rock Shelters in Menifee County Kentucky*. Department of Anthropology and Archaeology, Vol. 3, No. 4. University of Kentucky, Lexington.

Witthoft, John, and Wendell Hadlock

1946　　Cherokee-Iroquois Little People. *The Journal of American Folklore* 59(234):413–423.

2

BEDROCK MORTAR HOLE SITES AS ARTIFACTS OF WOMEN'S TASKSCAPES
Late Archaic and Early Woodland Chaîne Opératoire on the Upper Cumberland Plateau of Tennessee

Jay Franklin, Lucinda Langston, and Meagan Dennison

More than 500 prehistoric archaeological sites have been recorded on the Upper Cumberland Plateau (hereafter, the UCP) of Tennessee in Southern Appalachia over the course of 18 years of fieldwork (Figure 2.1). This work represents the first *long-term,* systematic prehistoric archaeological research in the region (Franklin 2002, 2006a, 2006b, 2008a, 2008b; Franklin and Bow 2008; Bow and Franklin 2009; Langston and Franklin 2010; Franklin et al. 2010; Franklin et al. 2012; Franklin et al. 2013; Langston 2013). The work has mostly concentrated along the western escarpment of the plateau. The vast majority of these sites are rock shelters because they dominate the landscape of the region. There are tens of thousands of rock shelters in the region—a geological reality that is quite unique to this landform.[1] The original purpose of this research was to identify and investigate prehistoric archaeological sites in order to define and write the culture history of this region (Franklin 2002, 2006a, 2006b). This first step is important because it has been demonstrated that the cultural chronological sequences of adjacent lowland river valleys cannot be used to interpret the cultural sequences on the Upper Cumberland Plateau. More recently, however, our work on the UCP has emphasized site formation processes, functional studies, mobility patterns, and predictive modeling of settlement practices and informed choices made by prehistoric hunter-gatherers (Franklin et al.

Figure 2.1. Upper Cumberland Plateau study area.

2010, 2012; Dye et al. 2010; Langston 2013; Dennison 2013). This work has largely been carried out from a gender neutral perspective.

We attempt to reinvestigate certain aspects of this recent research on the UCP from an agency perspective, with a focus on women as decision makers for site selection and use. We specifically focus on investigating the distribution of bedrock mortar hole sites (BRMs), assuming these are the products of women's labor. We first review ethnographic data dealing with bedrock mortar holes and the division of labor among hunting and gathering groups. We then discuss previous research on the Cumberland Plateau and nearby regions that has found evidence of women's work and ritual. After justifying the attribution of bedrock mortar to women's activities, we turn our attention to the archaeological record of the UCP of Tennessee and discuss the distribution of bedrock mortar hole sites and rock shelter sites with BRMs from a macro-perspective and how these landforms relate to activities directed and conducted by women during the Late Archaic and Early Woodland periods.

We wish to stress that there are some limitations to this research. First, the ethnographic data utilized here may not be representative of the groups that created the prehistoric record on the UCP. Despite this, ethnographic analogy is still useful to archaeologists as it provides a baseline from which to work when interpreting the archaeological record. Further, we emphasize the fact that in the world over, gathering and plant processing was largely the domain of women, while hunting and other higher risk behaviors were typically associated with men. This seems to be documented well enough (Hollenbach 2009; Homsey et al. 2010:190). Second, the study of bedrock mortar holes is limited in that chronological and cultural context for these features in many cases is not presently known, which can present problems in interpretation. Despite these limitations, we suggest that the archaeological record of bedrock mortar hole sites on the Upper Cumberland Plateau is largely an artifact of women in the Late Archaic and Early Woodland periods selecting and using the region as a taskscape for the intensive collecting and processing of acorns. Our interpretations are couched within a *chaîne opératoire* theoretical perspective.

Beyond Flaked Stone Tool Technologies: The *Chaîne Opératoire*

A detailed explication of the *chaîne opératoire* is beyond the scope of this chapter. However, it is important to note that in the *chaîne opératoire*, social and technical acts are not differentiated (Leroi-Gourhan 1993). The *chaîne opératoire* in its holistic sense as laid out by Leroi-Gourhan (1993) is similar to Ingold's (1993) "taskscape." A taskscape is "the entire ensemble of tasks, in their mutual interlocking. . . . Just as the landscape is an array of related features, so—by analogy—the taskscape is an array of related activities. . . . [T]he taskscape is to labour what the landscape is to land" (Ingold 1993:158). Gamble (1999:86) has essentially equated the taskscape to *chaîne opératoire*. We also use it synonymously with Pelegrin's (1993) "*manières de faire*," or ways of doing. As the landscape is essentially an array of related geologic and topographic features (the myriad rock shelters, bluff overhangs, caves, and open sandstone bedrock exposures of the UCP), the taskscape is a collection of related social and technical activities (e.g., hunting, foraging, and nut processing) (Gamble 1999:137). The notion of a taskscape is a concept that links locales, or sites, to a region, in an analytical sense (Gamble 1999:68, 87). Leroi-Gourhan espoused a group approach to analysis, which of course is quite consistent with an anthropological approach that employs both comparative and holistic evaluation. Nothing has meaning in isolation. "Everything humans make—tools, gestures, and products alike—is impregnated with group aesthetics. . . Individuals introduce their personal variations into the traditional framework and, safe in the knowledge of belonging to the group, draw some of their sense of existing as individuals from the margin of freedom allowed them" (Leroi-Gourhan 1993:253). This is important given the nature of archaeological assemblages and our analyses of (technological) traditions. When we analyze assemblages, we are looking at palimpsests of the actions of multiple individuals over an undefined period of time (Leroi-Gourhan's "group aesthetics").

The *chaîne opératoire* has largely been applied to the study of lithic technology. It has also been criticized for not being holistic in application in the sense that the use of the *chaîne opératoire* fostered great understanding of the organization of production but not the social contexts in which it was conceived and generated (Edmonds 1990). Further, other researchers point to a lack of attention in the *chaîne opératoire* to human interactions with their environments (de la Torre and Mora 2009:21). We believe we have a great opportunity here to apply the *chaîne opératoire* in its holistic conception initially outlined by Leroi-Gourhan. This has important implications for the interpretations offered concerning the archaeological resolution of gender and gender roles on the UCP in prehistory because we suggest that not only were these bedrock mortar hole sites used primarily by women, but in fact the sites, and by extension, taskscapes were initially selected by women. Women identified, selected, and manipulated their environments in both social and technical ways.

Ethnographic Background

This paper is one of several in this volume, each citing regional ethnographic information, that finds that women focused attention on bedrock outcrops or boulders (Introduction, chapter 1, 3, 4, 5, 6 and 7). There is also ethnographic information available on the use of mortars by women in the southeastern United States.

Division of Labor in Foraging Groups

Investigations of subsistence practices can help inform interpretations of mobility and social organization of hunting and gathering groups.

Intertwined in this realm of investigation is the division of labor between men, women, children, adolescents, and the elderly. While interpretations of the exact workings of these roles may remain elusive in many archaeological contexts, using what is known from ethnographic data may help to increase the resolution of different tasks of individuals that occurred in the past.

In order to interpret the archaeological record on the Cumberland Plateau with an eye toward a woman's gaze across this landscape, we must first consider ethnographic sources of information on the kinds of activities that may have been conducted by men, women, and children in the past. While no ethnographic analogy will be completely representative of any archaeological assemblage because communities of practice are historically situated, this kind of information may help to elucidate certain aspects of prehistory that would otherwise remain unknown. Ethnographic data on foragers in the southeastern United States is nonexistent. Instead, accounts of indigenous peoples from this region are based on groups that practiced maize agriculture and who were later included in activities related to the spread of capitalism to the New World (e. g., the trading, cash economy). These ethnographic accounts should not be dismissed, however, as they may represent some historical continuity with the people that inhabited the Cumberland Plateau during the Late Archaic and Woodland time periods.

Some indigenous North American groups were still foragers at the time of contact, however. These people may not be historically related to southeastern groups but may help us to better understand the group dynamics of prehistoric North American foragers. Additionally, there are many groups worldwide who have been extensively observed by anthropologists and archaeologists alike. These data serve as important reference points for how *most* hunting and gathering societies divide tasks, time, and foraging activities among males and females of different ages and abilities. Again, the data do not fit perfectly with the archaeological record of the Southeast; however, it is important to establish a baseline for the interpretations that follow. Below we briefly highlight aspects of southeastern agriculturalists, North American foragers, and consistent patterns seen on a large scale.

Southeast

It is well documented that at the time of European contact, women were primarily in charge of agricultural-based subsistence activities (Adair

2009; Swanton 1946). These include hoeing, planting, weeding, harvesting, and processing, although men likely shared in some of this responsibility. Perdue (1999) notes that among the Cherokee, men assisted women with the initial planting of crops, largely removed themselves for matters of war and hunting for most of the growing period, but returned again to assist with harvesting. Skeletal analysis of pre-contact Mississippian populations corroborates this—women tended to have well developed arm and leg bones, as well as characteristic features on the forearms indicative of maize processing (Bridges 1989:391–392). Men were less involved in subsistence related activities at the time of contact, except for hunting, but were more focused on politics and warfare. It has been assumed by many that this trend of women's foraging activities centering on plant food gathering and processing has deep historical connections in the Southeast (Fritz 1999; Watson and Kennedy 1998), even as early as the Paleoindian Period (Hollenbach 2009). For this paper, we assume that women were primarily responsible for plant food gathering and processing.

Broad Trends

Anthropology as a discipline has moved well beyond the days of classifying men's and women's roles in traditional societies as mere binaries of division of labor. Nonetheless, certain tendencies may be highlighted. Women are not strictly gatherers, nor are men strictly hunters, but men and women forage based on criteria of the predictability of resources, risk involved, and social factors, such as sharing and prestige. This is noted in ethnographic data from groups located in Oceania (Bliege Bird 2008) and South America (Hawkes 1990). As several authors point out, men tend to target risky resources; however, when acquired, these resources are more likely to be shared (Hawkes 1990; Kelly 2007; Panter-Brick 2002) and processed by women. Women, on the other hand, tend to target reliable and predictable resources, which allows for adjustments in time allocation and resource exploitation as needed to meet required caloric intake (Bliege Bird 2008).

Bedrock Mortar Holes

W. D. Funkhouser and William S. Webb (Funkhouser and Webb 1929, 1930, 1932; Webb and Funkhouser 1929, 1936) were the first to intensively document bedrock mortar holes in the southeastern United

States (but see Myer 1924, 2014, 1928). They investigated at least 44 rock shelter sites on the Cumberland Plateau of Kentucky and identified two archaeological cultures in their work. The earlier culture was found within the often thick ash beds of the shelters and was characterized by mortar holes and nutting stones, "flints," remains of early plant cultigens, burials, and occasionally rock art. It is this culture that Claassen has argued had fertility shrines and menstrual retreat shelters (Chapter 1). Webb and Funkhouser tentatively suggested an Algonquin association. The latter culture they believed was ephemeral and represented only cursory visits to the shelters. It was largely characterized by woven textiles and relatively few fragments of pottery either scattered on the surface or in deposits just above the great ash beds. It seems fairly clear that Funkhouser and Webb (1929) associated this latter culture with historic groups, namely the Cherokees, based on perceived similarities in pottery styles. In fact, they thought it possible that neither archaeological culture was necessarily prehistoric, although they did suggest that the former may have been of great antiquity. In actuality, the two archaeological cultures recorded by these early pioneering archaeologists represent the Archaic and Woodland, broadly speaking. It is also clear that there was

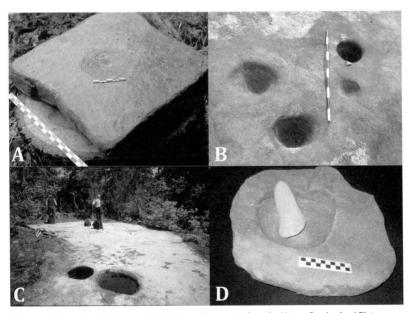

Figure 2.2. Examples of nut processing features documented on the Upper Cumberland Plateau: A) nutting stone, B) bedrock mortar holes, C) kettle holes, and D) portable mortar.

Table 2.1. Bedrock Mortar Hole Sites on the UCP of Tennessee.

SITE[1]	# OF FEATURES	NUTTING STONES	CLASSIC MORTARS	KETTLE HOLES	ASSOCIATED VEGETATION
Upland Open-Air Exposures					
Balam Beaty Rock	62		*		Northern Red Oak
Neely Farm Rock(s)	40		*		Hickory
Sandy Rock	26		*		Northern Red Oak
Mother HoleRock	20		*	*	Northern Red Oak
Mossy Rock	19		*	*	Northern Red Oak
Norman Rock	14		*		Northern Red Oak
Tinch Rock	10		*		Northern Red Oak
Backyard Rock	9		*		Northern Red Oak
Indian Kettle Holes Site	6	*		*	Multiple red oak species
Prickly Pear Rock	6		*		Northern Red Oak
Paul Tench Rock 1	6			*	Northern Red Oak
Cookin' Rock	4			*	Northern Red Oak
Paul Tench Rock 3	4				Northern Red Oak
Minner' Branch Rock	3		*	*	Northern Red Oak
Old Sunbright Rock	3		*		Northern Red Oak
Golf Course Rock	3		*	*	Hickory
Barn Rock	2		*	*	Northern Red Oak
Hull Rock	2		*		Hickory
Paul Tench Rock 2	2		*		Northern Red Oak
Creek Bend Hole	1		*		Hickory
Garage Rock	1		*		Northern Red Oak
SP2	1		*		Northern Red Oak
Rock Shelter/House or Cave					
Gwinn Cove Shelter	13	*	*		Northern Red Oak
Sachsen Cave Shelter	12	*			Northern Red Oak
Narrows Point Rock House	7	*			Hickory
Roaring Gamble Rock Shelter	6		*		Hickory
Ward Rock House	6	*			Hickory
Cross-Slide Shelter	5	*			Northern Red Oak
Barn Creek Rock Shelter	4	*			Hickory
Rock Creek Mortar Shelter	3	*	*		Hickory
Jerry's Rock House	3	*			Hickory
Low Bluff Shelter	3	*			Northern Red Oak

Site	No.				Vegetation Community
Yellow Creek Falls Rock Shelter	3	*	*		Northern Red Oak
The General's East Shelter	3		*		Hickory
Fire in the Hole Shelter	3	*			Hickory
Goat Bluff Rock Shelter	3	*			Hickory
Snakebite Cave	2		*		Northern Red Oak
Hull Cave	2		*		Hickory
Tevepaugh Rock Shelter	2	*			Northern Red Oak
Raven Cave	2	*			Hickory
White Oak Rock Shelter	2		*		Hickory
Long Branch Shelter 1	2	*			Northern Red Oak
Four Dog Rock Shelter	2	*			Hickory
Hemlock Falls Rock House	2	*			Hickory
Ward Bluff	2	*			Hickory
G81	2	*			Hickory
Duck Under Rock House	2	*			Northern Red Oak
Moccasin Gap Rock Shelter	2		*		Hickory
Great Oak Shelter	1	*			Northern Red Oak
Fatty Point	1	*			Hickory
A.J's Shelter	1	*			Northern Red Oak
G64	1	*			Northern Red Oak
Indian Rockhouse	1	*			Hickory
Lonesome Hole Rock Shelter	1		*		Hickory
Burned Out Shelter	1		*		Hickory
Big Rock House	1	*			Northern Red Oak
On Top of a Rock Shelter/Cave					
Winningham Rock	92	*	*		Northern Red Oak
Calf Rock	41	*	*	*	HIckory
Cooktown Site	22		*		Hickory
Gernt Shelter Cave	13	*	*		Hickory
S16B	1		*		Hickory
Isolated Find					
J10	1	*			Northern Red Oak
40FN12	1	*			Northern Red Oak
Rockcastle Creek Boulder	1	*			Hickory

1. The total number of features (i.e., one feature equals one nutting stone OR one classic mortar hole OR one kettle hole) per site is provided. An asterisk (*) indicates which type(s) of features were recorded. Additionally, the associated vegetation community (using modern soil surveys as a proxy) for each site is listed. White Oak is ubiquitous in the region and therefore all but one BRM site (Indian Kettle Holes) is in close proximity to vegetation communities of this species.

some Mississippian, or late prehistoric, pottery recovered based on some vessel forms and the presence of features, such as strap handles.

Bedrock mortars are holes ground directly into *in situ* sandstone, usually, and limestone much less frequently (they were frequently ground in granite bedrock in California). They are permanent site furniture in that they are ground (or perhaps cut) into geologic features, such as sandstone outcrops and large immobile breakdown clasts resulting from the mechanical weathering of bedrock. These are differentiated from nutting (lap) stones that are small depressions or pits worked into the flat surfaces of portable sandstone rock fragments. These two types of ground stone facilities differ in the typical size of the ground depressions (small and very shallow on nutting stones; more variable but deeper in bedrock mortar features) and in their portability (Figure 2.2; see Table 2.1 herein for measurements). However, Funkhouser and Webb (1930) documented portable mortars in Kentucky, and we have documented at least two cases of portable or semi-portable mortars in our survey work (Figure 2.2D). So perhaps the differences are ones of degree rather than kind, at least in certain cases. In any case, the two types of features (that is nutting stones *vis a vis* BRMs) have different implications for site selection and use.

Given that the vast majority of bedrock mortars are permanent features, the implication is that prehistoric peoples intensively used these sites and invested great time in generating these features. The pits on the smaller nutting stones are always very shallow and could have been created fairly quickly. Therefore, nutting stones have little implication regarding either the intensity or duration of site use. Nutting stones are found almost exclusively in rock shelters on the UCP and were likely used for hickory nut processing as we show later.

Among bedrock mortar holes, variability in diameter and depth can be great. It is generally assumed that "hominy holes," a common term first introduced into the archaeological literature by Webb and Funkhouser (1929) early in the 20th century, were used for grinding corn and/or nut mast, such as acorns, hickory nuts, walnuts, and chestnuts. In fact, Webb and Funkhouser postulated that not only were these features used for grinding, but they were also used for percussion crushing of vegetable materials. This is consistent with ethnographic accounts from California. "There is the notion that acorn flour is created by 'grinding'; the process is strictly one of pounding or hitting and crushing the acorns" (Ortiz 1996:73). In their surveys, they recovered limestone pestles and pestle fragments in the bottom of several hominy holes and wooden pestles and stone pestles in shelter fill. Humbard and Humbard (1964) were skeptical concerning the use of these features as mortars. They conducted experiments and concluded that grinding corn in hominy holes was virtually impossible while walnuts were easily ground into meal. Their experiments raise a valid point. Therefore, these features are more appropriately termed bedrock mortars or BRMs. In point of fact, Myer recognized this before other researchers (1924, 2014, 1928b:498). Henson and Martz (1979) suggested that they may (also) have been used to catch rainwater. Other early researchers suggested that perhaps they were used as support holes for the placement of totems or poles (e.g., suggestion by Cox, cited in Parris 1946 and Hassler 1946:61). We have recorded two sites with evenly spaced ground holes on vertical faces of enormous breakdown boulders immediately in front of shelters that may have served as support holes for some sort of temporary structure or wind break (Franklin 2002:116, 126). In any case, the tangible evidence, including their form and association with grinding handstones (pestles), overwhelmingly indicates that these features are the result of grinding (manufacture) and pounding (function) grinding.

We have also identified a different type of hole on the UCP of Tennessee that we refer to as "kettle holes" (Figure 2.2C). One of our sites, located in the Big South Fork National River and Recreation Area just across the border in Kentucky, is called Indian Kettle Holes Site (with a posted sign even). The site also has classic BRMs and a portable mortar (Franklin 2002:189). Webb and Funkhouser apparently did not record such features, and Ison (2001, pers. comm.) indicates they are not present in the Daniel Boone section of the plateau in Kentucky. However, they have been recorded elsewhere (Bartlett 1984; Schwegman 2003). In our study area, kettle holes typically range from 30–60 cm in diameter and 20–70 cm deep, clearly outside the range of classic BRMs. Franklin (2002:178, 180) offers a number of plausible explanations for their function. Given that virtually all of the kettle hole sites also have classic (smaller) BRMs in association, they almost certainly functioned for acorn processing (leaching, boiling, and parching).

Finally, we include features that we are calling rinsing holes. Rinsing holes are located in the bedrock of small creeks and streams in direct spatial association with BRM sites. In some cases, the holes are underwater year round (e. g., Winningham Rock). In other cases, they are located in wet weather stream or erosion channels. It is our opinion that they are not natural features. We have never seen such features in creeks or streams that are not located in direct spatial association with BRM sites. They were almost certainly used for cold water leaching of acorns to remove the tannins (Petruso and Wickens 1984:362; Jackson 1991:305; Ortiz 1996:100, 103). Such features possess basins to hold acorn meal but also allow for a continuous supply of cold water to run over and through the meal to remove tannic acid. Cold water allows for better retention of nut oil as well (Jackson 1991:305).

Modern Research on BRMs in the Eastern Woodlands

The BRM sites that Webb and Funkhouser (1929:702, 709) initially recorded were in the uplands of the Green River drainage in Kentucky, and they initially suggested that perhaps such sites did not occur outside of this area. They went so far as to suggest that this limited distribution of bedrock mortars might indicate a particular ethnic group. Just a few years later, however, they recorded similar sites in eastern Kentucky in the Red and Kentucky River drainages on the Cumberland Plateau (Funkhouser and Webb 1929, 1930; Webb and Funkhouser 1936). In the years since, Ison (2001, pers. comm.) observed many such sites in the Daniel Boone National Forest north of the Kentucky River but only one bedrock mortar site south of the river. Ison (1996) described an affiliation between bedrock mortars, petroglyphs, and incipient horticulture. In fact, he suggested a Terminal Archaic cultural affiliation for bedrock mortar sites within the Daniel Boone Forest and Green River areas of Kentucky. Ison also suggested that these sites reflect the beginnings of matriarchal societies in the uplands of Southern Appalachia. While several of the sites are multi-component, in the many cases where bedrock mortar hole sites possess only a single component, it is always Terminal Archaic (Ison 1996; Cecil Ison 2001, pers. comm.).

Humbard (1963) documented bedrock mortars at the Stanfield-Worley Rock Shelter in north Alabama. Likewise, Henson (1964) recorded a bedrock mortar site in northwest Alabama. Later, Henson and Martz (1979) documented 18 petroglyph sites in north Alabama. Nine of these locations also contain bedrock mortars. Most of these sites possess glyphs that display classic Mississippian iconography, and some are multi-component. More recently, an association of bedrock mortar holes and Mississippian red ochre pictographs has been seen in the Mud Puppy Shelter in northeastern Alabama (Alan Cressler 2014, pers. comm.).

Bartlett (1984) documented a bedrock mortar hole, or "kettle" hole, site in the mountains of southwest Virginia. Diagnostic artifacts indicate that the shelter is multi-component although, the most intensive occupation appears to have occurred during the Woodland period (Bartlett 1984:186). However, some of the diagnostic artifacts he used to make this affiliation are Lamoka and Merom projectile points, typically associated with the Late Archaic period (Justice 1987). This feature, then, could be associated with the Late/Terminal Archaic rather than or in addition to the Woodland period.

Several bedrock mortar hole sites have been identified in the uplands of southern Illinois. In all, at least six sites have been found. Five sites are open air sandstone exposures and one is a prehistoric rock shelter site. One of the open sites also possesses extremely large kettle holes in association with the mortar holes (Schwegman 2003).

BRMs on the Upper Cumberland Plateau Region of Tennessee

Until several years ago, virtually no BRM sites had been identified in the Cumberland Plateau/Escarpment region of Tennessee (or anywhere else in the state, for that matter). Myer (1924, 1928:498) referred to several bedrock mortar "Indian towns" in the area, including Winningham Rock (Myer 2014, 1928:498; Franklin 2002:159–160, 176–178). Working with Myer, Hassler (1946) also described Winningham Rock in some detail (Figure 2.3; Figure 2.4, northernmost site). However, he was writing from memory of archaeological investigations conducted some 30 years prior (Hassler 1947:42). Myer (1924) also makes mention of at least two others in the Cumberland Plateau region of Tennessee. One such shelter, locally known as the Dirt-Rock House (40FN17), was described by Myer as having a large mortar hole capable of holding a gallon of water; petroglyphs were also found inside the shelter.

Franklin (2002:174–195) details 20 BRM sites on the UCP including several open air sandstone bedrock exposures with great variation. Since then, that number has more than tripled as more BRM sites have been discovered on the UCP during subsequent surveys. Franklin (2002:193) suggested that these BRM sites were likely associated with certain vegetation communities, namely oaks, and that BRM sites on the UCP were used for processing acorns. Often multi-component, where only one component was recorded, it was either Late Archaic or Early Woodland, seemingly in accordance with BRM sites in the Cumberland Plateau region of Kentucky (Ison 1996; Claassen 2011). However, only one BRM site, Gernt Shelter Bluff, on the UCP of Tennessee is associated

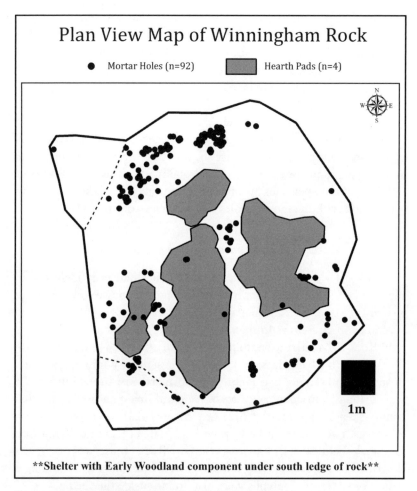

Figure 2.3. Plan view map of Winningham Rock, March 2013.

with rock art (though Myer believed the glyphs at Winningham Rock were ancient).

Thus far, we have documented at least 64 nut processing sites on the UCP of Tennessee (Table 2.1). Based on the features recorded at these sites, three common types of nut processing sites were identified: portable nutting stone sites (rock shelters), classic bedrock mortar hole sites, and kettle hole sites (Figure 2.2). These three site types are not nearly mutually exclusive and, in many cases, features from at least two of the three types were documented at the same site. We recognize that

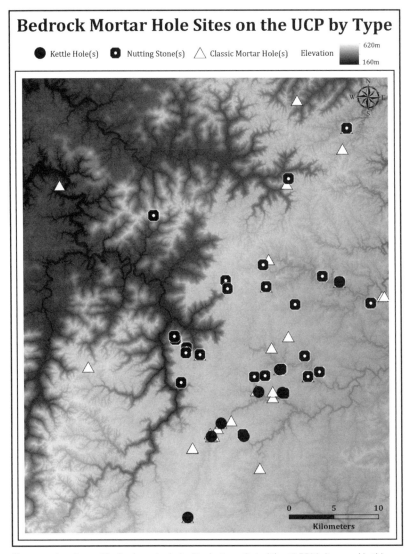

Figure 2.4. Locations of bedrock mortar hole sites by type. Out of the 58 BRM sites used in this study, kettle holes were recorded at 8 sites, nutting stones at 28 sites, and classic mortars at 32 sites.

these features often represent functional and perhaps gender-related differences and that these three site types cannot account for the full range of variation both within and between groups. However, the separation of these sites by "type" serves as a starting point from which to analyze and discuss their geographic distribution and function across the UCP.

Lessons from California BRMs

Bedrock mortar holes are more abundant and better understood in California where Native American populations have been observed using bedrock mortars for processing acorns (Gifford 1936; Jackson 1991; Haney 1992; Ortiz 1996). While ethnographic research indicates that BRMs were used for a variety of resources such as berries and dry meats (Davis 1965) and a variety of nuts, berries, medicinal plants, and dried meat and fish (Barrett and Gifford 1933), it seems clear enough that most were used for pounding and processing acorns. Their ubiquity, storability, and thus, reliability leave little doubt (Jackson 1991:303; Haney 1992:104). The social importance and tradition of pounding acorns has also been well documented (Jackson 1991; Ortiz 1996). For this project, some general observations concerning BRM site distribution and variability in the western U.S. can be related to the UCP region. These observations include ideas about variation in configuration and distribution of BRMs in relation to environmental factors.

First, while some studies suggest that depth variation of BRMs is due to sociocultural differences, the hardness of base rock, and how much/often a BRM was used (White 1985; Johnson 1967), more empirical studies have related variability in the depths of individual mortar holes to functional differences (Barrett and Gifford 1933; Voegelin 1938; McCarthy et al. 1985; Jackson 1991; Ortiz 1996). From their work with the Western Mono populations, McCarthy et al. (1985) developed a typology for mortar holes based on hole depths in relation to functional differences: acorn starter holes (0–5.5 cm), acorn finishing mortars (5.51–9.5 cm), and seed mortars (9.51+ cm). While such a typology may not correlate with BRM sites in the eastern U. S., *sensu stricto*, it does provide an empirical baseline by which to evaluate our BRM sites on the UCP. For instance, the BRMs used for acorn processing in California (e. g., the McCarthy et al. typology) are overall larger in diameter but shallower than those found in Kentucky (Ison 1996:4; see Claassen Table 1.2 for dimensions of BRM holes on the plateau in Kentucky). Our BRM (and kettle) holes on the UCP are much more variable and thus comparable to both the California sites and the Kentucky sites. An obvious possibility is that early cultigens do not appear to have been important on the UCP in Tennessee (we have recovered none) as has been well documented on the plateau in Kentucky (Cowan et al. 1981; Gremillion 1996, 1997).

Clearly, suitable exposures of bedrock are important, and this has also been documented at California sites (Haney 1992:97–98; McCarthy et al. 1985:307). However, we argue that proximity to certain plant communities was more important on the UCP because vast exposures of suitable bedrock are myriad just like the rock shelters.

A final point may be made from reference to California BRM studies, that of social and political issues. BRM sites are not portable commodities like other goods or items. They are fixed places on the landscape (again, just like rock shelters). Of course environmental factors were important. However, the selection of sites almost certainly lies in the domain of women. "The arrangement of mortar features on the landscape, then, is basically the result of decisions by the women who made and used these facilities" (Jackson 1991:314). This is essentially the equivalent of a taskscape. Further, BRM sites provide a suitable environment in which to monitor children. It also provides for interactions with children (Jackson 1991:317). Because these sites could not be traded or handed down in the conventional sense, "some accommodation of property rights must have been necessary when the fixed bedrock mortar facilities were incorporated into the society's material culture" (Jackson 1991:318). Thus, with the selection, use, and inclusion of these sites into the taskscapes of women, we may be seeing indications of matriarchal, or at least matrilocal, cultures. A sense of place then becomes important. This is a sentiment echoed by others, too. "Every woman has her own special rock" (Ortiz 1996:59).

In sum, archaeological and ethnographic work in California has indicated that BRMs were overwhelmingly used to pound and process acorns because they require intensive preparation in order to make them palatable. The costs invested in intensive processing of acorns are more than outweighed by their caloric content, storability, and reliability. Further, because BRM sites are fixed places on the landscape, these sites have implications for ownership and/or a sense of place which appears, in most cases, to have resulted in matrilocal communities. Women passed along property (BRM facilities) and associated tools (pestles, sifting baskets, etc.) essentially the same way people pass along heirlooms. "Like acorn trees, the mortars are owned by an individual or family, each one handed down through the generations" (Ortiz 1996:59). There are social implications as well. Women chose certain rocks to process acorns depending on whether they wished for solitary time or whether they wished to be together (Ortiz 1996:35–36). We believe the spatial associations of BRM rocks on the UCP fit well with this idea of individual rocks and group rocks.

BRM and Women on the Cumberland Plateau

Closer to our study area, few research projects have been conducted on the Cumberland Plateau that address the distinctive roles of women and men; however, two notable exceptions present cases which suggest that the actions and activities of women are visible in the archaeological record. Both studies involve the use of BRMs. Ison (2004) suggests that BRM rock shelter sites located in Kentucky in association with rock art and early domesticates indicate a rise in status of women centering on food production beginning during the Terminal Archaic period. Similar to what we see on the UCP of Tennessee, Ison (2004:179, 187) notes a dramatic increase of sites beginning in the Terminal Archaic, many associated with bedrock mortar holes. However, unlike what is noted on the plateau in Kentucky, we do not typically see the association of rock art with BRMs. Nor do we have evidence of early cultigens on the UCP, much less an association of earliest cultigens with BRMs. This is curious given the proximity of these two areas that occupy the same landform. In fact, it seems only a modern state line separates the two. Ison notes that despite intensive survey, only one BRM site has been discovered in Kentucky south of the Kentucky River. We have recorded one site in Kentucky along the Big South Fork of the Cumberland River, the Indian Kettle Holes Site. Ison believes these areas dominated by BRMs may be culturally bounded regions based in matrilineal kinship. While we tend to agree with Ison, we believe these boundaries were fluid through prehistory and thus the bounding of certain elements (e.g., rock art and early cultigens) may not always correspond to the distribution of others (e.g., BRMs). We also agree with Ison that BRM sites likely reflect the predominance and perhaps ownership by women of these facilities. The lack of rock art and early cultigens does not preclude the fact that intensive acorn processing constitutes a substantial if not dominant contribution by women to the overall subsistence base. Thus our sites on the UCP of Tennessee, like the ones Ison (2004) and Funkhouser and Webb (1930) describe on the plateau in Kentucky likely represent matrilocal/matrilineal communities and "women-owned" sites if not "women-only" sites. Ison's (2004) study, while apparently drawing from a large dataset, is not readily accessible to the archaeological community.

Claassen (2011) also attributes BRM features, rock art, and early cultigens to women but suggests that they and several other identifying features may also be related to rock shelter sites that served as women's retreats (e. g., women-only). Furthermore, Claassen (2011) suggests that cord-marked pottery recovered in these contexts may also be associated with these separation rituals. While Claassen's ideas are compelling and should be explored in furthers studies, this earlier study is plagued by sample size issues. We note here that in our work in the rock shelters on the UCP of Tennessee, like was the case for the features Ison identified, we do not see a similar pattern. Our work indicates shelters were occupied and used by entire family groups for a variety of activities (Franklin et al. 2010, 2012, 2013). That being said, our earlier work was not necessarily designed to explore the division of labor. We have recorded at least one site where we have only recovered pottery. The vessel, however, is plain (not cord-marked) and represents a Late Woodland vessel. The site could perhaps represent a women's retreat of some ilk. In any case, while we do not have the exact associations that Ison and Claassen document on the plateau in Kentucky, we have myriad BRM sites on the UCP of Tennessee that correspond chronologically with their sites (Terminal Archaic and Early Woodland). Further, they have both made cases for sites that significantly represent the activities of women, which Claassen elaborates on in Chapter 1 mustering a larger sample size. In the *chaîne opératoire* we lay out below, we also believe that our BRM sites reflect the selection, use, and perhaps ownership by/ of women.

Chronology of Bedrock Mortar Hole Sites on the UCP of Tennessee

Like Ison (2004) and Claassen (2011), we believe BRM sites reflect activities during the Late/Terminal Archaic and Early Woodland, though it is possible that the use of these continues through the Woodland. In fact, many of our sites are multi-component, ranging from the terminal Pleistocene through the Mississippian. However, where only one or two components have been recorded, it is always Late Archaic and/or Early Woodland. Table 2.2 lists radiometric determinations from sites with BRMs in association. Diagnostic artifacts recovered from Calf Rock include an undifferentiated Late Archaic stemmed biface base, an Early Woodland Greenville biface recovered on site (in both cases from sediments within the holes themselves), and an early Middle Woodland McFarland biface recovered from nearby the rock. Diagnostic artifacts from Calf Rock Cave below range from the Early Archaic through the Mississippian (Franklin 2002). One accelerator mass spectrometry (AMS) determination from the cave is Early Woodland (Table 2.2).

Winningham Rock and Shelter contain artifacts from the Woodland and Mississippian periods. However, most of the material is Early to Middle Woodland, and we have both an AMS and a luminescence date that reflect this (Table 2.2). Charred hickory nut was recovered and dated here, but we also recovered nutting stones in the tiny shelter.

The last site we mention is Rock Creek Mortar Shelter. It is a multi-component site but has a thick Late Archaic midden with both charred acorn and hickory. One nutting stone was recovered from the midden during testing. Two mortar holes are located on the shallow sandstone shelf in the back of the shelter. One AMS determination has a median probability of B.C. 887 (Table 2.2). We also have several new dates that extend this midden back to B.C. 2500 (Franklin et al. 2015). The chronology of our BRMs is curious given research by others that indicate significant efforts at nut processing and the use of rock shelters and caves during the early Middle Archaic (Walthall 1998; Miller 2014; Homsey-Messer 2015). We address this curiosity later in the chapter.

Table 2.2. Radiometric Dates Associated with BRM Site on the UCP of Tennessee.

SITE	SAMPLE #	LAB #	METHOD	MATERIAL	MEASURE	INTERCEPT/ 2 SIGMA MEAN
Calf Rock Cave	CRC1	AA45684	AMS	mammal bone	2371 ± 33 BP	2413 BP
Winningham Rock Shelter	By1-1	Beta-350452	AMS	charred hickory nut	2500 ± 30 BP	2611 BP
Winningham Rock Shelter	By1-OSL2	LB1181	OSL	chalcedony tempered, cord-marked body sherd	293 ± 89 AD	n/a
Rock Creek Mortar Shelter	SP234_PP42	Beta-350456	AMS	charred acorn	2750 ± 30 BP	2850 BP

Distribution of Bedrock Mortar Hole Sites on UCP

Because bedrock mortars are more or less permanent features, the implication is that these sites were intensively used and a great deal of time was invested in generating them. Though BRMs have been documented in the region, little research has been conducted concerning their role in prehistoric hunter-gatherer behavior on the UCP. Further, little to nothing is understood about their spatial distribution in relation to similar features or other archaeological sites. Also, there is great variability in the configuration and context of these features and no previous studies have addressed such variability spatially. Lastly, access to specific vegetation communities that would yield food resources (i.e., nut mast) have most definitely influenced the geographic placement of BRMs, and the importance of these communities should be underscored. The analysis to follow is an attempt to understand the spatial patterning of BRM sites based on their geographic location, configuration, and proximity to specific vegetation communities. This will provide some empirical context for the hypothetical *chaîne opératoire* to follow and will demonstrate the features that women looked for when creating these facilities.

After eliminating spatial outliers, 58 of the 64 BRM sites on the UCP were used to conduct spatial and statistical analysis. The distribution of the three types of BRM sites (Figure 2.4)—portable nutting stones (recorded at 28 sites), classic mortars (recorded at 32 sites), and kettle holes (recorded at 8 sites)—was investigated using statistical tools in ArcGIS 10.0 (ESRI 2011) and SPSS (IBM 2011). The spatial statistical analysis employed *Ripley's K Function* to analyze clustering for each of the different site types and a Hot Spot Analysis for identifying archaeological "hot spots" based on BRM feature density. Lastly, a discriminant analysis was conducted in SPSS (IBM 2011) to determine if variables relating to the proximity of specific resources (vegetation communities and water) could be used to discriminate between the different types of BRM sites.

BRM Site Size and Type

Before conducting any spatial analysis, the density of holes per site was used as an indicator of site size based on McCarthy et al.'s (1985) ethnographic work with the Western Mono populations. McCarthy et al. (1985:308) developed a typology for categorizing site type and/or site

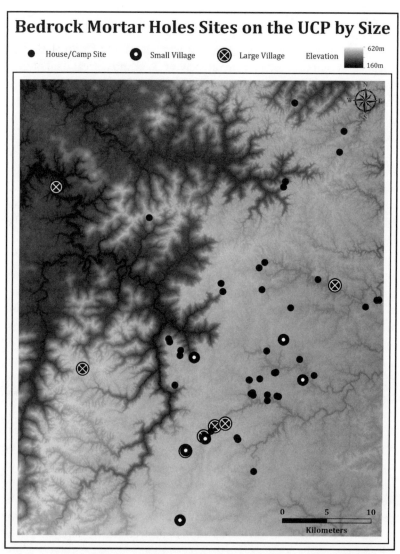

Bedrock Mortar Holes Sites on the UCP by Size

● House/Camp Site   ◉ Small Village   ⊗ Large Village   Elevation   620m / 160m

0   5   10
Kilometers

Figure 2.5. Distribution of bedrock mortar hole sites by size. Using McCarthy et al.'s (1985:308) method of estimating site size based on the number of BRM holes per site, a total of 45 house/ camp sites, 6 "small villages," and 7 "large villages" were identified.

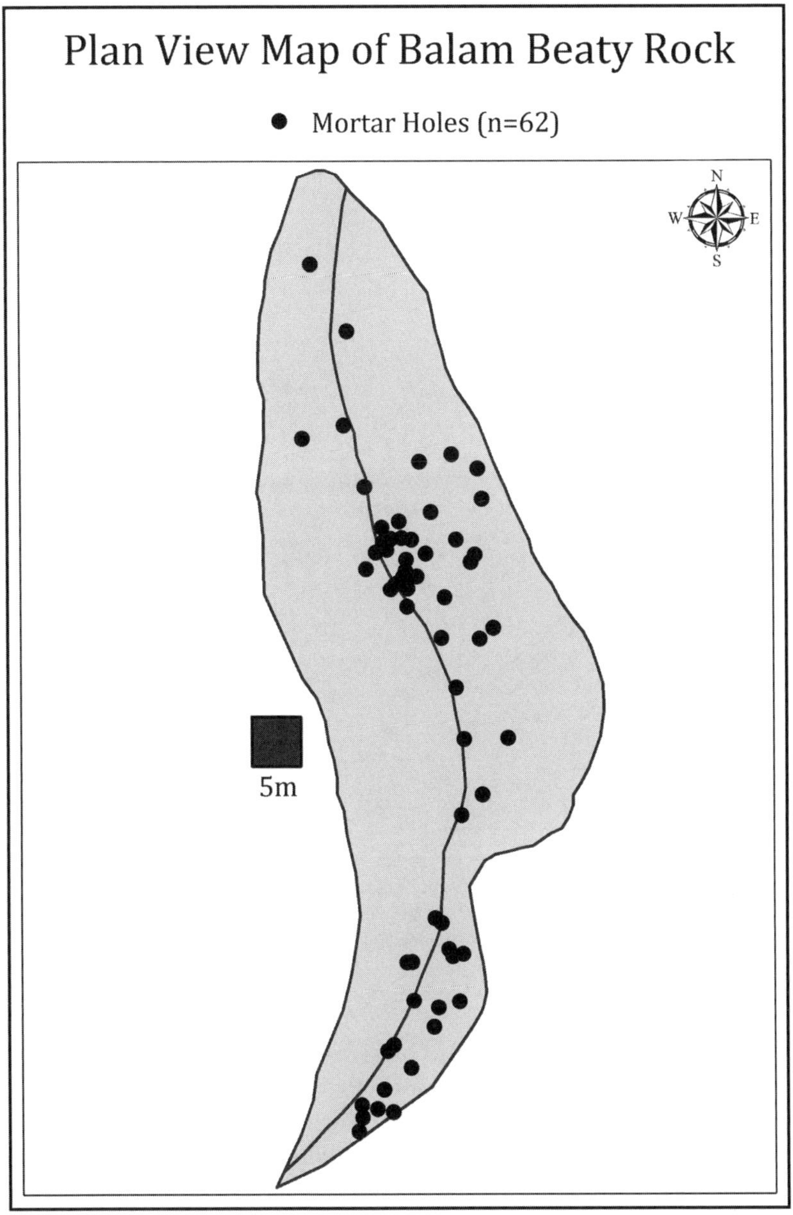

Plan View Map of Balam Beaty Rock

● Mortar Holes (n=62)

5m

Figure 2.6. Plan view map of Balam Beaty Rock, January 2006. A total of 62 classic mortars were recorded at this large open-air bedrock exposure. The line running down the center of the rock indicates a slight crest from which the rock slopes to the east (towards a creek nearby).

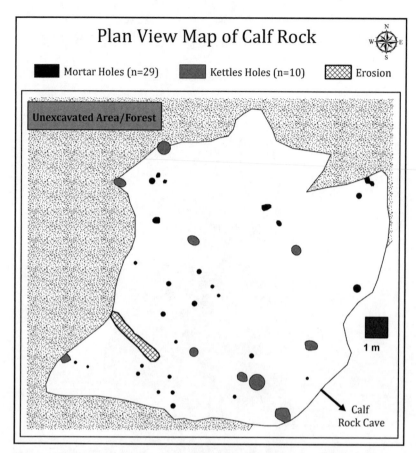

Figure 2.7. Plan view map of Calf Rock, June 2003. Calf Rock is situated above Calf Rock Cave. A total of 39 features—10 kettle holes and 29 classic mortars—were recorded on Calf Rock, and two nutting stones were found in association (Calf Rock Cave).

size based on the density of BRM holes recorded at a site (i.e., one rock shelter or one open-air rock exposure) where 1 to 7 holes represent a house/camp site, 8 to 19 holes indicate a small village, and 20 or more holes suggest a large village. This same typology was applied to the UCP of Tennessee in an effort to better understand the geographic distribution of BRM sites and the implications this might have for the exploitation of resources. It represents our first efforts at developing a working typology for these sites on the UCP as suggested by Franklin (2002).

Using McCarthy et al.'s (1985:308) typology, 45 house/camp sites, 6 small villages, and 7 large villages were identified for our study area

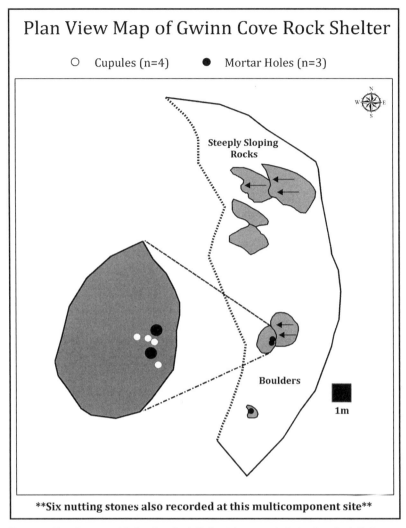

Figure 2.8. Plan view map of Gwinn Cove Rock Shelter, May 2004. At Gwinn Cove Rock Shelter, a total of 13 BRM features were recorded: 3 classic mortars, 4 smaller mortars or cupules, and 6 nutting stones.

(Figure 2.5). For the sites classified as "large villages," four are open-air rock exposures (Figure 2.6) and three sites form the roof of a rock shelter or cave (see Figures 2.2 and 2.7). We propose that these sites possibly represent areas of long-term and intensive use and/or occupation. In the case of Calf Rock, this is clear given that both Late Archaic and Early

Woodland artifacts were recovered in direct spatial association. For the other "large villages," only archaeological testing might reveal the nature and duration of these sites. For the "small villages," four are open-air rock exposures and two are rock shelters/caves (Figure 2.8); nutting stones were also documented at the two shelter sites and kettle holes were recorded at one of the rock exposures. For a majority of the house/camp sites (n=25), only nutting stones were documented making them seemingly isolated features. Only at three sites were both nutting stones and classic mortars recorded. Also, 25 of the 45 sites are rock shelters.

Cluster Analysis

The *Ripley K's Function* tool in ArcGIS (ESRI 2011) was used to explore the geographic distribution of the three BRM site types in order to look for significant patterns (i.e., clustering). Based on the output of the *Ripley's K Function,* classic BRM sites are more significantly clustered together across the UCP than nutting stone site locations. All sites where nutting stones were recovered are rock shelter sites (n=28). Considering that sandstone rock shelters on the UCP of Tennessee are myriad, sandstone nutting stones are just as ubiquitous. They represent transient, expedient, and intensive occupations of rock shelters along the rims of the gorges where it would be possible to access the limited and scattered stands of hickory found mainly in the middle slopes of the region. The nutting stones sites are less clustered than the classic mortar hole sites because they are expedient items used to exploit and process hickory (see Hinkle 1989). On the other hand, classic bedrock mortars indicate intensive site activity that most likely represents a logistically organized strategy for acorn exploitation and processing. Because of the widespread availability or acorns in the region, prehistoric peoples would not have needed to travel very far in order to exploit this particular resource—making these sites more clustered overall than the nutting stone rock shelter sites, which are also fixed places on the landscape. So it may be that the spatial patterning of classic bedrock mortar hole sites versus portable nutting stone sites reflects the relative and comparative investment of labor and processing of particular resources, such as acorns and hickory.

Hot Spot Analysis

Following *Ripley's K Function,* a Hot Spot Analysis was conducted in ArcGIS 10.0 (ESRI 2011) to identify significant hot and/or cold spots for all bedrock mortar hole locations using the total number of features per site. The *Getis-Ord Gi** (or simply Gi*) statistic was used to run the Hot Spot Analysis; this statistic calculates hot spots based on a weighted set of features. A hot spot is not necessarily a point but an area of a certain size that represents a spatial cluster of points with values higher

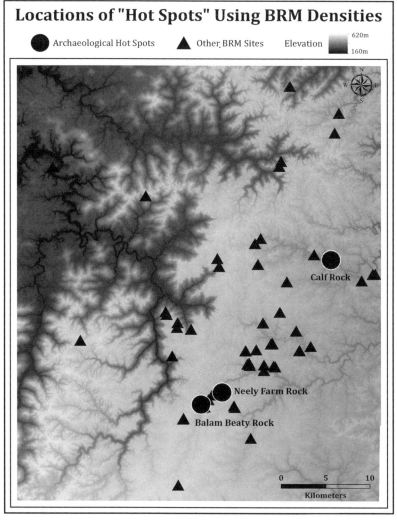

Figure 2.9. Archaeological "hot spots" identified for the Upper Cumberland Plateau. The number of BRM holes per site was used to conduct a hot spot analysis. Three sites were identified as potential areas for intensive prehistoric occupation and use: Balam Beaty Rock (62 classic mortars), Neely Farm Rock (40 classic mortars), and Calf Rock (29 classic mortars, 10 kettles, and 2 associated nutting stones).

in magnitude than would be found at random. The statistic is a Z score. "Hot spots" are identified as areas where features in close proximity to each other have similar high values (positive Z score value) whereas "cold spots" are reflective of concentrations of low values (negative Z score values). Z score values near zero demonstrate no similarity in values. Hot spot analysis is rare in archaeological research, but this project attempts to demonstrate its usefulness in identifying prehistoric "hot spots" based on bedrock mortar hole locations. A total of three archaeological hot spots were identified using the Hot Spot Analysis. These three hot spots correlate with the locations of Neely Farm Rock, Calf Rock, and Balam Beaty Rock (Figure 2.9).

Neely Farm Rock is an upland open-air rock exposure that includes several small and large rock outcrops. A total of 40 BRMs ranging in diameter and depth were recorded at this site. Similar to Neely Farm Rock, Balam Beaty Rock is classified as an open-air rock exposure although it consists of a single large rock exposure; 62 small-to-medium mortar holes were documented at this site (Figure 2.6). Calf Rock is much smaller than both Neely Farm Rock and Balam Beaty and is situated on top of a rock shelter. At this site, both classic mortars (n=29) and kettle holes (n=10) were recorded (see Figure 2.7). Additionally, two portable nutting stones were documented in the shelter below. This is the only site in which all three BRM types have been recorded in association.

The results of the Hot Spot Analysis most likely have implications for identifying central areas where specific resources were being intensely exploited by large groups of women. Identifying "hot spots" using BRM densities provides a baseline from which we can attempt to determine resources important to prehistoric hunter-gatherers and to what extent they travelled to access those resources processed at those facilities.

Discriminant Analysis

Following the spatial analysis, a discriminant analysis was conducted in SPSS (IBM 2011) to determine which factors, if any, contribute to the spatial variation and distinction of BRM sites. The standardized canonical discriminant function coefficients can be used to gauge the significance that each variable has in discriminating between groups. The variables used in the discriminant analysis were designed specifically to address the proximity to resources, such as vegetation communities and water, and to possibly identify the resources most likely processed at these facilities.

Modern soil surveys can be used as a proxy for determining food sources that might have been present in prehistoric times. Depending on their properties and features, different soils can support different tree and plant species. Women and animals in the past would have been particularly interested in nut- and fruit-bearing trees and plants. Three genera were identified as potentially significant food resources: *Quercus* (oak), *Carya* (hickory), and *Juglans* (walnut). Five *Quercus* species were present in the study area: chestnut oak, northern red oak, southern red oak, white oak, and scarlett oak. Two species of *Juglans*, *Juglans nigra* (black walnut) and *Juglans cinerea* (butternut) occur in the area although they are not widespread. *Carya* was mainly identified at the genus level.

In ArcGIS (ESRI 2011), the modern soil surveys of the UCP were used to determine "supporting zones" for the above vegetation types; GIS layers were generated for each of these vegetation communities. After combining the vegetation data and other GIS layers (e.g., surfaces representing elevation and slope on the UCP), cost distance surfaces were generated. The final variables (Table 2.3) represent the time required to access supporting zones of different species of oak, walnut, and hickory. These zones have the potential to represent a direct (e.g., gathering nuts for human consumption) or indirect (e.g., to hunt game) food resource for prehistoric hunter-gatherers. An additional variable representing the amount of time required to access a water resource (blue-line stream) was also included in the final variables.

The first discriminant analysis, which was not successful, attempted to separate the different categories of BRM hole sites (e.g., portable nutting stones, classic mortars, and kettle holes) using the variables discussed above. These findings may be the result of such a small sample size, especially in the case of the kettle hole sites (total of 8 sites with kettle hole versus 28 sites with nutting stone and 32 sites with classic mortar). However, it is also not surprising as many of these different features are found in spatial association at the same sites (e. g., Calf Rock and Sachsen Cave

Table 2.3. Variables Used to Explore Spatial Variation of BRMs

VARIABLES REPRESENTING ACCESS TO EXPLOITABLE RESOURCES[1]
Cost Distance to Black Oak
Cost Distance to Black Walnut
Cost Distance to Butternut
Cost Distance to Chestnut Oak
Cost Distance to Chinkapin Oak
Cost Distance to Hickory
Cost Distance to Northern Red Oak
Cost Distance to Southern Red Oak
Cost Distance to Scarlett Oak
Cost Distance to White Oak
Cost Distance to Water

1. Eleven variables, each representing the amount of time required (in minutes) to reach a specific resource, were used to run discriminant analyses on the BRM dataset in SPSS (IBM 2011).

Shelter). The same variables were used to run a second discriminant analysis between the different site types based on McCarthy et al.'s (1985:308) typology for BRM features—the 45 house/camp sites, 6 small villages, and 7 large villages. As with the first discriminant analysis, none of the variables qualified for the analysis and are therefore not significant in discriminating between the three site types.

It is possible that the results of the discriminant analysis are related to issues of typology. Even within the "groups" of BRMs that are discussed in this chapter, there is much variation in the configuration of these features. It is likely then that these three groups of BRMs (nutting stones, classic mortar holes, and kettle holes) are not enough to address the subtle variations.

BRM Sites and Rock Shelter Archaeology on the UCP

BRM Sites and Access to Vegetation Communities

Further investigation of the BRM sites in respect to vegetation communities stands to contribute to a better understanding of the distribution of BRMs and resource exploitation on the UCP. The proximity of BRM sites to vegetation communities of oak and hickory and mapped water resources in the region indicate that people situated themselves in areas that allowed for intensive exploitation of specific resources. The BRM sites, on average, occur either within or in very close proximity to communities of northern red oak, white oak, and hickory. Southern red oak is less ubiquitous than northern red oak and white oak and only occurs on the eastern and western boundaries of the study area. Similarly, scarlett oak is more confined to the northeastern portion of the UCP and is not as widespread as the other oak and hickory species.

White oak is the most widespread on the UCP occurring on upper and lower slopes and at almost every elevation. The BRM sites are, on average, four minutes away from zones of white oak with a maximum travel time of 18 minutes; these areas are where most of the probable house/camp sites (based on the typologies outlined previously) occurred. Additionally, the BRM sites average approximately 12 minutes from zones of northern red oak. While more travel time is required to access northern red oak, this is perhaps more significant than access time to white oak because northern red oak is far less prevalent in the region than white oak. All seven of the "small villages" occurred closer to zones of northern red oak than any other vegetation community. Last, hickory occurs more on the western portion of the UCP and is much less wide-spread than white oak and northern red oak (see Hinkle 1989). Eighteen of the 64 BRM sites are situated within zones of hickory, three of which are "large villages" and one of which is a "small village." This differential patterning of where the small and large villages occur in respect to the different vegetation communities may represent differences in resource exploitation and group size needed to support exploitation.

Rock Shelter Site Selection on the UCP

In a recent study, Langston (2013) used data collected from two archaeo-logical surveys on the western escarpment of the UCP of Tennessee: the East Obey River gorge (Franklin 2002) and Pogue Creek gorge (Langston and Franklin 2010) to develop and evaluate a site location model for prehistoric rock shelter selection and occupation. The resulting model also has implications for the distribution of BRM sites and stands to contribute to a better understanding of the prehistoric taskscape of the UCP of Tennessee and even possibly Kentucky and Alabama. Though several research objectives were addressed through the development of the UCP model, the primary goal was to gain insight into the logistics of gathering in this upland region that is dominated by rock shelters.

Using a combination of spatial and traditional statistics and geo-spatial analysis, Langston (2013) explored rock shelter selection on the UCP by examining 1) accessible resources (e.g., vegetation communities and water) that may have been important to people selecting residential and processing sites and 2) the amount of exposure or shelter that the surrounding landscape provides. Oak and hickory species are important sources of food for humans and wildlife so it is foreseeable that hunter-gatherers would have situated themselves in rock shelters close to areas where food sources (both for gathering nuts and hunting wildlife) were plentiful.

The discriminant analysis discussed in the previous section of this paper incorporated four of the variables Langston (2013:138) used to generate the final model of rock shelter selection on the UCP: *Cost Dis-tance to Northern Red Oak, Cost Distance to Southern Red Oak, Cost Distance to Hickory,* and *Cost Distance to Water.* As pointed out before, white oak is ubiquitous on the UCP indicating that access to supporting zones of white oak would not be a significant factor in shelter selection. The *Cost Distance to Northern Red Oak* variable was one of the most significant variables in the UCP site location model. On average, the UCP rock shelters are about 10 to 20 minutes away from areas likely to support northern red oak. However, rock shelter sites are closer on average to areas of southern red oak than non-site locations on the UCP. This indicates a trend towards locating sites closer to areas that support southern red oak. Interestingly, oaks aside, sites are situated closer to supporting zones of hickory than any other vegetation type used in this study. This is not surprising given that the rock shelter sites used for this model are virtually all located in the bluff lines that rim the Obey River and Pogue Creek gorges thus allowing the shelter occupants to easily exploit the limited stand of hickory primarily located on middle slopes (Hinkle 1989:127) Out of the four vegetation types, it is probable that the proximity of rock shelters to southern red oak and hickory had the greatest influence on site selection choices (Langston 2013:138).

Cost Distance to Water proved not to be a significant variable in the UCP site location model (Langston 2013:139). This is almost certainly due to the fact that the GIS cannot take into account unmapped seeps, springs, and intermittent streams that are myriad on the UCP.

Other variables included in the development of the UCP site location model that proved to be statistically significant in determining site location included measures of exposure/shelter (Langston 2013:139–140). Though the rock shelters provide shelter in the sense that they are ready-made structures, there are varying degrees of exposure of the overhang related to the surrounding landscape and vegetation. Locally (within a 100 meter radius from each rock shelter), the UCP rock shelter sites are located in extremely sheltered areas. These habitats provide protection from some natural elements (winter winds and rain/snow) but also receive abundant sunshine. However, at a regional scale (within a 1,000 meter radius from each rock shelter), the rock shelter locations are very exposed. This is not a contradiction and instead indicates that though the sites are sheltered locally, when compared to the rest of the plateau, they are situated higher and offer better views of the overall landscape. So whereas the steep gorges offer some protection from the natural elements (at least more so than being on top of the plateau), those locations also offer prime viewing locations—similar to vantage points. This seems to be in agreement with Mickelson's (2002) contention that early horticulturalists on the plateau were selecting shelters that afforded views of their garden plots below. We would point out, though, that we have not identified any evidence of early cultigens in our area of the Cumberland Plateau. Further, it is important to point out that some of the most sheltered rock shelter sites are located in horseshoe-shaped gorges and do not provide wide views of the landscape.

Correlation of BRM Sites and Rock Shelter Sites on the UCP

Based on the geospatial and statistical analysis, BRM sites (as processing facilities) on the UCP were selected by women based on their proximity to certain nut-producing tree communities. Obviously, bedrock geology is very important, too. However, prehistoric hunter-gatherers in the region did not have to look far for large, open exposures of sandstone, and they chose those exposures or rock shelters in close proximity to the resources they sought. In the case of white oak trees, this was not difficult given its ubiquitous distribution. The selection of sites in close proximity to the less common northern red oak may have been a more significant decision then. While white oak acorns can be eaten (and enjoyed) without processing, red oak acorns, on the other hand, require processing before they can be eaten. Many long-time residents on the plateau tell us they routinely eat white oak acorns after picking them up but red oak acorns taste extremely bitter. In any case, the proximity of BRM processing sites to northern red oak communities stands to reason and is supported by our GIS model. Proximity to hickory is also important and reflects the overall importance of this resource to southeastern hunter-gatherers.

Rock shelter sites were also selected, in large part, based on their proximity to nut-producing tree communities. Both rock shelter sites and BRM sites tended to be selected for their proximity to northern red oaks. In other words, the selection choices of BRM locations mirror the overall selection of the thousands of rock shelter sites more generally. Nearness to southern red oak communities was also important for shelter selection as was hickory. Both hickory and southern red oak communities tend toward the escarpments of the plateau where most of the rock shelters are located in the stream gorges. The selection of certain shelters by women along the rims of these gorges allowed for exploitation of hickory downslope and red oaks in the rolling uplands just above.

As we noted above, *Cost Distance to Water* was not significant in our GIS models entirely because we were not able to include water sources beyond blue line streams. We point out, though, that the average cost-distance time to mapped water sources for rock shelter sites is 33 minutes. For BRM sites, it is only 17 minutes, almost half. This may reflect the importance of water at BRM sites for leaching (red oak) acorns for removal of tannic acid and/or cooking and boiling of nut meats for oil in the larger kettle holes. For now, this must remain an idea for future testing.

In sum, both the rock shelter and BRM site selection GIS data indicate that prehistoric hunter-gatherers on the UCP were targeting specific resources, namely nut mast. Thus, the taskscape was one focused on the acquisition and processing of nut mast. The rock shelters were mostly selected for their proximity to hickory stands, and the BRM facilities for their proximity to mixed oak species, although many shelters exhibit evidence of both (e.g., Sachsen Cave Shelter and Rock Creek Mortar Shelter). Again, the selection of shelters mostly along the rims of gorges allowed for easy exploitation of both oaks and hickory. If we accept that foraging and nut/plant processing were primarily conducted by women, then the Late Archaic/Early Woodland archaeological record of the UCP of Tennessee would seem to overwhelmingly represent the taskscape of groups of women. This would perhaps be consistent with Claassen's (2011) contention that some rock shelter sites on the Cumberland Plateau in Kentucky largely served as women's retreats during which nut processing and mast and medicinal plant gathering occurred in conjunction with this ritual specific behavior. She also offers physical selection criteria for those shelters in Chapter 1. We stress again, though, that our excavations strongly suggest subsistence-related activities rather than ritual activities, though as Leroi-Gourhan (1993) pointed out, social and technical acts are not necessarily differentiated.

Prehistoric *Chaîne Opératoire* and BRM Sites on the UCP: The Taskscape

We now present a hypothetical *chaîne opératoire* for bedrock mortar hole use on the UCP. We mean this in every sense of the term from specific *chaînes opératoires* for how the variable sites and site types functioned to *chaîne opératoire* in the broadest sense, that of the taskscape. Again, we emphasize the fact that the world over, gathering and plant processing was largely the domain of women while hunting and other higher risk behaviors were typically associated with men. This seems well enough documented, and we will not belabor the point here (Ison 2004; Hollenbach 2009; Homsey et al. 2010:190). Given that there were more than 10,000 shelters to choose from, we also believe that women were probably responsible for decision making involved in shelter selection on the UCP. If there are thousands to choose from, how does one go about deciding? We have demonstrated elsewhere that basic characteristics, such as depth aspect (shelter facing direction), distance to water, and shelter size and configuration were not important factors for shelter selection on the UCP based on their ubiquity as opposed to other environments where they occur with much less frequency (Langston and Franklin 2010; Langston 2013, 2014). Instead, we believe that women on the UCP selected particular shelters based on their proximity to certain tree communities, namely hickory and red oaks (Langston 2013). In this regard, the diet of people who inhabited the UCP prehistorically was not novel; hickory nuts and acorns were, of course, staple foods for southeastern Indians for thousands of years. What is more peculiar about the UCP is the intensive focus on acorn processing beginning in the Late Archaic. In contrast, several scholars arguing from different lines of evidence maintain that intensification tied to (hickory) nut processing began in the early Middle Archaic (Walthall 1998; Miller 2014; Homsey-Messer 2015).

There was a dramatic increase in the number of sites on the UCP from the Middle to the Late Archaic (Franklin 2002:219–222). This seems to have been a pan-southeastern occurrence, too (Anderson 1996:157; Miller 2014). Anderson (1996:165–166, 175) not only argues for significant population increase in the Late Archaic but also for "landscape filling" in the Southeast generally and Tennessee specifically. That is, large numbers of people occupied all physiographic provinces and elevations. While Miller (2014:164–166) finds Anderson's (1996) data useful, he argues there are both taphonomic and equifinality issues involved. He therefore employed an Ideal Free Distribution (IFD) model to examine population density and suitability of habitat. In the end, he was able to corroborate Anderson's assumptions using data from the Duck River Drainage. By the Late Archaic era, sites were evenly spread across all physiographic provinces, including the Cumberland Plateau, consistent with increasing populations. Further, by this time, there was little to no open habitat available (Miller 2014:189–190).

Thus, while it is clear that the plateau was not nearly abandoned during the Middle Archaic as suggested by some scholars (e. g., Des Jean and Benthall 1994), there were far more people on the UCP during the Late Archaic (Franklin 2002). There are also indications of intensive resource exploitation on the UCP during the Terminal Archaic in the form of deep cave chert mining (Simek et al. 1998; Franklin 1999, 2001). Modern climatic regimes were reached after 5,000 years ago, and this almost certainly was an influencing factor. Changes in forest composition in the rolling uplands of the plateau were, in part, due to the changing climatic regimes. About 4,000 years ago, the plateau was dominated by mixed oak species (Delcourt and Delcourt 1987:251; Hinkle 1989). Hinkle (1989:127) goes so far as to suggest that the term oak-hickory forest should not be applied to the rolling uplands of the Cumberland Plateau in Tennessee.[2] Hickory has been of limited importance in our study area, namely Fentress County (McCarthy 1976), but it appears to have been more important in ravines and middle and lower slopes (Hinkle 1989:129). This no doubt influenced rock shelter selection on the UCP (Langston 2013). In short, however, oaks have dominated the landscape here in the last 4,000 years with white oak, scarlet oak, and black oak being the most common. Their dominance is unquestionable on the rolling uplands of the plateau (Hinkle 1989). It is on this upland landscape where we most commonly find bedrock mortar hole sites in close proximity to inhabited shelters. These sites do not occur in isolation. The thousands of rock shelters, vast upland sandstone rock exposures, and the dominance of oak species are what makes the UCP a very unique landscape. There can be little doubt that they are associated with mass processing of acorns beginning in the Late Archaic. But why would there have been such an intensive focus on acorns?

As previously mentioned, Walthall (1998) notes the presence of myriad pits and processing features being used in rock shelters in uplands of the eastern Woodlands during the Middle Archaic. We simply do not see this phenomenon in the shelters of the UCP. We do see this phenomenon in the Late and Terminal Archaic (Franklin et al. 2010, 2012, 2013, 2015). By examining archaeological features, Homsey-Messer (2015) documents evidence of significant nut (hickory) processing during the Middle Archaic at Dust Cave, Stanfield-Worley Bluff Shelter, and Modoc Rockshelter. Significant oak expansions in the broader region have been documented by B.C. 5000(Delcourt 1979; Wilkins et al. 1991). However, we wonder if there was a time-transgressive nature to this expansion. The UCP shelters occur at significantly higher elevations than the sites examined by Walthall (1998) and Homsey-Messer (2015), on the order of 160–300 meters higher. Perhaps significant oak (and hickory) stands were not present on the UCP until much later, i.e., the Late Holocene.

Another, but not necessarily mutually exclusive, possibility is that the Late Archaic in central Tennessee represents a "bust" period. Miller (2014) employed a historical ecological approach to Archaic settlement and subsistence using various models to examine boom and bust periods in prehistory. By the early Middle Holocene, all available evidence points to significant warming in which oak/hickory forests greatly expanded.

This made for very good deer hunting conditions, too. Instead of competing with deer for acorns, humans intensively focused their efforts on hickory nuts. However, by the Late/Terminal Archaic Wade phase, deer were smaller and perhaps less abundant (Wade Phase bifaces are prevalent in our site assemblages on the UCP). Oak/hickory forests contracted due in part to a decrease in mean annual temperature, which would have had a much more significant impact on the availability of hickory than oak trees because oaks numerically dominated. Also, due to dramatic population increases and landscape filling during this period, humans may have had to compete with deer (and other species) for acorns (Miller 2014:199–204). Since the UCP was dominated by mixed oak species by this time, strategies were developed for mass processing of acorns (Franklin 2002:193). This would also be one reason why acorns would have been exploited even if they were not optimal resources (Miller 2014:204, 209). Paleoecological conditions remain to be tested in the immediate area of the UCP, but we have identified sites where we may address this issue moving forward.

Procurement and processing of acorns do not jibe with most models of optimal foraging theory (Gremillion 2002). However, they can be procured in vast quantities and perhaps stored for as long as ten years (Ortiz 1996:110). Acorns are also very reliable resources. Further, the very thing that makes them harder to process, the presence of bitter tannins, is also what makes them more resistant to other species of animals that eat acorns. Many species of animals will leave red oak acorns on the ground for months, meaning they are often still available in significant quantities well into the winter (Petruso and Wickens 1984). Nutmeats contain more calories than beef and venison. Individual oak trees could provide up to 20 kg of edible nutmeat (Delcourt and Delcourt 2004:69) and seven trees could potentially sustain a person for an entire year (Gardner 1997). It has also been demonstrated that processed acorn meal stores for much longer than the acorns themselves even after parching or roasting. This would help to explain the intensive efforts at making bedrock mortar features. Informal experiments we have conducted indicate that bedrock mortar holes can also be fashioned rather easily. A 20 cm diameter by 5–7 cm deep hole can be made in two hours using a chalcedony nodule and a little water (Joe Tevepaugh 2013, pers. comm.).[3] This produces a uniformly rounded and dished hole (Figure 2.10). A single person working an eight-hour day could therefore produce a hole two to three times the diameter and three to four times the depth, a kettle hole, for example. In short, the intensive efforts spent making mortar and kettle holes to process acorns

Figure 2.10. Experimental bedrock mortar hole and chalcedony grinding nodules in various states of use.

by leaching is more than offset by the massive yields of acorns and their long-term storability and reliability (Gremillion 2002:154, 159). All of the available evidence points to intensive and extensive acorn exploitation and processing beginning in the Late Archaic and continuing into the Early Woodland on the UCP.

Selection of rock shelter sites located under the bluff lines of the precipitous gorges of the UCP allowed Late Archaic and Early Woodland women to exploit the hickory stands that lie below the shelters on middle slopes but also the red oak stands just above in the rolling uplands. The presence of only a single to a few BRMS in these shelters along with nutting stones suggests that individual women (and perhaps their nuclear family members) were responsible for their manufacture and use. This type of site is exemplified by locales such as Gwinn Cove Shelter and Rock Creek Mortar Shelter. Sites, such as Winningham Rock and Calf Rock, were places occupied by small groups of women and their offspring. Processing was variable. At Winningham Rock, as evidenced by the shallow burnt red hearth pads, it appears that acorns were likely parched in these combustion features (e. g., Homsey et al. 2010). At least one "rinsing hole" below the spring at Winningham indicates cold water leaching of acorn meal, too. At Calf Rock, kettle holes were used with cold water to leach the tannins from acorns. It is also possible that stone boiling could have been used, but unlike at Winningham, we have not recorded evidence of heat or combustion at Calf Rock.

These sites were not simply functional processing sites, but also social locations and gatherings. Myer (2014:56) suggested this nearly 100 years ago for Winningham Rock, "The women and girls gathered around the mortar holes on this old stone and with songs worked their pestles in unison, while near were some of the men fashioning their weapons or some of their paraphernalia. . . "His suggestion was largely based on ethnographic accounts from California. Winningham Rock is situated on the periphery of a large open upland habitation site. There are also many other rock shelters and burial caves in close proximity. The rock affords a breathtaking viewshed looking south out over the spring and a big bend in the Obey River (now Dale Hollow Lake). While Winningham Rock likely did not serve as a women's retreat as those identified by Claassen (2011), it almost certainly reflects women's space somewhat removed but not disconnected from the larger site. Other mortar holes were once exposed in the nearby field and there are also other fire pad rocks nearby, though we have been unable to relocate these.

Two site complexes reflect both social and communal gatherings, at least in part geared toward the intensive large scale processing of acorns, but also solitary spaces perhaps owned and operated by particular women. Balam Beaty Rock and the associated sites of Prickly Pear Rock, Norman Rock, and Barn Rock represent one such complex. Balam Beaty Rock was a communal processing center. It stretches nearly 100 meters and possesses at least 62 BRMs of small and medium size (starter and finishing holes for processing acorn meal). There is also at least one rinsing hole in the small stream nearby. One-half kilometer to the east is Prickly Pear Rock with several small (starter) BRMs located in closer proximity to the North Prong of the Clear Fork River. Here smaller groups of women gathered to process acorns. One hundred meters to the southwest is Norman Rock, a small bedrock exposure that is perched and looks out over the Clear Fork. This was likely the pounding rock of an individual woman. It measures approximately 8 × 5 meters and has eight small (starter) holes. Just to the southwest of Norman Rock is Barn Rock, an exposure with a small BRM and a rinsing hole. Thus, at this site complex were a variety of facilities: a large communal one, another for smaller groups of women, and at least two more likely the property of one or two women. There are also several rock shelters in immediate proximity. This is quite consistent with ethnographic accounts for these facilities among California Yosemite Miwok/Paiute Indian women.

> Grandmother had three rocks where she pounded. When she was by her-self early in the morning, she pounded on a special, low-to-the-ground rock. . . When she (Julia) and Grandmother wanted to pound without in-terruption, they climbed atop a rock nearly 17 feet high with four or five mortar holes. Eventually, other young women got interested and began to help with the pounding on a third bedrock mortar, close to the ground and with many holes. (Ortiz 1996:33–34).

Thus, it seems that there were not simply functional differences between BRM facilities but also social ones. Some of the social differences may also reflect ownership of certain rocks by individual women or perhaps their families.

While not included in our statistical analyses here, we recently re-corded another BRM multiple facility complex in January 2014. The Paul Tench Site has at least three rocks that reflect different functional and social activities. The southernmost rock has at least six large kettle holes, one of which is 65 cm deep. It is possible there are smaller BRMs here, but we have only recorded the site and have much clearing yet to do. Approximately 300 meters to the northeast is a single BRM that lies on a small ledge above a shallow rock shelter. Two hundred meters to the northeast of this BRM feature is a small stream that flows west toward Brushy Fork. Here along the edges of the stream are at least four rinsing holes. On the rolling upland ridge that bisects these facilities is a large open air site where large numbers of flaked stone tools have been collected by the property owners. There are also large and small rock shelters in very close proximity to this complex. Pounding and process-ing of acorns could have taken place at the first and second facilities, and then the resulting meal taken to the rinsing hole features so that cold water could be continually run over and through the meal in the rinsing holes without fear of the meal being transported downstream or still water retaining the tannins.

Conclusions

We have addressed de la Torre and Mora's (2009) concern that stud-ies employing a *chaîne opératoire* approach omit humans' interactions with their environments. We can therefore propose that as the climate ameliorated and mixed oak species came to dominate the uplands of the UCP by the Late/Terminal Archaic Period about 4,000 years ago, populations in Southern Appalachia significantly increased and expanded. The foraging spectrum intensified, perhaps during a "bust" period (Miller 2014). In conjunction with this, women came to play an increasingly important, if not dominant, role in in providing food for their families and communities. As such, women were the ones selecting rock shelter sites and associated sandstone bedrock exposures where they could procure and process reliable nut mast resources. As women's roles in foraging became increasingly critical with this intensification, cultural landscapes, or taskscapes, became matrilocal. At a certain point, as suggested by Ison (2004), Southern Appalachian cultures became matriarchal. However, on the UCP, we do not think this is necessarily associated with early cultigens and the beginnings of horticulture. We have yet to recover early cultigens at any of our sites, though they date to the same time period as the shelters on the plateau on Kentucky. Nor are our sites associated with rock art. This stands in contrast to the cultural associations recorded by Ison (2004). While we believe the archaeological record of the UCP during the Terminal Archaic and Early Woodland reflects the informed and conscious selection and decision making on the part of women, it does not manifest itself in the same way as do the sites in Kentucky with the association of BRMs, rock art, and early cultigens. Interestingly, boulders in particular, as well as rock shelters and cliff faces were used for women's fertility rituals not only to the north on the Cumberland Plateau but also in the eastern Ozarks, the subject of Duncan and Diaz-Granados in Chapter 3, in the northern Plains as discussed by Greer and Greer and Kehoe in Chapters 5 and 6, and in southern California (Roth Chapter 7). And while we believe we can detect women's *spaces* on certain sites (c. g., Winningham Rock and the Balam Beaty complex), we have not been able to detect the retreat *places* suggested by Claassen (2011 and Chapter 1). Our rock shelter excavations indicate palimpsests of activities conducted by both men and women (Leroi-Gourhan's group aesthetics). However, men can fashion and maintain stone tools and other activities in any rock shelter while foraging for and processing of nut mast is better done in close proximity to where these nut resources naturally occur. Hunting of primary game species, such as white-tailed deer and turkey, is also likely better in and near these same tree communities. Thus, while our excavation work appears to reflect the activities of both men and women (and their families), we believe site selection was in the domain of women.

The Late/Terminal Archaic and Early Woodland archaeological record of the UCP of Tennessee largely reflects the economically and socially functional taskscape of pioneering women. In short, women identified, selected, and manipulated their environments in both social and technical ways, and these ways of doing are reflected as the artifacts we call bedrock mortar holes.

We will direct future research toward excavations at some of the large open BRM sites in order to refine chronology, differential activity areas, and the gendered use of space. We will also continue to survey these sites. There are likely hundreds more that have been covered by earth related to historic agriculture and secondary forest growth. It is also very likely that many BRMs have been destroyed by timbering and strip mining. Like the rock shelters themselves, the vast open sandstone exposures of the UCP were once myriad and reflected a complicated (sensu Gamble 1999:26) social and technical cultural landscape.

We believe the *chaîne opératoire* we have developed and presented here reflects Leroi-Gourhan's original conceptions of the term as it relates to group aesthetics, albeit one directed by women on the Late Archaic and Early Woodland Upper Cumberland Plateau. This *chaîne opératoire* is also quite consistent with ethnographic accounts of acorn exploitation and the archaeological record of these sites on the UCP. Moving forward we will pursue paleoecological studies to augment the taskscape we have proposed herein.

Acknowledgments

We would not know of most of these sites without the enthusiasm, support, and detective work of Joe Tevepaugh. Joe also got the ball rolling for the experimental production of BRM features. He has been a tireless field worker and a hugely tolerant friend. We are very grateful to Malcolm Colditz for his enthusiastic support of this work and for permission to conduct excavations at Sachsen Cave Shelter. We also greatly appreciate Malcolm and Harriet Colditz for the warm hospitality in welcoming us into their home, often feeding us wonderful meals, and quietly tolerated dirty boots and numerous intrusions in their lives for weeks at a time. We would like to thank the Estate of Bruno Gernt, Inc. for permission to conduct archaeological investigations on their land holdings as well. We are particularly indebted to Jerry Gernt for his interest, enthusiasm, hospitality, and support. Jay Franklin thanks Jan Simek for encouraging him to account for the variability in BRM features on the UCP and to develop a typology for them. Jay Franklin also wishes to thanks the Research Development Committee, Office of the Vice Provost for Research and Sponsored Programs, the College of Arts and Sciences, and the Department of Sociology and Anthropology at East Tennessee State University (ETSU) for funding and material support. Funding was also provided in the form of several competitive survey and planning grants awarded to Jay Franklin for the survey work in Pogue Creek Canyon State Natural Area, Pickett State Park, and Pickett State Forest by the Tennessee Historical Commission. We would also like to extend our sincere thanks to Tennessee State Parks and Forests, in particular, Alan Wasik, John Froeschauer, Travis Bow, Brandon Taylor, and David Todd for their unbridled support of this work and sincere hospitality. Lucinda Langston would like to thank the Tennessee Council for Professional Archaeology for a competitively awarded research grant that helped to fund the BRM site research. We owe a debt of gratitude to Marshall Parris for allowing us to conduct work at Winningham Rock. Jerry Huffman and Luke and Sandy Stowers also allowed us access to important BRM sites on their properties as did the Hull family. The late Mr. Henry Norman also allowed us to conduct archaeological work on several BRM sites on his property. Christina Bolte, Jacob Wall, Rachel Witt, and Sierra Bow assisted with mapping BRM sites. Archaeological survey and testing permits were granted by the Tennessee Division of Archaeology where necessary. Jay Franklin would also like to thank the numerous ETSU students who participated in the Pogue Creek and Pickett State Park and Forest archaeological surveys. The AMS determinations were done by the NSF-Arizona AMS Facility and Beta Analytic, Inc. (all radiocarbon measures were calibrated using Calib 7.0 with Intcal 09 atmospheric data). The luminescence date was calculated by Sachiko Sakai and Carl Lipo at IIRMES, California State Long Beach.

NOTES

1. We must emphasize that there are tens of thousands of rock shelters on the UCP. If we take the area of Fentress and Pickett counties alone and divide it by two (assuming at least half upland rolling terrain—though there are many shelters in the rolling uplands), it comes to 331 square miles, or 211, 840 acres. We recorded more than 100 rock shelter sites in Pogue Creek Canyon State Natural Area alone (approximately 3,000 acres). Pickett State Forest covers more than 21,000 acres. We have therefore projected that we will likely record more than 1,000 rock shelter sites in the forest (we have already recorded more than 150 in two and half seasons of survey). Taking this projection one step further and applying it to the

more than 211,000 acres of Fentress and Pickett County area proposed above, then there are likely more than 10,000 rock shelter sites here (This this estimate does not include Morgan, Scott, Overton, and Cumberland counties portions of the UCP. There could be 30,000 rock shelter sites on the UCP). This is not at all an unreasonable estimate as Ison and others have estimated 20,000 rock shelters in the Daniel Boone National Forest portion of the Cumberland Plateau in Kentucky.

2. Nor was chestnut an important forest constituent on the UCP during prehistory (Hinkle 1989:128). We have not recovered chestnut remains from any archaeological site on the UCP. It was likely more important to the east in the Southern Appalachian mountains (Miller 2014:45) and also perhaps later in time during the protohistoric and early historic eras. Chestnut was not an influencing factor in prehistoric site selection on the UCP.

3. Though not in direct spatial association with BRM features, we have recovered smoothed or polished and almost perfectly rounded chalcedony nodules from sites on the UCP. Until our informal experiments in making a BRM feature, these rounded nodules puzzled us. We now believe the most plausible explanation for their configuration and appearance is that that they were used to make bedrock mortar holes. A rough chalcedony nodule can become rounded and smoothed in this way in less than an hour.

REFERENCES CITED

Adair, James

2009   *The History of the American Indians.* University of Alabama Press, Tuscaloosa.

Anderson, David G.

1996   Approaches to Modeling Regional Settlement in the Archaic Period Southeast. In *Archaeology of the Mid-Holocene Southeast*, K. E. Sassaman and D. G. Anderson, editors, pp. 157–176. University Press of Florida, Gainesville.

Barrett, S. A., and E. W. Gifford

1933   Miwok Material Culture. *Bulletin of the Public Museum of the City of Milwaukee* 2(4): 117–377.

Bartlett, C. S., Jr.

1984   A Plateau Rock Shelter "Indian Kettle" Site—44WS6. *Archeological Society of Virginia Bulletin* 39(4):182–188.

Bliege Bird, Rebecca

2008   Fishing and the Sexual Division of Labor among the Meriam. *American Anthropologist* 109(3):442–451.

Bow, Sierra M., and Jay D. Franklin

2009   Luminescence Dating and the Pogue Creek Archaeological Survey. Paper Presented at the 21st Annual Current Research in Tennessee Archaeology Meeting, Nashville, TN.

Bridges, Patricia

1989   Changes in Activities with the Shift to Agriculture in the Southeastern United States. *Current Anthropology* 30(3):385–394.

Chatters, James C.

1987   Hunter-Gatherer Adaptations and Assemblage Structure. *Journal of Anthropological Archaeology* 6:336–375.

Claassen, Cheryl
2011   Rock Shelters as Women's Retreats: Understanding Newt Kash. *American Antiquity* 76(4):628–641.
Cowan, Wesley, Edwin Jackson, K. Moore, A. Nickelhoff, and T. Smart
1981   The Cloudsplitter Rockshelter, Menifee County, Kentucky: A Preliminary Report. *Southeastern Archaeological Conference Bulletin* 24:60–75.
Davis, E. L.
1965   An Ethnography of the Kuzedika Paiute of Mono Lake, Mono County California. *Anthropological Papers* 75:1–55.
de la Torre, Ignacio, and Rafale Mora
2009   Remarks on the Current Theoretical and Methodological Approaches to the Study of Technological Strategies of Early Humans in Eastern Africa. In *Interdisciplinary Approaches to the Oldowan*, E. Hovers and D. Braun, editors, pp. 15–24. Springer, Amsterdam.
Delcourt, H. R.
1979   Late Quaternary Vegetation History of the Eastern Highland Rim and Adjacent Cumberland Plateau of Tennessee. *Ecological Monographs* 49(3):255–280.
Delcourt, Paul A., and Hazel R. Delcourt
1987   *Long-Term Forest Dynamics of the Temperate Zone.* Springer-Verlag, New York.
2004   *Prehistoric Native Americans and Ecological Change: Human Ecosystems in Eastern North America since the Pleistocene.* Cambridge University Press, Cambridge.
Dennison, Meagan E.
2013   Faunal Analysis of Sachsen Cave Shelter: A Zooarchaeological Approach to Site Function. Master's thesis, Department of Anthropology, University of Tennessee, Knoxville. http://trace.tennessee.edu/utk_gradthes/1606.
Des Jean, Tom, and Joseph L. Benthall
1994   A Lithic Based Prehistoric Cultural Chronology of the Upper Cumberland Plateau. *Tennessee Anthropologist* 19(2):115–147.
Dye, Andrew D., Jay D. Franklin, and Maureen A. Hays
2010   Lithic Technology and Site Function at Early Times Rock Shelter, Upper Cumberland Plateau, Tennessee. Paper presented at the 67th Annual Meeting of the Southeastern Archaeological Conference, Lexington, KY.
Edmonds, Mark
1990   Description, Understanding, and the Chaîne Opératoire. *Archaeological Review from Cambridge* 9:55–70.
ESRI
2011   ArcGIS Desktop. Redlands, CA: Environmental Systems Research Institute.
Ferguson, Terry A., Robert A. Pace, Jeffrey W. Gardner, and Robert W. Hoffman
1986   *An Archaeological Reconnaissance and Testing of Indirect Impact Areas Within Selected Development Sites of the Big South Fork National River and Recreational Area.* Final Report of the Big South Fork Archaeological Project. Submitted to U.S. Army Engineer District, Nashville, TN.
Franklin, Jay D.
1999   The Rime of the Ancient Miners. Master's thesis, Department of Anthropology, University of Tennessee, Knoxville.

2001   Excavating and Analyzing Prehistoric Lithic Quarries: An Example from 3rd Unnamed Cave, Tennessee. *Midcontinental Journal of Archaeology* 26(2):199–217.

2002   The Prehistory of Fentress County, Tennessee: An Archaeology Survey. Doctoral dissertation, Department of Anthropology, University of Tennessee, Knoxville.

2006a   Prehistoric Culture Chronology on the Upper Cumberland Plateau of Tennessee. Paper Presented at the 63rd Annual Southeastern Archaeological Conference, Little Rock, AR.

2006b   An Archaeological Reconnaissance Survey of the Bluffs and Gorges of the South Sides of Fletcher Branch and North White Oak Creek to the Confluence of Mill Seat Creek, Fentress County, Tennessee. Report Submitted to Holbrook and Peterson, PLLC, Knoxville, TN and the Estate of Bruno Gernt, Inc, Allardt, TN.

2008a   Luminescence Dates and Woodland Ceramics from Rock Shelters on the Upper Cumberland Plateau of Tennessee. *Tennessee Archaeology* 3(1):87–100.

2008b   Big Cave Archaeology in the East Fork Obey River Gorge. In *Cave Archaeology of the Eastern Woodlands: Essays in Honor of Patty Jo Watson*, David H. Dye, editor, pp. 141–155. University of Tennessee Press, Knoxville.

Franklin, Jay D., and Sierra M. Bow

2008   The Upper Cumberland Plateau Archaeological Luminescence Dating Project. Paper Presented at the 65th Annual Southeastern Archaeological Conference, Charlotte, NC.

Franklin, Jay D., Maureen A. Hays, Sarah C. Sherwood, and Lucinda M. Langston

2012   An Integrated Approach: Lithic Analyses and Site Function, Eagle Drink Bluff Shelter, Upper Cumberland Plateau, Tennessee. In *Contemporary Lithic Analysis in the Southeast: Problems, Solutions, and Interpretation*, Phillip J. Carr, Andrew P. Bradbury, and Sarah E. Price, editors, pp. 128–145. University of Alabama Press, Tuscaloosa.

Franklin, Jay D., Meagan E. Dennison, Maureen A. Hays, J. Navel, and A. D. Dye

2013   The Early and Middle Woodland of the Upper Cumberland Plateau, Tennessee. In *Early and Middle Woodland Landscapes of the Southeast*, A. Wright and E. Henry, editors, pp. 71–88. University Press of Florida, Gainesville.

Franklin, Jay D., Renee B. Walker, Maureen A. Hayes, and Chase W. Beck

2010   Late Archaic Site Use at Sachsen Cave Shelter, Upper Cumberland Plateau, Tennessee. *North American Archaeologist* 31(3–4):447–479.

Franklin, Jay D., Frédéric Surmely, Maureen Hays, Ilaria Patania, Lucinda Langston, and Travis Bow

2015   Migration Terminus? Late Pleistocene and Early Holocene Archaeology at Rock Creek Mortar Shelter (40Pt209), Upper Cumberland Plateau, Pickett State Forest. Paper Presented at the 27th Annual Current Research in Tennessee Archaeology Meeting, Nashville.

Fritz, Gayle

1999   Gender and the Early Cultivation of Gourds in Eastern North America. *American Antiquity* 64(3):417–429.

Funkhouser, William, and William Webb

1929   The So-called "Ash Caves" in Lee County, Kentucky. *Reports in Archaeology and Anthropology* 1(2):37–112.

1930   Rock Shelters of Wolfe and Powell Counties, Kentucky. *Reports in Archaeology and Anthropology* 1(4):239–306.

1932   *Archaeological Survey of Kentucky. Reports in Archaeology and Anthropology* 2.

Gamble, Clive

1999   *The Palaeolithic Societies of Europe*, Cambridge University Press, Cambridge.

Gardner, Paul S.

1997   The Ecological Structure and Behavioral Implications of Mast Exploitation Strategies. In *People, Plants, and Landscapes: Studies in Paleoethnobotany*, Kristen Gremillion, editor, pp. 161–178. University of Alabama Press, Tuscaloosa.

Gifford, E. W.

1936   California Balanophagy. In *Essays in Anthropology Presented to Alfred L. Kroeber*, R. H. Lowie, editor, pp. 27–98. University of California Press, Berkeley.

Gremillion, Kristen

1996   Early Agricultural Diet in Eastern North America: Evidence from Two Kentucky Rockshelters. *American Antiquity* 61:520–536.

1997   New Perspectives on the Paleoethnobotany of the Newt Kash Shelter. In *People, Plants, and Landscapes: Studies in Paleoethnobotany*, Kristen Gremillion, editor, pp. 23–41. University of Alabama Press, Tuscaloosa.

2002   Foraging Theory and Hypothesis Testing in Archaeology: An Exploration of Methodological Problems and Solutions. *Journal of Anthropological Archaeology* 21:142–164.

Haney, J. W.

1992   Acorn Exploitation in the Eastern Sierra Nevada. *Journal of California and Great Basin Anthropology* 14(1):94–109.

Hassler, E. F.

1946   Sandstone "Hominy Holes." *Tennessee Archaeologist* 2(3):61–62.

1947   Rock Shelter Explorations. *Tennessee Archaeologist* 3(3):42–43.

Hawkes, Kristen

1990   Why Do Men Hunt? Benefits for Risky Choices. In *Risk and Uncertainty in Tribal and Peasant Economies*. Elizabeth Cashdan, editor, pp. 145–166. Westview Press: Boulder, CO.

Henson, B. B.

1964   Stone Markings by Aborigines of North Alabama. *Journal of Alabama Archaeology* 10(2):61–65.

Henson B., and J. Martz

1979   *Alabama's Aboriginal Rock Art*. Alabama Historical Commission, Montgomery.

Hinkle, C. R.

1989   Forest Communities of the Cumberland Plateau of Tennessee. *Journal of the Tennessee Academy of Science* 64(3):123–129.

Hinkle, C. R., W. C. McComb, J. M. Safley, Jr., and P. A. Schmalzer
1993   Mixed Mesophytic Forests. In *Biodiversity of the Southeastern United States: Upland Terrestrial Communities,* W. H. Martin, S. G. Boyce, and A. C. Echternacht, editors, pp. 203–253. John Wiley & Sons, New York.

Hollenbach, Kandace R.
2009   Foraging in the Tennessee River Valley, 12,500 to 8,000 years ago. University of Alabama Press: Tuscaloosa.

Homsey, Lara K., Renee B. Walker, and Kandace D. Hollenbach
2010   What's for Dinner? Investigating Food-Processing Technologies at Dust Cave, Alabama. *Southeastern Archaeology* 29(1):182–196.

Homsey-Messer, Lara
2015   Revisiting the Role of Caves and Rockshelters in the Hunter-Gatherer Taskscape of the Archaic MidSouth. *American Antiquity* 80(2):332–352.

Humbard, R. A.
1963   Mystery Holes in Rock. *Journal of Alabama Archaeology* 9(1):30–33.

Humbard, R.A. and J. R. Humbard
1964   Mystery Holes in Rocks—Part II. *Journal of Alabama Archaeology* 10(1):36–37.

IBM Corp.
2011   IBM SPSS Statistics for Windows. IBM Corp., Armonk, NY.

Ingold, Tim
1993   The Temporality of the Landscape. *World Archaeology* 25(2):152–174.

Ison, Cecil R.
1996   Hominy Holes, Petroglyphs, and the Cogswell Phase: Rethinking Terminal Archaic Sedentism. Paper Presented at the 53rd Annual Meeting of the Southeastern Archaeological Conference, Birmingham, AL.

2004   Farming, Gender, and Shifting Social Organization, A New Approach to Understanding Kentucky's Rock-Art. In *Rock-Art of Eastern North America: Capturing Images and Insight,* Carol Diaz-Granados and James R. Duncan, editors, pp. 177–189. University of Alabama Press, Tuscaloosa.

Jackson, Thomas L.
1991   Pounding Acorn: Women's Production as Social and Economic Focus. In *Engendering Archaeology,* Margaret Conkey and Joan Gero, editors, pp. 301–327. Routledge Press, London.

Johnson, J. J.
1967   The Archaeology of the Camanche Reservoir Locality California. *Sacramento Anthropological Society,* Paper No. 6.

Justice, Noel
1987   *Stone Age Spear and Arrow Points of the Midcontinental and Eastern United States.* Indiana University Press, Bloomington.

Kellar, J. H.
1958   *An Archaeological Survey of Perry County.* Indiana Historical Bureau, Indianapolis.

Kelly, Robert L.
2007   *The Foraging Spectrum: Diversity in Hunter-Gatherer Lifeways.* Percheron Press, New York.

Langston, Lucinda M.

2013   Site Location Modeling and Prehistoric Rock Shelter Selection on the Upper
        Cumberland Plateau of Tennessee. *Electronic Theses and Dissertations.*
        Paper 1157. http://dc.etsu.edu/etd/1157.

2014   GIS Analysis and Spatial Patterning of Bedrock Mortar Holes on the Upper
        Cumberland Plateau of Tennessee. Paper Presented at the 26th Annual
        Current Research in Tennessee Archaeology Meeting, Nashville.

Langston, Lucinda M. and Jay D. Franklin

2010   Archaeological Survey of Pogue Creek State Natural Area: A GIS Perspective.
        Paper presented at the 67th Annual Meeting of the Southeastern Archaeo-
        logical Conference, Lexington, KY.

Leroi-Gourhan, André

1993   *Gesture and Speech,* reprinted from 1964 edition. Anna Bostock Berger,
        translator. MIT Press, Cambridge, MA.

McCarthy, Helen, Clinton M. Blount, and Robert A. Hicks

1985   A Functional Analysis of Bedrock Mortars: Western Mono Food Processing
        in the Southern Sierra Nevada. In *Cultural Resources of the Crane Valley
        Hydroelectric Project, Madera Country, California,* Vol. 1, pp. 303–356.
        Theodoratus Cultural Research, Inc.

Mickelson, Andrew

2002   Changes in Prehistoric Settlement Patterns as a Result of Shifts in Subsistence
        Practices in Eastern Kentucky. Doctoral dissertation, Department of Anthro-
        pology, Ohio State University, Columbus.

Miller, Darcy Shane

2014   From Colonization to Domestication: Historical Ecological Analysis of Pa-
        leoindian and Archaic Subsistence and Landscape Use in Central Tennessee.
        Doctoral dissertation, School of Anthropology, University of Arizona, Tucson.

Myer, William Edward

1924   Catalogue of Archaeological Remains in Tennessee. Unpublished manuscript
        on file at the Smithsonian Institution, Washington, DC and the Tennessee
        Division of Archaeology, Nashville.

1928   *Indian Trails of the Southeast.* Bureau of American Ethnology, 42nd Annual
        Report, 1924–1925. Smithsonian Institution, Washington, DC. Reprinted
        1971 by Blue & Gray Press, Nashville, TN.

2014   Stone Age Man in the Middle South and Other Writings. Edited by Donald B.
        Ball. Borgo Publishing, Tuscaloosa, AL.

Ortiz, Beverly R. (as told by Julia F. Parker)

1996   *It Will Live Forever: Traditional Yosemite Indian Acorn Preparation.* Heyday
        Books, Berkeley, CA.

Panter-Brick, Catherine

2002   Sexual Division of Labor: Energetic and Evolutionary Scenarios. *American
        Journal of Human Biology* 14:627–640.

Parris, W. G.

1946   A Cave Site in Pickett County. *Tennessee Archaeologist* 2(3):59–60.

Pelegrin, Jacques

1993   A Framework for Analysing Stone Tools Manufacture and a Tentative
        Application to Some Early Stone Industries. In *The Use of Tools by Human*

and Non-human Primates, A. Berthelet and J. Chavaillon, editors, pp. 302–314. Oxford University Press, New York.

Perdue, Theda

1999   *Cherokee Women: Gender and Culture Change, 1700–1835*. Bison Books, University of Nebraska Press, Lincoln.

Perkins, Dexter, Jr. and Patricia Daly

1968   The Potential of Faunal Analysis. An Investigation of the Faunal Remains from Suberde, Turkey. *Scientific American* 219(5):96–106.

Petruso, Karl M. and Jere M. Wickens

1984   The Acorn in Aboriginal Subsistence in Eastern North America: A Report on Miscellaneous Experiments. In *Experiments and Observations on Aboriginal Wild Plant Food Utilization in Eastern North America*, Patrick J. Munson, editor, pp. 360–378. Indiana Historical Society, Indianapolis.

Reitz, Elizabeth J., and Elizabeth S. Wing

2008   *Zooarchaeology*, 2nd edition. Cambridge University Press, Cambridge.

Schwegman, J. E.

2003   Prehistoric Man-created Bedrock Holes of the Eastern Shawnee Hills, Southern Illinois. *Transactions of the Illinois State Academy of Science* 96(3):163–175.

Simek, Jan F., Jay D. Franklin, and Sarah C. Sherwood

1998   The Context of Early Southeastern Prehistoric Cave Art: A Report on the Archaeology of 3rd Unnamed Cave. *American Antiquity* 63(4):663–677.

Swanton, John R.

1946   *The Indians of the Southeastern United States*. Bureau of American Ethnology Bulletin 137. Government Printing Office, Washington, DC.

Voegelin, Erminie

1938   Tubatulabal Ethnogeography. *University of California Anthropological Records* 2(1).

Walthall, John A.

1998   Rockshelters and Hunter-Gatherer Adaptation to the Pleistocene/Holocene Transition. *American Antiquity* 63(2):223–238.

Watson, Patty Jo, and Mary C. Kennedy

1998   The Development of Horticulture in the Eastern Woodland of North America: Women's Role. In *Reader in Gender Archaeology*, Kelley Hays-Gilpin and David S. Whitley, editors, pp. 255–275. Routledge, London.

Webb, W. S., and W. D. Funkhouser

1929   The So-called 'Hominy Holes' of Kentucky. *American Anthropologist* 31(4):701–709.

1936   Rock Shelters in Menifee County, Kentucky. *Reports in Archaeology and Anthropology* 3(4):105–167. University of Kentucky, Lexington.

White, David R. M.

1985   *Settlement Pattern Implications of Bedrock Milling Implement Analysis: An Example from the Kern River, California*. Paper presented at the Southwest Anthropological Association meetings, Chico, CA.

Wilkins, Gary R., Paul A. Delcourt, Hazel R. Delcourt, Frederick W. Harrison, and Manson R. Turner

1991   Paleoecology of Central Kentucky Since the Last Glacial Maximum. *Quaternary Research* 36(2):224–239.

3

ROCK ART, GENDER,
AND THE DHEGIHAN LANDSCAPE

James R. Duncan and Carol Diaz-Granados

A review of the literature concerning vision quests, economics, and societal organization, especially some recent contributions (Kelly et al. 2008; Kelly and Brown 2012; Lepper 2004) have interested the authors by their excellent constructions of spiritual journeys. It is the purpose of this chapter to examine the iconography of the Missouri rock art and reconstruct its ideology with a more gender sensitive perspective. This will be done in view of the complex exchange systems of the Western Mississippians. This system formed an integral part of their cosmology. Therefore, our approach will be to employ the ethnography in the interpretation of the iconography associated with the rock art and landscape.

The American Indian people of the Eastern Woodlands shared a basic ideology. The layered cosmic model is a major facet of this these beliefs. There seemed to be a general understanding and acceptance of this basic belief system. Although it was widespread, it contained variations among the linguistic groups. However, the Dhegihan cosmos was probably one of the more intricate and encompassing examples. This Dhegihan model is likely the one employed by the people responsible for the large mound centers located along the Mississippi River corridor between the Missouri and Ohio rivers. The Dhegihan cosmos was the creation of a singular invisible creative power that animated all things, from the multiple universes that make up the cosmos to the smallest mote floating in the heavens (Figure 3.1). A word of caution is necessary here—this power is addressed by modern Dhegihans as Wa-kon'-da, a spiritual being, something to be "sensed" but never to be seen (Bailey

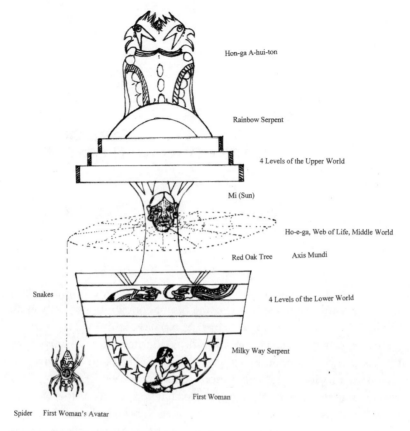

Figure 3.1. The Osage Dhegihan Cosmos.

1995:31). Also, it is impossible to separate the spiritual worlds from the secular world in Dhegihan ideology because they function in tandem.

This complex cosmos contained two basic realms: the daytime sky, which was assigned the male gender, and the night sky, which was considered to be feminine. These entities were the parents of spirit beings who were in turn parents of the Dhegiha. The principal male spirit, First Man, resided in the Sun and was often thought to be synonymous with the Sun and the daytime sky. First Woman, the Earth, resided in the Moon and was synonymous with both the night sky and the earth (Ponziglione 1897:11–13; Bailey 1995:33; Duncan 2011:21).

To the Siouan (Dhegiha) the system of mutual reciprocity is related to and reflects the cosmos. Just as the cosmos is a balanced affair, the exchange of goods reflects the societal values of this balanced system (Bowers 1950:91). An interesting anecdote of this rigidly adhered to system is an account by Maximilian of Wied-Neuwied. "Generosity was a highly valued trait among those tribes, generosity and bravery were the twin pillars of social status for the men among the Plains tribes. In an implied lesson in good manners for the prince, the prominent Mandan chief Mate-Tope, or Four Bears, pointedly informed Maximilian about what the Mandan regarded as the boorish behavior of George Catlin in 1832. Four Bears had disgustedly returned Catlin's inappropriate and trivial gifts, informing Catlin that he must be so "poor" that the artist obviously needed those trinkets more than did the insulted chief" (Wood, Porter and Hunt 2002:46). Still today, the Dhegiha, especially the Osage, follow this precept of generosity and reciprocity during their rites (Mathews 1961:783). This system of exchange between hosts and visitors had and still has absolutely nothing to do with a western European styled market.

In order to explicate and illustrate the thesis of this chapter, we will discuss two "groups" of Missouri's rock art—two contrasting groups with respect to the media, the style of the imagery, and the possible chronological difference between them (Figure 3.2). The first site is the Maddin Creek site (23WA26), a Missouri State Parks managed site in the Big River valley of the eastern Ozarks. This site is one of a group of five that share close affinities in location, media, and style. They are petroglyphs rendered on sandy dolomite glade outcrops. These five petroglyph sites (see The Big Five, Diaz-Granados and Duncan 2000) are not as concerned with realistic proportion as with delineating important iconographic motifs.

The second site is in the Little Bourbeuse River valley. It is the Rattlesnake Bluff/ Willenberg Shelter group (23FR95) and (23FR96), which we now believe to be a single entity; two separate groups of motifs relating to the same rite. The Rattlesnake Bluff/ Willenberg sites are pictograph sites, meaning that they are painted. The imagery at Willenberg is painted in red and black pigments on sandstone shelter walls. There are some clues that the Bourbeuse River group might be earlier than the Big Five in the Big River valley.

The Role of Women in this Scenario

Some archaeologists have imagined a construction for the exchange of goods as a cross between a modern farmers' market and a Parisian flea market, occupying the plaza areas of Western Mississippian villages

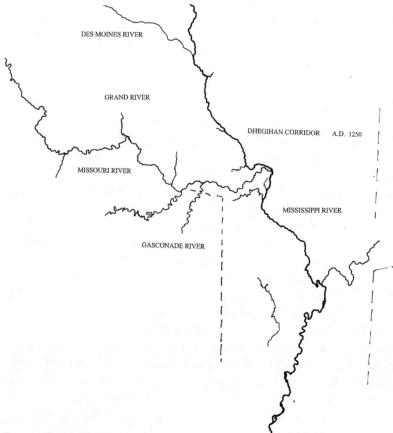

Figure 3.2. The Dhegihan Corridor.

and major mound centers, especially in the Cahokia area, but nothing could be farther from the truth. That being said, what did the exchange of prestige craft objects and valuable goods entail? Where did commerce and exchange take place? What did the ritual event look like to visitors? For starters, we will describe the suitable objects of exchange from ethnographic description and the archaeological record. Beginning with the most valuable gift, a high-ranking female relative of the giver, a woman who is usually a sister, a daughter, or even a wife would be the exchange item. These relationships are not always for lengthy periods; they can be of short duration. In the first half of the nineteenth century, during the adoption of a Kansas chief, the grand "White Hair" chief of the Osage, named Iron Necklace, gave his sister as a wife to the Kansas leader (Louis Burns, 2002, pers. comm.). Osage historian, Louis Burns, was emphatic in using this incident as an example of the adoption of the Kansas leader as a brother by the White Hair and that the most important reciprocal act expected of the Kansas, other than some magnificent gifts, was the Kansas' alliance in war with Iron Necklace and the Osage.

This same scenario was witnessed by the Spanish in the spring of 1541 where a temporary peace was brokered between the leaders of Pacaha, Casqui, and Hernando deSoto. According to the accounts, wives, sisters, and daughters were exchanged between the leaders. It was an uneven exchange, of course, because deSoto had no female relations with him on the trip (Phillips, Ford, and Griffin 1951:358). The location of the towns of Casqui and Pacaha, south of the mouth of the Ohio River, was part of the domain of the expansive Dhegiha, especially the Quapaw (Morse 1990:82).

The LaSalle expedition met the Quapaw living in a town called Kappa near the mouth of the Arkansas in 1682. The French were greeted by a large contingent of men who brought them poles for shelters, firewood, and food. Dances and polite ceremonies were performed for the French, no doubt the adoption rite, and the French were allowed to enter the village plaza where they were surrounded by women and children (Taylor 1956:219–220).

A review of the ethnographic literature indicates that these women were essential in cementing close familial ties between the adopted "brothers" (Bowers 1992:91–92). Usually the woman's status was high enough that she had participated in the gathering of goods and presents for the acquisition, for themselves and by male relatives, of religious offices and bundle privileges. Often these women possessed skills in manufacturing ritual objects, skills acquired through purchase. Thus, a woman was not considered as chattel but as a partner in religious rites (Bowers 1951:71–72; see also Christie [Chapter 8] and Mueller and Fritz [Chapter 4] for the role of women in Dhegihan production and exchange). When the adoptive brethren/children visited a Dhegihan town, the wa'-wa-thon or pipe dance was performed to celebrate the sacred relationship between the relatives (Bailey 2010: 24). Adoption, where the son or brother represents a deceased relation, was also a widespread and essential rite among Western Mississippians and their neighbors (Hall 1997:45–47).

The Maddin Creek Site

The Maddin Creek Site is relatively near the large mound centers at the confluences of the Missouri and Mississippi rivers and the Ohio and Mississippi rivers. It is located in the eastern Ozarks, a heavily karstic region of many springs, streams, and rivers. On its eastern margin, along with several large salt springs concentrated atop ridges along the Meramec River, are extensive deposits of high quality chert. East of the central uplift are deposits of galena and hematite and to the south are the basalt dikes of the St. Francois Mountains. All of these resources were used by the Western Mississippians (Kelly and Brown 2012:109).

The Maddin Creek site is a large and important site on a small stream that is part of the Big River drainage. Maddin Creek was mapped and surveyed in the 1950s by Frank Magre and Benedict Ellis. It might be appropriate at this time to reiterate that the Dhegihan Sioux language has no word for "art" (La Flesche 1975:232). What we do find is the term, xthe-xthe which means to mark or tattoo an object, supernatural being, or person in such a manner as to consecrate and/or bestow honor upon that thing or being (La Flesche 1975:220). The xthe-xthe marking of the sandy dolomite outcrops at the Maddin Creek site express the holy or sacred nature of the imagery, iconography, and the setting. While the Maddin Creek site is badly vandalized and worn, nine vulvar motifs and at least two female figures giving birth are graphically carved among the groups of petroglyphs at the site (Figure 3.3). These will be discussed further along.

When looking at a sketch map of the many panels at Maddin Creek, there seems to be distinct groups of motifs, at least eleven or so, surrounding a larger core group of symbols around a large natural depression. Roughly south of the natural depression is a core group, a vignette, where two anthropomorphs are displaying weapons and flank a large upside down (dead or overpowered) anthropomorph with a "spade" or serpentine shaped head (Figure 3.4). We believe that this group is a "freeze frame" of the two sons/nephews (Stone and Gray Wolf) of Morning Star (Hawk) who have vanquished the principal "giant" (Snake Hide) who has a snake skin tied to his upper left arm. The giant (Snake Hide) is head down with a right foot carved on his back, very possibly the foot of one of the triumphant brothers. By integrating this one vignette with the entire site, it creates a cosmogram with various elements of the "Earth Making" rites, assigned to the Tsi'-Zhu or Sky People (Fletcher and La Flesche 1992:171–172). Using Dhegihan ethnography, especially the

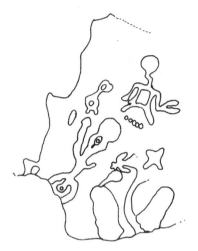

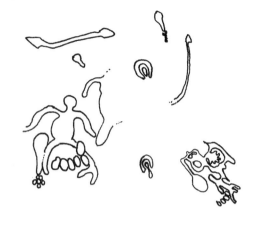

Figure 3.3. Feminine motifs at Maddin Creek.

Osage and Omaha sources, as well as related peripheral sources, we present a shorthand version of the oral tradition of this important rite, the "Making of the Earth," Mon-thin-ka Gaxe (Duncan 2015:209–237, Fletcher and La Flesche 1992:171–172).

Figure 3.4. Stone and his brother Gray Wolf battle the Great Serpent.

The Making
of the Earth

"Way beyond this time," before the Middle World was created, First Man[1] and some companions who lived in the sky, were enticed into joining the "Children of Snake Hide" in several games of chance. First Man and his followers won all but one of the games. First Man was coerced into betting his head and lost it in the final game. The Children of Snake Hide took the shining, but bloodied head west, to their town and the daytime sky fell into darkness. The largest of Snake Hide's children, the one with the beaver tail, swallowed First Man's companions. They were engulfed by darkness and death.

First Woman who was busily working and singing in her lodge (the Moon), awaited the coming of her husband's beautiful face (the Sun). She was saddened when he did not appear. First Woman went looking for First Man whom she finally found headless, wondering about blindly in the darkness. She took the blind and helpless First Man to her lodge and grew old feeding him from her magic pot. Snake Hide and his sons brought game and guarded First Woman's lodge. She would not eat the game, as it was not hers to eat. As First Woman grew old and feeble, her grandsons Stone and Gray Wolf bribed Snake Hide with food and visited their grandmother, First Woman. She gave them powerful weapons, two ancient bows with quivers of lightning arrows and two powerful war clubs—possibly hafted spuds—with thunder power. The boys placed their hands on First Man's hands and chest getting his strength and power, thus they became the most powerful spirits in the cosmos.

Gray Wolf, a great scout, traveled south for a long time and found the town of Snake Hide and his children. He was followed by his grandmother, First Woman, disguised as a spider and carrying her grandson, Stone, on her back. First Woman made food and fed her grandsons. After they had eaten, she dressed and painted them with powerful warrior symbols and they attacked the town of Snake Hide. Snake Hide's children were dancing around the pole on which First Man's head was displayed when the two brothers attacked. The boys' lightning arrows pierced the wicker shields carried by Snake Hide's children. The snakes jabbered among themselves in confusion as they fell, writhing in pain and vomiting blood. Finally Gray Wolf and Stone confronted Snake Hide himself. Gray Wolf and Stone both shot him with arrows and as he was falling to the ground, Stone and the Gray Wolf struck him with their war clubs. Although Snake Hide could not be killed, he had thus been vanquished and disarmed.

In the throes of pain from the many arrows shot into his body, Snake Hide's beaver tailed child disgorged the companions of First Man. These companions appeared as armed warriors, wolves (True Dogs) with deer antlers on their heads. These wolves hunted down, slew, and captured many more of Snake Hide's children. These warriors avoided hurting Snake Hide as Stone and Gray Wolf had tied a bull snake hide to his upper left arm signifying that he was now da'-gthe, a captive to be kindly treated (Duncan 2015:223–224).

While the twins, Stone and Gray Wolf, were fighting, First Woman sat and sang tremolos, brave heart songs to encourage her grandsons in their fight. As she sang, she grew younger and more beautiful. She threw off her ragged and dusty old robe so that all could see her gorgeous red-painted body and beautiful white-painted face.

The two boys took the head of First Man from the pole in Snake Hide's town. Dancing and singing victory songs, they carried it back to First Woman's lodge. To their grandmother they gave the captive, Snake Hide. She would conduct the "walking" ritual in order that she might become the vessel of his powers of resurrection and immortality (Bowers 1950:284–285). The two boys gave a feast and presents to the da'-gthe Snake Hide for the "walking" rite that he performed with their grandmother. First Woman then had intercourse with her husband, First Man, whose body and head had been reunited. After intercourse, First Man was reborn. Preceding First Man in the miraculous rebirth, was his first born son, Hawk. Hawk assists his father and together they burst forth from First Woman's mat covered house.[2]

The two brothers, Stone and Grey Wolf, sing and show the resurrected First Man how they will help him to travel across the daytime sky. The eldest son, Hawk or Morning Star, stands on the vanquished body of Snake Hide and becomes the great Red Oak Tree that pushes the Upper World away from the Lower World (Figure 3.5). First Woman, once again as a spider, begins weaving the Middle World, the Ho'-e-ga, the web which will hold all of the life that makes up this fleeting world that human beings will live in, in the center, the Middle World (Figure 3.6). As the eldest son, Hawk, ascends, carrying the newly resurrected Sun into the sky, he becomes the axis of the cosmos. As his spirit ascends, he embraces his sister, the resurrected evening star. When he stands on the body of the Great Serpent, the rainbow of the upper sky, with his sister Evening Star, the two together become Hon'-ga A-hui-ton, the powerful unifying spirit of the dawn, the new beginning (Figure 3.7). The Middle World was now ready to receive the spirits of the Dhegiha, the star people.

The narration of the Earth Making rite—other details are available in Chapter 4—was the property of all the clans, each clan or fire having a segment of the rite. The clan priests sang their parts, all at the same time so that the songs were a cacophony of sounds, inaudible to the uninitiated listeners. After the death of John Wilson, in 1901, who brought the peyote church to the Osage, several clan priests, under the leadership of the chief, Fred Lookout, made a shortened version of the ancient "Earth Making" rite a part of the Osage peyote church (Louis Burns, 2009, pers. comm.). This ritual is still a part of the fifteen hour rite of vigil of the Osage Native American Church. It is now time to analyze the story behind the Earth Making rite and to further examine the concepts encoded in this most important oral tradition and the rite's influence on the landscape and rock art.

First, the adoption rite is a key component of this ritual. In the oral tradition, this shorthand version that we have related is only a small part of the rite. Some of the songs from this portion of the rite have survived on the periphery of the Western Mississippian world, especially among the Chiwere-speaking Ho-Chunk (Winnebago) and the Ioway. Bits and pieces have been collected among the neighboring Caddoan speakers and other Siouan speak-

Figure 3.5. The triumphant eldest son.

ers, even among the southeastern Muskogee speakers (Radin 1948; Skinner 1925; Bowers 1950, 1992; Swanton 1929; Lankford 1987).

The adoption rite charters the brother-brother relationship between "Stone" and "Gray Wolf" (Fletcher and La Flesche 1992:171; Lankford 1987:165–173; Duncan and Diaz-Granados 2000:9–12). Let us return to the relationship between Maximilian and Four Bears. This relationship was certainly viewed by Four Bears as a brother-brother adoption. While Maximilian's war exploits as a cavalry commander during the Napoleonic wars were most certainly told to Four Bears, the war record of Four Bears was likewise made known to Maximilian. Four Bears had personally slain five enemy chiefs in battle, and he had taken at least 14 scalps, one being that of his brother's slayer, an Arikara, who he killed and scalped on a lone mission of revenge. These feats were probably not duplicated in the nineteenth century by any other prairie/plains warrior (Bowers 1950:34, 70, 123; Wood, Porter, and Hunt 2002:72–73). The gifts exchanged by these "brothers" were many and Maximilian's collection still contains several of them to this day. Four Bears received many rich presents from Maximilian, including a very fine double barrel hunting gun. These presents were best exchanged in the presence of

Figure 3.6. The Spider, First Woman's alter-ego/avatar.

many onlookers, beautifully encased or displayed during a period of public feasting.

Figure 3.7. Hon-ga A-hui-ton, Wulfing Plate from Dunklin County, MO.

From the Mandan standpoint, Four Bears was an "Okipa Maker," a most important religious leader among his people. Four Bear's military record was only a part of his unique leadership qualifications. His father, "Good Boy," had also been a well-liked leader, a chief. Four Bear's household contained several female relatives. His family of industrious female relations were augmented by adopted "daughters," war captives, who helped to prepare food and goods needed for the rites under his jurisdiction. Four Bears was the head of a corporate group, largely female, engaged in the myriad roles of procurement, manufacture, and disbursement (Bowers 1950:34, 166–167, 298).

So what was the allure of the limestone and dolomite glades of the eastern Ozarks on which this imagery appears? Why were they the favorite "canvas" for petroglyphs, xthe-xthe on the landscape—the body of the First Woman? To answer these questions, one must remember that these glades were different prior to the coming of the Europeans. The Native Americans had long used fire as a tool to improve the productivity of their environment (Steyermark/Yatskieviych 1999; Schroeder 1983). These annual burnings in the late winter/early spring hastened the warming of the earth and promoted biodiversity. . . . advantageous plant growth for animals and humans. Burning also restricted the growth of large red cedar trees. Instead, the stony, relatively fire free glade areas were conducive to red cedar growth. The red cedar has long been recognized as a sacred tree to the Dhegiha and their neighbors (Fletcher and La Flesche 1992:42, 457–458; Bailey 1995:37, 234–235). What better place to encounter Stone and Gray Wolf, the Thunder Boys, the Children of the Sun, who were attracted to red cedar glades and who were sought during rites of vigil? "Lucky vigil keepers" were adopted by these powerful spirit beings, and their help and advice were instrumental in insuring a long life, many children, or success in warfare. Young women, as well as young men, were favored by the Thunderers in these glades and they made vision quests into them (La Flesche in Bailey 2010:102). These quests and pilgrimages were among many Native American practices intended to promote fertility and acquire knowledge (Claassen Chapter 1 and 2013; Patel Chapter 9). Often, these rituals employed a rock shrine, such as documented here and by Greer and Greer (Chapter 5) and Roth (Chapter 7) as well as sacred trees (Claassen 2013).

The rite of fasting and vigil, or the vision quest, in which an individual sought the help of a spirit being or beings, was practiced by women as well as men in Dhegihan society (Ponziglione 1897:13–17). To be adopted by a powerful spirit being was ascertained only after an examination and review by the vision advisers and priests. Gifts had to be made before and after the vision quest. Additional gifts were made for the manufacture of ritual objects to be used to access the adoptive supernatural being or beings. Only individuals from large, ambitious families and clans could engage in frequent vision rites and the accompanying feasts. Suitable gifts from the women of a clan involved in vision quests consisted of food, woven containers, pottery, metal items, tanned robes and hides, clothing, textiles, both trade and native, those woven by the women as garments, and blankets to name several (Drooker 1992:72–77). The man in Osage society with plural wives "was accustomed to receive more gifts both in public and private religious ceremonies" (Fitzgerald 1939:229). Polygamy was definitely an economic asset in Dhegihan society.

Visits to the Ozark glades with their petroglyphs were catalytic in bringing about the rounds of gift exchanges and payments for the rites accompanying these visits. Not only were these visits of a sacred nature, there was also a strong economic incentive, the acquisition of nearby, valuable mineral resources. There were probably clans who "owned" the rights to gather these resources, particularly salt and the basalt from the dikes in the St. Francois Mountains (Kelly and Brown 2012). This "ownership" was allocated to individuals, families, and clans (Bowers 1950:212–216). These visiting groups intent on acquiring the resources not only paid for the rights to gather them from the owners, both human and supernatural beings (Greer and Greer, Chapter 5, mention offerings left at Indian Lake Medicine Boulder), they also received reciprocal payments during the exchange of the materials. Acquisition of these powers to acquire and exchange was a costly enterprise. Prominent families who possessed the rights to the acquisition had to be compensated. To this day, the impressive displays of costly Pendleton woolen blankets, groceries, beautiful horses, and fine wearing apparel during the ritual exchange associated with the I'n-Lon-Schka drum, during the June solstice dances, still excite the admiration of the Dhegihan participants.

Rattlesnake Bluff and Willenberg Shelter

Rattlesnake Bluff and Willenberg Shelter are most likely contemporaneous and probably earlier than the eastern Ozark glade sites previously discussed that contrast with them. Rather than being rendered in a petroglyphic format, the imagery is painted in red and black pigments on sandstone shelter walls. Because the style at Rattlesnake Bluff involves a realistic portrayal of the figures, we see connectors between these images and a continuum with the Braden style that originated in the lower Missouri River and its confluence with the Mississippi River, namely the greater Cahokia area (Brown 2007:219; Diaz-Granados 2011:66–68).

Rattlesnake Bluff and the Willenberg shelter are on opposite sides of a small valley at the junction of the Little Bourbeuse River and Three Mile Creek. The sites were first reported by Robert Elgin in 1958 (MAS Site Files). Since then Dale Henning in 1960 and R. Bruce McMillan in 1965 have visited the sites and filed additional site reports. Fletcher Jolly III wrote an article about the Willenberg shelter, published by the Central States Archaeological Society (1982). When we first visited these sites with Robert Elgin, the Willenberg site alone had evidence of clandestine digging. On our last visit with Frank Magre, both of the sites had been extensively vandalized. The alluvial bottom between the sites has a large, elevated terrace with evidence of human occupation over a long period of time. Several prehistoric and historic artifacts were found eroding from the west bank of the Little Bourbeuse River opposite the Willenberg shelter.

The Little Bourbeuse River valley region has resources that are similar to those available to visitors to the eastern Ozark petroglyph sites with two notable differences: there are no basalt dikes and this area is rich in flint clay deposits. One of these deposits, not yet identified, is the probable source of the red flint clay used in the manufacture of the large figurines found in and around Cahokia (Emerson et al. 2002:313; Emerson et al. 2003:288–291) and discussed in detail by Mueller and Fritz in Chapter 4.

We will first look at the Rattlesnake Bluff site on the west side of the Little Bourbeuse River. The sandstone bluff has somewhat protected the pictographs from weathering and also forms a shallow shelter at its base. At the northern edge of the composition is a skillfully drawn or painted rattlesnake in black pigment, over 80 centimeters in length and realistically undulating in a serpentine fashion. Above this image is another, much fainter, image. Neither has a distinct head or tail. Accurately depicted belly scutes and the distinctive pattern of the scale pattern on the dorsal surfaces can be easily seen. The bottom image is the most realistic depiction of a rattlesnake in Missouri's rock art inventory (Figure 3.8). The serpentine body seems to be traveling from north to south. About five meters to the south of the rattlesnakes is a red painted male figure with a rectangular, wicker-style shield in his left hand and a crown shaped mace or war club in his right hand (Figure 3.9). This figure is one meter tall. This vignette is so placed on the bluff as to be illuminated by the light from the dawn or early morning sun.

On the opposite side of the valley is Willenberg, a deeper sandstone shelter. On the sloping wall of this shelter are several figures painted or drawn in dark red, red-orange, and black pigments. The most prominent group is made up of two principal figures: one, a large round eyed figure with large cat-like ears and displaying a clawed left "hand." In this figure's right "hand" is a bilobate paddle-shaped mace or war club (Figure 3.10). Directly above the first figure is an atypical figure with attributes of a horned owl with outspread wings and extended talons. The "owl" is painted in red to red-orange pigment while the other figure is painted with a darker red pigment. On the south side of the two largest figures is a small anthropomorph in red pigment holding a drawn bow with an arrow in his right hand and a mace shaped war club with an unusual diamond shaped head in his left hand (Figure 3.11). Just inside the shelter on the west wall is a wonderful elk (wapiti), realistically painted in red pigment, with at least two arrows in its body (Figure 3.12). To the east of the cat-like figure and the owl, on the ceiling in red pigment is a cruciform within concentric circles next to a crescent moon (Figure 3.13). Near the principal figures there are faint, scattered enigmatic markings, one possibly a profile of a human head with a fore-and-aft feather headdress and an anthropomorphic figure in black. Willenberg shelter and Rattle Snake Bluff are somewhat unique in style. The realistic Braden style of the silhouetted anthropomorph at Rattlesnake Bluff is most reminiscent of the figures at Picture Cave.

To begin the interpretation, we are sure that the two sites are contemporaneous and complimentary. They form an interesting cosmological structure. The deeper shelter with the owl and other characters is west facing and would be illuminated by the setting sun. The triumphant red painted warrior figure and rattlesnake images on the bluff opposite

Figure 3.8. Rattlesnake pictograph from 23FR95.

Figure 3.10. Vignette of three figures from 23FR96, Willenberg Shelter site.

Figure 3.11. Anthropomorphic figure at Willenberg Shelter.

Figure 3.9. Dancing Warrior from 23FR95.

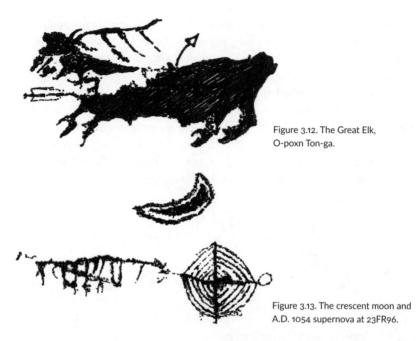

Figure 3.12. The Great Elk, O-poxn Ton-ga.

Figure 3.13. The crescent moon and A.D. 1054 supernova at 23FR96.

are lit up by the early morning sun. We have put together an interesting scenario in an attempt to explain the purpose of these two sites.

We think that the most important symbol is the cruciform within concentric circles next to the crescent; it likely depicts the crab nebula super nova next to the crescent moon that occurred on July 4–5 in A.D. 1054. A stellar event of this magnitude would certainly have caused some sort of ritual response to affect supernatural beings thought to be responsible for such a unique happening. Knowing that the Moon was the lodge of the First Woman (the Earth), who might the bright star be that tried to rival the Sun in its brightness and was so close to First Woman's lodge? The Sun had just started moving southward (after the summer solstice) in the daytime sky when the A.D. 1054 supernova occurred. This spectacular new star appeared in the Milky Way in the night sky. The great serpent's tail, the great rift in the Perseid arm, the brightest part of the Milky Way, was in the southern sky, and the constellation Cassiopeia—the great serpent and his four sons—was closer to the northern horizon at dawn. The pictograph of the body of the Rattlesnake is southwest of the group in the shelter, just as it is in the night sky. The feline figure at the Willenberg shelter, which may represent the Great Puma, the alter ego of the Great Serpent, is northeast of his "body," the Milky Way, just as he (the middle star, of Cassiopeia) was at dawn on July 5 in A.D. 1054.

The red painted "Dancing Warrior" is undoubtedly Morning Star or the Symbolic Man, who would be moving south from the northernmost position he occupied at the solstice. This one meter tall figure is the only monumental Braden style image of Morning Star that has survived (and barely at that). The first light of the sunrise on July 5 in A.D. 1054 would have illuminated this figure as he moved away from the headless body of the Rattlesnake. With a wicker style shield and brandishing his war club, he danced south, in the direction of First Woman's lodge.

The figure of the Great Puma in Willenberg shelter is being attacked by a smaller, red-painted figure with a bow and arrow and a war club or mace. This small, red painted anthropomorph is probably "Stone," one of Morning Star's nephews/sons. While he is not accompanied by his brother, Gray Wolf, we are fairly certain of this figure's identity. The Owl, the dominant figure just above the Great Puma, is spectacular. With its wings outspread and legs extended with their talons, this bird seems to be on the attack. Who does the owl represent, and who is being attacked? Is this the owl of oral tradition who is the antagonist of Hawk (Swanton 1929:152; Bailey 2010:145)?

There are three clues that might just help solve this puzzle. The first clue is the absence of an identical brother depicted as Stone as we see at Maddin Creek and Picture Cave. Can it be that Gray Wolf has another shape that he can assume? During the Okipa rite of the Mandan, First Man's counterpart, the Foolish One is painted to resemble the night sky, he is often called Owl, the opposite of the Hawk in the daytime sky. More importantly, the Mandan oral tradition states that the Foolish One killed the sacred Snakes and the evil woman (Deer Woman) who made men stray from their wives. This important spirit being is OxinhEdE, or Little Foolish One, the son of the Sun (Bowers 1950:365). The third clue is the small head worn on the head of the human/hawk copper plate from Malden in Dunklin County, MO. This small head displays the terraced design commonly associated with the Upper World. Can it be the head of Morning Star's alter ego, Gray Wolf, who also represents the night sky (Figure 3.14)? This Braden style copper plate probably represents the Morning Star at dawn on the first day of the creation of the Middle World, displaying the head of his alter ego owl as the symbol for the displaced night (Figure 3.15).

The two groups of pictographs in Willenberg Shelter and Rattlesnake Bluff, form a cosmogram, representing the moment of the creation of

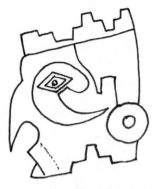

Figure 3.14. Detail of head rattle on head-dress of Wulfing Plate from Dunklin County, MO. Courtesy of Kemper Art Museum, Washington University, St. Louis, MO.

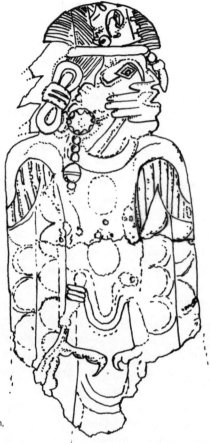

Figure 3.15. Anthropomorphic copper plate from Wulfing set of eight plates, Dunklin County, MO. Courtesy of Kemper Art Museum, Washington University, St. Louis, MO.

the Middle World, the dawn of the first day. The Dhegiha believed that the cosmos was a constantly changing and evolving system where com-memorative rituals aided individuals and communities in connecting with the invisible powers (Bailey 1995:30–31).

Conclusions

A comparison of these two sites reveals more similarities than differ-ences. One relevant point is that both are located south of Cahokia, a direction associated with a set of cosmic concepts including "women." While the Maddin Creek site has symbolism related to First Woman, the Little Bourbeuse River sites have only one possible female figure, the peculiar figure in black pigment who might represent First Woman on her back with her knees drawn up, a coital position (Figure 3.16). The general subject matter common to both sites seems to be a conflict between cosmic forces, Morning Star and his related supernatural beings fighting the Great Serpent and his family. Metaphorically, it is the two major divisions of the cosmos, upper and lower worlds, light and darkness, in combat, which represent the prelude to the creation of the Middle World. While the arrangement at the Little Bourbeuse River sites is clearly cosmological, its subject matter is a little enigmatic when compared to the more specific imagery at the Maddin Creek site. With regard to chronological differences, we believe that the Little Bourbeuse River sites are older than the Maddin Creek site because of their more realistic portrayal of the human and animal figures. This realism is the hallmark of the Braden style (Phillips and Brown 1978:69–76; Brown 2011:37–38).

Although Cahokia and the East St. Louis mound group do not have any known directly associated rock art, the western mound group that was situated where downtown St. Louis is today did have rock art on a limestone ledge on the Mississippi River bank. For the Dhegihan peoples, the direction west also was associated with female elements in the cosmology. In the first half of the 19th century, this very important ledge bore a realistic pair of human foot prints. It was removed and transported to New Harmony, IN (Figure 3.17) (see Diaz-Granados and Duncan 2000:11, 15, 73). The foot prints were associated with a cave, an entrance to the beneath world (the vulva of the First Woman). The modern Osage West Moon peyote church at Hominy, OK, has a similar pair of foot prints at the opening of a west facing vulvar shaped altar (Mathews 1961:747, 753). This altar represents the vulva of First Woman where the Sun and his son, Morning Star, will enter at sunset. Foot prints and caves/shelters are explored by Claassen in Chapter 1, which she connects to fertility rites.

In the balanced cosmos of the Dhegiha, how many pilgrims from surrounding centers, towns, and hamlets came to participate in the rites of the birth of the Sun and his eldest son, Morning Star? With the singing of the Wa'-wa-thon during the times of heightened ritual activity and visits, how impressive must have been the stacks of beautifully displayed gifts, most the work of industrious female relations of the elite visitors. There is little doubt that visiting delegations from distant nations also brought quantities of rich gifts, presents, and food to impress their adoptive relations. The amount of archaeologically re-corded items from far-flung sources found at the greater Cahokia region is well documented. Likewise, the sheer amount of material produced in the Mississippi corridor and the Dhegihan homeland and found on sites scattered from Florida to Iowa is astonishing.

While the elite seem to have been the preferred recipients of the pres-tige goods, being elite meant, in part, having numerous female relations, both actual relations and adoptees who were willing to participate in manufacturing goods and providing food stuffs. Women cannot effi-ciently farm when the male relatives are few, lazy, or non-participating. While men successful in warfare kept the women safe, in Dhegihan so-ciety the captives brought home to be adopted were the warrior's most important contribution. These additional members were essential for a thriving, achieving clan. The twin pillars of Dhegihan society, bravery and generosity, place a successful warrior/priest at the head of a suc-cessful clan. But, he could only achieve this with the help of industrious female relatives who were motivated by their high regard for him.

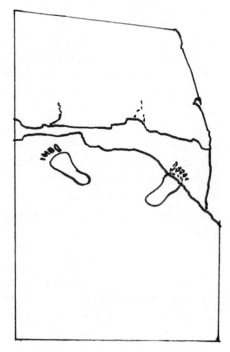

Figure 3.16. Anthropomorphic figure at Willenberg Shelter.

Figure 3.17. Petroglyph foot prints, originally located on St. Louis Riverfront, now in Posey County, IN.

There is an interesting account of the dispersal of goods and food to the deserving members of Dhegihan society. Not all men were successful warriors, some perished, often leaving aging relatives and parents with no source for offspring, real or adopted. The Dhegihans gave relief to those unfortunates with periodic gatherings. One such gathering was recorded—an event in a grove of timber where all members of the band, especially those who had lost relatives in warfare, received carefully allocated shares of the goods accumulated by the elite (Ponziglione 1897:261–262). Due to the conflict during the expansive period of the Dhegiha, war captives would also be available to allocate.

Perhaps the most important role of ritual sites, rock art sites in particular, was in the gathering of spiritual power through vision quests and related rites. This is seen today among Dhegiha participating in prayer groups and peyote church rites. Officiating religious leaders receive gifts and they in turn reciprocate. Large numbers of guests are fed, many of them non-participants. Dhegihan protocol has two major precepts: all are welcome, even outsiders, and an abundance of food is prepared and provision is made for all to take home food after the ritual. At these events, the women who are the "cooks" and the men who tend the cooking fires are in turn rewarded with food and gifts by those sponsoring the rite.

We believe that in-depth and continuing study of the ethnographical resources are essential, even critical, in recognizing and interpreting the iconography found in rock art as well as on portable artifacts. A deeper understanding of these icons and graphic scenarios employed by ancient Native Americans can be used to reconstruct cultural systems, especially complex ones, laden with symbolism and metaphors as we find in the Western Mississippian societies. The complexity and charting of the interaction between those subjected to the mores and protocols of a culture are encoded in the oral traditions of that culture and on the landscapes on which they placed their symbols, stories, and beliefs. Brought into focus by these rock art sites are the economic and spiritual contributions of women, as well as men, and a personified landscape.

Acknowledgments

We wish to thank Charles RedCorn, Kathryn RedCorn Lynn, Mary Carter, John Maker, William S. Fletcher, Eddie RedEagle, Dudley Whitehorn, and the late Andrew (Bud) RedCorn, Cora Jean Big Elk Jech, Louis F. Burns, Charles Pratt, Leonard Maker, Preston Morrell and Raymond Red Corn, Sr. We also wish to sincerely thank Cheryl Claassen for bringing together this important volume and for her patience in seeing it to fruition.

REFERENCES CITED

Bailey, Garrick (editor)

1995   *The Osage and the Invisible World: From the Works of Francis La Flesche.* University of Oklahoma Press, Norman.

2010   *Traditions of the Osage.* University of New Mexico Press, Albuquerque.

Bowers, Alfred

1950   *Mandan Social and Ceremonial Organization.* University of Chicago Press, Chicago.

1992   *Hidatsa Social and Ceremonial Organization.* University of Nebraska Press, Lincoln.

Brown, James

2007   Sequencing the Braden Art Style within Mississippian Period Art and Iconography. In *Ancient Objects and Sacred Realms*, F. K. Reilly and J. F. Garber, editors, pp. 213–245. University of Texas Press, Austin.

Claassen, Cheryl

2013   Fertility, A Place-based Gift to Groups. In *Género y Arqueología en Meso-américa. Homenaje a Rosemary A. Joyce*, María J. Rodríguez-Shadow and Susan Kellogg, coordinators, pp.198–225. Centro de Estudios de Antropología de la Mujer, Las Cruces, NM.

Diaz-Granados, Carol

2011   Early Manifestations of Mississippian Iconography. In *Visualizing the Sacred*, George Lankford, F. Kent Reilly, and J. F. Garber, editors, pp. 64–98. University of Texas Press, Austin.

Diaz-Granados, Carol, and James Duncan

2000   *The Petroglyphs and Pictographs of Missouri.* University of Alabama Press, Tuscaloosa.

Drooker, Penelope

1992   *Mississippian Village Textiles at Wickliffe.* University of Alabama Press, Tuscaloosa.

Duncan, James R.

2011   The Cosmology of the Osage. In *Visualizing the Sacred*, George Lankford, Kent Reilly, and Jim Garber, editors, pp. 18–33, University of Texas Press, Austin.

2015   Identifying the Characters on the Walls of Picture Cave. In *Picture Cave: Unraveling the Mysteries of the Mississippian Cosmos*, Carol Diaz-Granados, James R. Duncan, F. Kent Reilly, editors, pp. 209–237, University of Texas Press, Austin.

Duncan, James R. and Carol Diaz-Granados

2000   Of Masks and Myths. *Midcontinental Journal of Archaeology* 25:1–26.

Emerson, Thomas, Randall Hughes, Mary Haynes, and Sarah Wisseman

2002   Implications of Sourcing Cahokia–Style Flint Clay Figurines. *American Antiquity* 68(2):287–313.

Fitzgerald, Mary

1939 *Beacon on the Plains*. Saint Mary College, Leavenworth, KS.

Fletcher, Alice, and Francis La Flesche

1992 *The Omaha Tribe*, Vols. I and II, reprinted from 1911 edition. University of Nebraska Press, Lincoln.

Hall, Robert

1997 *An Archaeology of the Soul*. University of Illinois Press, Urbana and Chicago.

Jolly, Fletcher

1982 The Willenberg Shelter. *Central States Archaeological Journal* 29(2):68–74.

Kelly, John, and James Brown

2012 In Search of Cosmic Power: Contextualizing Spiritual Journeys between Cahokia and the St. Francis Mountains. In *Archaeology of Spiritualities*, K. Roundtree, Christine Morris, and Alan Peatfield, editors, pp. 107–109. Springer, New York.

Kelly, John, James Brown, and Lucretia Kelly

2008 The Context of Religion at Cahokia: The Mound 34 Case in *Religion, Archaeology and the Material World*, L. Fogelin, editor, pp. 298–316. Center for Archaeological Investigations, Occasional Paper No. 36. Southern Illinois University Press, Carbondale.

La Flesche, Francis

1975 *A Dictionary of the Osage Language*. Smithsonian Institution, Bulletin No. 109, Bureau of American Ethnology, 43rd Annual Report 1925–1926. Washington, DC.

Lankford, George

1987 *Native American Legends*. American Folklore Series. August House, Little Rock, AR.

Lepper, Bradley

2003 The Newark Earthworks: Monumental Geometry and Astronomy at a Hopewellian Pilgrimage Site. In *Hero, Hawk, and Open Hand: American Indian Art of the Ancient Midwest and South*, R. Townsend and R. V. Sharp, editors, pp. 73–82. Art Institute of Chicago and Yale University Press, New Haven, CT.

Mathews, John

1961 *The Osages*. University of Oklahoma Press, Norman.

Morse, Dan

1960 The Nodena Phase. In *Towns and Temples Along the Mississippi*, David Dye and C. A. Cox, editors, pp. 69–97. University of Alabama Press, Tuscaloosa, AL.

Parkman, Frances

1986 *The Discovery of the Great West*, William Taylor, editor. Greenwood, Westport, CT.

Phillips, Philip, and James Brown

1978 *PreColumbian Shell Engravings, Part 1*. Peabody Museum Press, Peabody Museum of Archaeology and Ethnology, and Harvard University, Cambridge, MA.

Phillips, Philip, James A. Ford, and James B. Griffin

1951 *Archaeological Survey in the Lower Mississippi Alluvial Valley, Vol. XXV*. Peabody Museum of Archaeology and Ethnology and Harvard University, Cambridge, MA.

Ponziglione, Paul

1897   The Osages and Father John Schoenmakers, S. J., Interesting Memoirs Collected from Legends, Traditions and Historical Documents. Handwritten manuscript on file at Midwest Jesuit Archives. St. Louis, MO.

Radin, Paul

1948   Winnebago Hero Cycles: A Study in Aboriginal Literature. *International Journal of American Linguistics*, Indiana University Publications in Anthropology and Linguistics, Memoir 1, Waverly Press, Baltimore, MD.

Schroeder, W.

1983   *Presettlement Prairie of Missouri.* 2nd edition, Natural History Series, No. 2, Missouri Department of Conservation, Jefferson City.

Skinner, Alanson

1925   Traditions of the Iowa Indians. *Journal of American Folklore* 38:425–506.

Yatskievych, G. (editor)

1999   *Steyermark's Flora of Missouri,* Vol. 2. Missouri Department of Conservation, Jefferson City.

Swanton, John

1929   *Myths and Tales of the Southeastern Indians*, Bureau of American Ethnology. Bulletin 88, Smithsonian Institution, U.S. Government Printing Office, Washington, DC.

Wood, Raymond W., Joseph C. Porter, and David C. Hunt

2002   *Karl Bodmer's Studio Art.* University of Illinois Press, Urbana and Chicago.

4

WOMEN AS SYMBOLS AND ACTORS
IN THE MISSISSIPPI VALLEY
Evidence from Female Flint-Clay Statues
and Effigy Vessels

Natalie G. Mueller and Gayle J. Fritz

Introduction

Native women probably domesticated the seed-bearing plants that came to be economically important across a large swath of precolonial eastern North America. Women were the major, if not sole, producers and local breeders of the tropical crops, especially corn (*Zea mays* ssp. *mays*), that sustained their families and fed the invading armies and colonists who came from the Old World after 1500 A.D. Acknowledgment of the dominant role played by American Indian women in agriculture is explicit in a number of publications, including those by Watson and Kennedy (1991); Smith (1993); Fritz (1999); Mueller (2013); and Scarry and Scarry (2005). By extension, the contributions made by women to environmental transformations caused by farming can be assumed if not specified (Fritz 2000; Hammett 2000; Wagner 2003). Men were instrumental in the initial clearing of wooded areas for new fields, but most Mississippian farmers were not primarily shifting agriculturalists. Instead, they probably planted crops in fields that, following initial clearance of woody vegetation, were open permanently or at least for decades. Farmers shifted plots around within these spaces as needed to rest the soil but not allow mature forests to regenerate (Doolittle 1992). In addition to the considerable labor involved in keeping fields open and productive, women augmented the productivity of harvested wild and managed fruits from bushes, small trees, and herbaceous plants growing at the edges of fields and habitation areas. Furthermore, as gatherers and harvesters, women participated in the maintenance of orchard-like groves of nut- and fruit-bearing trees near farmsteads, villages, and towns located in suitable environmental zones. Most of the settlements themselves were probably enhanced by home gardens where an array of edible and medicinally valuable plants could be readily accessed. Since the landscape of both cultivated and "wild" but managed food-bearing plants was associated with women and their work, we expect that the propitiation of the forces of fecundity would employ feminine symbols.

Less obvious in the literature, but growing in volume, is appreciation of the roles played by living women where ideological, ritual, socioeconomic, and physical elements of the landscape intersect (Claassen 2011; DeBoer 2001; Duncan and Diaz-Granados 2004; Galloway 1997). We expand this conversation by focusing on two prominent classes of Mississippian art: (1) Cahokia-style female flint-clay "fertility" statues and (2) ceramic Kneeling Woman effigy vessels from the central Mississippi River Valley region. These remarkable works combine themes from realms that we, non-Native social scientists, might view as mythic and spiritual, agricultural, mortuary, and connected to human reproduction. The flint-clay itself came from the cedar glades of the Missouri Ozarks (Duncan and Diaz-Granados Chapter 3). Duncan and Diaz-Granados discuss the possibility that journeys to harvest flint clay also served as pilgrimages to boulder and rock shelter fertility shrines. Creation, renewal, and regeneration are associated both with the raw material and with the iconographic content of these objects. One spiritual personage—Old Woman Who Never Dies or Grandmother—connects the beliefs and behaviors that we think involved and sometimes combined commemoration, supplication, and devotion. We begin by looking into the spiritual and agricultural roots of the domesticated landscape in which Mississippian farmers lived. Traces of the gendered institutions that maintained this landscape, both practically and spiritually, are suggested by Mississippian iconography and ritual spaces. We have used one mythical figure, Grandmother or the Old Woman Who Never Dies, as a cipher to guide our understanding of these traces.

Woodland Roots of a Gendered Landscape

Grandmother is, in Siouan Plains Village mythology, "the custodian of all vegetation that ripens or sheds its leaves in the fall and is 'rejuvenated' in the spring with the northern flights of the waterbirds, which she accompanied" (Bowers 1992:338). As such, rites performed on her behalf, or seeking her blessing and aid, may have preceded the domestication of crops in the Eastern Woodlands, and devotion to her probably long predated the intensification of maize. The retreat shelters and marked crevices of the Ozarks and Cumberland Plateau discussed by Claassen in Chapter 1 may have been Late Archaic and Early Woodland expressions of the Grandmother propitiation (Duncan and Diaz-Granados Chapter 3). Whether or not this can ever be recognized archaeologically, we argue that women were active participants, not only in the planting and tending of gardens and fields that produced the chenopod, knotweed, maygrass, sunflower, sumpweed, squashes, and other crops grown in significant amounts during Middle Woodland times (200 BCE–400 A.D.) but also in the large gatherings that took place in those years at Hopewellian mound centers located across the Midwest.

Mueller (2013) has recently made a plausible case for the exchange of seed stock as explaining key aspects of the archaeobotanical assemblage at Mound House, a floodplain mound complex in the lower Illinois River valley dating to the early first millennium A.D. The exchange of plant products including crop seeds was very likely dominated by women, who would not only have spread attractive varieties to new regions but would also have broadcast knowledge essential to successful production of unfamiliar crops, along with processing and preparation techniques. We see this exchange as including actions such as offerings, prayers, performances, and bundle-opening ceremonies and taking place within the ritually-charged backdrop of multi-community feasting, mound building, and world renewal rites. Thus, the significance of these seemingly lowly grains extended well beyond the purely domestic, economic, and functional spheres.

The building of Hopewellian mounds and other earthworks ceased during Late Woodland times (400–850 A.D.), but production of native Eastern Agricultural Complex (EAC) crops was intensified, and populations in the midcontinent grew in density as villagers applied successful skills for the farming, hunting, and management of wild plant resources. Ceramic technology and storage practices clearly improved in conjunction with evolving agricultural intensification (Braun 1983; Buikstra et al. 1986). We assume that early spiritual beliefs and traditions of previous generations persisted and evolved throughout the second half of the first millennium A.D., in spite of the reduced visibility of large-scale, multi-community ceremonialism and long-distance exchange networks.

The spread of maize into eastern North America, often viewed by archaeologists as a hallmark of economic transformation, does not appear to have had a major impact on either Late Woodland subsistence or ritual practice although the exact timing of that event is still being fine-tuned, and the causes and consequences of the process continue to be debated (Hart et al. 2013; Smith and Cowen 2003). Between 850 and 1050 A.D., however, Emergent Mississippian farmers set the stage for dramatic subsequent events (Kelly 1990), notably the coming together of tens of thousands of people at Cahokia Mounds and the surrounding bottomland and upland region of eastern Missouri and western Illinois during the eleventh century A.D. (Pauketat 2009). By this time, maize was an important component of the subsistence economy, balanced by maygrass, chenopod, knotweed, sunflower, squash, and other EAC crops. The dynamics of feeding—not to mention otherwise integrating—this unprecedented density of people, many of whom appear to have relocated from hundreds of kilometers away (Slater et al. 2014) and belonged to linguistically and culturally diverse societies must have been challenging.

Grandmother, with her long mythic history, emerges as a key figure in the ritualized Mississippian landscape (Duncan and Diaz Granados 2004). She is manifested across the landscape at rock art sites and within settlements close to Cahokia where special structures have been interpreted as world renewal temples. We turn now to the female flint-clay statues and effigy vessels that, through the symbolism they project and the contexts in which they were uncovered, speak to the roles played by women in the social and productive transformation of the Mississippian landscape.

Mississippian Women as Symbols

Aspects of a Dominant Symbol

Images of women in Mississippian art potentially reflect both the referents of women as symbols and the prerogatives of women as actors. In linguistics, the referent is the object or concept that is invoked by a word (or symbol, in this case). Complex concepts can often be referred to by many different symbols. For example, a crown of thorns and a cross both invoke the story of the crucifixion of Jesus and all of the abstract meanings associated with it. Conversely, a symbol can be polysemous: it can have many different specific referents depending on the context in which it is deployed. A polysemous symbol with a complex and culturally important suite of referents can be manipulated to perform a variety of social actions. A cross can also designate a sacred space, declare a religious affiliation, or act as a talisman to ward off evil. Is it possible to recover the nuances of representation intended by Mississippian people from their symbols?

In his classic scheme for parsing symbols, Victor Turner described three aspects of symbolic meaning: *exegetical, positional,* and *operational* (1967:50–52; Figure 4.1). For Turner, exegetic meaning was obtained from conversations with informants or other testimony from within the symbolic community. It is the meaning consciously invoked by a person using the symbol in a given context. As archaeologists, we receive our exegetic meanings indirectly and imperfectly from the oral histories and ethnographies of descendent communities. But through archaeological context, we have fairly direct access to positional meaning, which is contingent on the interaction of multiple symbols, and operational meaning, which is dependent on how and by whom a symbol is deployed (Turner 1967; Figure 4.1). Turner's classic scheme helps us to bring both ethnohistorical and archeological observations to bear on our analysis of the two different types of Mississippian woman effigies: flint-clay figurines and hooded effigy vessels.

Ethnographies and oral histories of descendent communities are imperfect reflections of the beliefs consciously held by the communities who created Mississippian symbols. Yet by comparing many different mythologies and rituals from later communities, it may be possible to

DOMINANT SYMBOLS	EXEGETICAL	OPERATIONAL	POSITIONAL
According to Turner	Obtained from informants: What meanings do people consciously associate with symbols	Obtained from observing informants: How is the symbol used? Who uses it, and who is excluded from using it? What is the affective quality of performances using this symbol?	Obtained from observing symbols in relation to other objects and persons: What is the web of relationships surrounding a symbol? How is the meaning of a symbol affected by its context?
In archaeology	Obtained from ethnography or oral history of descendant communities, or, with less reliability, from historical accounts	Inferred from archaeological context, but only the final deployment of the symbol is usually accessible	Inferred from associated symbols, objects, and structures

Figure 4.1. Victor Turner's (1967) scheme for parsing dominant symbols, adapted for archaeologists.

triangulate what Turner called *dominant symbols* by taking note of motifs that are particularly widespread and consistent in their associations. According to Turner, "each dominant symbol has a 'fan' or 'spectrum' of referents, interlinked by what is usually a simple mode of association, its very simplicity enabling it to interconnect a wide variety of *significata*" (1967:50). One seemingly dominant symbol from Plains and eastern American Indian lore is Old Woman Who Never Dies, or Grandmother.

Grandmother in Myth and Legend: Exegetical Aspects of Meaning

In Siouan mythology Grandmother is an important mythological figure who was responsible for teaching people how to live well on earth by growing and gathering food and hunting game. Grandmother in Siouan myth is the patroness of all vegetation and is honored in springtime festivals that celebrate rejuvenation. She is a protagonist in the Sacred Arrow myth, her part beginning when the culture hero Grandson falls from the sky with his mother, who dies in the descent. Grandmother takes in the lost child. She gives him food from her garden and teaches him how to hunt. She can call game with her sunflower whistle, or drive it away, depending on her whims. She brings rain in the summer and snow in the winter. Her consorts are giant water snakes, and she owns vessels that magically refill themselves (Bowers 1992:333–338). She is also mythically entangled with Two Men, the Siouan manifestation of the archetypal twins, who appear in many New World mythologies. In the Hidatsa version, Two Men want to marry Grandmother, but she refuses and becomes angry, using her magical whistle to bring winter storms and drive away their game (Bowers 1992:335–336). After many years of living among the people as a teacher, she tires of their constant demands and retires to an island. Her retreat is fabled to be near the mouth of the Mississippi River and guarded by her serpent consorts (Bowers 1992:336). She is immortal; she bathes in the river and becomes young again. It is by observing this power that Grandson knows "that she is the one who has control of the vegetation, causing it to grow each year when the water birds come north and the snakes appear" (Bowers 1992:335). (Other details of Old Woman Who Never Dies can be found in Duncan and Diaz-Granados, Chapter 3).

While clearly a multifaceted character, we hope to demonstrate that she is *not the same as* the Corn Mother of eastern Woodlands mythologies, a character who dies in various ways while giving corn and/or fertile ground to the people. In this analysis we would like to point out what appears to be an important dichotomy in traditions related to women and plant fertility in eastern and plains traditions. An important woman deity, sometimes old, sometimes young and beautiful, also appears in the traditions of Muskogean, Iroquoian, Caddoan, and some Algonquian tales recounting the origins of maize, but her role is different. Corn Mother's body *is* (or gives rise to) maize and other crops. In some myths, she rubs her feet or body, and her skin turns into the first kernels of corn. In others, she dies in childbirth and her body gives rise to corn, beans, and squash. There are also versions of the myth where Corn Mother dies or is killed and her children have to drag her body around in order to make the soil fertile for the first maize or other crops (Lankford 2011:1557).

This latter group of myths *may be* derivative of or younger than the story of Grandmother and the Orphan because in Corn Mother tales an adopted child is sometimes also a part of the tale. When this occurs, the child is usually tasked with killing and/or manipulating the dead body of Corn Mother so as to produce more corn (e.g., Grantham 2002:62). This version of the myth has been "merged with the Grandmother-Orphan legend" writes George Lankford, who also recognizes the Grandmother/ Corn Mother distinction (2011:157–158). The division of these two mythical figures is not always clear cut, as the preceding quote implies. For example, in the Hidatsa story recounted by Bowers there is no mention of what happens to the body of Grandson's mother (a version of Sky Woman) after she dies in her descent from the Sky World (Bowers 1992:334), yet in other versions the body of the Sky Woman is buried in Grandmother's garden and confers fertility (Duncan and Diaz-Granados 2004:200). In the Seneca creation myth, Sky Woman falls from the sky to an island and *does not die*, instead becoming the Grandmother figure in the myth. In this tale, it is Sky Woman's daughter who dies, and maize, beans, and squash grow from her body (Cornplanter 1963:19–25).[1] Despite the complexity of the mythical landscape, it seems that we can distinguish between Corn Mother and Grandmother on the basis of immortality: Grandmother is an eternal, ageless figure whereas Corn Mother's death is instrumental to her story. While it is impossible to prove, we can at least suggest that the spread of Corn Mother stories across the landscape accompanied the spread of maize as an important crop, merging with older tales of Grandmother in myriad unique ways. As suggested by Claassen in the Introduction, the spread of both maize and these stories also indicates that women traveled widely.

While Grandmother is often associated with Siouan mythology, she also appears in southeastern lore, in a different but highly enlightening narrative context. In several similar tales from the Yuchi and Alabama, two men attempt to bring their dead wives back from the Sky World. Along the way, they encounter an old woman who is working in her garden. She feeds them from food that replenishes itself, helps them pass by monstrous snakes unharmed, and gives them seeds to bring back to their communities (Swanton 1929). All of these actions, as well as the story's form—a prolonged interaction with a pair of adventuring men—link this Old Woman to the Siouan Grandmother. But these stories add a new set of enlightening referents. According to the Yuchi and Alabama, the old woman helps the men find the spirits of their wives. She catches the women's spirits and traps them inside of gourds. Then she tells the men that they can only be reunited with their wives if they bring the gourds home and smash them on the dancing grounds in their own village. One man is too impatient to see his wife and opens the gourd right away while the other is obedient and is able to resurrect his wife (Grantham 2002:167–177). In this set of myths, Grandmother is not only a symbol of regeneration and an immortal being, but she is also capable of resurrecting the spirits of the dead. The snake, a symbol closely associated with Grandmother, similarly invokes resurrection among the (Siouan) Osage: in legend, the snake assures the people "even though the little ones [people] pass into the realms of spirits, they shall, by clinging to me and using my strength, recover consciousness" (La Flesche 1932:368).

A survey of oral histories and ethnographies reveals at least two dominant woman symbols shared by many of the possible descendants of Mississippian people. Corn Mother is usually associated with maize and/or specific domesticated plants, whereas Grandmother is the patroness of *all vegetation* and is associated specifically with the actual work of cultivating. Unlike Corn Mother, she knows how to grow plants but does not personify or create them. She is also repeatedly associated with the guidance over time of an orphaned child and/or the entire community, whereas Corn Mother usually dies in the act of becoming an important figure. Grandmother also appears in epic tales of both Siouan and southeastern tradition; she is a dynamic character in the mythology, whereas Corn Mother's potency usually lies in a single act of creation. Corn Mother's death is often central to her story, whereas Grandmother is eternal (hence the moniker "Old Woman Who Never Dies"). Grandmother is invoked in regeneration, which is not the same as birth. The act of regeneration implies the entire cycle of life, including old age and death. We agree with Duncan and Dias-Granados (2004:197) and Witthoft (1949:2) that new rituals and symbols likely accompanied maize kernels as they diffused throughout the eastern Woodlands, but we do not think that Grandmother was one of these new symbols. The fact that she is associated with all plant life, yearly renewal, and themes of resurrection and immortality—and that these referents are consistent among many linguistically and geographically disparate groups—makes us suspect that she is an older symbol with roots in the pre-maize ritual and subsistence systems of eastern North America (see also Fox 2004).

Iconography: Positional Aspects of Meaning

The positional and operational elements of Grandmother symbols (their spatial contexts, and their interactions with other symbols and actors) allowed Mississippian people to understand which aspect of this poly-semous symbol was being invoked. We begin by reviewing the icono-graphic content of the Cahokia-style female flint-clay figures and the Kneeling Woman hooded effigy vessels. Specifically, we are concerned here with what Turner referred to as positional meaning, which are nuances of meaning that are derived from the interaction of several symbols.

These two classes of artifacts are united by their central theme: both depict kneeling women. Female flint-clay figurines are both rarer and more commonly covered in the literature. The corpus currently consists of no more than nine objects, but several articles, site reports, and the-ses discuss their meaning and significance (Colvin 2012; Duncan and Dias-Granados 2004; Emerson 1982, 1997; Emerson and Boles 2010; Emerson and Hughes 2000; Emerson and Jackson 1984; Emerson et al. 2000, 2003; Galloway 2001; Jackson et al. 1992; Prentice 1986; see Figure 4.2). There are many other flint-clay figurines that depict male or neuter persons. We do not review those here. Figure 4.2 summarizes the contexts and iconographic content of the nine figurines that depict women. Conversely, hooded effigy vessels depicting women are com-mon but not very widely discussed in the literature. They appear in catalogues of finds from southeastern Missouri and elsewhere in the central Mississippi valley, unpublished theses, and two book chapters (Duncan and Diaz-Grandados 2004; Hatchcock 1976; Holmes 1884; Phillips et al. 1951; Sharp et al. 2011; Sobel 1989). The two types of artifacts we are focusing on are separated by both time and space. The

FIGURE	SITE	COUNTY/STATE	PROVENIENCE	ASSOCIATED ARTIFACTS AND HUMAN REMAINS
Schild	Schild	Greene, IL	Burial 96, one of hundreds in a Mississippian cemetery	Hooded frog effigy bottle "killed" Ramey incised jar Mussel shell spoon Adult male flexed burial Fragments of an infant's skeleton
Exchange Avenue	East St. Louis	St. Clair, IL	In s shallow pit filled with 2cm of red ochre, near the eastern wall of Feature 181, a 6.9 X 4.1 m wall trench structure that was destroyed by fire.	Red cedar (used to construct F 181), possibly woven cane mats or baskets, acorns, maize, lumps of tempered and untempered Koalin clay, a 1m concentration of red ochre, Mill Creek hoes and other lithic tools and projectile points
Birger	BBB Motor	Madison, IL	Northern focus; shallow pit	None
Keller			Northern Focus; Head and upper torso: a pit in Structure 87 (F150); Base and right hand: Feature 38, a pit 3m to the south	Structure 87: "Exotic" material; galena; jimsonweed seeds; red cedar charcoal; maize; erect knotweed; maygrass; two gourd effigy jars Feature 38: galena; maize, chenopod, sunflower, maygrass, erect knotweed, black nightshade, wild beans
Sponemann	Sponemann		Fragments from: Structure 282, third and final floor level of a building destroyed by fire. Feature 183, a large pit exterior to Structure 282	Structure 282:Unique ceramic forms; hooded human effigy bottle fragment; quartz crystal; Mill Creek hoe cache; metates, various utilitarian ceramics and chipped stone tools, red cedar charcoal, maize; wild-sized sunflower, tobacco, chenopod; maygrass, and wild bean seeds Feature 183: Red ceder, maize
Willoughby				
West				
Westbrook	Opossum Fork Bayou Mound	Desha, AR	Central burial in a mound, at the bottom of a 1.91 m shaft	Disarticulated (headless) "small and fine-boned" individual; conch shell

Figure 4.2. Table of female or probably female flint-clay figurines and associated contextual and iconographic details.

DESCRIPTION	GRAND-MOTHER AS-SOCIATIONS	RITUALLY "KILLED"?	SOURCE(S)
Platform pipe depicting a kneeling figure (no secondary sexual characteristics are depicted) with a snake wrapped around the its base. The right hand holds or is inserted into a bag or vessel. The left hand rests over the heart.	Snakes Vessels Children	Yes, burned.	Perino 1971: 25;117-118
Kneeling woman holds half shell or gourd bowl in front of her knees. No secondary sexual characteristics are shown, but the costume and hair style strongly suggest that the figure is a woman.	Plant fertility (?) Gourd vessels (?)	Possibly burned before destruction of F181, but did not fracture.	Emerson and Boles 2010
Kneeling woman strokes or strikes a feline-headed serpent with a hoe held in her right hand, while resting her left hand on the serpent's body.. She wears a backpack. Squashes are draped over her back. A broken flower element on the left side of her head may be a sunflower.	Plant fertility Sunflow-ers (?) Snakes Women's work/ agriculture	Possibly. Weathered breaks may have come from historic plowing.	Emerson and Jack-son 1984; Figure 3
A woman kneels on a mat or bundled objects (reeds?), a rectangular object that has been interpreted sacred bundle or basket lies in front of her knees. Her hand rest atop an elongated-rounded element which may an element of a sacred bundle or the lid of the basket.	Plant fertility Sunflowers Bundles OR Women's work/ basketry Gourd vessels	Yes, broken and depos-ited in two different pits.	Emerson and Jack-son 1984; Figure 5
Upper torso and head of a woman with up-turned palms. Stems or vines with evident nodes extend up from her palms, a broken ele-ment on the left side of her head is probably a flower, but cannot be identified as a sunflower. Upper torso and head of woman with both arms upraised, holding a square plates or palettes up to her head. A vlne or stalk runs up her right side and encircles her head. On the left side of the figure's head is a broken element which may be a flower. Base fragment depicts kneeling legs atop an elaborate square paneled basket. Head and upper torso of a woman with at least two rattlesnakes coiled around her. She holds the head of one snake in her hand, another is coiled around her head.	Plant fertility Sunflowers Women's work/ basketry Snakes	Yes, broken then burned	Jackson et al. 1992; Figure 5
A kneeling woman holds pointed objects in both upturned hands. Rounded stems extend upwards from both hands; the stem on her left side ends in a sunflower draped over her left shoulder. The other pointed objects have been interpreted as maize, but see text for a counter argument. A basket or bundle is suspended from her back.	Plant fertility Sunflowers Bundles OR Women's work/ basketry	Yes, broken	Colvin 2012; Figure 4

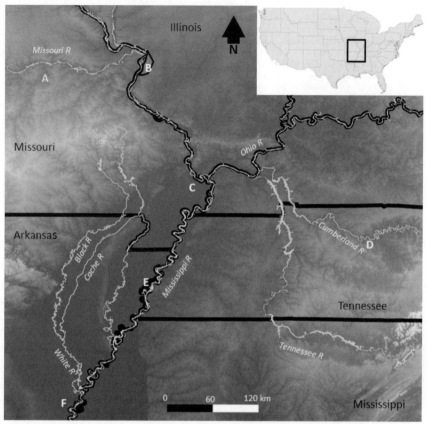

Figure 4.3. Map of the study area. A) approximate source area for flint clay; B) the American Bottom, BBB Motor, and Sponemann sites; C) the Cairo lowlands and Sandy Woods site; D) Nashville area sites surveyed by Sharp et. al.; E) Lowlands of northeastern Arkansas, Nodena site; F) Confluence of the Arkansas and Mississippi rivers and approximate location of the mound containing the Westbrook figurine.

flint-clay figurines were probably produced in the greater American Bottom region, but not necessarily at Cahokia Mounds, using flint clay from deposits in eastern Missouri (Emerson and Hughes 2000; Emerson et al. 2003). Those artifacts with known provenience date to the Stirling Phase, ca. 1100–1200 A.D. (Emerson and Jackson 1984; Jackson et al. 1992) and come from the American Bottom, Lower Illinois valley, and the Middle Mississippi valley, respectively (Figure 4.2; Figure 4.3). On stylistic grounds and considering those objects that have been scientifically excavated, the Kneeling Woman effigy vessels date from the Middle Mississippian to the Protohistoric period and mostly come from the four-state area around the confluence of the Ohio and Mississippi rivers (Sharp et al. 2011; Figure 4.3).

Female Flint-Clay Figurines

Without Grandmother as a bridge, these two classes of artifacts are only weakly connected by the posture and gender of their subjects, but both have clear iconographic connections to Grandmother. The connection is most evident on the most famous and iconographically rich of the corpus, the flint-clay Birger figurine (Duncan and Diaz-Granados 2004:196; Colvin 2012; Figure 4.4). Her adornments include squashes and probably a sunflower, the latter plant being so strongly associated with Grandmother that it was a part of her sacred bundle among the Mandan and Hidatsa (Bowers1992:345–346). Like Grandmother, she is actively engaged in cultivation, wielding a hoe. She sits atop a round base reminiscent of an island, surrounded by a feline-headed serpent, invoking both Grandmother's mythical retreat and her consorts (Figure 4.4). A much less fragmentary rendition of the sunflower headpiece appears on the flint-clay Westbrook figurine (Figure 4.5) while references to diverse plants are to be found on many members of the flint-clay corpus (Figure 4.2; Figure 4.6).

While both specific and generic plants are portrayed on these figurines, we would like to stress that maize is never depicted. While the objects in the hands of the Westbrook figurine bear some resemblance to maize in photographs, they have no kernels, they are not attached to the stems by shanks, and diagonal lines below the distal points do not enclose the alleged ears in the manner of corn husks. We argue that it is impossible to interpret these elements as corn because the outer wrappings extend around part of the circumference of the adjacent stems, whereas real corn husks do not wrap around any section of the main stalk; instead, the husks enclose only the ears above the shank during all stages of development. We point out these inconsistences because when the creators of these figurines wished to accurately portray a specific plant, they were more than capable of doing so. This is evident in the beautifully rendered sunflower on the very same figure (Figure 4.5) and in the squashes on the Birger figurine (Figure 4.4), which are rendered in such great detail that it is possible to identify them to species. On the basis of their thickened peduncle and the corky ridges along the upper parts of the fruit, the artist was most likely representing green-striped cushaw (*C. argyrosperma* ssp. *argyrosperma*), a squash domesticated in Mexico but introduced to eastern North America by the Lohmann phase (A.D. 1050–1100) (Fritz 1994).

These figurines are linked to Grandmother by two other iconographic tropes in addition to plant imagery. Three of the figurines—Schild, West, and Birger—are holding or are entwined by snakes. Several others include references to women's work. These include representations of tools used to plant, tend, harvest, and prepare seed crops (e.g., hoes and baskets) (Figure 4.2). Arguably, all of the female flint-clay figurines are depicted with either plants, snakes, or tools associated with food production. Some iconographic elements, however, are open to multiple interpretations. For example, the Exchange Avenue figurine may be holding either a shell or a gourd bowl. The Keller figurine may be kneeling either on a woven mat, bundles of reeds, or some other object(s). Her hands rest atop what is probably a large basket, possibly something similar to historic Natchez *petaca*, which were special lidded baskets with hide lids that were used to store precious or sacred objects (Horton and Sabo, [2017]; Figure 4.6). The Schild figure is holding a small bag or vessel, which might hold seeds or represent Grandmother's gourd ves-

Figure 4.4. The Birger Figurine, side and back views, showing serpentine base, hoe, and squashes identified as green stripe cushaw (C. argyrosperma ssp. argyrosperma.) Images courtesy of the Illinois State Archaeological Survey, University of Illinois.

sels. Some female figurines are less strongly linked to Grandmother than others, but we include them all in Figure 4.2 to facilitate comparison. The variety of plants depicted on these figurines, as well as the specific depiction of sunflowers, snakes, and agricultural tools, all suggest an association with Grandmother rather than Corn Mother.

Figure 4.5. The Westbrook figurine. Front: stalk elements that have been mistaken for maize. Inset: Close-up of sunflower element. Photos courtesy of David Dye.

Figure 4.6. From left to right: The Sponemann figurine showing vine element around head and stalk element in right hand; the Keller figurine showing grinding stone and possible mat base that has been mistakenly identified as maize; the Willoughby figurine showing vine element on right side of head and fragmented flower element on left side of head. Images courtesy of the Illinois State Archaeological Survey, University of Illinois.

Kneeling Woman Hooded Effigy Vessels

The corpus we refer to as Kneeling Woman hooded effigy vessels is defined by several characteristics. The vessels depict females explicitly through modeling of the breasts. The opening is positioned on the neck of the vessel, which is the back of the effigy's head. For this reason, these vessels are referred to as "hooded" and are understood to double as gourd effigies since bottle gourds were cut in the same way (Figure 4.7). Often, but not always, these figurines depict hump-backed individuals

Figure 4.7. From left to right: Gourd effigy vessel, Sandy Woods, MO; Gourd-women effigy vessel, New Madrid County, MO; Kneeling Woman effigy vessel, Gray's Farm site, TN. Showing the progression of forms connecting gourd effigies to kneeling woman effigies. Images courtesy of the Peabody Museum of Archaeology and Ethnology, Harvard University.

Figure 4.8. Kneeling Woman effigy vessels. Left: Negative-painted effigy vessel, Mr. Grower's Place, TN, showing "patterned shawl" characteristic of many Tennessee vessels (Sharp et al. 2012), placement of orifice, hump-back, and modeled vertebrae. Right: Negative-painted effigy vessel, Noel Cemetery, TN, showing front view of "patterned shawl" and modeled breasts. Images courtesy of the Peabody Museum of Archaeology and Ethnology, Harvard University.

with clearly modeled vertebrae, a characteristic that led some to draw parallels between them and similar hump-back effigies in the Southwest and in northern Mexico (Figures 4.7–4.10; Phillips et al. 1951:164). The hump-backed individuals also tend to be "pleasingly plump" (Phillips et al. 1951) while straight-backed individuals tend to be slender (e.g.,

Figure 4.9. Left: Slim, straight-backed vessel, Arnold, TN. Right: Plump, hump-backed effigy vessel, provenience unknown. Images courtesy of the Detroit Institute of Arts and the Peabody Museum of Archaeology and Ethnology, Harvard University.

Figure 4.10. Effigy vessel from eastern Arkansas, Arkansas State University Museum, Jonesboro, AR, showing possible tattoos including two rattlesnakes etched around her neck. Photos courtesy of David Dye.

Moore et al. 2006: Figure 8). Some are painted in distinctive ways while others are burnished (Figures 4.7–4.10; Sharp et al. 2011).

The most obvious connection between the female effigy vessels and Grandmother is that many such vessels depict a hump-backed woman. The most parsimonious explanation for this feature is that it is meant to depict advanced age. Yet straight-backed examples are also common. Moreover, Sharp and colleagues (2011) have convincingly argued that both the straight-backed and hunch-backed vessels depict the same mythological figure on the basis that both are sometimes decorated with identical, patterned shawls. The fact that the same woman is being depicted as both young and old may allude to Grandmother's ability to make herself young again.

Then there is the form of the vessel to consider: all of the female effigy vessels are also hooded vessels. These vessels were inspired by gourds, which were cut in the same way historically and used as water bottles that were carried with one finger hooked into the top of the gourd through the side opening (Sobel 1989:38–40). As we have described above, Grandmother is associated specifically with magical gourd vessels in both Siouan and southeastern mythology.

Archaeological Context: Operational Aspect of Meaning

Contexts of Flint-clay Figurines

If Grandmother is the referent of these symbols, then their creators may have meant to invoke any one of her mythological attributes and abilities. Some aspects of their archaeological context may help us to understand how she was used as a symbol by Mississippian people. Five of the flint-clay statues were found ritually killed in or near ceremonial buildings at two sites in the immediate vicinity of Cahokia, BBB Motor, and Sponemann (Emerson and Jackson 1984; Jackson et al. 1992). These two sites have been interpreted by their excavators as early manifestations of Green Corn or World Renewal ceremonialism and as part of the "architecture of power" in rural Cahokia (Emerson 1997c; Jackson and Emerson 1984). Both sites date to the Stirling phase, but Sponemann is probably slightly later. They are less than 2 km apart. Romain (2015:37) has recently argued that these two sites are linked to each other and Monk's Mound by a lunar alignment and suggests that lunar alignments in general at Cahokia reference an archetypal Earth Mother.

The BBB Motor site was, prior to construction of I-255, located on a low rise beside a small lake called Robinson's Lake between the Edelhardt Meander Scar, immediately to the west, and the bluff line that bounds the American Bottom floodplain (Emerson and Jackson 1984:4). This bluff lies less than 2 km to the east, and the Grand Plaza of central Cahokia Mounds lies 3 km to the west-south-west of the site. Emerson and Jackson (1984:4–5) describe the topographic relief in the Robinson's Lake locality as very low and the soils as not optimal for agriculture due to their slow permeability and the risk of flooding. Higher, more friable and better-drained soils were available nearby, on the colluvial veneer and alluvial fan area at the foot of the bluff. Robinson's Lake itself would have been a source of fish, waterfowl, and edible plants, such as water lotus. Emerson (1997b:95) suggests that "Prehistorically, the site area may have been an 'island' surrounded by open water and marsh. The topography consists of a number of low-lying ridges surrounded by marshes, sloughs, ponds, and lakes." If this characterization is correct, the site's setting may have invoked Grandmother's island retreat, especially during spring floods.

At BBB Motor, two figurines (Keller and Birger) were recovered from the northern focus of the site: a series of Stirling phase structures, pits, and wall trenches. Structure 87 was a rectangular building with 16.5 m² of interior space and probably a central post. The head and upper torso of the Keller figurine came from a pit excavated into the floor of this structure (Emerson and Jackson 1984:209). The feature containing the figurine fragment held few artifacts and no plant remains but was adjacent to a larger (roughly 4 m²; Emerson and Jackson 1984:203) feature that contained both "exotic" material (Emerson and Jackson 1984:209) and two carbonized jimsonweed (*Datura* cf. *stramonium*) seeds, as well as maize, maygrass, and erect knotweed (Whalley 1984:329–30). Structure 87 also yielded two gourd effigy vessels from the same occupation surface—the only vessels of this type recovered from the site (Emerson and Jackson 1984:289). The base and right hand of the Keller figurine were found in Feature 38, 3 m to the south of Structure 87, along with "a considerable amount" of ceramic and lithic objects (Emerson and Jackson 1984:217). Archaeobotanical remains from this feature include 24 kernel fragments, 112 corn cob fragments, 2 chenopod, 1 sunflower, 41 maygrass, 1 erect knotweed, 8 black nightshade (*Solanum nigrum*), and 6 wild beans (*Strophostyles helvola*) seeds (Whalley 1984:330)—in other words, a variety of important food plants including sunflower and one potential medicine.

The Birger figurine is the most famous and well published of the corpus. While it is certainly an extraordinary artifact, its context is relatively unremarkable. It was recovered from a shallow pit 8 m distant from the nearest structure, a mere 40 cm below the surface. No other artifacts or plant remains were recovered from this context. Although the Birger figurine was damaged by earth moving equipment during excavations, two additional breaks showed signs of weathering. Either they were made by earlier plowing or this figurine, too, was ritually killed before being deposited (Emerson and Jackson 1984:258).

The BBB Motor site has been interpreted as an early manifestation of the Green Corn ceremony or busk (Emerson 1997a:177), an important summer festival associated with world renewal and absolution among many groups who historically lived in the East. We will return to this interpretation below, but here it will suffice to say that if ceremonies at BBB Motor were focused on renewal and growth, aspects of these rituals also dealt with death. A minimum of nine individuals were recovered from an area of burial pits closely associated with the northern focus of the site, where the figurines were deposited (Emerson and Jackson 1984:208–217). All of the human remains were fragmentary: they were probably dismembered, defleshed, then bundled and buried. One feature was interpreted as a possible "grave house"—BBB Motor was not just a burial ground but also a site of ongoing mortuary ritual. Interestingly, an infant and an adolescent were identified among the highly fragmented remains in these mortuary features (Milner 1983:395). The association of the figurine with the internment of children is a detail of operational meaning that links the two flint stone figurines found at BBB Motor to the Kneeling Woman vessels from later and further south, as we will discuss below.

The Sponemann site is located just south of Schoolhouse Branch and east of Cahokia Creek on a well-drained natural levee of the Edelhardt meander channel. It is 1 km north of BBB Motor and 4 km northeast of central Cahokia's Monks Mound. Sponemann is a much larger site than BBB Motor (15.5 ha as compared to 0.5 ha), and most of it was not within the right-of-way of I-255/270. Therefore, it was not fully excavated as part of the FAI-270 project, and much of it still exists in farmland. Fortier (Jackson et al. 1992:17) describes the numerous advantages of Sponemann's location as follows: "Proximity to aquatic resources, easily worked and fertile floodplain soils, relatively high ground, available supplies of fresh water from Schoolhouse Branch, as well as a meandering Cahokia Creek within the old channel scar, and easy access to the nearby uplands were no doubt key factors in the selection of this important locality for long-term settlement." Kin groups who lived there in early Mississippian times may well have acquired or increased their social prominence in part as a result of successful agricultural and other pursuits.

At the Sponemann site, excavators found a precinct that was interpreted as a ceremonial complex consisting of 8 structures and 23 exterior pit features (Jackson et al. 1992). Most of the more than 500 flint-clay figurine fragments recovered from this site came from the third and final floor level of Structure 282, the "ceremonial and symbolic focal point" of the site, according to its excavators (Jackson et al.1992:70). Structure 282 was destroyed by fire. The final floor of this structure yielded a number of unusual finds apart from the hundreds of figurine fragments recovered. These included the only fragment of a hooded human effigy bottle recovered from the site (only its head was recovered, so its sex is unknown), a number of other unique ceramic forms, a quartz crystal, and a cache of Mill Creek hoes (Jackson et al. 1992:55). Diverse plant remains were also recovered, including foods (maize, sunflower, chenopod, maygrass, and wild beans) and ritual plants (red cedar and tobacco). The majority of the sunflower achenes recovered from the site come from Structure 282 (n=35) (Parker 1992:315). A number of other features also contained fragments of figurines, including a large exterior pit 12 m southeast of this structure—Feature 183—which contained two flint-clay figurine fragments, and like Structure 282 yielded red cedar charcoal. The density of maize kernel and cob fragments was extremely high in the 30 liters of floated fill analyzed from Feature 183, hence the interpretation as "a possible communal busk pit" (Jackson et al. 1992:97).

The Exchange Avenue figurine was recovered from a shallow pit filled with red ochre inside of a large wall trench structure. The structure, Feature 181, is located on the "northern fringe of the [East St. Louis] mound center's residential zone adjacent to the Cahokia Creek channel" (Emerson and Boles 2010:479). This structure is interpreted as a temple that was ritually destroyed by burning: it was partially constructed of red cedar and full of unusual items including powered red ochre, cane mats or baskets, and a Ramey incised jar. The presence of debitage, abraders, possible pressure flakers, and numerous projectile points suggest that flint knapping occurred within the structure (Emerson and Boles 2010:480–481). Raw materials for potting and weaving (lumps of Kaolin clay and masses of split cane) as well as Mill Creek hoes were also recovered, suggesting that types of crafting historically associated with women either took place in Feature 181 or were being referenced as part of its ritual destruction.

Outside of the American Bottom, female flint-clay figurines are very rare. There are three exceptions: the Westbrook figurine, the Schild figurine, and the newly discovered New Madrid figurine.[2] The Westbrook figurine was recovered from a burial in a mound, reinforcing the relevance of burials to the operational meaning of these symbols. It was found nearly 600 km south of Cahokia, in southeastern Arkansas. This figurine was dug up by nonprofessionals in the 1960s during an episode described by Colvin (2012:49) as "looting." An interview was conducted in April 2006 by Dr. John House of the Arkansas Archeological Survey with one of the collectors who was present during the episode. Information recorded during the interview sheds some light on its context. Apparently the Westbrook figurine came from a burial at the bottom of a deep (1.91 m) shaft at the center of a mound at a site in Desha County alternatively known as the Opossum Fork Bayou Mound, Richland Mound, or DeSoto Mound. The collector remembered two curious things about the skeleton: it was "small and fine-boned" and lacking a head, instead having a conch shell above the shoulders (Colvin 2012:48–50). In this fragmentary description, the themes of postmortem processing and, possibly, the burial of children or adolescents surface again.

The Schild figurine accompanied the burial of an adult man at a large Mississippian cemetery in the lower Illinois valley. The Schild figurine is sculpted in less detail than all of the other female figurines, so the fact that it lacks clearly modeled breasts may or may not be significant (Perino 1971:117–118). It also differs from the other members of the corpus in that it is a platform pipe. While executed in a different style and for a different purpose, the Schild figurine also depicts a kneeling figure entwined by a snake. Although it was not broken, it was burned before being deposited in the burial along with the fragmentary remains of an infant (Perino 1971:25).

Contexts of Kneeling Woman Hooded Effigy Vessels

The Kneeling Woman hooded effigy vessel was a common motif for potters in the villages of southeastern Missouri, northeastern Arkansas, and the Cumberland and Tennessee river valleys, as well as the Ohio River valley up to its confluence with the Wabash River, beginning ca.

1200 A.D. and continuing into the Protohistoric period in some sub-areas (Figure 4.3) (Morse 1990; Morse and Morse 1983; Sharp et al. 2011). This same area shared broader ceramic traditions and materials during the Mississippian period. For example, Smith (1990:136) refers to roughly the same area just described as "an oversized unit . . . the Cairo Lowland tradition."

Human effigies were created by Mississippian potters throughout the Midwest and the Southeast, so that determining the spatial extent of a particular form is complicated because researchers have used different features to classify them. Phillips et al. offer an exhaustive list of Mississippian human effigies that were known in 1950 from museum collections and early excavations (1951:183–190). Of 169 examples, 161 were recovered from the four state area pictured in Figure 4.3. The exceptions come from Alabama, Louisiana, Florida, and Oklahoma, do not depict females explicitly, and are not hooded vessels (Phillips et al. 1951:198–190). Those that Phillips and colleagues definitely identify as female or as hooded were disproportionately recovered from sites in three specific regions, represented in Figure 4.3 by the Sandy Woods site, near the confluence of the Ohio and Mississippi rivers, the Nodena site, between the St. Francis and Mississippi rivers, and the Averbuch cemetery site in the vicinity of Nashville, on the Cumberland River (Figure 4.3). Of course, this early list may reflect sampling bias more than true distribution. If a more recent comprehensive survey existed, it might turn up other concentrations. Unfortunately, because so many interesting and beautiful ceramic forms were crafted by Middle and Late Mississippian people in these areas, including head pots, rim-effigy bowls, and compound forms, pot-hunters have targeted this region for over a century. Many Kneeling Woman female effigy vessels have been looted or haphazardly excavated.

It is possible that the flint-clay figurines of the American Bottom inspired the later effigy vessels. By ca. 1100 A.D., inhabitants of sites in the Cairo Lowlands were clearly in contact with the American Bottom; Varney ceramics, a style characteristic of southeastern Missouri and northeastern Arkansas, have been recovered both from Cahokia proper and from peripheral sites dating to this period (Pauketat 2003:54). At the same time, Varney style hooded gourd effigies, though not yet human effigies, were already being produced at sites like Zeebree, AR, a Mississippian village located on prime agricultural land on the shores of a backwater lake. Researchers have proposed that these hooded bottles may have been trade items and/or seed containers (Morse and Morse 1983:219–220).

Over the next two centuries, the population density of the Central Mississippi valley increased and large, palisaded villages with multiple mounds sprang up (Morse and Morse 1983:236). Hooded vessels (and ceramics in general) became increasingly elaborate and figurative. The earliest members of the corpus of Kneeling Woman effigies probably date to this period (ca. 1200–1350 A.D.) and come from sites like Sandy Woods, a 22 ha fortified village with nine mounds situated on a ridge amid a series of meander belts (Potter 1880). Evidence that farmers were intensifying food production during this period include the placement of sites on prime agricultural soils, the increasing ubiquity of maize, and possibly the domestication of one member of the Eastern Agricultural Complex, knotweed (*Polygonum erectum.*) At the same time, during the Thurston phase (ca. 1250–1450 A.D.) in the Cumberland River valley, settlements were also growing in size and were often bounded by palisades (Moore et al. 2006:91). All of the Kneeling Woman effigy vessels identified by Sharp and colleagues from this area date to this period, so the form may be somewhat later here than in the lowlands of southeastern Missouri and northeastern Arkansas (Sharp et al. 2011:180). Perhaps we are seeing the spread of a symbol which began in the Cahokia area into a much wider area to the south of Cahokia. If so, its spread was coincident with agricultural intensification and the continued successes on the part of women to breed desired characteristics into local and foreign plants.

Kneeling Woman effigy vessels continued to be produced in the Central Valley up until and perhaps after contact with Europeans. For example, a Kneeling Woman effigy vessel was recovered from the Upper Nodena site and probably dates to ca. 1400 A.D. Also recovered from this site were polishing pebbles and a pottery anvil in association with a female burial, lending some material support to the notion that women were potters during this period (Morse and Morse 1983:90–91). In the only analysis to focus specifically on the burial contexts of Kneeling Women effigies, Sharp and colleagues identified two dozen examples of Kneeling Woman effigies interred in stone lined burials. *All* with known proveniences came from the burials of children or sub-adults (Sharp et al. 2011:180), a choice which may link these objects to the burials associated with some of the flint-clay figurines.

Previous Interpretations

Maize Goddesses and Green Corn: A Rebuttal

Most archaeologists can agree that figures of women with plants or agricultural tools represent deities or ancestors responsible for ensuring plant fertility and enhancing productivity. Some have made the further inference that they must be associated with maize agriculture. The terms "Earth Goddess," "Earth Mother," "Corn Mother," and "Corn Maiden" have been applied to these figures, and plants or plant-like parts carved on four of the statues have been suggested to depict or directly reference corn (Emerson 1982, 1997; Fortier 1992; Reilly 2004). "Green Corn ceremonialism" is a term that has been used to describe the events at BBB Motor and Sponemann. This interpretation is based on the presence of large pit features containing the remains of both crop plants and psychotropic, medicinal, or ritual plants such as jimson weed, black nightshade, and red cedar, concentrations of fancy artifacts, such as Ramey Incised ceramics and crystals, and on the interpretation of the flint-clay figurines as Corn Mother fertility figures.

At Green Corn ceremonies of the recent past and present, the kindling of the New Fire, offering plant material by burning, and ingesting various medicines (though not hallucinogens) all play central roles in the proceedings. The example of large-scale burning most pertinent to remains at BBB Motor and Sponemann comes from Bartram's 1777 description of an Atassi Busk in Alabama: "They collect all their worn out cloathes [*sic*] and other despicable things, sweep and cleanse their house, squares, and the whole town, of their filth, *with all the remaining grain and other old provisions*, they cast together into one heap and consume it with fire" (quoted in Grantham 2002:77, emphasis added). Notice that in this relatively early account, all remaining foods from the previous season are offered, not just corn—a detail which is in line with the diverse plant remains recovered from both sites. Adair recounts a "first fruits" ceremony among the Creeks, in which "a beloved old woman" brings a basket full of newly ripened fruits to offer to the New Fire (Grantham 2002:79). These accounts hark back to what Grantham refers to as a more ancient "first fruits" rite. As we have argued above, corn is not depicted on any of the flint-clay figurines, while other plants explicitly are, and a variety of burned plant remains were recovered from nearby features, including hundreds of maygrass seeds and lesser amounts of other EAC crops.

If the flint-clay figurines were part of a precursor to a ceremony similar to Green Corn, they may reflect this older tradition. We are not alone in suggesting the pre-maize origins of plant fertility ceremonialism. Emerson (1982:10) wrote that "the Birger Figurine is a representation of a very old mythological concept in the Eastern Woodlands that precedes the introduction and widespread acceptance of maize in Late Woodland/Mississippian times." Reilly (2004:137) likewise acknowledges the "Woodland-period matrix" from which the symbolism of what he calls the Mississippian Art and Ceremonial Complex (including the Cahokia-style flint-clay figurines) was derived. If the prominence of maize in historic first fruits ceremonies is a reflection of its economic importance to historic southeastern people, then we might expect maize to have played a smaller part at Cahokia than in Colonial period ceremonies since maize in the American Bottom was one component of a diverse and balanced, multicropping system that included native EAC grains (Fritz and Lopinot 2007; Simon and Parker 2006).

However, we find it difficult to link the contexts of the flint-clay figurines securely to Green Corn ceremonialism as it was practiced historically. In all of the descriptions of Green Corn, there is no mention of destroying dozens of beautifully crafted art objects, much less effigies of the Corn Mother herself. Nor is the Green Corn ceremony associated with Corn Mother, despite its name. Instead, the patron of the ceremony is a celestial/solar being associated with breath (Swanton 1931:85). Green Corn ceremonies take place outdoors in a carefully swept square where the New Fire is kindled. While the layout of the structures at BBB Motor and Sponemann do not preclude such a central square, they do not strongly suggest it either. Token amounts of maize and tobacco were sometimes burned in the New Fire as offerings, but the mass burning of last year's plant material described by Bartram would have taken place outside of this purified space. At Sponemann, the largest feature containing plant materials was located within what would have been the central courtyard while at BBB Motor the largest feature was inside of a small structure and contains other special items that are not easy to characterize as "detritus." At both BBB Motor and Sponemann, parts of the "killed" figurines were recovered from inside structures with a floor area of 16 m^2 or so. This corresponds to the kind of exclusivity or restricted access posited by Emerson, but it is antithetical to Green Corn ceremonies, which are intensely public and involve the entire community, albeit rigidly separated by gender.

The Female Statues as Tools of an Elite-Centered Priesthood

In addition to their emphasis on the busk, the discussions of "red goddesses" by Thomas Emerson and colleagues, as laid out in Emerson (1997a, b, c) and elsewhere, include arguments that the ritual precincts at BBB Motor and Sponemann manifest the institutionalization of a priestly cult that served Cahokia's elite. This "chiefly warrior cult," or "cult of the nobility" (Emerson 1997b:216) is cast in opposition to "the communally based fertility cult." The chiefly warrior cult is seen as effectively neutralizing the communally based fertility cult as a base of power. In this scenario, the structures and associated hearths and pits in which the flint-clay statues and other ritual objects were deposited were temples, residences of priests, and surrounding features: "I think there can be little doubt that Sponemann was staffed by religious specialists who were part of a permanent priesthood" (Emerson 1997b:225). One concern of these priests was to aid elite leaders in domination of the commoners, which included appropriation of the fertility cult and its symbols:

> That expropriation of the fertility cult as part of the dominant ideology by the Cahokian elite during the Lohmann-Stirling phase transition was a major ideological tool in creating and sanctifying elite sacredness and consolidating elite *power over*. The manipulation of fertility cosmology through a system of 'rites of intensification' and associated symbols of authority served to naturalize the inherent social inequality that was a major hallmark of Stirling life. (Emerson 1997b:228)

Other archaeologists have accepted at least some elements of the power play theme. Reilly (2004:137), for example, places emphasis on emerging elites who used these exquisite images to convey "to their people the supernatural power and prestige inherent in the cosmos itself, which they purported to control." Although we did not find explicit references to the gender or genders of these Stirling phase priests, it seems unlikely that any of the authors who favor an elite usurpation of fertility symbolism and ceremonialism would suggest that Mississippian women in general assumed more control *after* the fertility cult was expropriated. Recently, this conception of power at Cahokia has been changing. The recognition of pervasive lunar alignments, coupled with the fact that many of the most striking pieces of representational art recovered from the American Bottom are female flint-clay figurines, has led Emerson (2015:59) to suggest that the Earth Mother cult and its priests *and priestesses* may have been central to Cahokian religion.

The Statues as Beings Central to Women's Age-Grade Societies

Recently, Matthew Colvin (2012) has made a strong case for the connection between Cahokia-style flint-clay statues and postcontact rituals involving Old Woman Who Never Dies as documented by ethnographers visiting the Hidatsa and Mandan villages during the nineteenth century and early twentieth century. He discusses the importance of Old Woman in rituals performed by members of Plains Indian village female age-grade societies, specifically the Goose Society, and the centrality of bundles containing objects that seem to be depicted on the Missouri flint-clay fertility figures or found in nearby archaeological contexts:

> This ceremony is conducted to retell the story of Old-Woman and prepare for her arrival during the planting season. . . . The bearer of the Old Woman bundle would also place an image of Old Woman outside their residence, indicating the location of the ceremony. The interpretation can be made that the flint-clay statues could be reminiscent of this practice. (Colvin 2012:82)

We obviously appreciate Colvin's emphasis on women as primary actors and his meticulous reading of both the ethnographies and the contextual complexities of the BBB Motor and Sponemann site structures and associated artifacts and ecofacts, especially the plant remains. His thesis inspired us considerably and serves as a foundation for key parts of our discussion. Like us, Colvin stresses the significance of sunflower symbolism, and he sees no depictions of maize.

The Structures at BBB Motor and Sponemann as Menstrual Houses

Galloway (1997) offers an intriguing alternative interpretation of the BBB Motor and Sponemann ritual structures, suggesting that some may have been menstrual huts or women's houses. She points to the presence of red ochre, a singular quartz crystal with a red impurity, the presence of *Datura stramonium* (which she suggests may have been used for childbirth or abortions), and the spatial segregation of these buildings from the rest of the village at BBB Motor. She goes on to suggest that Ramey ceramics may have been special vessels created by women for exclusive use during menstruation and after childbirth. She cites Emerson's characterization of Ramey decorations as simple and visible at a distance to argue that such designs might have been intended to "warn of pollution" (1997:60), noting that historically and up to the present, menstruating women in many Native American communities have used separate sets of eating utensils and vessels and observed various other taboos. If Mississippian women spent several days of each month in menstrual seclusion with other adult females of their kin-group, how did they spend their leisure time?

Galloway suggests that women may have spent their time crafting elaborate objects or special wares, such as Ramey Incised pottery, that could only be used by menstruating women. The woman-gourd effigies may also have served as special vessels reserved for women during menstruation or after childbirth. Menstrual seclusion by historic southeastern people was predicated on a belief that menstruating women were dangerous to the ongoing fertility of both plants and people: menstruating women were not to touch or go near men for fear of reducing their virility, nor did they work in or walk near their gardens (Galloway 1997:55). Given this cultural anxiety, women may have invoked the patroness of regeneration to ensure that their own fertility would survive the menstrual or post-birth period. Might they also have crafted the intricate flint-clay figurines during these periods for the same reason?

Galloway also suggests that women may have spent some of their time in seclusion gambling (1997:57). DeBoer (2001) provides an overview of dice gambling throughout North America and amply demonstrates that it was an activity dominated by women. The stakes in women's games were often small but valuable objects, such as exotic shells, jewelry, pots, and objects of personal adornment (DeBoer 2001:227–228). The life histories of both figurines and effigy vessels could include episodes as stakes in women's dice games. Claassen, in Chapter 1, found evidence of several other activities engaged in by women when in menstrual retreat. Based on the perishables found in Newt Kash and several other rock shelters in Kentucky, Tennessee, and the Ozarks, it appears that women might have engaged in basket stave making, cordage production, and nut oil rendering utilitizing flakes, burins, mortars, pestles, fire, etc. Whatever specific activities occupied their time, if Mississippian women practiced menstrual seclusion it seems certain that they would have shared food and knowledge with each other during these times. At Cahokia in particular, menstrual seclusion may have been an important institution for the diffusion of goods, techniques, and symbols between groups.

Object Life Histories: Gendered Symbols on a Changing Landscape

The fact that all of the flint-clay figurines that have been recovered seem to have been intentionally broken before deposition is an important operational aspect of their meaning. While ritually killed artifacts are common in the archaeological record of North America, the intentional breaking of artifacts is not a part of many of the ceremonies described in ethnographic or historical accounts reviewed for this paper. Perhaps this is because the ritual killing of objects marked a singular, rather than cyclical, event—a burial, closure, or rupture. This type of event would have been less commonly witnessed or shared with historical informants than annual public ceremonies, such as Green Corn.

Although we lack specific ethnographic analogues, the referent of resurrection or regeneration is suggested by another operational aspect of some of these artifacts: they were ultimately deployed in or near burials. The association of many of these effigies with burials is incomprehensible if we consider fertility and growth to be in opposition to death. But if we instead foreground the special abilities of Grandmother to enable regeneration, or even resurrection, this association seems natural. These words imply a cycle, the process by which something that has spent all of its creative energy can be made fertile again. Recall that in the Siouan myth, Grandmother is able to become young again by bathing in the river, and she has special vessels that magically refill with food or water when they are empty. In the southeastern myths, Grandmother has the same magically refilling vessels, and she is even able to put the souls of the dead into these special gourds and return them to the land of the living. In connection to these stories, the fact that the kneeling woman effigies double as gourd effigies seems telling. Their placement in burials, especially those of children, may reference Grandmother's role as a guide or caregiver to a lost child. Alternatively, these vessels may invoke the resurrection theme more literally, as a rite to ensure that future births would balance the loss of a child. At BBB Motor and Sponemann, the closure of one ritual space may have necessitated special rites to perpetuate the community elsewhere. This interpretation is in line with what Martin Byers has called "mortuary-mediated" world renewal ceremonies, in which each part of the mortuary cycle seeks to restore balance through regeneration or release (Byers 2013).

It is unlikely that either the figurines or the vessels were finally deployed in a cyclical ceremony, such as Green Corn. The ritual killing of figurines at BBB Motor and Sponemann and subsequent abandonment of these sites suggest a singular event while the deposition of the Westbrook figurine and the effigy vessels must have been associated with mortuary ceremonies. However, it is important to consider that these figurines probably had roles to play before they were finally broken, burned, and buried.

The figurines and effigies we have considered here may have been created for and/or deployed in a range of gendered activities—menstrual seclusion, annual activities of women's age-grade societies, or gambling. Any of these, because of their potential to facilitate exchange among women, may have had important economic outcomes for a society in the midst of an agricultural and symbolic transition. Ethnographically, Grandmother is associated with exchange, specifically of seeds. As noted by Colvin (2012), the richest exegetic record of Grandmother-related ceremonialism comes from the Siouan Mandan and Hidatsa Goose Society, an all-woman age-grade organization responsible for maintaining the Old Woman Who Never Dies bundle. The Goose society was made up of married women of child-bearing age. Its primary ceremony took place in the spring and involved the distribution of seed for planting (Bowers 1992:202–203).

Ceremonial exchange of seed in early spring was important to Mandan and Hidatsa farmers because it helped them to maintain special varieties and diversify their seed stock. For Mississippian residents of a multi-ethnic community at Cahokia, seed exchange ceremonies may also have facilitated the transfer of novel crops or landraces, from communities who had already been growing them for several generations to others who were still unfamiliar with the new varieties. In myth, Grandmother is several times associated with introducing new seeds to travelers or instructing people in methods of cultivation, and in ritual she is associated with the exchange of seed. Institutions associated with such a cult, if they were already in place by the Woodland-Mississippian transition, might have facilitated the introduction of tropical crops to eastern North America.

Another important juncture of ideological and functional gendered behavior involves allocation of field plots. Through his interviews with

Maxidiwiac (Buffalo Bird Woman), Gilbert Wilson (1987) recorded the conventions and sanctions used by late nineteenth-century Hidatsa women to lay out their plots and resolve disputes that sometimes occurred between farmers of adjacent gardens. All agricultural activities were spiritually imbued, necessitating balance, harmony, and reverence, and Grandmother was, as we have seen, the presiding supernatural presence.

If women's age-grade societies developed in the Mississippi River valley during Stirling phase times or earlier, they may have played a role in the distribution of agricultural land by forming social groups that cross-cut kinship ties and accommodated families that had disparate geographical roots. We argue that the lack of archaeobotanical evidence for an agricultural revolution in terms of new and different proportions of crops produced between 950 and 1100 A.D. (Simon and Parker 2006) indicates continuity in infrastructure, an essentially smooth economic transition underlying the dramatic changes otherwise manifested by Cahokia's Big Bang. This is not to deny the importance of status differences such as: (1) hierarchical ranking of clans; (2) importance of wealth, age, or prestige in gaining admission to a particular age-grade society; or (3) exclusivity of rights and leadership responsibilities in terms of bundle ownership and other ceremonial legacies. Still, it places women in charge of decision making where farming was concerned rather than transferring prerogatives to an abstract, "elite" sector of admittedly, very complex Cahokian society.

Finally, we address the issue of who made the effigy vessels and female flint-clay figures. Because women are acknowledged to have been the primary potters in the eastern Woodlands at, and probably long preceding, European contact, it seems obvious to us that the Kneeling Woman Effigy vessels were made by women. We think it is at least as likely that the flint-clay figurines were made by women as by men, given their iconographic content and potential symbolic uses. It is possible that these objects were not created for formal ceremonies at all. Grandmother is associated not just with plants but with women's work and skills. She was solicited by women as they worked in their homes and gardens. It is worth quoting Bowers at length on this subject:

> Probably no Mandan or Hidatsa myth is as widely related and discussed as that of Old Woman Who Never Dies. . . . Likewise, the varieties of ritual forms within one village were greater than for any of the other ceremonies. The simplest and most universal rites were performed by women as individuals or households of women and consisted primarily of simple offerings. . . . This was done without the benefit of public gatherings or payments to bundle holders. On other occasions a woman . . . set up

within her garden a high post on which a newly composed personal sacred bundle was hung as a "protector" of the garden. (Bowers 1992:340)

Even if they were finally deployed in public or semi-public ceremonies, they may have served many private ritual functions first. Before
they were broken and interred, might these figurines have served as
miniature protectors of gardens and homes or as elements in individu-
alistic personal bundles? Certainly each one is unique, both in style and
iconographic content.

Conclusions

The impacts of women on the landscape were extensive in Late Woodland and Mississippian times. They created and managed the fields
and groves where food was produced and harvested, thus changing
the ecology of the land and the rivers. We have argued that for women
primarily, the institutions and ritual practices associated with Grandmother structured women's work and thus their transformation of the
landscape. Grandmother is a figure commemorated in stories, places,
and things from North Dakota to the Gulf Coast. Women's marks of
adoration and supplication can be seen in caves, rock shelters, and rock
art sites (see Chapter 3 as well as in the expert crafting of effigy vessels
and the ceremonial deposition of these vessels. The residues of women's
participation in Mississippian ceremonialism can be detected both inside
burial mounds and within ritual precincts of densely settled habitation
zones, including areas that were intricately connected to Cahokia and
other important centers.

It is important to recognize multiple female characters in mythology
because each of these enriches our understanding of both the possible
referents of women as symbols and the preoccupations of women in the
societies we study. Grandmother is not only (or even primarily) a symbol
of fertility. She is a polysemous symbol with a fan of related concepts
and associated symbols that are fairly constant across thousands of miles
and between speakers of languages from at least four different families.
In some contexts, she seems to have been an accessible force solicited for
the most pragmatic reasons. She represents the life's work of women,
to cultivate their gardens and to guide and teach their children, which
is why she was honored by women in small personal ways, within their
homes and gardens. But she is also a symbol of the immortal or eternal,
a regenerative force that makes death a creative event.

Recognizing a major female supernatural personage—a prominent figure in precontact iconography and postcontact ethnology—makes the lives of Mississippian women potentially less murky and more interesting. We can never know definitively how these symbols were operationalized by their creators and owners. Given their iconographic richness and aesthetic appeal, we are confident that other researchers will continue to reinterpret their import for years to come. Our goal here has been to show how gendered symbolism can be used as a window on gendered institutions that structured the social and physical landscape during a transformational period. Thinking about institutions associated with Grandmother has led us to consider forces that may have maintained stability or facilitated the integration of communities via mutually comprehensible institutions. Women's age-grade societies could have structured the exchange of seed and agricultural knowledge and the distribution of plots for gardens. Menstrual seclusion may have allowed women to share stories and materials and learn each other's symbolic vocabulary. The ritual killing or burial of Grandmother symbols may have linked the continuity of communities and families to an ideology of regeneration with ancient roots. Gendered institutions and beliefs, and the artifacts that give us limited access to them, are an important element of the Mississippian story, characterized as it is by the spread and local adaptation of novel crops, social relations, and symbol systems.

Acknowledgments

We would like to recognize the precedence of Carol Diaz-Granados, Jim Duncan, and Matthew Colvin in pointing out the importance of Grandmother. Their work inspired us to reexamine these artifacts in a new light. John Kelly, S. Margaret Spivey, and Edward Henry read earlier versions of this paper and provided many helpful comments and critiques. Our sincere gratitude is extended to Tom Emerson, Director of the Illinois State Archaeological Survey, and Laura Kozuch, ISAS Curator, for not only granting permission to publish images of the figurines from BBB Motor and Sponemann but also furnishing newly acquired images to meet our stated needs, and to David Dye for providing images of Kneeling Woman Effigy vessels and the Westbrook figurine. We would also like to thank Elizabeth E. Dennison and Renee B. Walker for organizing the Southeastern Archaeological Conference symposium *Gender in Southeastern Archaeology and Beyond* (2013), where we presented this paper, and all of the participants in this symposium for their valuable feedback.

NOTES

1. Fox (2004) makes a strong argument that the Late Archaic Frontenac Island mortuary was believed by Middle Woodland peoples of the Lake Ontario region to be the place where Sky Woman landed and birthed her daughter.
2. A female flint-clay figurine with plant imagery was recently discovered from the New Madrid area. The details on this figurine's provenience and iconography are forthcoming (Boles 2014).

REFERENCES CITED

Boles, Steven L.

2014   Supernaturals in the Confluence Region. Paper presented at the Southeastern Archaeological Conference, Greenville, SC.

Bowers, Alfred W.

1992   *Hidatsa Social and Ceremonial Organization*. University of Nebraska Press,
[1963]   Lincoln and London.

Braun, David P.

1983   Pots as Tools. In *Archaeological Hammers and Theories*, J. A. Moore and A. S. Keene, editors, pp. 107–134. Academic Press, New York.

Buikstra, Jane E., Lyle W. Konigsberg, and Jill Bullington

1986   Fertility and the Development of Agriculture in the Prehistoric Midwest. *American Antiquity* 51(3):528–546.

Byers, Martin A.

2013   *From Cahokia to Larson to Moundville: Death, World Renewal, and the Sacred in the Mississippian Social World of the Late Prehistoric*. Newfound Press: The University of Tennessee Libraries, Knoxville.

Claassen, Cheryl

2011   Rock Shelters as Women's Retreats: Understanding Newt Kash. *American Antiquity* 76(4):628–641.

Colvin, Matthew H.

2012   Old-Woman-Who-Never-Dies: A Mississippian Survival in the Hidatsa World. Master's thesis, Anthropology Department, Texas State University, San Marcos, TX.

Cornplanter, Jesse J.

1963   *Legends of the Longhouse*. Empire State Historical Publication XXIV. Ira J. Friedman, Inc., Port Washington, NY.

DeBoer, Warren R.

2001   Of Dice and Women: Gambling and Exchange in Native North America. *Journal of Archaeological Method and Theory* 8(3):215–268.

Dellinger, S. C., and S. D. Dickinson

1940   Possible Antecedents of the Middle Mississippian Ceramic Complex in Northeastern Arkansas. *American Antiquity* 6(2):133–147.

Doolittle, William E.

1992   Agriculture in North America on the Eve of Contact: A Reassessment. *Annals of the Association of American Geographers* 82(3):386–401.

Duncan, James R., and Carol Diaz-Granados

2004   Empowering SECC: The "Old Woman" and Oral Tradition. In *The Rock-Art of Eastern North America: Capturing Images and Insight*, Carol Diaz-Granados and James R. Duncan, editors, pp. 190–218. University of Alabama Press, Tuscaloosa.

Emerson, Thomas E.

1982   *Mississippian Stone Images in Illinois*. Circular No. 6. Illinois Archaeological Survey, Urbana.

1997a   *Cahokia and the Archaeology of Power*. University of Alabama Press, Tuscaloosa.

1997b   Cahokian Elite Ideology and the Mississippian Cosmos. In *Cahokia: Domination and Ideology in the Mississippian World*, Timothy R. Pauketat and Thomas E. Emerson, editors, pp. 190–228. University of Nebraska Press, Lincoln and London.

1997c   Reflections from the Countryside on Cahokian Hegemony. In *Cahokia: Domination and Ideology in the Mississippian World*, Timothy R. Pauketat and Thomas E. Emerson, editors, pp. 167–189. University of Nebraska Press, Lincoln and London.

2015   The Earth Goddess Cult at Cahokia. In *Medieval Mississippians: The Cahokian World,* Timothy R Pauketat and Susan M. Alt, editors, pp. 55–60, Schools of Advanced Research, Santa Fe, NM. Press.

Emerson, Thomas E. and Steven L. Boles

2010   Contextualizing Flint Clay Cahokia Figures at the East St. Louis Mound Center. Illinois Archaeology: Journal of the Illinois Archaeology Survey 22(2): pp. 473–490

Emerson, Thomas E. and Randall E. Hughes

2000   Figurines, Flint Clay Sourcing, the Ozark Highlands, and Cahokian Acquisition. *American Antiquity* 65(1):79–101.

Emerson, Thomas E., Randall E. Hughes, Mary R. Hynes and Sarah U. Wisseman

2003   The Sourcing and Interpretation of Cahokia-Style Figures in the Trans-Mississippi South and Southeast. *American Antiquity* 68(2):287–314.

Emerson, Thomas E. and Douglas K. Jackson

1984   *The BBB Motor Site*. American Bottom Archaeology: FAI-270 Site Reports. Illinois Archaeological Survey, Springfield.

Emerson, Thomas E., Brad Koldehoff, and Timothy R. Pauketat

2000   Serpents, Female Deities, and Fertility Symbolism in the Early Cakokia Countryside. In *Mounds, Modoc, and Mesoamerica: Papers in Honor of Melvin L. Fowler*, Steve R. Ahler, editor, pp. 511–522. Scientific Papers, Vol. XXVII. Illinois State Museum, Springfield.

Fortier, Andrew C.

1992   Figurines. In *The Sponemann Site 2 (11-Ms-517): The Mississippian and Oneota Occupations*, Andrew C. Fortier, Douglas K. Jackson, and Joyce A. Williams, editors, pp. 227–303. University of Illinois Press, Urbana.

Fox, William

2004   Islands of Creation, Islands of Rebirth. *The Bulletin: Journal of the New York State Archaeological Association* 120:47–57.

Fritz, Gayle J.

1994   Precolumbian *Cucurbita argyrosperma* ssp. *argyrosperma* (Cucurbitaceae) in the Eastern Woodlands of North America. *Economic Botany* 48(3):280–292.

1999   Gender and the Early Cultivation of Gourds in Eastern North America. *American Antiquity* 64(3):417–429.

2000   Levels of Biodiversity in Eastern North America. In *Biodiversity and Native America*, Paul E. Minnis and Wayne J. Ellisens, editors, pp. 223–247. University of Oklahoma Press, Norman.

Galloway, Patricia

1997   Where Have All the Menstrual Huts Gone? The Invisibility of Menstrual Seclusion in the Late Prehistoric Southeast. In *Women in Prehistory: North America and Mesoamerica*, Cheryl Claassen and Rosemary Joyce, editors, pp. 47–64. University of Pennsylvania Press, Philadelphia.

Grantham, Bill

2002   *Creation Myths and Legends of the Creek Indians*. University Press of Florida, Gainesville.

Hammet, Julia E.

2000   Ethnohistory of Aboriginal Landscapes in the Southeastern United States. In *Biodiversity and Native America*, Paul E. Minnis and Wayne J. Elisens, editors, pp. 248–299.

Hart, John P., and William A. Lovis

2013   Reevaluating What We Know About the Histories of Maize in Northeastern North America: A Review of Current Evidence. *Journal of Archaeological Research* 21(2):175–216.

Hatchcock, Roy

1976   *Ancient Indian Pottery of the Mississippi Valley*. Hurley Press, Inc., Camden, Ar.

Holmes, William Henry

1886   *Ancient pottery of the Mississippi Valley*. US Government Printing Office.

Horton, Elizabeth T., and George Sabo III

[2017]   Baskets for the Ancestors: Sacred Bundles in the Great Mortuary at the Spiro Ceremonial Center. In *Sacred Bundles*, F. Kent Reilly III, editor. Universtiy of Texas Press, Austin.

Jackson, Douglas K., Andrew C. Fortier, and Joyce A. Williams

1992   *The Sponemann Site 2: The Mississippian and Oneota Occupations*. American Bottom Archaeology: FAI-270 Site Reports. Illinois Archaeological Survey, Springfield.

Kelly, John E.

1990   The Emergence of Mississippian Culture in the American Bottom Region. In *The Mississippian Emergence*, Bruce D. Smith, editor, pp. 113–152. Smithsonian Institution Press, Washington, DC.

La Flesche, Francis

1932   *A Dictionary of the Osage Language*. Bureau of American Ethnology Bulletin No. 109. Smithsonian Institution, Washington, DC.

Lankford, George E.

2011   *Native American Legends of the Southeast: Tales from the Natchez, Caddo, Biloxi, Chickasaw, and Other Nations.* University of Alabama Press, Tuscaloosa.

Lynott, Mark J., Thomas W. Boutton, James E. Price, and Dwight E. Nelson

1986   Stable Carbon Isotopic Evidence for Maize Agriculture in Southeast Missouri and Northeast Arkansas. *American Antiquity* 51(1):51–65.

Milner, George R.

1984   Human Skeletal Remains from the BBB Motor Site. In *The BBB Motor Site*, Thomas E. Emerson and Douglas K. Jackson, editors, pp. 395–398. American Bottom Archaeology: FAI-270 Site Reports. Illinois Archaeological Survey, Springfield.

Moore, Michael C., Emanuel Breitburg, Kevin E. Smith, and Mary Beth Trubitt

2006   One Hundred Years of Archaeology at Gordontown: A Fortified Mississippian Town in Middle Tennessee. *Southeastern Archaeology* 25(1):89–109.

Morse, Dan F.

1990   The Nodena Phase. In *Towns and Temples along the Mississippi*, David H. Dye and Cheryl Anne Cox, editors, pp. 69–97. University of Alabama Press, Tuscaloosa.

Morse, Dan F., and Phyllis A. Moore

1983   *Archaeology of the Central Mississippi Valley.* Academic Press, New York.

Mueller, Natalie G.

2013   *Mound Centers and Seed Security: A Comparative Analysis of Botanical Assemblages from Middle Woodland Sites in the Lower Illinois Valley.* Springer, New York.

Parker, Kathryn E.

1992   Archaeobotany. In *The Sponemann Site 2: The Mississippian and Oneota Occupations*, Douglas K. Jackson, Andrew C. Fortier, and Joyce A. Williams, editors, pp.305–324. American Bottom Archaeology: FAI-270 Site Reports. Illinois Archaeological Survey, Springfield.

Pauketat, Timothy R.

2003   Resettled Farmers and the Making of a Mississippian Polity. *American Antiquity* 68(1):39–66.

2009   *Cahokia: Ancient America's Great City on the Mississippi.* Penguin, New York.

Pauketat, Timothy R., Lucretia S. Kelly, Gayle J. Fritz, Neal H. Lopinot, Scott Elias, and Eve Hargrave

2002   The Residues of Feasting and Public Ritual at Early Cahokia. *American Antiquity* 67(2):257–279.

Perino, Gregory H.

1971   The Mississippian Component at the Schild Site (No. 4), Greene County, Illinois. In *Mississippian Site Archaeology in Illinois*, Vol. 1, pp. 1–148. Illinois Archaeological Survey Bulletin No. 8, Springfield.

Phillips, Phillip, James A. Ford, and James B. Griffin

1951   *Archaeological Survey in the Lower Mississippi Alluvial Valley, 1940–1947.* Peabody Museum of American Archaeology and Ethnology, Cambridge, MA.

Potter, William B.

1880   Archaeological Remains in Southeastern Missouri. In *Contributions to the Archaeology of Missouri by the Archaeological Section of the St. Louis Academy of Science: Part I. Pottery*, George A. Bates, editor. Naturalists' Bureau, Salem, MA.

Prentice, Guy

1986   An Analysis of the Symbolism Expressed by the Birger Figurine. *American Antiquity* 51(2):239–266.

Reilly, F. Kent, III

2004   People of Earth, People of Sky: Visualizing the Sacred in Native American Art of the Mississippian Period. In *Hero, Hawk, and Open Hand: American Indian Art of the Ancient Midwest and South*, Richard Townsend and Robert Sharp, editors, pp. 125–138. Art Institute of Chicago, Chicago.

Romain, William F.

2015   Moonwatchers of Cahokia. In *Medieval Mississippians: The Cahokian World*, Timothy R. Pauketat and Susan M Alt, editors, pp. 33–41. Schools of Advanced Research Press, Santa Fe, NM.

Scarry, C. Margaret, and John F. Scarry

2005   Native American "Garden Agriculture" in Southeastern North America. *World Archaeology* 37(2):259–274.

Sharp, Robert V., Vernon J. Knight, and George E. Lankford

2011   Woman in the Patterned Shawl: Female Effigy Vessels and Figurines from the Middle Cumberland River Basin. In *Visualizing the Sacred: Cosmic Visions, Regionalism, and the Art of the Mississippian World*, James F. Garber, F. Kent Reilly III, and George E. Lankford, editors, pp. 177–200. University of Texas Press, Austin.

Simon, Mary L., and Kathryn E. Parker

2006   Prehistoric Plant Use in the American Bottom: New Thoughts and Interpretations. *Southeastern Archaeology* 25(2):212–257.

Slater, Philip A., Kristin M. Hedman, and Thomas E. Emerson

2014   Immigrants at the Mississippian Polity of Cahokia: Strontium Isotope Evidence for Population Movement. *Journal of Archaeological Science* 44:117–127.

Smith, Bruce D.

1993   Reconciling the Gender-Credit Critique and the Floodplain Weed Theory of Plant Domestication. In *Archaeology of Eastern North America: Papers in Honor of Stephen Williams*, J. B. Stoltman, editor, pp. 111–125. Archaeological Report No. 25. Mississippi Department of Archives and History, Jackson.

Smith, Bruce D., and Wesley C. Cowan

2003   Domesticated Crop Plants and the Evolution of Food Production Economies in Eastern North America. In *People and Plants in Ancient Eastern North America*, Paul E. Minnis, editor, pp. 105–125. Smithsonian Books, Washington, DC.

Smith, Gerald P.

1990   The Walls Phase and its Neighbors. In *Towns and Temples along the Mississippi*, David H. Dye and Cheryl Anne Cox, editors, pp. 135–169. University of Alabama Press, Tuscaloosa.

Sobel, Elizabeth
1989   An Archaeological Study of Hooded Bottles from the Sandy Woods Site. Master's thesis, Anthropology Department, Yale University, New Haven, CT.
Swanton, John R.
1929   *Myths and Tales of the Southeastern Indians.* Bureau of American Ethnology Bulletin No. 88. Smithsonian Institution, Washington, DC.
1931   *Modern Square Grounds of the Creek Indians, with Five Plates.* Miscellaneous Collections Vol. 85, No. 8. Smithsonian Institution, Washington, DC.
Turner, Victor
1967   *The Forest of Symbols: Aspects of Ndembu Ritual.* Cornell University Press, Ithaca, NY.
Wagner, Gail E.
2003   Eastern Woodlands Anthropogenic Ecology. In *People and Plants in Ancient Eastern North America,* Paul E. Minnis, editor, pp. 126–171. Smithsonian Books, Washington, DC.
Watson, Patty Jo, and Mary C. Kennedy
1991   The Development of Horticulture in the Eastern Woodlands of North America. In *Engendering Archaeology,* Joan Gero and Margaret W. Conkey, editors, pp. 225–275. Basil-Blackwell, Oxford.
Whalley, Lucy A.
1984   Plant Remains from the Stirling Phase. In *The BBB Motor Site,* Thomas E. Emerson and Douglas K. Jackson, editors, pp. 321–335. Illinois Department of Transportation, Springfield.
Wilson, Gilbert L.
1987   *Buffalo Bird Woman's Garden.* Minnesota Historical Society Press, St. Paul.
Witthoft, John
1949   *Green Corn Ceremonialism in the Eastern Woodlands.* University of Michigan Press, Ann Arbor.

PART TWO
THE PLAINS

5

INDIAN LAKE MEDICINE BOULDER AND FERTILITY ON THE AMERICAN NORTHWESTERN PLAINS AT EUROAMERICAN CONTACT

Mavis Greer and John Greer

Native American women are not major players in written accounts of Northwestern Plains history from the 1800s when Euroamericans were moving into the region and interacting with the many tribes. Most histories focus on the warfare aspect of tribal life and on interactions of male Euroamericans and Natives, especially their conflicts. Diaries and remembrances of their younger years in the Wild West are mainly written by white men, and they mention Native women in passing more than as active participants. However, Native women who married or cohabited with Euroamerican males brought white men into the established societies of the region and helped integrate western culture into the Native landscape while still retaining aspects of the cultures they brought to the union. Marriages of Euroamerican men with Native American women have been considered in terms of benefits, both social and economic, these unions brought the husbands (Brown 1980:64; Harmon 1957) and in fewer cases the benefits these unions brought the wives (Mays 2004:212). However, in this chapter we are concerned with those unions in terms of social ritual retention by the wives, specifically as it relates to fertility and rock art sites. These sites are places in the regional landscape set apart from living areas making them distinctly different physical locations culturally modified with specific purposes in mind and used for performing specialized activities. Our focus is on how and why tribal beliefs related to fertility rituals conducted at boulder rock art sites may have been retained by Native women after marriage to Euroamerican men, and we look specifically at the Indian

Lake Medicine Boulder (24PH1008), located north of the Missouri River in northeastern Montana (Figure 5.1), and examine its place in the ritualized landscape of Native women at the time of contact.

Here we consider marriage and cohabitation as synonymous. Most early 1800s unions between white men and Indian women were recognized under Native customs of marriage and not legally sanctioned by the government or Christian churches (Sangster 2006:309). Marriages occurred for many reasons, and in many cases Native women were given in marriage by their fathers to white traders or trappers to solidify alliances from both sides (Mays 2004:212), but women also actively sought husbands that were traders (Van Kirk 1987:56–57). There are also cases of men choosing to marry to solidify alliances (Denig 1961). Although arranged marriages for economic benefit are often assumed to be between an older man and younger woman, this was not always the case on the frontier where many traders and trappers were young men. In 1802 George Nelson, who was 15 years old at the time, felt "pressed into marriage with the daughter of an Ojibwa leader on whom his subsistence and success largely depended" (Nelson 2002:3). Our interest here

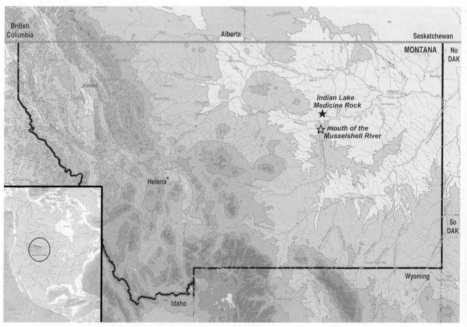

Figure 5.1. Map of Montana showing relative location of Indian Lake Medicine Boulder (24PH1008).

is not on the ages of the marrying couple or whether or not the union was forced on them, arranged with their consent, or one of mutual love and affection. Instead we are concerned about the reproductive life of these couples where at least the women were interested in assuring that children were born to the union and how that aspect of their lives was intertwined with their regional landscape.

In examining these marriages, we assess why a white husband would be more beneficial than someone from the woman's tribe or even another tribe and why women would want children with a foreign husband rather than with someone who shared their traditions and beliefs. At first glance it would seem the common culture and knowledge of rituals and where to preform those rituals within their landscape would be advantageous to assuring fertility. Nonetheless, a deeper look at changes occurring within this landscape at the time of white contact indicates that other factors in a husband were more important than the man's knowledge about fertility rituals and places to conduct them because this was something that a woman could fulfill from her side without his help. These other needs, however, were better met with a husband from the powerful incoming culture. As with white men, economic advantages for Native women are most evident, even though many women ended up being abandoned by their white husband when he left the trading life to return east (Harmon 1957:xxxix). Many couples continued to live a nomadic lifestyle with the wife's tribe, but even these unions could translate to better living conditions in terms of increased access to trade goods. The status of the Native wife within her tribe increased after her marriage to a trader, especially if the couple lived with or near her people, because it gave her more authority and prestige due to her ability to provide her family ready access to trade (Mays 2004:212). In many cases, by the end of the 1800s the couple lived at a fort where protection from warfare was aided by log structures, and women were provided some western clothing and household items that helped to lighten their workload (Denig 1961; Hampton 2011). There were also opportunities for the children's education, which provided a better opportunity for advancement in the changing world.

Better living conditions would be expected to result in reduced mortality, a long-term problem for hunters and gatherers in this region. These groups needed healthy children to perpetuate the tribe and help with many tasks (including warfare), and within tribes on the northwestern plains at the end of the 1800s mortality was becoming even more an issue due to devastating losses from diseases and increasing gun-based warfare. Smallpox, along with other European-introduced diseases, such as measles, influenza, cholera, and tuberculosis, affected not only babies but also a large number of people in their childbearing years (ca. 15–40 years old). Smallpox also had a direct effect on fertility as it caused conception failure in males and miscarriages for females (McFalls and McFalls 1984:533; Thornton 1987:54). Northwestern Plains Indian women were raised with the knowledge that rituals were necessary to assure the well-being of their tribe, and although not covered well by ethnographers and historians, to assure fertility of the group, which by extension included bison and other animals. Regardless of tribal affiliation, women who married white men "served as cultural mediators between Indian and European communities" (Mays 2004:212), and they usually retained at least some of their identity, language, dress, and customs. Additionally, they maintained ties to the landscape so they knew not only where to hunt or gather but also where to preform necessary rituals to aid in different aspects of their lives, such as vision quests for coming of age or ceremonies for fertility.

Although marriage to Euroamerican men could mean easier access to material goods at this time of declining bison populations, better protection from guns due to log houses and stockades, and better access to medicine, it did not completely alleviate every problem. Indian women were noted in ethnohistorical records as carrying on aspects of their traditional ways even when marriage brought them into a trading post or fort living situation. The diary of C. M. Lee, a young man trained in gun repair who lived at the confluence of the Musselshell and Missouri rivers in the late 1800s, often mentions Indian women at his trading community (Hampton 2011). He records women involved in subsistence activities (gathering wood and hunting) and associated with warfare, both of which indicate that women in this region did not stay sequestered in their small white settlement nor within their Indian village. Instead, some women roamed for miles from their living base to participate in these activities and had an intimate knowledge of their extended landscape. Lee seldom mentions anything relative to Native rituals, probably because he was not privy to them, which is the case for most ethnohistorical documents for the northwestern plains. However, the exception is rituals associated with mourning, as commented on by several diary keepers, remembrance writers, and ethnographers (Hampton 2011; McClintock 1992:150; Quaife 1973:124; Schmutterer 1989). Frequent comments on this topic occur because consequences of the ritual were so readily visible and so foreign to the white recorders.

[Lee Diary, April 24, 1870] A large party of Crow Indians at Musselshell in the morning. . . . They have mutilated themselves by cutting off their fingers and hair for their dead friends that were killed by the Sioux. They also destroyed a great many robes and lodges and reduced the size of a great many of their large lodges. They make a . . . sight to see them with their fingers tied up and their hands and face all bloody, and their hair cut off close, and their face blackened with coal. Only those that have lost relatives do these things. (Hampton 2011:75)

Indian women undoubtedly continued traditional methods of ritual for many aspects of their lives, and surely ones to assure pregnancy and live births were not abandoned. Such rituals, however, were not readily recorded for this area forcing us to search elsewhere for evidence of ritual practices as archeologists are beginning to recognize (Claassen 2013).

The area along the extended Missouri River corridor was one of increasing interaction between Indians and whites, most obvious from just after the Lewis and Clark expedition of 1804–1806 until the reservation period at the end of the century. The Indian Lake Medicine

Figure 5.2. General view of Indian Lake Medicine Boulder (DSCN0071), looking east.

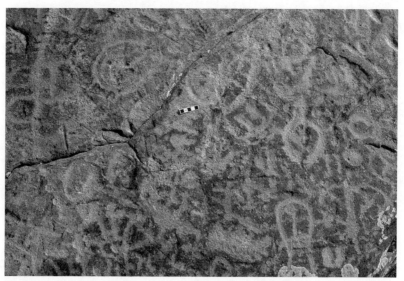

Figure 5.3. Indian Lake Medicine Rock surface (DSCN0089).

Boulder site (48PH1008) is a prominent rock on relatively flat terrain, and there is nothing for miles comparable in size or complexity (Figure 5.2). Extensive petroglyphs covering it attest to its cultural significance for generations of people in this region (Figure 5.3). The lack of written and oral histories associated with the site is surprising, but other methods of analysis help us infer a scenario of its use by Native women in the area during the late 1800s. Thus, we turn to our working hypothesis that Native women who married white men for whatever reasons, and stayed for benefits it afforded them and their children, continued to use particular petroglyph boulder sites in northeastern Montana for fertility rituals.

Rock Art Boulders on the Northern Plains

During the terminal Pleistocene large continental glaciers retreated from North America and left behind boulders known as erratics, smooth rocks generally consisting of transported non-local materials and ranging in size from small boulders that can be lifted by one person to those as large as a pickup truck; the Indian Lake Medicine Boulder is on the large end of the spectrum. Most boulders used for rock art are medium sized, about a meter tall and a meter wide. Erratics in northeastern Montana are of sandstone, granite, quartzite, and other crystalline substances from at least as far away as northern Manitoba. When used for rock art, the surface was either covered with individual images (mainly animal tracks), or the entire boulder was modified into a three-dimensional representation of a bison, often referred to as a *ribstone* (Greer and Greer 1999, 2000; Hoy 1969; Keyser and Klassen 2001; Steinbring and Buchner 1997; Sundstrom 1993, 2004).

About 25 rock art boulder sites are recorded in Montana (Figure 5.4). Although most sites have only one rock, four sites have two rocks, and one site has over 60 rocks. Boulder rock art sites with similar styles also occur in North and South Dakota, Alberta, and Saskatchewan (Keyser and Klassen 2001; Steinbring and Bucher 1997; Sundstrom 2004). Boulder rock art in this area has not been directly dated although an attempt was made to date a buried pictograph found during excavation around the base of a boulder in Saskatchewan in the 1990s, but the paint sample was not large enough for a C14 date (Steinbring and Buchner 1997:74). Several age estimates of boulder rock art have been made, and Keyser and Klassen (2001:177) place all petroglyph boulders within their Hoofprint tradition, which includes pecked hoofprints, bison heads, and human faces as well as ribstones. They suggest a date from the Late Prehistoric (as early as A.D. 500) to as late as A.D. 1800 (Keyser and Klassen 2001:1184). Their Hoofprint tradition includes Sundstrom's Tracks-Groove-Vulva style, which consists of deeply ground and abraded animal tracks and human vulvas (Sundstrom 2004:83). Her suggested date for this style is also from the Late Prehistoric to early historic period. Steinbring and Boucher (1997) have the most evidence-based dates from their excavations around the bases of rock art boulders in Saskatchewan and suggest a "florescence of rock art activity in the Avonlea/Besant time period" (1997:77), about A.D. 500. They found offerings in excavated context around boulders and suggested the offering tradition continued into the historic period. They thought boulder rock art was mainly made at the beginning of the Late Prehistoric period (A.D. 500), but the practice could have begun earlier.

Rock art on boulders has been the subject of study in California for many years, and Parkman (1992, 2007) has specifically examined the pit-and-groove petroglyphs in that area, focusing on their use as fertility shrines. He suggested, "that a Paleoindian culture with cultural associations on both the Plateau and in the Great Basin may have ventured out onto the Northern Plains and created some or all of the ribstones

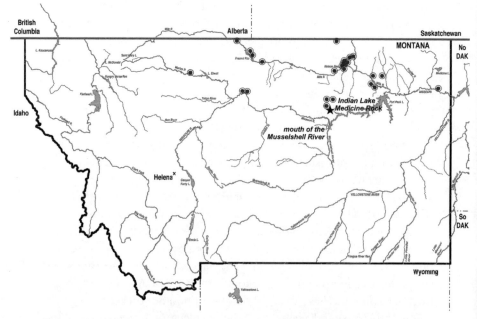

Figure 5.4. Map showing the distribution of known rock art boulder sites (dots) in Montana relative to the Indian Lake Medicine Boulder (24PH1008).

about 10,000 B.P." (Parkman 2007:10). Although we find no support for creators of boulder petroglyphs (including ribstones) on the Northern Plains to have come from the southwest, we agree that the beginnings of this form of rock art could date to the Paleoindian period based on the durable boulder surfaces, the deeply pecked images, and complete patination on the boulders. These characteristics argue for a long-time depth, and this is supported by similar heavily varnished images of hoofprints, vulvas, and grooves at Medicine Creek Cave (48CK48) in northeastern Wyoming. Medicine Creek's suggested minimum age of 6000–7000 years old is based on similar geological formations and the similarity of the varnish with dated Early Hunting style petroglyphs, which Tratebas points out may have ties to Siberia (Tratebas 1999:23–24, 2012).

Thus, for our purposes, boulder rock art was probably made for at least a thousand years before the contact period on the Northwestern Plains, and the practice of leaving offerings at these rocks—possibly considered sacred because of their old petroglyphs—dates back at least to A.D. 500. The Indian Lake Medicine Boulder is a good representation of this style of rock art, and offerings are still being left here, demonstrating the spiritual affiliation of this location with local Indian tribes and the retention to the present of this ritualized landscape.

Rock Art Boulders and Rituals

Culturally modified erratic boulders evoked some of the earliest references to rock art in historical sources for Montana. In an ethnography of the Gros Ventre tribe, Kroeber wrote, "A complete buffalo of stone, with hump, horns, ribs, and other parts, half of it underground, has been seen by the Gros Ventre, and many offerings and prayers have been made to it" (Kroeber 1908:281). In 1892 Grinnell (1926:263) noted that the Blackfeet left gifts around a Milk River-area boulder revered by all Plains Indians, and Ewers (1952:51) reported Blackfeet offerings at another boulder on the Marias River. Individuals and groups throughout northeastern Montana's prehistory and history made such offerings because they considered the boulders to be spiritually significant, capable of interceding with the supernatural on behalf of themselves or their group for a desired outcome, and offerings continue to be made at these shrines today (Gillette and Greer 2014). Offerings in the past included arrowpoints, pipes, and pieces of bone, mainly bison (Steinbring and Buchner 1997; Park 1990:46), while today offerings consist of bits of red cloth, tobacco, coins, and candles. It appears that the act of leaving an offering is an important part of the prayer ritual, and the kinds of offerings are limited in scope both in the past and today. The practice of prayers and offerings accounts for the application of the common term "Medicine Rock" applied to most rock art boulders throughout the Northern Plains from the time of first written records for the area.

The combination of vulvas and animal tracks in Northwestern Plains rock art has been recognized as associated with fertility (Keyser and Klassen 2001:186–189; Sundstrom 1993:294–295, 2002, 2004:83–98), and Sundstrom (2002:107) notes that, "A metaphorical relationship between hooves and vulvas is widespread in Native American cultural traditions. Both are symbols of women's reproductive powers, as well as the dangers of seduction." Although the vulva motif is fairly common in South Dakota, only two boulders with vulva representations are known in Montana—Monument Boulder, 24PH1005 (Figure 5.5), and Indian Lake Medicine Boulder, 24PH1008 (Figures 5.2 and 5.3). In both Montana cases the association is on very large boulders completely covered with figures, as opposed to the more common smaller rocks with only a few figures, further suggesting that the large boulders served a special function not practiced at other regional rock art sites. Today, Monument Boulder has been placed in a display shelter along Montana's Highway 2, so Indian Lake Medicine Boulder is the only one remaining in its original context.

Women's association with vulva and bison track rock art has been discussed in some depth by Sundstrom (1993:294–295, 2002, 2004:83–98) and in less depth by Claassen in Chapter 1. Sundstrom focuses on deeply ground and abraded animal tracks and human vulvas in the Black Hills of South Dakota and Wyoming. She also relies on ethnographic accounts for her explanation of the images that discuss a sacred connection between women and bison and rituals expressing that connection in Lakota culture. She suggests that the figures were made by and for women in their pursuit of the tribe's survival and notes that ambiguity between bison hoofprints and vulvas in regional rock art was intentional and a way of "expressing the close link between female identity and the mainstay of life" (Sundstrom 2004:88). Furthermore, she contends that the Track-Vulva-Groove style "expresses a connection between women's reproductive and nurturing potential" (Sundstrom 2004:98). The hoofprint-vulva association in Montana boulder rock art is stylisti-

Figure 5.5. Pecked figures on Monument Boulder (24PH1005) and modern offerings.

cally similar to those in South Dakota, and in many cases the areas were frequented by the same cultural groups, so it would not be unexpected for the functions that these images played in reproductive rituals to be similar.

A ritualistic landscape associated with fertility must include both a physical location and a ritual act. In this case, the location is Indian Lake Medicine Boulder, but the ritual act is not as readily identifiable due to a lack of historical documentation. However, outside the Northern Plains there are specific examples of rock art sites associated with fertility rituals. Most recorded in America are in California, and most of these are associated with pit-and-groove petroglyphs found in the softer rocks of northern California (Hays-Gilpin 2004; Hedges 1983; Gillette and Greer 2014:269; McGowan 1978:18; Whitley 2000:98). Among the California groups, the Pomo have been most cited as they were known to remove the powder from these soft chlorite schist, serpentine, and similar rock surfaces to mix into a paste for use in fertility rituals. The Pomo used the paste to mark the woman's body, ingest via the mouth, or insert into her vagina, but this ritual also involved fasting, prayers, and specific body movements. Fertility rituals have been recorded not only for California tribes but also for the Zuni in New Mexico, where on Corn Mountain they have a shrine known as *Mother Rock*, a place of a ritual similar to the Pomo (Parkman 1992:365; Slifer 2000:77). Fertility shrines that include petroglyphs are also discussed in the literature for other parts of the American Southwest (especially for the Yumans and Hopi) as well as Mexico (Bostwick 2004; Claassen, this volume; Hays Gilpin 2004, 2005, 2012; Ploeger 2012; Roth, this volume; Slifer 2000).

Thus, ritual landscapes that include both fertility and rock art occur in western America although details of rituals associated with most rock art sites are no longer known. Additionally, ritual studies today in cultures in the Americas, especially Central America, show that although ritual details may have changed over time, the underlying reasons for those rituals are still the same (Claassen 2013; Greer and Greer 2007, 2015). Rock art sites with vulva and hoofprint images used in historic times for fertility rituals by the Lakota (a branch of the Sioux) in South Dakota are not far removed geographically from the Indian Lake Medicine Boulder and are even closer culturally, providing support that these kinds of ceremonies were highly probable during the 1800s at this boulder although details of the rituals may have been different from those performed even the generation before.

Indian Lake Medicine Boulder (24PH1008)

Indian Lake Medicine Boulder is about 10 miles north-northeast of the Missouri River at its nearest point and about 20 miles north of the mouth of the Musselshell River, the historic location of the settlement of Musselshell (Figure 5.1). Today the mouth of the Musselshell River is under the Fort Peck Reservoir, completed in 1940. Indian Lake Medicine Boulder was first formally recorded and given a number (24PH1008) in 1970 as part of a road construction project although the site was well known as the largest petroglyph boulder in the region by all living in the general area. Today the site is fenced for public viewing, with an adjacent parking area, and the site is monitored by the Bureau of Land Management (BLM) for protection. However, in the past the boulder was subjected to several instances of filling the grooves with chalk or shoe polish for photographs (Figure 5.6), which today are not acceptable enhancement methods because of their detrimental effects on potential direct dating of the rock art and destruction of any remaining Native painting of the grooves. In 1968 Lloyd Pierson, an archeologist with the Denver Service Center, attempted unsuccessfully to remove lichen on the rock with Clorox. Despite these modern intrusions, the rock is still at its original location, and other than fencing and nearby roads, it has maintained its relatively pristine environmental setting and viewshed (Figure 5.2). The images are still clear enough that a visit to the site allows one to experience the rock art as it was when nomadic peoples made pilgrimages to this location (Figure 5.3).

This large quartzite boulder measures 9 ft × 11 ft (2.7 m × 3.35 m) across and 3 ft (0.79 m) tall with a wide, flat top and almost vertical sides. The top of the boulder, with its altar-like appearance, and the sides are completely covered with petroglyphs. Images are dominated by abstract figures, which may have been identifiable as representational images prior to intensive superpositioning by later prehistoric petroglyph additions. Recognizable images include hoofprints or tracks of bison and deer, vulvas, and glyphs that appear to be combinations of hoofprints and vulvas. As noted above, bison hoofprints and vulvas here are similar in style to those in South Dakota (Figure 5.7), providing support for the woman-bison fertility explanation for site function, at least during the early historic period. Other support for ritual practice at Indian Lake Medicine Boulder is found in the State Historic Preservation records for this site.

A 1969 memo by a BLM Natural Resource Specialist mentions that a man named Gene Barnard first saw the rock in 1948 and that Indians still visited it every year and would hang bright colored cloth on adjacent sagebrush and would polish the rock (Chamberlain 1969). A 1981 memo from the BLM Area Manager notes that Indians from the Fort Belknap Reservation, the home of the Gros Ventre and Assiniboine tribes, still performed religious ceremonies at the rock as recently as 1950 (Dahlen 1981). John Talks Different, an Assiniboine interviewed by Chamberlain (1972), noted that prayers offered in the early 20th century were not to the rock, but rather the rock was viewed as a medium to reach the one who placed it there. John Talks Different and his son Ira Talks Different said that they would place their hands on the rock while in prayer to gain strength through the rock and to prevent lichen from becoming too firmly attached. They related that prayers said at the rock were for a safe journey, happiness in marriage, good health, a successful hunt, fallen comrades in war, and a long life. During the years prior to Talks Different's explanation, there was little interest by the tribes in medicine rocks, so other explanations for past ceremonies or beliefs at the Indian Lake Medicine Boulder are not recorded and were not necessarily the same as those practiced by the Talks Different family in the early 20th century. However, the Talks Different men confirmed use of the rock

Figure 5.6. Chalking or shoe polish enhancement on Indian Lake Medicine Boulder.

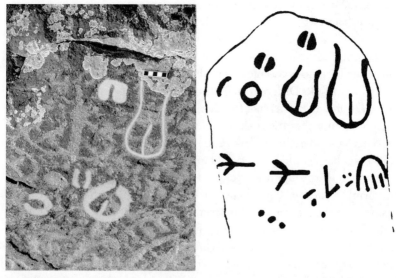

Figure 5.7. Computer highlighted vulva and bison hoofprints on the Indian Lake Medicine Boulder (5-cm scale) compared with a sketch of vulvas and bison hoofprints on a South Dakota boulder, 39SP10. Left photo by John Greer, 2000. Right photo from Sundstrom 1993:266.

by local tribes for spiritual help, including health and long life, both of which are associated with fertility. It is likely that if Chamberlain had talked with women from these tribes his answers about what was prayed for and by whom would have been different.

Native Women in the Indian Lake Medicine Boulder Region in the Late 1800s

There are no early ethnographic or ethnohistorical accounts of the rock's use, but such documents for nearby areas along the Missouri River in northeastern Montana in the 1800s provide information on who was in the area at that time, and it is most likely that they were the people using the site even if they were not the original makers of the petroglyphs. Therefore, a search for tribes in the area during the 1800s provides better information on who was actually present than generalized tribal distribution maps or even nearby present-day reservations.

Diaries are especially helpful in determining which tribes were in the area, and although men writing the diaries were mainly interested in male interactions, they saw a few women, and those they did see attracted their attention and were mentioned, especially as numbers. A typical recording by Lee living at the mouth of the Musselshell gave counts of Indians [August 22, 1870]: "About noon a party of 35 Rappahoes [Arapahos], 9 of them squaws, rode into Musselshell" (Hampton 2011:98). Personal information about individual actions of women is seldom noted, but there are records of spousal abuse (Hampton 2011:67), women escaping a raid (Hampton 2011:66–67), and women of one group attacking women and children in another and killing them (Beckwourth 1902:226).

Like most of America at the time of Euroamerican contact, diseases also arrived that resulted in dramatic population changes on the northwestern plains. David Jones, who studies epidemics at the time of Euroamerican contact throughout the Americas, reports that "Acute infections of smallpox, measles, and influenza dominated initial encounters" (Jones 2004:4), and the ethnohistorical documents of the area support this statement for the northwestern plains. Smallpox was especially a problem, and there are many references to women associated with the disease. In the settlement of Musselshell:

> [Lee's Diary: April 28, 1870] The Col. told me that his Crow woman came back last night in the night sick with the smallpox and that the Indians that came in with her left a[s] soon as they learned the nature of her sickness. The Col. is very much alarmed at the prospect of trouble with the Crow on account of the smallpox as they are terribly afraid of it and there will probably not be another Crow here for six months (Hampton 2011:76).

In this instance, it would be interesting to know who the Indians were with the Colonel's wife and what kind of excursion they were on.

As mentioned previously, one of the most important things we learn from ethnohistorical documents and not available elsewhere is what tribes were in an area during a particular period. At the mouth of the Musselshell Lee observed the following tribes during his short time there between 1868 and 1872 (Hampton 2011): Arapaho, Assiniboine, Blackfeet, Crow, Flathead, Gros Ventre, Pend d' Oreille, Piegan, and Sioux (Santee, Teton, and Yankton). Of these tribes, those most mentioned were Arapaho, Crow, Gros Ventre, and Sioux. Up the Musselshell River from 1878 to 1879, Andrew Garcia saw the following tribes: Assiniboine, Blackfeet, Blood, Cree, Crow, Gros Ventre, Nez Perce, Pend d' Oreille, Piegan, and Sioux (Garcia 1967). It is most notable that he did not mention Arapaho, and it may be that he was not able to distinguish them from their relatives the Gros Ventre, but this is doubtful since he recognized the nuances of so many tribes even when people from more than one group were traveling together. Therefore, it is most likely that he saw no need to separate or distinguish between these relatives. He also did not mention any particular divisions of Sioux. Garcia (1878–1879) wrote about a decade after Lee (1868–1872), and from a position farther up the Musselshell from Lee, where he mainly encountered Crow, Gros Ventre, and tribes from the Blackfoot Nation (Blackfeet, Blood, and Piegan). John Healy was at Fort Benton, further up the Missouri from the mouth of the Musselshell, from the late 1860s through the 1870s and traveled throughout the region of the Missouri and Yellowstone Rivers. He discusses tribes along the Missouri from Fort Peck to Fort Benton, including the mouth of the Musselshell, and records seeing the Blackfoot Nation tribes, Gros Ventre, Assiniboine, Crow, and Sioux (Robison 2003). These three histories of the area indicate that there were a number of diverse tribes using the Musselshell drainage at the end of the 19th century, but those most numerous in the area were the Gros Ventre and the Crow, with a later influx of Sioux.

As noted, interactions of women with the landscape and with each other are mostly absent from ethnohistorical diaries, and unfortunately, this kind of information is also limited in ethnographic studies of these tribes. Early ethnographies here were written shortly after the tribes were settled on reservations and while people were still alive that remembered their nomadic life on the plains. Life stories and related activities of both men and women were recorded but mostly as related to warfare. Stories told by women were usually from older women, and when associated with ritual were not about something as personal as fertility or birth but instead were like the example of the seven sacred bags of the Arapaho, where an old woman told how she obtained one (Kroeber 1902–07:30).

Edwin Thompson Denig, a fur trader on the upper Missouri in the 1800s who married two Indian women, is one of the most detailed recorders of this time. His remarks on disease and death set the stage for his comments on fertility (Denig 1930, 1961). Unlike most other early writers for this area, he is not intimidated about reporting on fertility issues. This may be due to his Native wives, who were able to provide him with information directly so he did not have to talk about these intimate issues with women he did not know.

In 1848 a number of Crow children died from smallpox, but in 1849 the tribe was hit even harder by a strain of influenza that killed 600 people, and among them "were some of the best warriors and wise councilors" (Denig 1961:186). He also notes that venereal disease was a problem in that it not only was fatal, but people with it could not procure husbands or wives. As such, the disease may have forced some women to seek white husbands. Lee notes [April 12, 1870], "one of the squaws at Col. Clendenin's, and known as Mrs. Bogg, died from the effects of venereal disease of long standing" (Hampton 2011:73).

Denig notes that abortion and infanticide were no longer acceptable to the Crow tribe by the 1800s and instead brought disgrace to both the mother and father. Although he notes that this change in social view did not completely stop the practices from happening, it did drive them underground. He recorded that prior to the loss of population due to warfare and disease, two-thirds of married women practiced abortion or infanticide, with abortions outnumbering infanticide. He said that those who knew about such activities within the Crow tribe at that time estimated that three-fourths of all women who died in the past did so due to an abortion not conducted properly (Denig 1961:186).

By the middle 1800s Denig estimated that two out of five children on the upper Missouri died before reaching adulthood. He attributed children's deaths to exposure to extreme weather conditions from a very young age and to their lack of access to food. He notes, "not that they often absolutely starve to death, but are rendered weak and unable to stand the hardship the life requires" (Denig 1930:513). He thought conditions were especially hard on women:

> It is evident that the hard labor the women perform after marriage ruins their constitutions. A woman is old on the plains at the age of 35 years, and seldom healthy. They have from 2 to 5 children, more are occasionally seen, but 7 or 8 is a rare occurrence. There are but few very old women. . . . A woman ceases to bear at 40 years, often earlier. Children have been produced by women at the age of 15, though this is uncommon; from 18 to 35 is the usual period. (Denig 1930:513)

Although religious practices and rituals associated with fertility differed from one plains group to another, they had the common underlying theme of calling on a higher power for help. Rites and ceremonies involved offerings of considerable value, fasting, body laceration, and prayers (Denig 1930:483). Although fertility is not specifically mentioned for ceremonies in this area, prayers and dances are often associated with asking for long lives and asking for the return of the bison. Based on Sundstrom's work connecting bison and women with fertility (1993:294–295, 2002, 2004:83–98), it is likely that one of the most pertinent ceremonies directed toward health and reproduction is a women's dance among the Gros Ventre and Arapaho. Kroeber (1908:231) relates that, "The women in their dance among both tribes represent buffalo, and the actions gone through in this ceremony are in both tribes probably more directly imitative of the animals symbolized than in any of the men's ceremonies." This suggests that ceremonies associated with fertility conducted at rock art boulders with bison hoofprints and vulvas were designed to protect the longevity of the tribe during a time of decreasing human and bison populations, and these were probably led, if not carried out, by women.

Thus, it appears that fertility ceremonies conducted at rock art sites on the northern plains were instigated and executed by women, but it does not appear that the boulder petroglyphs were made during those ceremonies. Rather, the boulder locations were likely used because they were recognized, from the old petroglyphs, as important sacred places. Patina formed over the petroglyphs at Indian Lake Medicine Boulder suggests these images long pre-date the time of contact. The hard surfaces were not conducive to making abraded grooves like the sandstone of the Black Hills area although the Yanktonai (a group of the Sioux from whom the Assiniboine separated by 1640 [Kessel and Wooster 2005:29]) were known to have carved drawings on the rocks (Sundstrom 2002:106), and the Assiniboine and several Sioux groups are known to have been in the Indian Lake Medicine Boulder area in the 1800s. The rock powder created at sites in California, which was subsequently eaten, rubbed over the body, and even inserted to cure sterility, could not be produced from the hard Indian Lake Medicine Boulder. Thus, instead of making the hoofprints and vulvas during fertility ceremonies at this site, it is more likely that the grooves were painted to enhance their visibility and renew the power of the image.

Scenario for Fertility Rites at Indian Lake Medicine Boulder

In developing a scenario for use of Indian Lake Medicine Boulder as a fertility ritual site, it is useful to examine how rock art sites made hundreds or thousands of years prior to the 1800s by different cultures for unknown (possibly fertility) reasons could come to function as part of this kind of ceremony after A.D. 1800. The process of "revitalization" as defined by Anthony Wallace (1956) is appropriate here. He proposed that when people realize something is happening to their culture that may cause it to become extinct, they try to do something about it. Revitalization occurs in response to cultural stress, typically the result of one culture coming into contact with a more dominant culture that threatens its extermination, such as the Euroamerican contact period on the northwestern plains. Adaptation is then attempted by self-imposed change, in this case by Native women entering into marriage with Euroamerican men and staying in those relationships with the hope that their children would have better living conditions, grow to adulthood, and be accepted by the new culture, providing them opportunities for prosperity and longer life. To assure this revitalization, fertility ceremonies were necessary.

Rituals that involved the leaving of offerings have been conducted at rock art boulders since at least 1,500 years ago (Steinbring and Buchner 1997). These offerings were left voluntarily, and based on the kinds of images that we now see on the boulders (vulvas and bison hoofprints in particular), they are obvious places for rituals to assure population renewal or population continuance. When offerings were left at places within the ritualized landscape they were undoubtedly made in conjunction with dances, prayers, and probably smoking, which was important to all Plains Indian tribes.[1] Also as part of the ritual, it is likely that the petroglyphs were painted, a trait practiced by many groups throughout the world, and paint can still be found in petroglyph grooves of some northwestern plains sites today (Greer and Greer 2003). Body painting was probably also part of the ritual although unlike the Pomo, the paint probably was not taken from the rock art boulder but instead was processed from mineral naturally available throughout central Montana and carried in small personal bags by many Indians on the plains. When women used the boulders for fertility pursuits in conjunction with relationships with men in the incoming dominating culture, they could envision a good outcome not only for themselves but for their future generations.

Fertility and continuation of the tribe are often under the jurisdiction of women although it is certainly a concern of the entire tribe, and as Claassen (2013) has pointed out, rituals associated with fertility can be a joint effort. On the northwestern plains, and especially in circumstances where the couple are from different cultures, it is most likely that women conducted or oversaw these rituals. They alone were familiar with which rock art sites within their regional landscape had the appropriate images for fertility rituals, and only they knew what rituals needed to be conducted since fertility rites were not part of daily life of their white Euroamerican male counterparts. With declining populations at contact, and concern that native cultures were being engulfed by incoming whites, women married to white men had already begun the process of assuring continuation of their genes in the most Darwinian manner of "survival of the fittest" by marrying into the dominating culture, but this may not have been enough to assure babies would come and young children would remain healthy. For women to assure continuation of their bloodlines, marrying white men of better economic status and access to goods was a rational decision, but they had to adhere to rituals that had been part of their heritage to guarantee conception and a subsequent healthy life. But even as they were reconstructing these rituals, other social changes that were bringing about the need for assurance of continued or increased fertility were forcing changes in how rituals were performed, as death claimed those experienced women most knowledgeable in the old ways. However, flexibility is one of the strengths of ritual behavior, and rituals can be adapted and changed as necessity demands (Claassen 2013; Greer and Greer 2007, 2015; Murray 2014; Turpin and Eling 2014). The women were from nomadic tribes and familiar with the kinds of sites needed for rituals as well as where those sites were located on the landscape. Sites with correct images or motifs could be adapted to fertility rites, but presumably not all petroglyph boulders were appropriate. Those with vulva and bison hoofprints, however, worked.

Conclusions

By the 1800s, Natives and outsiders, now equipped with guns and in the midst of diseases brought by incoming whites, were actively experiencing changing population dynamics on the northwestern plains. Death by firearms was common, more often the result of infected wounds due to bad aim and unreliable firing than a fatal direct shot, and most people killed were young men in their reproductive prime (Hampton 2011). This resulted in a shortage of tribal husbands and diminishing population numbers. Worse than guns were fatalities from diseases, which affected all ages and decreased the number of people in their childbearing years by either death or infertility. For some women the way to assure continuation of their bloodlines was to marry white men from the incoming dominant culture who could provide them with somewhat better protection from warfare and better access to food during this time of declining bison populations. But these unions did not assure healthy pregnancies and births.

Revitalization, or in some cases the continuation of traditional fertility rituals associated with vulva and bison hoofprint rock art boulders, which were used as altars for offerings and as portals to supernatural help through the petroglyph images, was a means of accomplishing this goal of individual and group continuance. Comparative evidence suggests that the Indian Lake Medicine Boulder was used for such a purpose by women from a variety of tribes, especially the Gros Ventre (and probably their Arapaho relatives who were often observed together during the 1800s), the Crow, and the Assiniboine, but possibly also the newly incoming Sioux groups from the southeast and the Blackfeet, Blood, and Piegan from the northwest. Thus, Native women were helping to save their tribes from extinction in the long term by working for their own benefit and that of their children in the short term. The mixed-heritage children would bridge the two cultures and allow Native culture to continue at least with some traditions and rituals while keeping the new culture from completely dominating and destroying it. Even though contents of rituals undoubtedly changed with this new generation of women living with men from different backgrounds and beliefs, and with the women probably separated from their kinsmen, tradition continued through the memories these women had of their learning as girls still living among their tribes about traditional ritual behavior, underlying reasons for the rituals, and locations where they should occur, such as rock art sites with appropriate symbolism.

Reviewing the past century we can see that revitalization of fertility practices was successful. Tribes that frequented the Missouri River area of northeastern Montana are still in existence today and with many of their cultural traditions associated with boulder rock art still active, particularly prayers and the leaving of offerings. Thus, there is support for the hypothesis that Native women who married white men for whatever reason(s), and stayed because of benefits it afforded them and their children, continued to use particular petroglyph boulder sites in northeastern Montana for fertility rituals, such as Indian Lake Medicine Boulder, thus keeping alive the ritualized landscape of their ancestors.

NOTES

1. Women's pipes in Northwestern Plains ethnographic collections are described as having a short, unrecessed stem and plain bowl (Van Stone 1996:18).

REFERENCES CITED

Beckwourth, James P.

1902   *The Life and Adventures of James P. Beckwourth, Mountaineer, Scout,*
    Pioneer, and Chief of the Crow Nation of Indians, Charles G. Leland, editor.
    Macmillian & Co., New York.

Bostwick, Todd W.

2012   Rock Art Research in the American Southwest. In *Discovering North*
    American Rock Art, Lawrence L. Loendorf, Christopher Chippindale, and
    David S. Whitley, editors, pp. 51–92. University of Arizona Press, Tucson.

Brown, Jennifer S. H.

1980   *Strangers in Blood: Fur Trade Company Families in Indian Country.*
    University of British Columbia Press, Vancouver.

Chamberlain, Lee C.

1969   Memo From Bureau of Land Management Natural Resource Specialist
    (Chamberlain) to the Bureau of Land Management Malta District Manager,
    dated 4/17/69. On file with the 24PH1008 site form at the Montana State
    Historic Preservation Office Records, Helena.

1972   The Medicine Rock of Malta. *Our Public Lands.* Volume 22, No.1, pp.
    8-11. Winter. Bureau of Land Management, US Department of the Interior,
    Washington, DC.

Claassen, Cheryl

2013   Fertility, A Place-based Gift to Groups. In *Género y Arqueología en Mesoa-*
    mérica, Homenaje a Rosemary A. Joyce, María J. Rodríguez-Shadow and
    Susan Kellogg, coordinators, pp. 198-225. Centro de Estudios de Antrop-
    ología de la Mujer, Las Cruces, NM.

Dahlen, Charles S.

1981   Memo from the Bureau of Land Management, Phillips Resource Area
    Manager, to the Bureau of Land Management, District Manager, Lewistown
    District, dated 3/12/1981. On file with the 24PH1008 site form at the
    Montana State Historical Preservation Office Records, Helena.

Denig, Edwin Thompson

1930   *Indian Tribes of the Upper Missouri.* J. N. B. Hewitt, editor. Forty-Sixth Annual
    Report of the Bureau of American Ethnology to the Secretary of the Smithson-
    ian Institution 1928–1929. Government Printing Office, Washington DC.

1961   *Five Indian Tribes of the Upper Missouri: Sioux, Arickaras, Assiniboines,*
    Crees, Crows. John C. Ewers, editor. University of Oklahoma Press, Norman.

Ewers, John C.

1952   The Medicine Rock of the Marias: A Blackfoot Shrine beside the Whoop-up
    Trail. *The Montana Magazine of History* 11(3):51–55.

Garcia, Andrew

1967   *Tough Trip through Paradise 1878–1879.* Comstock Editions, Sausalito, CA.

Gillette, Donna L., and Mavis Greer

2014   Spirituality in Rock Art Yesterday and Today: Reflections from the Northern
    Plains and Far Western United States. In *Rock Art and Sacred Landscapes,*
    Donna L. Gillette, Mavis Greer, Michele Helene Hayward, and William
    Breen Murray, editors, pp. 253–273. Springer, New York.

Greer, John, and Mavis Greer

2007   Rock Art Associated with Ritual Cave Use in the Southwest and Northern Mexico. Paper presented at the 72nd Annual Meeting of the Society for American Archaeology, Austin. http://greerservices.com/html/presentationsframeset.html.

2015   Rock Art Associated with Ritual Cave Use in the Southwestern U.S. and Northeastern Mexico. In *American Indian Rock Art*, Vol. 41, James D. Keyser and David A. Kaiser, editors, pp. 23–42. American Rock Art Research Association, Glendale, CA.

Greer, Mavis, and John Greer

1999   Northeastern Montana Boulder Rock Art. Paper presented at the Annual Meeting of the Montana Archaeological Society, Sidney. http://greerservices.com/html/presentationsframeset.html.

2000   Boulder Rock Art of Montana. Paper presented at the Joint Midwest Archaeological/Plains Anthropological Conference, St. Paul. http://greerservices.com/html/presentationsframeset.html.

2003   Dangling Legs Petroglyphs, Natrona County Wyoming. Paper presented at the Annual Meeting of the Wyoming Archaeological Society, Sheridan. http://greerservices.com/html/presentationsframeset.html.

Grinnell, George B.

1926   *By Cheyenne Campfires*. Yale University Press, New Haven, CT.

Hampton, Duane H. (editor)

2011   *Life and Death at the Mouth of the Musselshell, Montana Territory— 1868–1872. Featuring the Diary of C. M. Lee, Gunsmith, Merchant.* Stoneydale Press, Stevensville, MT.

Harmon, Daniel Williams

1957   *Harmon's Journal 1800–1819*. Touch Wood Editions, Surrey, British Columbia.

Hays-Gilpin, Kelley A.

2004   *Ambiguous Images: Gender and Rock Art*. Altamira Press, Walnut Creek, CA.

2005   From Fertility Shrines to Sacred Landscapes: A Critical Review of Gendered Rock Art Research in the Western United States. In *Discovering North American Rock Art*, Lawrence L. Loendorf, Christopher Chippindale, and David S. Whitley, editors, pp. 196–216. University of Arizona Press, Tucson.

2012   Engendering Rock Art. In *A Companion to Rock Art*, Jo McDonald and Peter Veth, editors, pp. 199–213. Blackwell Company Anthropology, Wiley-Blackwell, Hoboken. NJ.

Hedges, Ken

1983   A Re-examination of Pomo Baby Rocks. *American Indian Rock Art*, Vol. 9, Frank G. Bock, editor, pp. 10–21. American Rock Art Research Association, El Toro, CA.

Hoy, Judy

1969   Petroglyph Boulders in Phillips County, Montana. *Archaeology in Montana* 10(3):45–65.

Jones, David S.

2004   *Rationalizing Epidemics: Meanings and Uses of American Indian Mortality since 1600*. Harvard University Press, Cambridge.

Kessel, William B., and Robert Wooster (editors)

2005   *Encyclopedia of Native American Wars and Warfare*. Book Builders Incorporated, Facts On File, Inc. New York.

Keyser, James D., and Michael A. Klassen

2001   *Plains Indian Rock Art*. University of Washington Press, Seattle.

Kroeber, A. L.

1902–07 The Arapaho. In *Bulletin of the American Museum of Natural History*, Vol. XVIII, Pt. 1, pp. 1–150. New York.

1908   Ethnology of the Gros Ventre. In *Anthropological Papers of the American Museum of Natural History*. Vol. 1, Pt. 4. Order of the Trustees of the American Museum of Natural History, New York.

Mays, Dorothy A.

2004   *Women in Early America. Struggle, Survival and Freedom in a New World*. ABC-CLIO, Inc., Santa Barbara, CA.

McClintock, Walter

1992   *The Old North Trail: Life, Legends & Religion of the Blackfeet Indians*. University of Nebraska Press. Lincoln.

McFalls, Joseph A., and Marguerite Harvey McFalls

1984   *Disease and Fertility*. Academic Press, Orlando, FL.

McGowan, Charlotte

1978   Female Fertility Themes in Rock Art. *Journal of New World Archaeology* 2(4):15–27.

Murray, William Breen

2014   Deer: Sacred and Profane. In *Rock Art and Sacred Landscapes*, Donna L. Gillette, Mavis Greer, Michele Helene Hayward, and William Breen Murray, editors, pp. 195–206. Springer, New York.

Nelson, George

2002   *My First Years in the Fur Trade. The Journals of 1802–1804*, Laura Peers and Theresa Schenck, editors. Minnesota Historical Society Press, St. Paul.

Park, John A.

1990   The Simanton Petroglyph Hill Site (24PH2073): A Ceremonial Complex in Northern Montana. *Archaeology in Montana* 31(2):41–49.

Parkman, E. Breck

1992   Toward a Proto-Hokan Ideology. In *Ancient Images, Ancient Thought: The Archaeology of Ideology. Proceedings of the Twenty-Third Annual Conference of the Archaeological Association of the University of Calgary*, A. Sean Goldsmith, Sandra Garvie, David Selin, and Jeannette Smith, editors, pp. 365–370. University of Calgary Archaeological Association, Calgary.

2007   *Pit-and-Groove Antiquity in New World Prehistory*. Science Notes No. 89. California State Parks, Petaluma, CA.

Ploeger, Anndrea Dorothea

2012   *The Hopi Katsina Art and Ritual: Preserving a People of Peace*. Master's thesis, Department of Art History, University of Wisconsin-Superior.

Quaife, M. M. (editor)

1973   *"Yellowstone Kelly," The Memoirs of Luther S. Kelly*. University of Nebraska Press, Lincoln.

Robison, Ken (editor)

2003   *Life and Death on the Upper Missouri: The Frontier Sketches of Johnny Healy by John J. Healy*. Overholser Historical Research Center, Fort Benton, MT.

Sangster, Joan

2006   Native Women, Sexuality, and the Law. In *In The Days of Our Grandmothers: A Reader in Aboriginal Women's History in Canada*, Mary-Ellen Kelm and Lorna Townsend, editors, pp. 301–335. University of Toronto Press, Toronto.

Schmutterer, Gerhard

1989   *Tomahawk and Cross: Lutheran Missionaries among the Northern Plains Tribes 1858–1866. Including the Diary of Missionary Schmidt in North America and Autobiography of the Missionary to the Indians Carl Krebs.* The Center for Western Studies, Augustana College, Sioux Falls, SD.

Slifer, Dennis

2000   *The Serpent and the Sacred Fire: Fertility Images in Southwest Rock Art.* Museum of New Mexico Press, Santa Fe.

Steinbring, Jack, and Anthony P. Buchner

1997   Cathedrals of Prehistory: Rock Art Sites of the Northern Plains. In *American Indian Rock Art*, Vol. 23, S. M. Freers, editor, pp. 73–84. American Rock Art Research Association, San Miguel.

Sundstrom, Linea

1993   *Fragile Heritage: Prehistoric Rock Art of South Dakota.* National Park Service, South Dakota Historical Preservation Center, Vermillion.

2002   Stone Awls for Stone Age Plainswomen. *Plains Anthropologist* 47(181):99–119.

2004   *Storied Stone: Indian Rock Art in the Black Hills Country.* University of Oklahoma Press, Norman.

Thornton, Russell

1987   *American Indian Holocaust and Survival: A Population History since 1492. Civilization of the American Indian Series*, Vol. 186. University of Oklahoma Press, Norman.

Tratebas, Alice M.

1999   The Earliest Petroglyph Traditions on the North American Plains. In *Dating and the Earliest Known Rock Art*, Matthias Strecker and Paul Bahn, editors, pp. 15–27. Oxbow Books, Oxford.

2012   North American-Siberian Connections: Regional Rock Art Patterning Using Multivariate Statistics. In *A Companion to Rock Art*, Jo McDonald and Peter Veth, editors, pp. 143–159. Wiley-Blackwell, Hoboken, NJ.

Turpin, Solveig A., and Herbert H. Eling Jr.

2014   Trance and Transformation on the Northern Shores of the Chichimec Sea, Coahuila, Mexico. In *Rock Art and Sacred Landscapes*, Donna L. Gillette, Mavis Greer, Michele Helene Hayward, and William Breen Murray, editors, pp. 177–193. Springer, New York.

Van Kirk, Sylvia

1987   The Role of Native Women in the Creation of Fur Trade Society in Western Canada, 1670–1830. In *The Women's West*, Susan Armitage and Elizabeth Jameson, editors, pp. 53–62. University of Oklahoma Press, Norman.

Van Stone, James W.

1996   Ethnographic Collections from the Assiniboine and Yanktonai Sioux in the
            Field Museum of Natural History. In *Fieldiana: Anthropology, New Series,*
            No. 26. Field Museum of Natural History, Chicago.

Wallace, Anthony

1956   Revitalization Movements. *American Anthropologist* 58:264–281.

Whitley, David S.

2000   *The Art of the Shaman: Rock Art of California.* University of Utah Press, Salt
            Lake City.

6
GENDERED LANDSCAPES?
IF YOU SPEAK AN ALGONKIAN LANGUAGE

Alice Beck Kehoe

My point in this paper is to explicate "gender": "syntactical obligatory distinctions within a language: 'classes of nouns reflected in the behavior of associated words' (Corbett 1991:1, quoting Hockett). Conflating gender, a linguistics category, with cultural distinctions between men and women makes "gender" a metaphor. Its usage began as means to circumvent conventional connotations of "sex" with intercourse. Supreme Court Justice Ruth Bader Ginsburg explained, "I was doing all these sex-discrimination cases [in the 1970s], and my secretary said, 'I look at these pages and all I see is sex, sex, sex. The judges are men, and when they read that they're not going to be thinking about what you want them to think about' (quoted in Toobin 2013:42). Ginsburg then termed her cases "gender discrimination."

Other Realities

George Lakoff (1987:318–320) emphasizes that syntax encodes cognitive concepts and may structure them into systems such as noun classes. Indo-European's millennia-old syntactical gender implies, or some would say imposes, high saliency upon signs of sex. What is constantly salient in speaking, even if ordinarily not consciously noted, colors reality. Listening to the late George Kicking Woman on the Blackfeet Reservation, I was struck how a person's generation was more salient to him than whether the person was "he" or "she." Thinking in Blackfoot even as he spoke English, Mr. Kicking Woman talked about a *grandparent*, slipping between "he" and "she" as if they were synonymous. For him, living in a Blackfoot world, what was salient about the elder person was that person's age, actual and also relative to George.

Maya, Miguel Astor-Aguilera learned, have "a sense of place as marked by geographic markers and celestial bodies . . . . Nonhuman persons . . . are locatable around their quadripartitioned sky, ground, and inner earth. The Maya *j'meen* [ritual intercessors] can . . . bring forth ancestors and other nonhuman persons in order to consult with them. This is often done through their communicating objects," such as rocks, stelae, or crosses (Astor-Aguilera 2010:4, 245). Far to the north of Maya, Ojibwe[1] ritual specialists similarly recognize particular stones or rock outcrops used to link with nonhuman beings; in an interesting exercise, John Norder plotted 400 rock outcrops on waterways that looked suitable for pictographs, but he found only twenty of them actually did exhibit pictographs (Norder 2012:242). A. I. Hallowell, preeminent among ethnographers working with Ojibwe, meticulously discusses his consultants' knowledge of animate rocks (Hallowell 2010:44–50; 1992, Fig. 8, photograph of William Berens with one of these stones). Like Maya *j'meen*, the Ojibwe jessakid (*jaasakiid*) "conjuror" and the Wabano therapeutic dance host likely had one or more such stones in their ritual ground. An elder ritually naming a child might give the infant "a tiny cane, signifying that the infant protégé will live to old age; another gives a tiny gun signifying that the baby will become a mighty hunter; another gives a queer-shaped stone having mystic force" (Landes 1997[1938]:2–3). A Northern Cree man told Robert Brightman, "Any kind of thing can be a *pawākan* [non-human being helper]. Animals, fish, worms in water, water, ice, rock, wind. When people see them, they would look like a person" (Brightman 1993:77).

Sonya Atalay assists a Michigan Anishinaabe community working with the state to preserve a site with a large number of petroglyphs. Herself Anishinaabe, Atalay brokers the community's expectation that it will keep the site alive with proper ritual at summer solstice and prayers and offerings by Indian visitors. Like other beings, the rock requires water to live. Its protectors from the state, however, put a roof over it to keep water off. How the state's view of the rock as inanimate and its petroglyphs fossilized could be accommodated to the Ojibwe-speaking community's understanding of it as a being was an ongoing question when Atalay published her account (Atalay 2012:245–246).

Seeing a rock outcrop with old petroglyphs, versus seeing a landmark teaching knowledge, like Midéwiwin scrolls do, is the profound difference between the Michigan settler society and indigenous Anishinaabeg. Erving Goffman's concept of "presentation of the self" can be broadened to "actions, objects, or settings, 'while this image is entertained concerning the individual, so that a self is imputed to him, this self itself does not derive from its possessor, but from the whole scene of his action, being generated by that attribute of local events which renders them interpretable by witnesses'" (Wieder, Zimmerman, and Raymond 2010:152, quoting Goffman 1959:252). Landscapes present themselves to observers as do people and animals; that is to say, sensory input is cognized into fuzzy sets or images, which are labeled according to observer's language and experience (Lakoff 1987:440–447, 453–461). Algonkian speakers have been socialized to know that vitality is an innate property of the universe that vivifies organisms and may manifest to human senses in the form of beings. A rock that moves (perturbation is common in northern lands) or speaks through petroglyphs is seen to be a being. Ordinary commonplace rocks are likely not.

Sometimes a person walking hears a voice calling. Looking down, it comes from a stone, inviting the person to pick it up. On the Blackfeet Reservation, small ammonite and baculite fossils that look like bison, or like curled-up sleeping bison, can be found, especially around a lake in the northeast sector of the reservation. Called *iniskimiksi* (singular: *iniskim*), they were formerly ritually sung with to bring bison herds into corrals, as promised by the original *iniskim* that sang out during a famine to a woman collecting firewood:

> Yonder woman, you must take me.
> I am powerful.
> Yonder woman, you must take me,
> You must hear me.
> Where I sit is powerful (Wissler and Duvall 1908:85)

It was sitting in a little bed of bison hair and sage. The woman kept it wrapped in its bed, inside a pouch, until the community could gather in her tipi to learn the *iniskim*'s songs that bring the herds to the people. Today, people keep *iniskimiksi* to bring prosperity to their families; the miniature stone bison may be heirlooms, or part of other medicine bundles, or fortunate recent finds.

Bear-chief (NínoXkyàio), an Aamsskápi Piikuni born in 1857, recounted in 1911 to the Dutch linguist C. C. Uhlenbeck an experience he had had while hunting in the mountains:

> I heard, there was a sound . . . higher up the river. . . . I saw, there was a
> person. He was standing near the water, he was small, he had no clothes.

I then hid myself, I went around him, I looked up at him, who [then] was a rock. I then went to him, I got there. I told him: 'Now I shall take you, I shall bring you to my lodge.' I put him on my horse, I sat behind, then I went home. [The women] came out to [me], I gave them that person, [that was] a rock. They took him into my lodge. [An elder woman] . . . began to paint him. . . . She prayed to him, she wrapped him in a piece of cloth. He was one night in my lodge, and next morning we began to make a shelter for him. We broke camp and moved, we left him. . . . I told him, that he should keep watch. (Uhlenbeck 1912:216)

The potential for a rock to be a person, and vice versa, is reflected in the Blackfoot dictionary entry for "rock." *Óóhkotok,* defined as "large stone, rock," is animate as opposed to *Óóhkotok,* a "small stone, rock, pebble," which is inanimate (Frantz & Russell 1995:190–191, 426).

Many features of landscape are explained by actions of legendary personages. Blackfoot attribute a number of landmarks in their territory of Alberta and northern Montana to Napi, "Old Man"[2] (Figure 6.1):

Old Man came from the south, making the mountains, the prairies, and the forests as he passed along, making the birds and the animals also. He traveled northward making things as he went, putting red paint in the ground here and there—arranging the world as we see it today.

He made the Milk River and crossed it; being tired, he went up on a little hill and lay down to rest. As he lay on his back, stretched out on the grass with his arms extended, he marked his figure with stones. You can see those rocks today, they show the shape of his body, legs, arms and hair.

Going on north after he had rested, he stumbled over a knoll and fell down on his knees. He said aloud, "You are a bad thing to make me stumble so." Then he raised up two large buttes there and named them the Knees. They are called the Knees to this day. He went on farther north, and with some of the rocks he carried with him he built the Sweet Grass Hills.

Old Man covered the plains with grass for the animals to feed on. He marked off a piece of ground and in it made all kinds of roots and berries to grow: camas, carrots, turnips, bitterroot, sarvisberries, bull-berries, cherries, plums, and rosebuds. He planted trees, and he put all kinds of animals on the ground.

. . . When he had gone almost to the Red Deer River, he was so tired that he lay down on a hill. The form of his body can be seen there yet, on the top of the hill where he rested.

When he awoke from his sleep, he traveled farther north until he came to a high hill. He climbed to the top of it and there he sat down to rest. As he gazed over the country, he was greatly pleased by it. Looking at the steep hill below him, he said to himself, "This is a fine place for sliding. I will have some fun." And he began to slide down the hill. The marks where he slid are to be seen yet, and the place is known to all the Blackfeet tribes as "Old Man's Sliding Ground."[3] (Blackfeet Community College online)

Another prominent landscape feature, south of Calgary, is the Okotoks Erratic, a massive glacial erratic on the high plains (Figure 6.2). Napi put his robe on the rock to rest upon it and left, telling the rock it could keep the robe. Then, he changed his mind and grabbed the robe back. Angry, the huge rock rolled after Napi as his animal friends pecked and hit at it, leaving pieces that make what geologists term the Foothills Erratics Train, until finally they caused the rock to split and stopped it.

Napi is quintessentially impulsive male, horny and foolish. His marks upon the land color the places with his swaggering eager machismo. Yet no one thinks of his landscapes as masculine. Masculine/feminine is not a binary distinction for Blackfoot, along with most other American First Nations. Instead, a continuum is felt between conventional men's behaviors and conventional women's behaviors, with plenty of space for individuals to be flexible, or choose to comport themselves somewhat more like the other (biological) sex, or to assume, as part of ritual, dress or behavior usually seen among persons of the other sex (see Kehoe 1997 and other papers in that volume).

Individuals in Algonkian-speaking societies show a concatenation of behaviors that are normatively more or less "proper" to persons of their (biological) sex and age and family status, without constraint of a binary opposition between "man" and "woman." Beyond ordinary visible humans are ordinary animals, plants, rocks, and weather phenomena, all within a larger universe of usually non-perceived beings and forces. Darrell Robes Kipp, a Blackfoot scholar, told an audience at the 2010 Blackfoot History symposium on the Blackfeet Reservation that he no longer uses the term "culture" to distinguish his people's ways and understanding from those of other nations. Instead, he has come to realize that people in different societies may be living in different realities. That is why we should not project Indo-European gender into a universal.

Gendered Earth

In 1996, Sam Gill caused a ruckus in Native American Studies by exposing how tenuous and questionable is the idea that American Indians conceptualize the Earth as their Mother, a deity. Gill found that claims for this allegedly pan-Indian religious concept rest upon a chapter in *Myths, Dreams and Mysteries*, 1957, by the notoriously unreliable Mircea Eliade (Kehoe 2000:37–43), further developed by the Swedish romantic Åke Hultkrantz (Gill 1991:1–2). Gill traced an Indian "Mother Earth" to Charles Eastman's 1911 *The Soul of the Indian*, poetically describing Dakota religion by presenting Sun and Earth as metaphors for male and female principles and parents' roles raising children and to an 1885 statement by the Okanagon religious reformer Smohalla protesting colonists' taking over his nation's land (Gill 1983:153–157; Gill 1991:66–67, 135–136;). Not surprisingly, "Mother Earth" became popular with 1960s New Age spiritual seekers entwined with feminism.

When I was living in an Aymara village on Lake Titicaca, Bolivia, in 1988, I asked my hostess, and also Juan de Dios Yapita Moya, a professional linguist who is Aymara, about Pachamama, said to be Andean Indians' Mother Earth goddess. Both explained that the earth holds the female generative power vital for the growth of plants and animals, including humans. "Mother" is a metaphor for this power, as it was for Charles Eastman. Aymara and Quechua Indians swirl drinks in cups so that a few drops fall over onto the ground, a gesture assumed by tourists to be libations to Mother Earth, but my hostess laughed at this interpretation: "We do that because we pass the cup around, and swirling like that cleans the lip of the cup." Intangible powers and quasi-human beings such as vampires are recognized in Aymara reality, along with ordinary beings and things, without gender in the language. The lake, Titicaca, looms close by in the landscape, the Andes peaks ring the horizon, condors and pumas appear even in the church as in pre-contact temples, all infusing the landscape with sensed power organic to the Above, the land, and the Below.

Gill's 1983 sourcebook on North American Indian religious traditions richly illuminates "place" in several of these indigenous realities. The selection (in Gill 1983:20–27) from Robin Ridington's description of Beaver (Dunne-za) communities, a Dené nation in British Columbia, concisely relates parts of the landscape to Dunne-za webs of age, sex, family, and work. In common with so many societies where killing animals is frequent and economically important, Dunne-za see women's reproductive power to be antagonistic to hunting game. Therefore, women avoid hunting weapons and hunters' medicine bundles, lest female power negate hunting success. Female power being at its strongest during menstruation, menstruating women are particularly careful to observe these avoidances. Ridington explains how the opposition of killing and reproduction marks the bush as men's territory, and camps where women move freely as women's space. These are not so much "gendered" landscapes (aside from the fact that Dené languages lack gender) as domains of action. For example, a widowed or post-menopausal woman—a woman who will not reproduce life by bearing children—may hunt in the bush; women also tend fishnets in the watery domain and snare small animals around camps. Describing another Dené society, the Chipewyan, Henry Sharp agrees with what Ridington says about Dunne-za, "Women's lives are predicated on different principles than are men's, and each . . . thinks in the corresponding terms in the creation of their lives" (Sharp 1995:73).

What might these principles be? Kochems and Jacobs (1997), reviewing conventional and more recent studies of "gender" in First Nations ethnographies, have difficulty tabulating roles and statuses under English-language categories of "men" and "women." Probably the best explication of concepts common among American First Nations, they suggest, is the formulation worked out by Navajo anthropologist Wesley Thomas (1997:158): among traditional Navajo, there are men (*hastiin*,

Figure 6.1. Chief Mountain. Photo by Alice Kehoe.

Figure 6.2. Okotoks Rock, split and halted by Napi's friends as it chased him. Photo by Alice Kehoe.

"man") and women (*'asdzáán*, "woman") and *nádleeh* which indicates androgynous characteristics. Thomas emphasizes that this is not a case of "three genders" or "sexes"; Navajo know that "Everyone is of *sa'ąh* and *bik'eh hózhó*; everyone is a 'man-woman,'" i.e., with aspects of each social persona (Thomas 1997:183). The principles that Sharp refers to reflect the work necessary for survival, social reproduction, and pleasure. One brute fact of life is that only women can gestate and nurse infants; therefore, much of most women's lives reflects this role and centers them in the comparative safety of home. By default, men's role of sustaining societies includes hunting, in a pragmatic sense providing food, and in a larger sense, killing, which is contrasted to bearing and nurturing new life. Dené domains of men and women are constructed of tasks, are not sharply bounded, and may be bent or dissolved as situations indicate.

Linguists at Work

I began working on this paper with the knowledge that Algonkian languages are said to have gender as well as a syntactical distinction between animate and inanimate, signaled in Blackfoot by either animate (*-iksi*) or inanimate (*-istsi*) suffixes for noun plurals (Uhlenbeck 2013[1910]). For an example, I looked up "mountain" in the standard dictionary of Blackfoot by Donald Frantz and Norma Jean Russell (1995). According to Frantz, a professional linguist, and Russell, a speaker of Blackfoot, *miistak*, "mountain" takes the inanimate suffix. That did not seem right; my Blackfoot friends say mountains live very long, very slow lives, occasionally manifesting their vitality by changing shape. In 1992, Chief Mountain, *Ninaiistako,* in the heart of Blackfoot territory did this by sloughing off a large chunk. It was annoyed, people said, by the non-Indian rock climbers and New Age pilgrims invading its holy space where Thunder, *Ksisstsi'ko'm,* lives during the warm months. Surely *Ninaiistako* is not inanimate.

On August 20, 2013, I asked Marvin Weatherwax, Director of Blackfoot Language Studies in Blackfeet Community College, about mountains' gender. Weatherwax is familiar with academic linguistics and a member of the group of teachers of Blackfoot that meets regularly to discuss their work and agree on innovations. He is highly conscious of how his language reflects his people's reality. Other Blackfoot speakers I had talked with, Darrell Robes Kipp in Browning and Loma C. Beebe in Calgary, had told me that they did not think they would use *–istsi* with *miistak*; Beebe asked her Crowshoe (Aapátohsi Piikáni, Alberta Peigan) grandparents and they, too, said it would not sound right. Weatherwax, who is Aamsskáápi Piikuni (Montana Blackfeet), clarified the situation with a startling statement: Blackfoot does not have gender, the claim that animate/inanimate distinction constitutes gender in the language is an imposition by a professional linguist!

Donald Frantz, Weatherwax told me, was a young man of twenty-six when he came to the Blackfeet Reservation intending to compile a dictionary of the Blackfoot language. Marvin Weatherwax's grandmother, who lived in the southern portion of the reservation, permitted Frantz to camp near her house, later fixing up a shed so he could live in it. She asked Marvin, then a youth, and his cousin to introduce Frantz to elders who spoke Blackfoot well and to translate for him. Marvin did so for three years. Then, after five years working on the Montana reservation, Frantz went to Alberta, met Russell, and completed the dictionary by collaborating with her. It is Weatherwax's opinion that Frantz took for granted that Blackfoot, as an Algonkian language, would have animate/inanimate gender and imposed this in his dictionary.

The consensus of the Blackfoot speakers I spoke with is that the suffixes –*iksi* and –*istsi* are indeed used to indicate whether or not a noun has vitality but which suffix is used depends on context. When speaking of rocks that could be picked up and used for a tipi ring or today for construction, a Blackfoot likely would affix –*istsi*. When speaking of medicine rocks seen to have moved of themselves or sheltering Little Persons, Blackfoot would use –*iksi*. On a deeper level, my Blackfoot friends were uncomfortable with the idea that their language would govern meaning in an arbitrary way. Respect for individuals and their choices is very important for Blackfoot. So is admiration for fluent speaking graced with metaphors. Their language, they believe, reflects their philosophy.

Conclusions

Coming face to face with Blackfoot speakers insisting that context, not a syntactical feature of their language, governs which suffix they may use, I turned to a linguist who wrote his dissertation on Aamsskáápi Piikuni Blackfoot, Allan Taylor. Taylor clarified that "gender" is a conventional term in linguistics that came from the discipline's foundations in Indo-European studies, and its extension to other language stocks has been misleading. We are really talking about classes, or association groups, of morphemes, classes that linguists recognize as they analyze languages' structural features. Algonkian languages, Taylor explained, have two noun classes that linguists have labeled "animate" and "inanimate" because many, but not all, nouns in one of these classes refer to animate beings, and many in the other class refer to inanimate things (Taylor 2013). The noun classes and associated verbs may reflect, or give saliency to, Blackfoot reality in which people are conscious that there are many beings we do not ordinarily perceive, or perceive as alive. Bear-chief, for example, was hunting in the Sweet Grass Hills in 1888 when he thought that he saw three bison bulls sitting in a field, glittering in the sun. Then as he approached them, he saw they were three rocks. The Sweet Grass Hills are a holy place, and Bear-chief realized that the rocks *were* three bison bulls, powerful bulls that he could not kill. He and his companions prayed and placed offerings on the bull rocks. Later, Bear-chief was again in the area and went to see the bull rocks: they were gone! In their places grew three sunflowers. Bear-chief and his friends realized that the bulls turned to rocks, then sunflowers, were omens telling them the bison would be gone from their world (Uhlenbeck 1912:214–215).

Archaeologists should use ethnographies, particularly those of descendant communities, to read more from landscapes than geomorphology and plant species. A Western Enlightenment reality can be stretched only so far. Interpreting the archaeological record and its localities should bring in other realities recorded in ethnographies and living still in descendant communities.

NOTES

1. Ojibwe, Ojibwa, Ojibway, and Chippewa are variants of *očipwe*, referring to the widespread communities speaking this language. Contemporary members of these communities often use *anishinaabe* (plural, *anishinaabeg*), meaning "real people," as in Indian people speaking Ojibwe. Some groups in southern Manitoba were termed Saulteaux.

2. Napi is derived from the Proto-Algonkian *waap* "east, light," which in Blackfoot is the root *aap*. Hence Naapi is sometimes translated as Dawn Man, but in common usage, *napi* would be used for an elderly man (Allan R. Taylor, Oct. 7, 2013, pers. comm.).

3. Blackfeet Community College posts this Blackfoot creation legendary history online, based on narratives told to Ella Clark by Amskapi Pikuni (Montana Blackfeet) elder Chewing Black Bone.

REFERENCES CITED

Atalay, Sonya

2012   *Community-based Archaeology: Research With, By, and For Indigenous and Local Communities*. University of California Press, Berkeley.

Blackfeet Community College

2013   Blackfeet Creation Tale. http://www.montana.edu/wwwbcc/legend.html. Accessed 31 March 2013.

Brightman, Robert

1993   *Grateful Prey: Rock Cree Human-Animal Relationships*. University of California Press, Berkeley.

Corbett, Grenville

1991   *Gender*. Cambridge University Press, Cambridge.

Frantz, Donald G., and Norma Jean Russell

1995   *The Blackfoot Dictionary of Stems, Roots, and Affixes,* 2nd edition. University of Toronto Press, Toronto.

Gill, Sam D.

1983   *Native American Traditions: Sources and Interpretations*. Wadsworth, Belmont, Ca.

1991   *Mother Earth: An American Story*. University of Chicago Press, Chicago.

Goffman, Erving

1959   *The Presentation of Self in Everyday Life*. Doubleday Anchor, New York.

Hallowell, A. Irving

1992   *The Ojibwa of Berens River, Manitoba*. Harcourt Brace Jovanovich, Fort
        Worth, TX.

2010   *Contributions to Ojibwe Studies: Essays, 1934–1972*. University of
        Nebraska Press, Lincoln.

Kehoe, Alice Beck

1997   On the Incommensurality of Gender Categories. In *Two-Spirit People*,
        Sue-Ellen Jacobs, Wesley Thomas, and Sabine Lang, editors, pp. 265–277.
        University of Illinois Press, Urbana.

2000   *Shamans and Religion: An Anthropological Exploration in Critical Thinking*.
        Waveland Press, Prospect Heights, IL.

Kipp, Darrell Robes

[2010] Opening address, Blackfoot History Symposium, Cutswood School,
        Browning MT, August 20, 2010.

Kochems, Lee M., and Sue-Ellen Jacobs

1997   Gender Statuses, Gender Features, and Gender/Sex Categories: New Perspec-
        tives on an Old Paradigm. In *Two-Spirit People*, Sue-Ellen Jacobs, Wesley
        Thomas, and Sabine Lang, editors, pp. 255–264. University of Illinois Press,
        Urbana.

Lakoff, George

1987   *Women, Fire, and Dangerous Things*. University of Chicago Press, Chicago.

Landes, Ruth

1997   *The Ojibwa Woman*. University of Nebraska Press, Lincoln.
[1938]

Norder, John

2012   Landscapes of Memory and Presence in the Canadian Shield. In *Enduring
        Motives*, Linea Sundstrom and Warren DeBoer, editors, pp. 235–250.
        University of Alabama Press, Tuscaloosa.

Thomas, Wesley

1997   Navajo Cultural Constructions of Gender and Sexuality. In *Two-Spirit
        People*, Sue-Ellen Jacobs, Wesley Thomas, and Sabine Lang, editors, pp.
        156–191. University of Illinois Press, Urbana.

Toobin, Jeffrey

2013   Heavyweight: How Ruth Bader Ginsburg Has Moved the Supreme Court.
        The New Yorker 89(4):38–47.

Uhlenbeck, C. C.

1912   *A New Series of Blackfoot Texts*. Deel XIII No. 1, Verhandelingen der
        Koninklijke Academie van Wetenschappen te Amsterdam. Johannes Müller,
        Amsterdam.

2013   *Outline for a Comparative Grammar of Some Algonquian Languages*.
        Joshua Jacob Snider, translator. Mundart Press, Petoskey MI. (Original,
        Ontwerp van eene vergelijkende vormleer van eenige Algonkin-talen,
        *Verhandelingen der Koninklijke Akademie van Wetenschappen te
        Amsterdam*, Afdeeling Letterkunde, Deel 11 No. 3, Johannes Müller,
        Amsterdam 1910.)

Wieder, D. Lawrence, Don H. Zimmerman, and Geoffrey Raymond

2010   UCLA: Then and Now. In *The Social History of Language and Social Interaction Research*, Wendy Leeds-Hurwitz, editor, pp. 127–158. Hampton Press, Cresskill, NJ.

Wissler, Clark, and D. C. Duvall

1908   *Mythology of the Blackfoot Indians*. Anthropological Papers, Vol. 2, Pt. 1. New York: American Museum of Natural History. Facsimile edition, 1995, University of Nebraska Press, Lincoln.

PART THREE
THE GULF COAST AND WESTERN U.S.

7

GENDERED LANDSCAPES AND THE LATE PREHISTORIC OCCUPATION OF THE MOJAVE DESERT

Barbara J. Roth

The Late Prehistoric period in the Mojave Desert has usually been approached from the perspective of reconstructing hunter-gatherer adaptations to arid environments. "Landscapes," when considered, have primarily been addressed using water source locations and flora and fauna distributions. In this paper, I take a different approach in examining landscape use along Soda Playa in the Mojave Sink region. Recent survey and excavation projects in the Mojave Sink have documented seasonally-used sites that represent activities performed by different genders. The sites by themselves provide only limited information on prehistoric forager occupation of this region. Taken together, however, they provide significant insights into our understanding of how hunter-gatherers used the Mojave Desert landscape.

The Mojave Desert represents an environment that offered harsh challenges to hunter-gatherer groups. Many studies of the prehistoric occupation of this environment have thus, not surprisingly, focused on ecological aspects of hunter-gatherer adaptations to this arid and sparsely vegetated setting (Basgall 2000; Sutton 1996; Sutton et al. 2007; Warren 1984). Abundant ethnographic data from later Paiute occupants and other groups in the surrounding Great Basin point to the important role of social factors in influencing foraging behaviors; however, this aspect has not generally been pursued by researchers studying prehistoric occupations in the region. As a result, much of our understanding of foraging behaviors in this setting is tied to land use focused on key resources, such as water sources, game, and productive plants (e.g., mesquite).

Here I take a different approach in examining land use by prehistoric foragers in one portion of the central Mojave Desert. Using survey and test excavation data coupled with ethnographic data on the division of labor in foraging groups, I discuss the importance of gendered activities in structuring hunter-gatherers' use of this environment. I argue that prehistoric foragers made gender-based decisions on where and when to procure resources that are clearly visible in the assemblages recovered from sites in the region. Engendered activities structured seasonal movement and influenced the behavior associated with specific sites. This was apparently a necessary aspect of adaptation to the uncertainty of the Mojave Desert. By including social practices, such as engendered decision making, in our examination of past behavior, we can gain a better understanding of forager adaptations to this desert environment.

Background to the Study

The area discussed in this chapter is located at the terminus of the Mojave River in the east-central Mojave Desert and is referred to as the Mojave Sink (Figure 7.1). Pleistocene Lake Mojave once encompassed a significant portion of this area and is now represented by two dry lake beds, Soda Playa to the south and Silver Lake to the north. The Mojave River enters Soda Playa from the south and the playa contained water during wet periods throughout the Holocene (Warren 2010; Wells et al. 1989), but the alkalinity of the soil made this water non-potable. Springs are present throughout the area and would have provided reliable, albeit widely spaced, water sources. Vegetation is sparse and consists primarily of creosote bush, salt bush, and grasses. Mesquite its present adjacent to the springs and along the Mojave River and likely served as an important food source prehistorically. Game is surprisingly common, and includes big horn sheep, jack rabbits, and desert tortoises. Thomas (2011) noted that the dispersed nature of resources in the Mojave Sink affected forager movements and subsistence practices, and he argued that regional landscape use is more pertinent for addressing foraging behavior in this environment than a focus on specific sites. I use her approach as a starting point and expand it to incorporate ethnographic and archaeological data to argue that the landscape in this portion of the Mojave Sink was used in engendered ways that influenced movement and resource use.

This chapter uses data on sites dating to the Late Prehistoric period (A.D. 1200–contact) as the archaeological record for this time period in the Mojave Sink is relatively well documented compared to other

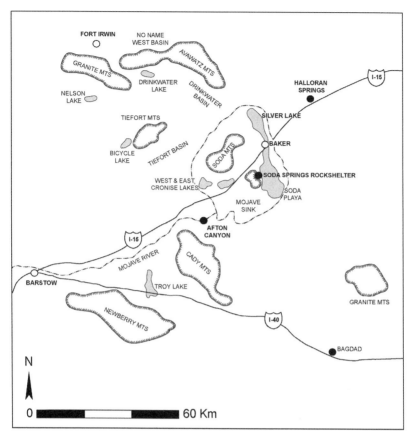

Figure 7.1. Mojave Sink.

portions of the Mojave Desert. Previous surveys and limited excavations of Late Prehistoric period sites have established that these groups practiced seasonal mobility based on resource availability, with seasonal camps located adjacent to reliable water sources and resource stands, such as mesquite (Thomas 2011). Ethnographic data on groups in the Great Basin are also available and can be used to explain patterns of movement and gendered activities.

Previous Approaches to Land Use

Before proceeding with the archaeological data to support the idea that the landscape in the Mojave Desert was used in engendered ways during the Late Prehistoric period, it is important to examine how land use has been addressed previously in this area. Previous work has taken the form of two general types of studies: 1) surveys for early "man" sites along the shores of Pleistocene lakes in the region, focusing on the distribution and geological context of sites with stemmed points and rarer fluted points (Campbell 1936; Campbell et al. 1937; Davis 1975, 1978; Warren and Decosta 1964; Warren and Ore 1978) and 2) studies of hunter-gatherer adaptations to the environment (e.g., Basgall 2000; Byrd 1998). Much of the work on early sites was done around Pleistocene Lake Mojave in the early decades of the 1900s by Elizabeth Campbell (Campbell 1936; Campbell et al. 1937). These studies focused on establishing the antiquity of occupation along Pleistocene Lake Mojave. Malcomb Rogers did more extensive surveys along the playas and recorded later sites, documenting the artifact assemblages associated with these later occupations (Rogers 1929, 1931). He was the first to document large sites dating to the Ceramic period (post A.D. 800) along the playas in the Mojave Sink. Later work at sites in the Cronese Basin (Drover 1979) established that these occupations were tied to Holocene lake stands. For the most part, however, the majority of archaeological investigations at Ceramic period sites in the Mojave Sink have been done along the Mojave River rather than along the playas (Rector et al. 1983; Schneider 1989).

The primary data on land use in this portion of the Mojave Desert has come from work done on Fort Irwin to the north of the Mojave Sink (Basgall 1993, 2000; Basgall and Hall 1992; Basgall et al. 1988; Jenkins 1985, 1986; Jenkins et al. 1984; Kelly and Warren 1984; McGuire and Hall 1988; Warren 1991). These studies have used survey and excavation data to examine forager adaptations to this very arid environment, documenting high mobility during dry periods and long-term reuse of well-watered areas.

Forager occupation of the Mojave Sink conforms to many of the patterns established by work at Fort Irwin. During the Pinto period (6000–2000 B.C.), groups were highly mobile and appear to have been occupying the region sporadically to hunt and gather small seeds, as indicated by the presence of milling stones at Archaic period sites in the area (Basgall et al. 1988; Warren 1994). Toward the end of the succeeding Gypsum period (2000 B.C.–A.D. 500), climatic conditions began to improve, and spring recharge led to an increase in forager use of the area, although it appears that much of that occupation involved hunting large game, especially big horn sheep.

The most substantial occupation of the Mojave Sink began during the Saratoga Springs period (A.D. 500–1200) and extended into the Late Prehistoric period. Sites dating to these time periods are characterized by the presence of brown ware and buffware ceramics and distinct projectile points. Rose Spring points are diagnostic of the Saratoga Springs period; Cottonwood Triangular and Desert Side-notched points are used to distinguish the Late Prehistoric period. Groups were apparently tethered to water sources during these periods and began to occupy the best-documented sites in this portion of the Mojave Desert, the Oro Grande site (Rector et al. 1983), Afton Canyon site (Schneider 1989), and shell midden sites in the Cronese Basin (Drover 1979). Elsewhere in the Mojave Desert, the Medieval Climatic Anomaly (MCA), a period of drought and climatic fluctuations that occurred from A.D. 800 to 1300, had a significant impact on Ceramic period groups (Jones et al. 1999), especially in the western portion of the desert, where large villages were abandoned and groups aggregated into sites located in areas that continued to contain resources (Gardner 2006; Sutton et al. 2007). The MCA would have impacted groups in the Mojave Sink as well, and it is likely that during dry periods groups abandoned the area and moved to portions of the desert that could sustain a resource base, most likely along the Mojave River.

Warren (2010) has argued that the early portion of the Late Prehistoric period was a wet period in the Mojave Sink, resulting in spring recharge, increased flow in the Mojave River, the presence of standing lakes in the Cronese Basin, and periodic standing water in Soda and Silver playas. The lakes in the Cronese Basin supported larger, more permanent settlements than were present in the Soda Playa area (Drover 1979; Wells et al. 1998). Standing water, although not potable, would have increased resource density along Soda Playa and Silver Lake, as tule reeds and other aquatic plants would have grown along the water's edge and migratory waterfall would have been present periodically. Arend and Roth (2016) note that increased resource density and spring recharge significantly affected the activities of prehistoric foragers in the area, resulting in more intensive occupation of the lakeshore during the Late Prehistoric period. Because this period is associated with wetter climatic conditions, evidence for subsistence diversification is present, including the incorporation of mesquite and a range of smaller game into the diet. Basgall et al. (1988) have documented more patterned seasonal movement in the Fort Irwin region during this period, which they tie to smaller annual ranges associated with this subsistence diversification. It is within this context of increasingly intensive seasonal exploitation and subsistence diversification after A.D. 1200 that we can examine engendered use of the landscape.

Engendered Landscapes

Forager adaptations to arid desert environments have not been the regular fodder for landscape studies, which have instead generally focused on characteristics of the built environment that served specific purposes within past societies (Anschuetz et al. 2001; Barton et al. 2004; Bender 1993; Crumley and Marquardt 1990; Whittlesey 1997; Zendeño 1997). Studies of prehistoric forager landscape use have often been artifact-based, using the spatial distribution of artifacts to address issues of movement and land use (Rossignol and Wandsnider 1992; Wandsnider 1998). However, several researchers have argued that a landscape approach is particularly useful for investigating foraging behavior in the Mojave Desert (Allen 2011; Arend and Roth 2016; Robinson et al. 2011). Examining behavior from this perspective provides a more holistic view of how hunter-gatherers were using the region than relying on individual site data alone. Using site distribution data gleaned from survey and excavation projects, they argue that a distinctive pattern of landscape use was present along Soda Playa during the Late Prehistoric period that focused on springs, dunes, and foothills. Basgall et al. (1988) refer to these kinds of landscape features as "magnet" locations in the Fort Irwin area.

Groups apparently identified a landscape based on the location of water sources, subsistence resources, and geography, then moved in response to seasonally available food resources, and repeatedly occupied areas with abundant and reliable resources. This patterned exploitation may be the fundamental means by which foragers adapted to the Mojave Desert environment (Arend and Roth 2013).

This general pattern of landscape use does not take into account how gendered decisions and activities impacted land use and ultimately influenced forager adaptations to this environment. Many of the recorded sites contain artifact assemblages and features that can be used, in concert with ethnographically-derived correlates, to reconstruct gendered activities. The distribution of these sites can in turn be used to gain an understanding of how Late Prehistoric foragers moved across the landscape and to address how gendered activities influenced decisions on where and when to move. One caveat must be given before presenting the data, however; preservation at these sites is limited and sites have often experienced substantial mixing, especially those located in dunes, making the definition of discrete feature areas with associated artifacts difficult. The lack of perishables is especially problematic because ethnographic data indicate that much of the material culture used by Great Basin foragers was perishable, including items that would be directly pertinent to this study, such as digging sticks and winnowing baskets. Despite these difficulties, it is possible to use the archaeological record combined with ethnographically-documented behaviors to reconstruct gendered behaviors and examine their distribution across the landscape.

Modeling Movements Using Ethnographic Data

Ethnographic data on Great Basin forager land use and subsistence practices can serve as a model with which to compare the archaeological assemblages from sites along Soda Playa. I have used this same type of modeling elsewhere to model gendered activities associated with the adoption of agriculture in the Southwest (Roth 2006). The basic premise of this approach is that cross-cultural ethnographic patterns (artifact and feature use and site locations) can be compared with archaeological data to determine if similar activities are indicated by the archaeological record, and from this gendered activities and movements can be discerned.

Abundant ethnographic data exist illustrating that gender was the basic social division within Great Basin forager society (Fowler 1986). This is similar to what has been documented cross-culturally by Murdock and Provost (1973), whose analysis of 185 ethnographic groups showed the association of women with gathering, processing, and storing plants, and men with hunting (especially large game), trapping, and fishing. Great Basin ethnographies also document men's association with manufacturing hunting equipment. Smaller game was taken by both men and women of all ages, while some resources such as piñon and agave were gathered during special forays by family groups where women would gather the plants while men hunted.

Most of the data come from Paiute groups because Paiute ethnographers regularly discussed the division of labor. Ethnohistoric records indicate that several different groups occupied the central Mojave Desert just prior to contact, including the Chemeheuvi (southern Paiute) and the Vanyume (Desert Serrano) (Earle 2005; Schneider 1988). Schneider (1988:38) notes that few ethnographic data are available on food-gathering and subsistence practices for these ethnohistoric groups, however. For this reason, the following discussion focuses on Paiute and Shoshone groups in the Great Basin.

The Southern Paiute are one of the best documented of these groups and they occupied similar environmental settings to the Mojave Sink (Kelly and Fowler 1986). Like other Great Basin foragers, their social structure was based on a flexible division of labor. Women harvested seeds, roots, and berries and processed the plants using manos, metates, mortars, and pestles (Kelly and Fowler 1986; Knack 1995). Seeds were gathered in conical baskets and parched with coals in willow trays. Seasonal variation in plant availability dictated group movement, and plants comprised the majority of the diet (60–70 percent). Often family groups would travel together to gather piñon nuts in the uplands, which the women would then process and cache (Knack and Stewart 1999). Deer were hunted by men in the summer and fall, and movements were somewhat dictated by game availability, but Southern Paiute men primarily hunted and trapped small game, especially rabbits. This activity could be done at any of the seasonal camps.

Although the Northern Paiute occupied a different setting than the southern groups and thus exploited different resources, their seasonal movements were predicated on a gendered division of labor as well. The Northern Paiute maintained residential bases in the marshes where women gathered cattails and bulrush but moved from there to exploit other resources including desert seed plants, piñon, and roots in the uplands. Men hunted waterfowl and fished in the marshes and hunted deer and bighorn sheep in the surrounding uplands, primarily during the fall. Family groups would move to the uplands in the fall where women would gather piñon and where antelope and jackrabbit were hunted communally, with all members of the group participating (Fowler 1992).

Western Shoshone groups had a similar division of labor and followed well-defined seasonal rounds focused on plant resources, including piñon in the north and mesquite in the south (Steward 1938, 1941). These staple plants were gathered and processed by women. Thomas et al. (1986:267) note that "game contributed far fewer calories than plant procurement," but a variety of game was taken, including bighorn sheep and antelope. Bighorn sheep were hunted in the fall and winter by males who used rock walls and hunting blinds for cover in upland side canyons. Antelope were hunted in communal drives with both men and women participating.

These ethnographies reveal a flexible but important role of the division of labor in insuring that subsistence pursuits were successful and efficient. These patterns can be used to examine prehistoric cultural activities to determine if similar practices existed in the past. In order to do this, it is important to look at the material culture that would be associated with these gendered activities.

Women's plant gathering and processing activities are primarily done with perishable materials and, as noted above, gathering activities are especially difficult to see archaeologically as they involved the use of digging sticks, wooden seed beaters, baskets, and hide bags. Even when these were preserved, they would likely be returned to base camps rather than left at procurement locations. Processing technology, such as ground stone, is more likely to be preserved in the archaeological record and would generally be left at the place of use. Plant processing features, such as roasting pits and parching areas, are also likely to remain. As I noted in my study of the adoption of agriculture in the Southwest (Roth 2006), in all of the ethnographies of arid land hunter-gatherers and farmers, these kinds of processing features signified the activities and work sites of women. In the Great Basin ethnographies, men's hunting activities were also associated with specific technologies, including the bow and arrow, a variety of snares and traps, and in some cases, hunting blinds. While bows and arrows would most often be taken back to base camps unless they broke during use, snares, traps, and hunting blinds would generally mark hunting localities.

These data can be used to engender activities practiced by prehistoric foragers along Soda Playa and to examine how these gendered activities were patterned across the landscape. In the following section, data from a sample survey and test excavations along Soda Playa are used to examine how gender influenced prehistoric land use.

Gender and Land Use along Soda Playa

The majority of Late Prehistoric sites along Soda Playa have been found in dunes along the western shore, along the eastern flanks of the Soda Mountains, and in the Mojave River Wash area (Thomas 2011; Figure 7.2). In addition to these sites, artifact scatters dating to this period have been found dispersed throughout the area and likely represent short-term procurement activities. Camp sites contain diverse artifact assemblages with projectile points, other stone tools, ground stone, ceramics, and hearth and roasting pit features. Based on the ethno-graphic models and cross-cultural research on foragers, these sites represent family camps comprised of men, women, and children. All of the camp sites are located in mesquite-covered dunes and/or near springs, supporting previous work indicating that resource abundance was a critical factor for choosing site locations. Their presence near plant resources but somewhat distant from bighorn sheep localities indicate that women's gathering activities apparently served as the primary anchor for camp site locations while men's hunting activities required greater mobility away from the base camps. This would have been the strategy used during the late spring, late summer, and early fall, when mesquite and seasonal grasses were available and game was also plentiful.

In addition to these family camps, specialized seasonally-used procurement and processing sites are present across the landscape. These include quarry sites, lithic reduction sites, and hunting camps located in the foothills of the Soda Mountains and gathering camps located in the mesquite-covered dunes on the eastern and western shores of Soda Playa. Artifact assemblages and features recovered from these sites point to specialized procurement activities, and they appear to have been gender-specific. The quarry, lithic reduction, and hunting sites all contain evidence of predominantly male activities, represented by projectile points, occasional hunting blinds, and lithic reduction materials. The hunting blinds are similar to those used by Shoshone men to hunt bighorn sheep. Specialized gathering sites contain ground stone, stone tools associated with plant processing, and features associated with plant processing, indicative of their predominant association with women's activities. These sites were most likely occupied during periods when base camps were located away from Soda Playa and during periods of drought when more reliable water sources were located along the Mojave River.

Excavations at two sites along Soda Playa provide additional data on the kinds of gendered activities taking place at these specialized seasonal procurement sites. Test excavations and archival research at Soda Springs Rockshelter (Figure 7.3), located on the southwest shore of Soda Playa next to Soda Springs (a reliable water source), indicate that this shelter was used from the Middle Archaic through the Late Prehistoric period (Schroth 1982; Roth and Warren 2008, 2009). The recovered artifact assemblage and prevalence of large mammal remains reveal a focus on hunting, primarily bighorn sheep, which were hunted in the adjacent foothills and processed at the site. Although the deposits were not well stratified, it appears that the exploitation of smaller game such as jack rabbits, cottontail rabbits, desert tortoises, and perhaps waterfowl increased over time. The lithic assemblage was dominated by projectile points, bifaces, retouched flakes and debitage. The projectile point styles date from the Middle Archaic through the Late Prehistoric period. Three hearths were excavated outside the shelter (by archaeologists from the University of California, Fullerton in 1982). These were stratigraphically distinct and they, too, document the repeated use of the site from the Archaic through the Ceramic periods (Schroth 1982). The quantity and diversity of faunal remains and the lithic assemblage

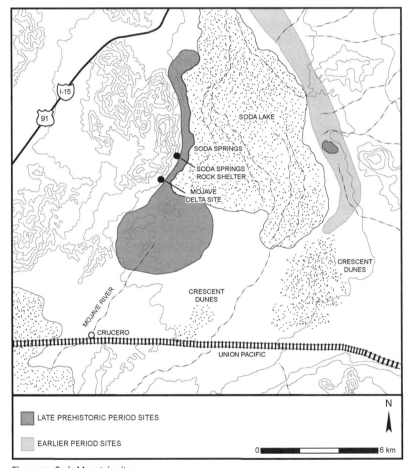

Figure 7.2. Soda Mountain sites.

Figure 7.3. Soda Springs rockshelter.

indicate that this was a specialized hunting camp used over a very long period of time, suggesting long-term stability in land use practices.

The Mojave Delta Site is located on dunes south of Soda Springs and west of the point where the Mojave River entered Soda Playa (Figure 7.2; Roth and Thomas 2011). Surface collections and test excavations indicate that the site was occupied primarily during the Late Prehistoric period. The recovered artifact assemblage consisted primarily of ground stone and ceramics; one chopper and four small biface fragments were the only flaked stone tools recovered.

Ground stone dominated the recovered assemblage, with six metates, 15 metate fragments, five manos, and three mano fragments recorded during fieldwork. The ground stone was found associated with two excavated hearths and six clusters of fire-cracked rock (probably deflated hearths). Portions of a small Desert Topoc Buff jar that was probably used for water storage were found associated with one hearth. The features and artifact assemblage indicate a focus on plant-processing activities, but unfortunately flotation samples from the excavated hearths did not yield anything but wood charcoal. Spring annuals are abundant in the dunes where this site is located, so it is likely that they were the focus of the occupation, with women moving seasonally to exploit them, likely from base camps located away from Soda Playa.

The patterning of the camps sites and specialized procurement sites coupled with data from excavations at Soda Springs Rockshelter and the Mojave Delta Site indicate that land use along Soda Playa was conditioned by both seasonal resource availability and the gendered division of labor. Reliable water sources were clearly the primary consideration in any land use decisions. However, beyond that, understanding land use in this region can be strengthened by examining the ways that gendered land use was patterned. It appears that, much like what has been documented in ethnographic groups in the Great Basin and other arid environments, women's gathering activities influenced site locations and movement (see also Guenther 1991).

The presence of seasonally occupied camp sites in mesquite-anchored dunes adjacent to reliable water sources indicates that family camps were located to take advantage of critical plant resources (e.g., mesquite) while other gender-specific tasks such as hunting could be done from these as anchor points. This strategy also explains the distribution of small specialized hunting camps and lithic quarry and reduction sites in the Soda Mountain foothills adjacent to these camps, where men could have gone on short-term hunting and lithic procurement forays.

Alternate land use strategies occurred during seasons (mid-summer, late fall/winter, early spring) or periods of drought when it was not a viable strategy to maintain camps in this portion of the Mojave Sink. Both the Mojave Delta Site and Soda Springs Rockshelter represent specialized use by mobile groups who maintained camps elsewhere. The available data indicate that these were predominantly the domains of different genders. The Mojave Delta Site was repeatedly reoccupied for plant procurement, likely spring annuals, but each individual occupation was short-term. It appears that the women were there briefly and then moved to other specialized gathering camps or returned to camp sites located in areas away from Soda Playa. Previous work at the Oro Grande site (Rector et al. 1983) along the Mojave River has documented a large camp site with evidence for generalized hunting and gathering activities occupied from A.D. 800–1300. Other camp sites like this were present along the river and these may have served as base camps for families from which specialized hunting and gathering activities occurred. It is also likely that groups moved into upland settings during certain times of the year to exploit other critical resources, such as agave. Soda Springs Rockshelter appears to have been a specialized hunting camp, and it could have been occupied primarily during the fall when big horn sheep would have been available and at the peak of their desirability in terms of fat reserves. The presence of water fowl in the faunal assemblage supports this, as they may have been hunted during fall migration. Again, it is likely that groups were maintaining camp sites outside this portion of the Mojave Sink, and male foragers may have returned to the camps after hunting in the Soda Mountains and adjacent playa shores.

Discussion

Previous models of prehistoric forager adaptations in the Mojave Desert have largely focused on environmental adaptations and the role of water sources and big game in adaptive strategies. This is not surprising given the harsh and arid setting as clearly the environment put significant constraints on foraging behavior. However, beyond simply examining the distribution of sites within the landscape, it is possible to use archaeological data to address the ways that gendered activities influenced land use. This is particularly useful in this setting because the division of labor structured many of the activities that occurred, and thus, it is possible to investigate how gendered activities were patterned to gain a better understanding of foraging behavior.

Survey and excavation data from Soda Playa indicate that engendered use of the landscape varied seasonally, with multi-gender family camps present in the late spring, late summer, and early fall to take advantage of seasonally abundant plant resources and reliable water sources. This changed during other seasons and during dry periods as groups moved their base camps elsewhere, perhaps to the nearby Cronese Basin, which contained a more reliable water source and denser resources during parts of the Late Holocene (Drover 1979) and also along the Mojave River where again resources were more reliable and abundant. This movement changed the way that the landscape along Soda Playa was used, resulting in patterned gendered behavior, with male hunting and lithic procurement camps present in the foothills and women's gathering camps present in dunes along the shoreline. By the end of the Late Prehistoric period, ca. A.D. 1500, the region had become so arid that it was no longer inhabited; ethnohistoric accounts indicate that other areas, such as the Mojave River, continued to be occupied, but Soda Playa was abandoned until later in the historic period.

Another possibility suggested by these data, although less clearly visible in the archaeological record as the gendered activities, is the potential that these sites also represent a different way of looking at the landscape, that there was a "gendered gaze" that influenced where sites were located and how they were used (Claassen, Introduction). Lithic procurement and hunting sites tied to male activities are usually located in upland settings away from the lake shores. When males looked across Soda Playa, it is likely that their gaze focused on the gravel-covered slopes, scanning for outcrops and herds of big horn sheep (Figure 7.4). By climbing these hillsides, they would have learned the best habitats for both small and large game and followed the trails created by re-peated game movements. This gaze may have periodically moved to the sky during fall when migratory waterfowl came through the area. The

Figure 7.4. Big horn sheep.

distribution of special-use male activity sites suggests that this upland and upward view of the landscape shaped how they perceived what was going on in the Mojave Sink and how they responded to the environmental challenges. It is likely that some of these hunting sites were used as training grounds for young boys and thus had significance beyond simply hunting. These sites also played an important role in reinforcing cultural values, including gender roles.

Unfortunately, few ethnographic data are available on the use of features like caves in this area. An exception is Newberry Cave, located in the Newberry Mountains to the east of the Mojave Sink, which contained many ritual items that show a focus on hunting rituals dating from 1100–2100 BC (Davis and Smith 1981). This ritual cave was most likely the domain of male hunters. If this was a pattern throughout the Mojave Desert, then it is possible that Soda Springs Rockshelter represents not only a gender-specific site but the integration of male activity (hunting) with male ritual (significance of caves and rock shelters). No studies of the distribution of these kinds of features and activity performance have been done, but this is clearly something that would be important for future research.

In contrast, the female gendered gaze would have focused on dunes, lake shores, river terraces, and springs. These lower elevation settings provided the lifeblood, water. Thus, when women looked at Soda Playa, they had a different perspective than males. As with the initiation of young males, young females likely went regularly with their mothers to gather, thus reinforcing their focus on what was taught to be important to them—water and plants. Rock art located at key points in these lowland settings, especially adjacent to springs and along trails leading to springs, may have been important components of this gendered gaze, marking important areas on the landscape. Again, no studies have been conducted linking the rock art to specific behaviors so this is another important avenue for future work.

Although this concept of a gendered gaze is difficult to fully operationalize, it may help to explain the overall landscape focus documented in the archaeological record, especially in the gender-specific distribution of sites. This gendered gaze was likely influential enough that it is possible to use it as a starting point to look at where sites will be located and what kinds of material culture can be expected from them. Given the general similarities of land use between the Fort Irwin area and the Mojave Sink, it is likely that this gendered gaze was characteristic of adjacent valleys as well and would have influenced group movements and activities as they entered new environments. The different way that the landscape was viewed would have been the first step in dividing up activities as groups moved to new areas; the gendered gaze was likely one of the major ways that groups ensured that they could successfully adapt to these settings.

Conclusions

Our understanding of the way that the landscape was used can be substantially enhanced by moving beyond mere site distributions to examine the kinds of activities that took place and the people who performed these activities. These data also illustrate the value of connecting ethnographic and archaeological data as they provide new ways of looking at the archaeological record. Future studies of sites in other portions of the Mojave Desert and Great Basin may benefit from taking this engendered approach, as the wealth of ethnographic and ethnohistoric data document that gender was a crucial aspect of forager behavior. It should come as no surprise to us that this extended well back into prehistory; something that researchers can and should investigate with future work in the area.

REFERENCES CITED

Allen, Mark
2011   Of Earth and Stone: Landscape Archaeology in the Mojave Desert. *California Archaeology* 3:11–30.
Anschuetz, Kurt F., Richard H. Wilshusen, and Cherie L. Scheick
2001   An Archaeology of Landscapes: Perspectives and Directions. *Journal of Archaeological Research* 9:157–208.
Arend, Tiffany A., and Barbara J. Roth
[2016]   Landscapes and Land Use along Soda Playa in the Mojave Desert. *California Archaeology*, forthcoming.
Barton, C. Michael, Joan Bernabell, J. Emili Aura, Oreto Garcia, Steven Schmich, and Luis Molina
2004   Long-term Socioecology and Contingent Landscapes. *Journal of Archaeological Method and Theory* 11:253–295.
Basgall, Mark E.
1993   *The Archaeology of Nelson Basin and Adjacent Areas, Fort Irwin, San Bernardino County, California.* Report on file, U.S. Army Corps of Engineers, Los Angeles.
2000   The Structure of Archaeological Landscapes in the North-Central Mojave Desert. *Archaeological Passages: A Volume in Honor of Claude Nelson Warren*, Joan S. Schneider, Robert M. Yohe II, and Jill K. Gardner, editors. Western Center for Archaeology & Paleontology Publications in Archaeology, No. 1, 123–138.

Basgall, Mark E., and Matthew C. Hall

1992   Fort Irwin Archaeology: Emerging Perspectives on Mojave Desert Prehistory. *Society for California Archaeology Newsletter* 26:1–7.

Basgall, Mark E., Matthew C. Hall, and William R. Hildebrandt

1988   *The Late Holocene Archaeology of the Drinkwater Basin, Fort Irwin, San Bernardino County, California.* Reported submitted to the U.S. Army Corps of Engineers, Los Angeles District.

Bender, Barbara (editor)

1993   *Landscape, Politics, and Perspective.* Berg, Providence, RI.

Byrd, Brian F.

1998   *Springs and Lakes in a Desert Landscape: Archaeological and Paleoenvironmental Investigations in the Silurian Valley and Adjacent Areas of Southeastern California,* Vol. 1. Report on file, San Bernardino County Museum Archaeological Information Center, Redlands, CA.

Cameron, Constance

1984   *The West Pond Report: Archaeological Investigations at SBR-363C, Soda Springs (Zzyzx), California.* Occasional Papers of the Archaeological Research Facility, California State University, Fullerton.

Campbell, Elizabeth W.

1936   Archaeological Problems in the Southern California Deserts. *American Antiquity* 1:295–300.

Campbell, Elizabeth W., William H. Campbell, Ernst Antevs, Charles Amsden, Joseph A. Barbieri, and Francis D. Bode

1937   *The Archaeology of Pleistocene Lake Mohave: A Symposium.* Southwest Museum Papers No. 11, Southwest Museum, Los Angeles, CA.

Crumley, Carole, and William H. Marquardt

1990   Landscape: A Unifying Concept in Regional Analysis. In *Interpreting Space: GIS and Archaeology,* K. M. Allen, S. W. Green, and E. B. W. Zubrow, editors, pp. 73–79. Taylor and Francis, London.

Davis, C. Alan, and Gerald A. Smith

1981   *Newberry Cave.* San Bernardino County Museum Association, Redlands, CA.

Davis, Emma Lou

1975   The "Exposed Archaeology" of China Lake, California. *American Antiquity* 40:39–53.

1978   *The Ancient Californians: Rancholabrean Hunters of the Mojave Lakes Country.* Natural History Museum of Los Angeles County Science Series No. 29, Natural History Museum of Los Angeles.

Drover, Christopher E.

1979   The Late Prehistoric Human Ecology of the Northern Mojave Sink, San Bernardino County, California. Doctoral dissertation, Department of Anthropology, University of California, Riverside. University Microfilms International, Ann Arbor, MI.

Earle, David D.

2005   The Mojave River and the Central Mojave Desert: Native Settlement, Travel, and Exchange in the Eighteenth and Nineteenth Centuries. *Journal of California and Great Basin Anthropology* 25:1–38.

Fowler, Catherine S.

1986   Subsistence. In *Handbook of North American Indians, Vol. 11, Great Basin*, Warren L. D'Azevedo, editor, pp. 64–97. Smithsonian Institution, Washington DC.

1992   *In the Shadow of Fox Peak: An Ethnography of the Cattail-Eater Northern Paiute People of Stillwater Marsh*. Cultural Resource Series No. 5, Fish and Wildlife Service, Stillwater National Wildlife Refuge, Fallon, NV.

Gardner, Jill K.

2006   The Potential Impact of the Medieval Climatic Anomaly on Human Populations in the Western Mojave Desert. Doctoral dissertation, Department of Anthropology, University of Nevada Las Vegas, Las Vegas.

Guenther, Todd R.

1991   The Horse Creek Site: Some Evidence for Gender Roles in a Transitional Early to Middle Plains Archaic Base Camp. *Plains Anthropologist* 36: 9–23.

Jenkins, Dennis L.

1985   *Rogers Ridge (4-SBr-5250): A Fossil Spring Site of the Lake Mohave and Pinto Periods—Phase 2 Test Excavations and Site Evaluation*. Fort Irwin Archaeology Project Research Report No. 18. Report on file, National Park Service, San Francisco. Reprinted and published by Coyote Press, Salina, CA.

1986   *Flood, Sweat, and Spears in the Valley of Death: Site Survey and Evaluation in Tiefort Basin, Fort Irwin, California*. Fort Irwin Archaeology Project Research Report No. 17. Report on file, National Park Service, San Francisco. Reprinted and published by Coyote Press, Salina, CA.

Jenkins, Dennis L., Claude N. Warren, and T. Wheeler

1984   Test Excavation and Data Recovery at the Awl Site, SBr-4562: A Pinto Site at Fort Irwin, San Bernardino County, California. Report on file, Interagency Archaeological Services Division, National Park Service, San Francisco.

Jones, Terry L., Gary M. Brown, L. Mark Raab, Janet L. McVikar, W. Geoffrey Spaulding, Douglas J. Kennett, Andrew York, and Phillip L. Walker

1999   Environmental Imperatives Reconsidered: Demographic Crises in Western North American during the Medieval Climatic Anomaly. *Current Anthropology* 40:137–170.

Kelly, Isabel T., and Catherine S. Fowler

1986   Southern Paiute. In *Handbook of North American Indians, Vol. 11, Great Basin*, W. L. A'Azevedo, editor, pp. 368–379. Smithsonian Institution, Washington, DC.

Kelly, Michael S., and Claude N. Warren

1984   An Evaluation of 22 Selected Sites in No Name West Basin, Fort Irwin, San Bernardino County, California. Fort Irwin Archaeology Project Research Report No. 10. Report on file, National Park Service, San Francisco. Reprinted and published by Coyote Press, Salina, CA.

Knack, Martha C.

1995   The Dynamics of Southern Paiute Women's Roles. In *Women and Power in Native North America*, L. F. Klein and L. A. Ackerman, editors, pp. 146–158. University of Oklahoma Press, Norman.

Knack, Martha C., and Omer C. Stewart

1999   *As Long as the River Shall Run: An Ethnohistory of Pyramid Lake Indian Reservation.* University of Nevada Press, Reno.

McGuire, Kelly R., and Matthew C. Hall

1988   *The Archaeology of Tiefort Basin, Fort Irwin, San Bernardino County, California.* Report on file, U.S. Army Corps of Engineers, Los Angeles.

Murdock, George P., and Caterina A. Provost

1973   Factors in the Division of Labor by Sex: A Cross-Cultural Analysis. *Ethnology* 12:203–225.

Rector, Carol H., James D. Swenson, and Philip J. Wilke

1983   *Archaeological Studies at Oro Grande Mojave Desert, California.* San Bernardino County Museum Association, Redlands, CA.

Robinson, David W., Jennifer E. Perry, and Gale Grasse-Sprague

2011   Landscape Archaeology in Southern and South-central California. *California Archaeology* 3:5–10.

Rogers, Malcolm Jennings

1929   *Report of an Archaeological Reconnaissance in the Mohave Sink Region.* The San Diego Museum of Man Archaeological Papers 1(1), San Diego.

1931   Report of Archaeological Investigations in the Mohave Desert Region during 1931. Bureau of American Ethnology, National Anthropology Archives, Catalog Number 2104, Washington DC.

Rossignol, Jacqueline, and LuAnn Wandsnider (editors)

1992   *Space, Time, and Archaeological Landscapes.* Plenum Press, New York.

Roth, Barbara J.

2006   The Role of Gender in the Adoption of Agriculture in the Southern Southwest. *Journal of Anthropological Research* 62:513–538.

Roth, Barbara J., and Tiffany Thomas

2011   Archaeological Investigations at CA-SBR-01989 on the Shore of Soda Playa near Zzyzx, California. Report submitted to the National Park Service, Mojave Desert Preserve, Barstow, CA.

Roth, Barbara J., and Claude Warren

2008   On the Shores of Pleistocene Lake Mojave: Excavations at the Soda Springs Rockshelter. In *Proceedings of the Second Three Corners Conference,* L. Perry and M. Slaughter, editors, pp. 211–226. Bureau of Reclamation Publication Series, Bureau of Reclamation, Boulder City, NV.

2009   Archaeological Investigations at Soda Springs Rockshelter (CA SBR 363), Zzyzx, California. Report submitted to National Park Service, Mojave National Preserve, Barstow, CA

Schneider, Joan S.

1988   Late Prehistoric Times in the Central Mojave Desert: Some Problems. *Pacific Coast Archaeological Society Quarterly* 24:30–44.

1989   *The Archaeology of the Afton Canyon Site.* San Bernardino County Museum Association, Redlands, CA.

Schroth, Adella

1982   Progress Report—1982 Season at the Soda Springs Rockshelter: CA-SBR-363B. Report on file, San Bernardino State Museum, San Bernardino, CA.

Steward, Julian

1938   *Basin-Plateau Aboriginal Sociopolitical Groups.* Bureau of American Ethnology Bulletin 120, Washington DC.

1941   *Culture Element Distributions, XIII: Nevada Shoshone.* University of California Anthropological Records 4(2):209–360, Berkeley.

Sutton, Mark Q.

1996   The Current Status of Archaeological Research in the Mojave Desert. *Journal of California and Great Basin Anthropology* 18:221–257.

Thomas, David H., Lorann S. A. Pendleton, and Stephen C. Cappannari

1986   Western Shoshone. In *Handbook of North American Indians, Vol. 11, Great Basin*, Warren L. D'Azevedo, editor, pp. 262–283. Smithsonian Institution, Washington DC.

Thomas, Tiffany A.

2011   A Landscape Approach to Late Prehistoric Settlement and Subsistence Patterns in the Mojave Sink. Master's thesis, Department of Anthropology, University of Nevada Las Vegas, Las Vegas.

Wandsnider, Luann

1998   Regional Scale Processes and Archaeological Landscape Units. In *Unit Issues in Archaeology: Measuring Time, Space, and Material*, A. F. Ramenofsky and A. Steffen, editors, pp. 87–102. University of Utah Press, Salt Lake City.

Warren, Claude N.

1984   The Desert Region. In *California Archaeology*, Michael Moratto, editor, pp. 339–430. Academic Press, Orlando.

1991   *Archaeological Investigations at Nelson Wash, Fort Irwin, California.* Fort Irwin Archaeology Project Research Report No. 23. Report on file, National Park Service, San Francisco. Reprinted and published by Coyote Press, Salina, CA.

2010   *Holocene Lakes and Prehistory in the Mojave Desert.* Unpublished manuscript in possession of the author.

Warren, Claude N., and John Decosta

1964   Dating Lake Mohave Beaches and Artifacts. *American Antiquity* 30:206–209.

Warren, Claude N. and H. T. Ore

1978   The Approach and Process of Dating Lake Mohave Artifacts. *Journal of California Anthropology* 5:179–187.

Wells, Stephen G., Roger Y. Anderson, Leslie D. McFadden, William J. Brown, Yehouda Enzel, and Jean-Luc Miossec

1989   *Late Quaternary Paleohydrology of the Eastern Mojave River Drainage, Southern California: Quantitative Assessment of the late Quaternary Hydrologic Cycle in Large Arid Watersheds.* Technical Report on file, New Mexico Water Resources Institute, Las Cruces, NM.

Wells, Stephen G., Kirk C. Anderson, and Roger Kriedberg

1998   Late Quaternary Geology and Geomorphology of the Lower Mojave River/Silurian Valley System and Southern Death Valley Area, Southeastern California. In *Springs and Lakes in a Desert Landscape: Archaeological and Paleoenvironmental Investigations in the Silurian Valley and Adjacent*

Areas of Southeastern California, Brian F. Byrd, editor, pp. 137–259. ASM Affiliates, Inc. Report on file, U.S. Army Corps of Engineers, San Diego, CA.

Whittlesey, Stepahnie M.

1997   Archaeological Landscapes: A Methodological and Theoretical Discussion. In *Vanishing River, Landscapes and Lives of the Lower Verde Valley*, Stephanie M. Whittlesey, Richard Ciolek-Torrello, and Jeffrey H. Altschul, editors, pp. 17–28. SRI Press, Tucson, AZ.

Zendeño, Maria Nieves

1997   Landscapes, Land Use, and the History of Territory Formation: An Example from the Puebloan Southwest. *Journal of Archaeological Method and Theory* 4:67–103.

8

PHYSICAL VERSUS SOCIAL SETTINGS
*Two Case Studies—Kwakwaka'wakw,
Northwest Coast, and the Hawai'ian Islands—
of Gender and Landscape Constructions*

Jessica Joyce Christie

I will investigate how the Kwakwaka'wakw/Kwakiutl[1] people on the Pacific Northwest Coast and the Hawai'ian islanders have constructed social space and their natural settings through the lens of gender. I will begin by clarifying my methodology and how I approach concepts of space, landscape, and gender. The following sections will sketch out the geographical, climatic, and biological settings of the Northwest Coast and then of Hawai'i as well as traditional forms of social organization. I will explore, compare, and question the multi-faceted relations, including gender, drawn in indigenous storyscapes between people and their natural environment. This chapter is developed from information coming from storyscapes obtained through ethnography since archaeological data from the regions covered are sparse.[2]

Some Clarifications about "Ground Rules"

To begin with, I explain how I address such deceptively common terms as landscape, place, space, and gender. During the past decades, landscape studies has emerged as an immensely popular and contested field (see Ashmore and Knapp 1999; Smith 2003; Christie 2009; Gulliford 2000; Janowski and Ingold 2012; Moore 2005; and Tilley 1994 as selected examples). One of the major insights to come out of these discussions has been that landscape and space are fundamentally socially constructed and are no longer seen as universal, absolute, or timeless. The word *landscape* is derived from the field of painting and implies that we are looking at a picture, a painted scene of nature that was by definition reconfigured by an artist. Denis Cosgrove and Stephen Daniels (1988:1) define a landscape as "a cultural image, a pictorial way of representing, structuring or symbolis[z]ing surroundings." They confirm the multiplicity of meanings for landscape in postmodern thinking from the standpoint of human geography (Cosgrove and Daniels 1988:7–8).

Christopher Tilley (1994:7–34) and others have explored the notion of space further and have juxtaposed it to "place": whereas "space" denotes the larger and more abstract spatial containment, "place" is the concrete, humanly defined locale. Henri Lefebvre's rigorous study of the *Production of Space* (1991) adds an economic dimension by further analyzing activities of production.[3] I have found Adam T. Smith's (2003:69–77) model of relational space, which was influenced by Lefebvre's work, more useful. After critiquing absolute and subjective notions of space, Smith (2003:30–77) replaces them with a relational ontology which emphasizes that space is only established when subjects and objects exist and relate to each other. Instead of theorizing the essential nature of space, Smith (2003:69) calls for investigating the social, cultural, and political practices that create, validate, or overturn particular spatial configurations. He follows Lefebvre (1991:38–46) in adopting a three-dimensional framework for describing spatial practices based upon the intersection of experience, perception, and imagination. Spatial experience describes material practices, the movement of bodies and things through physical space and the technologies of its construction. Spatial perception is concerned with the sensual interaction between actors and physical spaces and thus moves into the mental realm as it is shaped by impressions of the material world. Spatial imagination leads beyond physical form and constitutes analytic discourses about spaces that may be pictorially represented or described in storyscapes (Smith 2003:73–75). I will apply such a model of relational networks between human actors and living beings of the natural world to explore the cultural construction of landscapes and associated gender roles in oral narratives of Kwakwaka'wakw society in the Pacific Northwest and then of Hawai'i.

Gender is distinguished from sex in that the latter is biological and the former is social. Gender is not about the physical distinctions of the human anatomy that define sex, but it is socially performed and assigned as a set of roles and behaviors in different societies (Kearney

2014; Nelson 1997:15–16). It follows that archaeologists often encounter great difficulties in reconstructing gendered activities from material remains. Selected storyscapes in ethnography, on the other hand, can be rich sources of male and female referents reflecting the gendered social perceptions of those who narrated them. Here I will use gender as one tactic in the processes of spatial perception and spatial imagination of Smith's model, not advocating a specifically male or female view. This chapter will lead to a critical comparative analysis of gender as reflected in the Pacific-based settings of the two regions and socially constructed by two versions of chiefly societies.

The Natural Setting of the Northwest Coast

The cultural region of the Northwest Coast extends from Oregon northward along the Pacific shoreline all the way into Alaska (Figure 8.1). The land is oriented toward the west and sunset, which has framed Northwest Coast cosmology. The region covers an immense distance from approximately N 42°16' in southern Oregon to N 61°33' in northern Alaska. As one moves north, the daily cycle of daytime light and nighttime darkness changes toward periods of twenty-four hours of summer sunlight and twenty-four hours of winter darkness in the Arctic. For example, in Haida Gwaii night falls around 4:30 p.m. during the wintertime and daylight does not dawn until 8:30 a.m. Such extreme cycles have impacted people's worldview as well as physical and psychological health. Indigenous peoples concentrated their efforts on subsistence activities during the summer and dedicated the winter months to ceremonial cycles.

The land of the Northwest Coast presents a most beautiful tapestry of land and water (Figure 8.2): as the traveler moves north from Oregon, the coastline opens up into innumerable inlets and fjords and breaks into multitudes of larger and smaller islands. The climate is cool and moist with annual precipitation levels oscillating between 60 to over 100 cm depending on location. Rainfall originates in cloud cover, and along the Northwest Coast the number of clear days with full sunshine is limited. On most days, the sky is concealed from human eyes by layers of fog and mist soaked in cool fertile moisture. This type of climate and latitude nurture a lush and dense forest vegetation providing habitat for abundant wildlife and rich flora.

Following general archaeological assessments, indigenous people have populated the Northwest Coast ever since the first Asians crossed the Bering Strait and entered the American continent more than 10,000 years ago (see, for instance, Berlo and Phillips 1998:175–177). They built their villages on the beaches facing the ocean and lived in traditional wooden plank houses sectioned into individual family units (Nabakov and Eaton 1989:227–285). Canoes dotted the shoreline. The main food sources of Northwest Coast peoples have come from the sea; they were skilled whalers and fishermen and put to use all raw materials provided by the ocean: fish oils, shells for decoration, fish bones fashioned into tools, and even the intestines of certain sea mammals were turned into waterproof clothing in the far north. In the summer months, many families moved inland, traveling upriver in their canoes and taking house planks with them to construct temporary shelters. In the upland forest environment, they could supplement their diet with hunting and collecting berries and nuts. When the temperatures began to fall and the days grew shorter, they returned to their beachfront villages and began to prepare for the ritual season. Agriculture was never a major source of subsistence before the European invasion.

The center of Kwakwaka'wakw territory is Queen Charlotte Strait on the central coast of British Columbia, Canada. Groups have resided in northern Vancouver Island, the many small islands between it and the mainland, as well as further inland. Contact was first made between

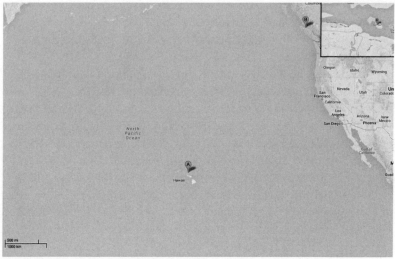

Figure 8.1. Map showing the location of the Northwest Coast (B) in relation to the Hawai'ian Islands (A). From Google Earth.

Figure 8.2 Landscape of the Northwest Coast. Photo by Brian Garrett.

the Kwakwaka'wakw and Europeans in 1786 when the British trader James Strange encountered indigenous people while traveling in Queen Charlotte Strait. After the 1780s, contact rapidly increased. The Hudson's Bay Company became an important intermediary in Native–white interactions after it established trading posts throughout the region of present British Columbia. Native peoples were eager to visit these posts in order to trade goods. In 1849, the Hudson's Bay Company set up a trading post in Kwakwaka'wakw territory on Beaver Harbour, which grew into the newly created village of Fort Rupert. Several high-ranking tribes moved to Fort Rupert, and it functioned as the center of commercial and ceremonial activities for the rest of the nineteenth century. Today Fort Rupert is a quiet community with mixed Native and white populations and a conspicuous ceremonial big house.

Alert Bay, the other principal Kwakwaka'wakw community situated on Cormorant Island at the end of Queen Charlotte Strait and a 30-minute ferry ride from Port McNeill, was established in 1870 when a cannery opened there. Alert Bay became better known than Fort Rupert after 1900 when the governmental Kwawkewlth Agency and a residential school located in the village and has continued to be more prominent

Figure 8.3 Alert Bay, British Columbia, harbor. Photo by Brian Garrett.

(Codere 1990:361–363). My own contacts and field observations are in Alert Bay (Figure 8.3).

Kwakwaka'wakw Social Organization

Most of the published information about traditional Kwakwaka'wakw social organization was recorded by Franz Boas in the late nineteenth century.[4] Boas participated in numerous expeditions to various indigenous communities in the Pacific Northwest connected with stays over multiple months. His objective was to collect and publish Native languages, narratives, and songs with the help of local assistants. Kwakwaka'wakw culture became a focus of his fieldwork, and he worked with multiple consultants in Fort Rupert as well as in Alert Bay. From a critical contemporary perspective, Boas' extensive documentative and interpretative work has not been adequately historicized especially in regards to gender (Wickwire 2001). We will return to this point later in this chapter. The following presentation of Kwakwaka'wakw social organization and ceremonial system is based upon Boas' recordings and the ways these have been paraphrased and cited by succeeding writers (Suttles 1990). These historical sources are complemented by my own field observations and contacts with Kwakwaka'wakw friends made since the 1990s.

Today the Kwakwaka'wakw, that is the Kwak'wala speaking people, are divided into seventeen tribes (www.umista.org). The most basic social group within each tribe is the "*numaym*" (Suttles 1991:86; Codere 1990:359, 366).[5] According to Lévi-Strauss (1982), the numaym was a type of "house" organization similar to the aristocratic houses of York or Lancaster in medieval English society. It was a social entity whose members could own more than one plank house and several seasonal sites where they held rights to harvest resources. Most importantly in the context of this chapter, each numaym claimed its own tradition of origin identifying its first ancestor who established rights to resource sites, hereditary names, and ceremonial privileges. The numaym was subdivided into a head chief, lesser chiefs, and commoners, including all members of their families. The position and associated authority of the head chief was validated by being publicly recognized as the direct descendant of the founding ancestor and the recipient of his powers. Numaym organization was somewhat open in the sense that families with other origins might be included (Boas [1935] in Suttles 1991:86) following shifting population numbers over time.

Chiefs were and continue to be the primary agents to build relational networks between social groups, with the natural world, and with outsiders. Looking through the lens of gender, the position of chief was transmitted from father to the oldest child, in theory independently from whether it was a son or daughter. However, in the historical records chiefs are usually listed as male. Mothers could assume temporary chiefly authority for underage sons. Chiefs also functioned as the mediators or more specifically were permeable membranes to the natural world. Such a relation with the beings of nature is grounded in the fact that the very status of a chief was derived from the founding ancestor of the numaym and that these ancestors were mythical beings who could transform and freely traverse the human, animal, and spiritual worlds (see below). In this manner, social status and the living landscape were inextricably intertwined and each constructed the other. This issue is paramount to gender analysis: men as chiefs could lay ancestral claims to territories and thus established personal relations with land on a level that traditional social organization did not allow for females. Numayms were not static entities, but chiefs constantly attempted to add new resource sites as well as new ceremonial names and privileges to their control. Such privileges were traced back to mythic times. All places in the natural environment as well as names, songs, narratives, and dances were personified by ancestral mythic beings who had to be approached and performed following a socially prescribed protocol of relations.

The most common way of opening relations with other social groups and acquiring new ceremonial property and privileges was the marriage system (Codere 1990:367–368). In Kwakwaka'wakw society, marriage was and is not only the way to build a new nuclear family but marriages have been the primary means through which ceremonial names and privileges are transmitted. In historical documents, individuals often carry a bewildering array of names (Suttles 1991:78–85): the transfer of names not only affects the bride and groom but may extend to their children from a prior marriage and to in-laws. Today most Kwakwaka'wakw individuals have at least one ceremonial name in addition to their English name.

For these reasons, marriages were often arranged. In the nineteenth century, such marriage arrangements were carefully negotiated alliances and had to proceed in socially prescribed steps that involved visits, exchanges of gifts, and name giving between the two families. The line of transmission was from father-in-law to son-in-law and thus women became vital links in traditional social organization: they were the vehicles through whom names could be transmitted and property circulated. To initiate a marriage, the groom had to give the woman's father a bride price. After she went to live with him, her father had to repay the bride price, which could occur in multiple payments and over time. Following repayment of the bride price, a marriage could be dissolved. The husband could pay another bride price for the same woman and marry her back or he could live single. The bride's father could then accept the marriage proposal of another groom. For both, men and women, having been married multiple times increased their ceremonial names and privileges and added to social status (Suttles 1991:94). This flow of ceremonial rights, privileges, and properties through the marriage system was an ongoing dynamic process of critical importance for the continuance of traditional Kwakwaka'wakw society. Indeed Boas (1966:55) makes the fascinating comment that if a man had no daughter and therefore no way of transmitting privileges through a real marriage, he might do so through a fictitious marriage. He could declare part of his body a woman and then marry this female part off to a fictitious son-in-law.

Through the transfer of ceremonial privileges, the marriage system forms the link between social organization and the ceremonial system. The concept of ceremonial privileges includes mythic and supernatural beings, material objects with their depictions, narratives, names, songs, and dances. It interweaves the human world with the land, the natural setting, animals, the sky, and the cosmos, and it is through this lens that we must approach the complex relational network between people and the landscape in traditional Kwakwaka'wakw society. Let us note that this is fundamentally different from all Western understanding of private property.

The Ceremonial System as Mediator between Social Organization and the Natural Setting

The gendered actors and agents in the ceremonial system and associated privileges are humans, animals, and mythic beings. In this section, I will paraphrase selected narratives to demonstrate the general animism of the homeland and then lead into the analysis of gender in the following section. In Northwest Coast cosmology, the universe consists of multiple realms including the sky world, the undersea or water world, the human, land, and forest world, and the spirit world. Here we can clearly see how in Smith's terms (2003:73–75) the physical experience of the natural environment on the Northwest Coast generates the cultural perception of the various realms. Spatial imagination constructs discourse about space that Kwakwaka'wakw people personify in a parade of gendered partly human, partly animal, and partly mythic beings. These agents communicate with the natural world, bind it to the social system, and in their colorful ritual performances and storyscapes explain the universe and people's place within it so that all makes sense. In the undersea and sky worlds, beings maintain the external appearance of a sea animal or bird but behave like humans and live in houses and villages.[6] Similar worldviews are documented throughout this book (see Claassen, Chapter 1).

It becomes clear that the boundaries between these worlds are blurred and permeable, and constant interactions between inhabitants of two or more domains take place (Wyatt 1999:7–10). Most important are the origin events narrated in creation storyscapes, which took place long ago at the beginning of time when the membrane separating the real and supernatural worlds was still fluid and had not yet hardened. Animals and mythic beings from the sky and undersea worlds crossed over to the middle realm of forests and engendered human beings. They became the founding ancestors of a numaym or tribe and then established the rank of its chiefs in Kwakwaka'wakw social hierarchy (Codere 1990:373).

Oral narratives of Transformer figures outline the transparent boundaries between the realm of the forest and the sky world. The following is a paraphrased Transformer story of the Nuu-chah-nulth people (not a Kwakwaka'wakw tribe) on the west coast of Vancouver Island.

> In the beginning, only birds and "other animals" lived on earth. They knew that one day they would be transformed into people and "real animals." When word arrived that two Transformers had descended from the sky and were coming, Son of Deer decided to resist them. He sharpened a pair of mussel shells to use as weapons to kill the Transformers. But the Transformers appeared in human form, tricked him, mounted the shells on his forehead as antlers, and turned him into a deer. Then the Transformers visited existing villages and transformed all living beings into animals and people. They gave people different languages and provided them with food and subsistence strategies. Chiefs still pray to the Transformers living in the sky to make them rich, as they had been taught (Boas 2002:245–246 [1895]).

This narrative vividly illustrates the complex transitions between animals, mythic beings with supernatural powers, and humans. The majority of actors and agents are male. We will see that women appear in many stories assuming roles as wives and daughters as a direct reflection of Northwest Coast social organization. The Transformer narrative then demonstrates how—in this case the Nuu-chah-nulth people—explained the existence and interrelationships of humans and animals on earth.

Oral narratives abound in place names that bind them to local landscapes. The homeland of the Nimpkish people (a Kwakwaka'wakw tribe) is the northeastern section of Vancouver Island. Many landscape features, for example, the Nimpkish River and Lake Nimpkish, carry their name. Narratives about numaym ancestors populate this homeland with protagonists who without effort transcend the membranes between the sky world and the world of people. For example, Tlalamin lived above the sun and the sky. He descended to the earth with his house and settled in a specific place above Lake Nimpkish. "The clouds were the roof of his house and above them was the sun. The sun's rays were his cape and he wore a big hat" (Boas 2002:325 [1895]). He moved to several places around Nimpkish Lake which can be identified. Later, Tlalamin returned to the sky and came back as the Kolos bird. His family owns the Kolos crest and uses the sun mask. He settled downstream from Lake Nimpkish, took on human form, and had a son. When the son grew up, Tlalamin sent him out to obtain supernatural powers. After the son had fasted and bathed, he encountered the spirit of the sea, Komokoa, who took him down to the bottom of the sea and hosted him in his house. The house of Komokoa is described as displaying seagulls, a Tsonokoa (female monster-like being, see below), carved men, sea-lions, and grizzly bears as crest figures. Later, Tlalamin wanted to dance but there was no one to sing for his dance. He invited a friend and then trapped many seagulls and transformed them into people. Tlalamin's numaym descends from them. Another son of Tlalamin constructed his house on an island in the Nimpkish River (Boas 2002:325–327 [1895]).[7]

These oral narratives about numaym ancestors (see also note 7) colorfully illustrate how the Nimpkish people have animated the physical experience of their natural surroundings constituted by mountains, forests, rivers, and lakes with ancestral protagonists who are at once human and yield superhuman powers and capabilities. On an imaginative level, they explain numaym histories, validate ceremonial privileges, and anchor traditional social organization in the natural landscape setting. Most of the toponyms recorded and mapped by Boas (1934) continue to be known in the twenty-first century and can be visited.

It is noteworthy that numaym ancestors are typically male. They empower the head chief with rights to numaym lands. Females are mentioned, for example, in the expanded Tla'lamin story, as daughters who are given away in marriage to establish new relations among numayms, exchange ceremonial privileges, and increase status. Thus it can be noted that in the social perception of Boas' consultants, men are more closely tied to specific territories and validate land rights (not to be confused with ownership in the Western sense). Females—at least traditionally—do not own land. In the model of Smith (2003:105–109), this finding forcefully projects the notion of authority-derived male power on the political landscape of the Northwest Coast.

A direct physical connection is constructed between the ancestor of another numaym and the Nimpkish River. This story relates that after the Flood, the former people were transformed into animals and stones. A sea monster rose from the ocean and brought a man to the mouth of the Nimpkish River. This man called himself NEmokyustalis (meaning "Having Come from the Earth as the Only One") and had a son. Father and son were visited by K'anigyilak. They tried to transform each other three times but always resumed their human shape. NEmokyustalis now took the name Guana'lalis. He agreed to be permanently transformed into a river by K'anigyilak. Guana'lalis became the Gua'ne River which is the Nimpkish River (Boas 2002:305–307 [1895]; Christie 2009).

The mythic genealogy continues with Guana'lalis's son Gyi'i who continued to live at the Nimpkish River. Gyi'i's son was Tsetlwalak-ame who had two wives with whom he lived at the mouth of the Nimpkish River. One wife was the daughter of the sun and the other the daughter of another numaym ancestor. One day the men went out to catch salmon and upon their return, the slaves decided to give more salmon to the daughter of the numaym ancestor than to the daughter of the sun. The latter became very upset and cried. Both women tried to transform each other into various animals but always regained human shape. Then the daughter of the sun who was pregnant decided to go home to her father. She went to the beach and walked on the water toward sunrise. As she came to Salmon River, she gave birth and threw the child into the sea near Seymour Narrows. Seymour Narrows, situated north of Campbell River and about 35 miles south from Salmon River, is still known for its dangerous rapids linked to this mytho-historical event (Boas 2002:307–311 [1895]).

In this oral narrative, the ancestor NEmokyustalis/Guana'lalis permanently transforms into the Nimpkish River along which his descendants continue to live. Today the Nimpkish River valley is sparsely populated and many Nimpkish people reside in Port McNeill and Alert Bay. Nevertheless, traditional individuals continue to perceive the Nimpkish region as their homeland. The ancestral narratives do not document Nimpkish history but are marvelous social constructions that interweave the land with Nimpkish society. The ancestors and other protagonists become mirror images of real humans with the difference that they harbor supernatural powers and relations with natural forces and the animal and sky worlds.

In the last story, the daughter of the sun is a woman of considerable authority. The actions the story attributes to her underscore that she does not feel jealousy against the other wife or motherly love for her baby. Her responses are guided by traditional and socially defined property rights and privileges as opposed to human feelings or biological instincts. Thus a rigidly defined social hierarchy, including the relationships between men and women, is pictured and overlaid on the natural surroundings to subject forces of nature to a human culturally defined order and thus tame them. Storied women largely assume their expected roles as intermediaries in the transfer of ceremonial rights and properties between families and numayms. Again, the daughter of the sun does not claim any specific land.

Thus the oral narratives illustrate the ceremonial system and construct it as a replica of human social organization. The animals Kwakwaka'wakw people encounter and experience in their daily routines are perceived as human-like agents who surpass human beings due to their magic powers to transform and to travel through space and time (see the Thunderbird and Wolf stories, footnote 6). These human-animal actors are imagined as living like people in parallel family and social structures. In this manner, the natural and social worlds are being integrated in order to make sense of human existence and to control and tame the world outside the villages. Thus the local landscape may be understood as a multi-relational cultural symbol. It follows that in this rational and very orderly system the construction of the female gender would roughly duplicate social norms. Surprisingly, there are mythic female characters who defy the rules of human society.

The Role of Gender in Kwakwaka'wakw Cultural and Natural Landscapes

While most females mentioned in the oral narratives by and large embrace their roles as daughters and wives in the vital transfer of ceremonial properties, there is a remarkable female character who does not fit social rules and lives in specific landscape zones: she is Tsono'koa. Tsono'koa/*Dzunuq'a* (both spellings) is described as a mythological being who is female, large, and stupid and has poor eye sight and hairy hands. The female members of the associated clan are represented with pendulous breasts, closed eyes as they are said to be sleepy, and rounded pursed lips because they utter "uh, uh, uh" sounds. They occasionally visit the villages to steal fish and unruly children whom they pack into a large basket on their back and carry away. In other circumstances, Tsono'koa bestows wealth on selected individuals (Boas 2002:311n36 [1895]). Tsono'koa continues to be popular in Alert Bay today: she is represented on totem poles in the Nimpkish burial ground (Figure 8.4) and animates the house posts of the communal big house.

Tsono'koa features in multiple oral narratives of the Kwakwaka'wakw. In the Nimpkish story of Ya'qstatl, Ya'qstatl and his brother catch salmon and dry them on a rack over the fire in their house. The salmon keeps disappearing mysteriously overnight and finally Ya'qstatl himself stays up to watch. During dawn hours, two huge Tsono'koa hands reach through the door screen, take the salmon from the drying rack, and stow them in a basket on her back. Ya'qstatl shoots his arrow into her breast. She cries and runs and knocks over large trees in her path. Ya'qstatl decides to pursue her and get his arrow back. He follows the fallen trees and finally arrives at a small lake where he sees a house. A young girl who is the daughter of Tsono'koa comes out of the house to fetch water. She talks to Ya'qstatl, thinking he is a shaman, and asks him to heal her ailing Tsono'koa mother. Nobody knows what she is suffering from because the arrow sticking in her breast is only visible to Ya'qstatl's eyes. He negotiates to receive the young girl as his wife and the water of life as payments and then heals the Tsono'koa woman, retrieving his arrow (Boas 2002:331 [1895]).[8]

The Comox recognize a cannibal woman T'al who appears to be the equivalent of Tsono'koa. She carries a basket slung over her back in which she catches humans. One day she finds a group of girls swimming

Figure 8.4 Totem pole displaying Thunderbird and Tsono'koa; Nimpkish burial grounds in Alert Bay. Photo by Brian Garrett.

in a lake. She snatches them, stuffs them into her basket, and carries them to her house where she wants to kill them. But the girls beg her to let them dance around the fire one more time. They take pitch and smear it in the face of T'al. The girls sing and beat time and tell T'al to go toward the fire and come back from the fire. As the cannibal woman performs these movements, the pitch begins to melt and glues up her eyes. When she cannot see anymore, the girls push her into the fire where she is burnt to death. The sparks shooting from her ashes transform into mosquitoes (Boas 2002:215–216 [1895]).

This oral narrative is important for several reasons: first, Tsono'koa/T'al is known among multiple Kwakwala speaking tribes; second, she can be overcome and killed; and third, she is vanquished by females. This is an eloquent case scenario in which two female roles and spatial realms are juxtaposed: T'al who eats humans and lives in the woods versus the girls who are integrated in human society and village life. Here human culture and associated values overcome the wild.

I think these observations also hold wider and more general relevance to Kwakwaka'wakw society. Oral narratives that explain the ceremonial system clearly differentiate between normal, socially integrated, and accepted versus wild, unruly, and asocial gender roles. On the female side, human daughters and wives versus Tsono'koa/T'al personify such roles. On the male side, the structural equivalents are fair and just traditional chiefs versus Hamatsa, the cannibal spirit and dancer (Boas 2002:338–339 [1895]; Suttles 1991:97–100; Joseph 1998:30–32). The Hamatsa is a young man who goes out into the woods, encounters the wild bird spirits, and becomes one with them and possessed by them. When he returns to his village, he has to be ritually tamed and reintegrated into human society. This dramatic performance has been and continues to be part of all Kwakwaka'wakw potlatches. Often female dancers assume lead roles in the taming process. With regard to the gender comparison, it must be noted that the female Tsono'koa and the male Hamatsa both personify wild forces of the outer natural surroundings. It is significant that Tsono'koa must be killed in order to be overcome whereas Hamatsa can be re-humanized, acculturated and returned into society. Viewed through this lens, I reason, Tsono'koa stands for indomitable and fearsome female powers. At the same time, females seem to be endowed with the power to vanquish such wild forces: the girls kill T'al/Tsono'koa and female dancers tame Hamatsa.

I argue that the binaries of gendered landscapes are fluid in Kwakwaka'wakw thinking. In recounting oral narratives, Boas' male consultants projected their social system onto the local landscape in attempts to validate ownership of numaym lands and to assert social and political control in their regions. Females and other living beings whom they could not directly control are imagined and visualized as wild forces of untamed nature. I discern a juncture versus disjuncture in the gendered storied landscapes versus economic and political landscapes. For men, storyscapes legitimized the economic and political landscapes in which they moved and performed; women did not own land and therefore storyscapes do not assign them specific places. Oral narratives and historical documents identify economic zones for women as the house, village, and inland areas for summer food collecting, but the legal rights to such places were maintained by male family members. Kwakwaka'wakw people have always been keenly aware of uncontrollable aspects and unforeseen events in human lives. The male narrators imagined and personified those as Tsono'koa and Hamatsa. Hamatsa, the male cannibal spirit dancer, shares the same sex as the narrators and can therefore be better related to and ultimately be tamed. Tsono'koa, on the other hand, is of the opposite sex and personifies all mysterious, unknown, and unpredictable elements of male existence and ultimately can only be overcome by integrated civilized females. It reinforces these observations that Boas defines one of the Nimpkish fishing grounds as *dzo'nogwade* meaning "having *dzonoq'wa*/Tsonok'oa." This fishing ground reaches from a house on the south side of Donegal head to the west end of Stubbs Island to the north end of Plumper Island and continues east to the south end of Swanson Island (Boas 1934:14, Map 19.15). Does this name with a confluence of female Tsono'koa aspects and male fishing practices suggest that some encounter with the unforeseen occurred there or should it be better seen as a male appropriation of Tsono'koa aspects to protect their fishing grounds?

A further consideration of gendered landscape constructions is that Northwestern ethnography has not been rigorously historicized or theorized. This means that most of Boas' writings have been cited at face-value from the standpoint of an early twentieth-century male researcher whose perspective is necessarily filtered by a male-centered Modernist worldview. Wendy Wickwire (2001) explores this issue in her gender-targeted analysis of the role of the grizzly bear in accounts of rituals associated with the birth of twins recorded by Franz Boas and his Native assistant James Teit. She documents significant discrepancies between the published accounts primarily authored and/or edited by Boas that focus on male, both human and animal, actors and the unpublished records, mostly Teit's field notes, in which he interviews a Nlaka'pamux woman about a female grizzly bear and in which he highlights female roles in the physical and ritual protection of twins. Teit's description appears to come much closer to an indigenous concept of the grizzly bear than Boas's who, as a cultural outsider, had limited exposure to the natural world and mostly worked with consultants. Wickwire (2001:448) calls on scholars to not simply rely on the published literature but invest more scrutiny in the field notes by Boas and his assistants. This type of archival work would surely lead to a more nuanced portrayal of gendered landscapes through the eyes of Northwest Coast peoples but is beyond the scope of this chapter.

A related supplementary approach consists of new and fresh consultations with Kwakwaka'wakw community members. My friend and consultant Trevor Isaac shares many stories about Village Island. The protagonist in one story is a woman: a lady from Village Island was visiting Nimpkish people and she was sitting on a boulder, she farted and the rock smashed to smithereens. True story. It turned into pebbles so that's why there are pebbles all over the place (Trevor Isaac April 2013, pers. comm.).

In this narrative, another female features in a context that is not within traditional socially accepted norms. She exercises supernatural powers of a type that is at once "disgusting" (to most outsiders) and ludicrous as well as a bit funny. We should remember that Kwakwaka'wakw oral traditions and ceremonies always set time aside for ritual humor. I interpret Trevor's story as another case in which a woman displays special powers that ignore common social norms. It is noteworthy that in both examples, Tsono'koa and the lady from Village Island, these females are portrayed in general negative terms: old, ugly, and monstrous or dirty.[9]

Comparative Outlook to the Hawai'ian Islands

In this section, I wish to take the unusual step of integrating a brief comparative discussion of gendered landscapes on the Hawai'ian Islands. Although the Pacific Northwest and the Hawai'ian Islands lie far apart geographically speaking, they both share institutionalized chiefly societies and human livelihood is intricately linked to the Pacific Ocean. I plan to show that their different geographic coordinates and ecological zones resulting in divergent flora and fauna and economic resources result in the construction of differing relational networks between people and their land as well as in different gender constructions.

Geographic and Climatic Settings, Traditional Social Organization, and History

The Hawai'ian Islands are situated in the northern Pacific Ocean, in northern latitude 18°54′ to 22°17′ and in western longitude 154 meridian 54′ (Figure 8.1). The islands of the Hawai'ian archipelago number ten; two of them as well as several small islets are uninhabited. The larger and most populated ones are Ni'ihau, Kaua'i, O'ahu, Moloka'i, Lana'i, Maui, Kahoolawe, and Hawai'i. Seasons change between the warmer dry season from April through October often cooled by refreshing trade-winds (*kona*) and the rainy season from November to April with high humidity and more rainfall. Throughout the year, temperatures rarely rise above the mid-eighties or drop below the mid-sixties degrees Fahrenheit.

The geological origin of the Hawai'ian Islands is volcanic, which is still visible by the fact that the larger part of the area of the islands is mountainous and exhibits numerous craters of extinct volcanoes as well as a continuously active volcano in the mountain-heights of Hawai'i. In native worldview, the land on the islands was spoken of as inland or upland (*uka*) and seaward (*kai*) (Figures 8.5a and b). The backbone of initial Hawai'ian social organization was the '*ohana* commonly described as an extended lineage whose members might reside in dispersed communities. It was customary for some members of the same 'ohana to live inland while others lived seaward so that they could exchange their respective products. Since the island terrain descends from the mountains to the coastline, land divisions were typically cut in sloping segments running from the shore back into the higher altitude zones. The smallest division was the '*ili*, a continuous narrow strip from shore to mountain top. Several 'ili composed the larger sub-division of the *ahupua'a*, which in turn was a section of a *moku* (island or district) (Handy and Pukui 1972:4). Indigenous cultigens are banana, plantain, coconuts, breadfruits, *ohias*, sugar-cane, arrow-roots, yams, sweet potatoes, *taro*—the staple of the Hawai'ian diet—strawberries, raspberries, and *ohelo* berries. Numerous other plant species–such as limes, oranges, mangoes, tamarinds, papaias or papayas, and guavas–that also flourish on the islands have been introduced through outside contacts during the nineteenth century.

Originally, the 'ili was probably the territory of one single 'ohana. It functioned as a self-sufficient unit since those living inland (uka) and those living along the shores (kai) exchanged their complementary products. The ahupua'a division was the domain of the *Alii'ai ahupua'a* Chief

Figure 8.5. Landscape on O'ahu, Hawai'ian Islands: (*above*) ancient Hawai'ian fishpond in the background; (*below*) upland flora. Photographs by Brian Garrett.

who in turn was the subject of the Ruling Chief or *Ali'i 'ai moku* of the moku district (Handy and Pukui 1972:4–5). The position and authority of the many Hawai'ian chiefs was rooted in mytho-history and validated by links with the past and selected supernatural beings. The position of some chiefs changed from that of a lineage head to a type of king around A.D. 1500. The status of women in traditional society was ambivalent: they were considered *noa* (common and free of *kapu,* which denoted high social status and privileges), but women in chiefly lineages could be vessels of very high rank, meaning they could contain such rank simply by being born into a high-ranking lineage. *Tabu* (prohibitions) pronounced by male kapu barred women from fully participating in sacrificial ceremonies or from eating together with men, but the fine mats and tapa cloth produced by women were indispensable items in chiefly rituals that cemented men's superior status. The ritual devaluation of women sprang from the notion of female pollution coming from menstrual blood that was said to drive the gods away (Linnekin 1990:13–24).

Hawai'ian history is being pieced together from oral narratives that provide a rich and colorful storyscape in which definitions of gods, supernatural beings, chiefs, and humans are quite fluid[10] and from a growing body of scientific work in archaeology. The research of Patrick Kirch brings both sources together in a compelling reconstruction on which I rely here (2012:288–333): a small group of Polynesians sailed north, possibly from the Marquesas Islands, in the 10th century and discovered the Hawai'ian Islands about A.D. 1000. This new island group was uninhabited and shared a similar climate and natural setting with their homeland. The Polynesian group settled and began to cultivate, grow, and expand, starting what Kirch (2012:288) calls a "microcosm" of social evolution without outside variables. By about 1400, the islands of Kaua'i and O'ahu as well as parts of Maui and Hawai'i were densely settled. Major irrigation systems for pondfields have been documented on O'ahu, Moloka'i, Kaua'i, Maui, and Hawai'i. Around 1500, a resulting change in social organization can be registered: the early Polynesians had lived by and large as egalitarian extended families led by chiefly lineage heads. Now certain chiefs took over management of the irrigation works and extracted agricultural surplus as tribute. Land was divided into hierarchical administrative units (see 'ili, ahupua'a, moku above), and new positions of land managers and full-time priests were instituted to collect tribute and perform worship of selected state gods. The chiefs themselves became full-time leaders. These developments in the 15th and early 16th centuries marked the transition from a society of chiefs to a state-like organization. Individual chiefs became kings of specific islands. By ca. 1700, limits of agricultural production were reached and surplus began to decline. Individual chief-kings engaged in invasions and territorial conflict to secure prime agricultural areas on adjacent islands and thus maintain their wealth economy. Social and political landscape construction was reoriented from an island-specific to an inter-island perspective. Captain Cook discovered the Hawai'ian Islands for the outside world on January 18, 1778, landing on Kaua'i and Ni'ihua (Kalakaua 1888:22–25). According to Kirch (2012:299), Cook encountered three archaic states, each ruled by a divine god-king: one was centered on Hawai'i and controlled parts of Maui; the second was governed from western Maui and included Moloka'i; the third was composed of O'ahu and Kaua'i. An alternate version of early Hawai'ian history relying solely on oral narratives was presented by King David Kalakua (Kalakaua 1888:19–32, see endnote 11).[11]

In 1795, Kamehameha I united all of the Hawai'ian Islands under his rule and assumed the title of king. His son, Kamehameha II, initiated a brief religious revolt during which he had most idols, shrines, and temples destroyed and the traditional priesthood removed from office. The lasting political and historical significance of this religious break was the abolition of *kapu* and associated *tabu* in 1819, which was a traditional Polynesian prerogative belonging exclusively to the priesthood and nobility (see Handy 1971:43). Kapu/tabu entailed the rights to issue commands—sometimes spontaneously and at will—to protect property and spaces that priests and aristocrats frequented. Violators were put to death. In the context of this chapter, I must repeat the contradictory status of women in reference to kapu/tabu: women as biologically defined were categorically *noa*—profane or free of kapu—whereas chiefly women as cultural constructions could be vessels/carriers of the highest kapu ranks and thus were indispensable in the processes of dynastic successions (Linnekin 1990:13–14). The lifting of the kapu/tabu weakened the traditional political and religious systems and left Hawai'ians ready and open to receive the Christian faith in the 1820s. The Kamehameha dynasty came to an end in 1873. One year later, David Kalakaua was elected to the throne by the Legislative Assembly and formally crowned with his queen on February 12, 1883. Here I have summarized the post-contact history of the Hawai'ian Islands as presented through his eyes (Kalakaua 1888:19–32).[12]

As suggested in this brief history, oral narratives and collective memory mesh gods and humans in a layered storyscape drawing relational networks between the large coastal islands of southern Asia, the intermediate Pacific islands and Hawai'i. The emergent chiefs and kings justified their authoritative positions through personal relations with certain supernatural beings and a guarded ancestor cult. Kamakau reinforces this notion in his words: "I am a stranger from foreign lands. . . . Those are our homelands. There are two big islands separated by a channel. Several ancestral chiefs sailed away a long time ago from these lands of ours. Haumea was the very first. She was a supernatural being with the character of a god. Pilika'aiea was a chief who came. Pa'ao was his priest . . . of their becoming the ancestors of chiefs and priests of Hawai'i" (Kamakau 1991:2).

The Hawai'ian Storyscape and Gender

Let us now turn to the Hawai'ian landscape from a gendered perspective and examine selected female characters. The first figure to be analyzed is the colorful Haumea, also known as Papa. It has been shown (see footnote 10) that her status fluctuates between being a goddess, supernatural, and human. She appears in important origin narratives and travel stories. In the larger context of Polynesian cosmology, Papa is identified with the "Earth-stratum" or lower shell that is always female. At the beginning of creation, sky and earth existed as two shells or strata lying on top of each other with a very confined living space between them. It has to be remembered that superior male and inferior female gender roles were assigned at this time (Handy 1971:16; see more in Linnekin 1990:16–17).[13]

In any discussion of a gendered Hawai'ian storyscape, it is vital to draw attention to the gendered and culturally biased mindset of the authors who report on the layered and obviously confusing oral narratives. Contrast Handy's interpretation—a male U.S. scholar active in the first half of the twentieth century—with the contemporary feminist reading of Lilikala Kame'eleihiwa, female director of the Center of Hawai'ian Studies at the University of Hawai'i at Manoa. She credits the beginnings of the ancient Hawai'ian world to Po, "the unfathomable and mysterious female night, [who] gives birth by herself, and without any male impregnating element, to a son and daughter . . . who by their incestuous mating create the world" (Kame'eleihiwa 1999:3). She claims that half of the Hawai'ian gods or *Akua* are female. "It is the female *Akua* that empower Hawaiian women. They are our ancestors; they are our inspiration; they live in us" (Kame'eleihiwa 1999:3). This contrasting comparison brings to the fore how important it is to include the training and gender of the researcher in any ethnographic analysis.

According to the genealogy of Wakea who is generally accepted as the husband of Papa/Haumea, Papa gave birth to the islands by birthing a gourd with its cover. Wakea threw various parts of this gourd up and by doing so, created the sky, the sun, the stars, the moon, clouds, rain, land, and the ocean (Kamakau 1991:125–126). Other accounts imply that Wakea and Papa were not the first ancestors who came to Hawai'i but belonged to the middle generations (Kamakau 1991:128; Handy 1971:20–21 see footnote 12). The island of Hawai'i is described as the first-born child of Wakea and Papa and the islands Kaua'i and Maui as children who followed (Kamakau 1991:128–129; Handy 1971:18). Numerous narratives mention that the marriage of Papa and Wakea did not remain happy and both took other lovers: "Wakea found favor with the beautiful *Hina*, and the island of Molokai was born of their embrace" (Kalakaua 1888:38). The small island of Lana'i was the offspring of Wakea and *Ka'ulawahine* (Kamakau 1991:129). Papa, in turn, mated with the warrior *Lua* and their product was the island of O'ahu (Kalakaua 1888:38; Kamakau 1919:129).

Papa/Haumea further features in adventure narratives, such as her delivery of the grandchild of Chief 'Olopana for the price of a flowering tree. Eventually the kapu/tabu in this tree is freed and carved into the idol and god Ku-ho'one'e-nu'u who became the god of the chiefs of O'ahu in early history (Kamakau 1991:6–8; see also Kame'eleihiwa 1999:4–5 on Haumea: she identifies Kuho'one'enu'u as female in her feminist reading of Hawai'ian cosmology!). Kame'eleihiwa (1999:5, 10) further refers to Haumea as a *Mo'o*, who are female Akua in the form of dragon or lizard gods to whom fish are attracted. They manifest themselves at water bodies, from waterfalls to fishponds, and at the surf in the ocean. Men build traditional fishponds where fish, a male element, are raised and attracted to the female Akua (Figure 8.5a).[14]

In short, Papa/Haumea is portrayed as a goddess linked to the creation of the Hawai'ian Islands and to the early history of its peoples. She can dispense multiple levels of supernatural powers and at other times, act as human. Similar to Northwest Coast ancestral figures, her godly, mythic, and human identities fluctuate but unlike the latter, she is a female goddess. I did not find major female mythological and god-like ancestors in Kwakwaka'wakw storyscapes.

The second and vital female figure in the gendered Hawai'ian storyscape is Pele, the Volcano Goddess. She is the deity most feared and

Figure 8.6. Kilauea Crater in Hawai'i Volcanoes National Park.

respected, especially on the Island of Hawai'i, since her favorite residence is the crater of Kilauea on this island (Figure 8.6). Traditionally she is assisted by five brothers and eight sisters all of whom display special powers associated with the dispersal of volcanic forces (see the list of the supreme and principal deities of the Hawai'ian group, Kalakaua 1888:48–50). Tribute and offerings to Pele had to be thrown into the crater of Kilauea and of other volcanoes.

Kalakaua (1888:139–154) makes the very important distinction between the goddess Pele and Pele the mortal. There is historical evidence that the Pele family came to Hawai'i during the second wave of migration in approximately A.D. 1175 (Kalakaua 1888:139–154). The Pele family was of chiefly blood and of priestly lineage; since the head of the family had fallen in battle, the eldest son Moho took the lead. They found open land to settle in the valleys and foothills of Mauna Loa, including the crater of Kilauea. As the volcano continued to be active, local residents had vacated the area. The Pele family was quickly perceived as standing under supernatural protection and being endowed with special powers for their boldness to settle in such unstable terrain. They established a small colony and cultivated their lands in peace. Pele is described as a courageous and very beautiful woman.

Kamapuaa, a traveling adventurer and warrior from O'ahu, became interested in marrying Pele but she refused. When he continued to urge his marriage proposal, Pele expressed contempt for him and insulted him. Kamapuaa's feelings of love turned into bitter anger, and he devised a plan to take Pele by force assisted by his companions. Moho knew that they could not hold their houses and therefore led his family to take refuge in volcanic caverns up in the mountains. Kamapuaa discovered their hideout by following a family dog. He and his followers had made several attempts to take out the Pele family when the volcano began to erupt and a flood of burning lava and half-molten boulders sent them running to their canoes on the beach. They barely made their escape and upon leaving, Kamapuaa saw that the cavern in which the Pele family had been hiding was deeply buried by the lava and debris.

Local people refused to accept that Pele and her family had perished but interpreted the events that Pele had invoked the eruption to make Kamapuaa leave the region. They believed that she had allowed her lands to be destroyed because her plan was to take up residence in the crater of Kilauea. Such interpretations spread and grew into a priestly cult dedicated to Pele, the goddess of fire. Pele continues to hold her place deep in the hearts of traditional Hawai'ian people. According to Kalakaua (1888:42–43), the last public recognition of the powers of Pele occurred on the island of Hawai'i in 1882. The town of Hilo was threatened by a slowly advancing broad stream of lava from Mauna Loa. The old chiefess Ruth, sister of the fourth and fifth Kamehamehas, traveled from Honolulu to Hilo with a large number of attendants. She had an altar erected in front of the advancing lava and made supplications and offerings to Pele. The stream of fiery destruction was halted, which the natives attributed to the intervention of Pele. Offerings to Pele have been thrown into the crater of Kilauea throughout the nineteenth century (Kalakaua 1888:17).

It is intriguing to unpack the ways in which the many editions of Hawai'ian oral narratives have been historicized and theorized. It is obvious that David Kalakaua writes from the educated and Christian position of a nineteenth-century Hawai'ian king who exudes a sense of superiority over Hawai'ian traditionalists. On the other hand, through the collaborative works of the U.S. researcher Craighill Handy and Mary Kawena Pukui, Pukui speaks with the loving heart of a Hawai'ian native toward her land and past, vividly illustrating the role of landscape in her identity formation.

Mary Kawena Pukui was born and raised in Ka'u, the southern and most rugged district of the island of Hawai'i, above which looms the Mauna Loa volcano. Furthermore, her lineage is from the chiefs and priests of Ka'u and its neighboring district Puna. The many beautiful names given to her, for example, *i-ka-poli-i-Pele* or in-the-bosom-of-Pele, testify to her heritage of the Pele clan. With deep insights imparting indigenous feelings toward natural elements as persons as opposed to things, they describe Pele as a much loved though awe-inspiring powerful woman (Handy and Pukui 1972:28–29). She is called *Pele-honua-mea* (Pele-the-sacred-earth person) and *Wahine-o-ka-Lua* (Woman of the Crater) because she lives deep inside the craters of Mauna Loa. Originally she had come from Kahiki together with her brothers and sisters. Before settling in Ka-'u, Hawai'i, she had probed the other islands Kaua'i, O'ahu, and Maui by digging craters with her staff *Paoa* in her search for a dry place for her eternal fires.

As a human, Pele had an extensive family clan. There were multiple brothers; her father was named *Kane-hoa-lani* (male-friend-of-Heaven) and her mother Haumea. Handy and Pukui (1972:30) comment that "Haumea had many bodies, one of which was the low lying breadfruit tree." Through the goddess Haumea, Handy and Pukui connect Pele with the origin mytho-histories and the beginnings of the Hawai'ian Islands. Pele is thus included among the creator gods.

One additional female figure deserves mentioning due to her multiple associations with nature: *Hi'iaka*, Pele's younger sister. She appears as a dancer in the *hula* dance-ritual; she can be a healer and guardian, a spirit of the ocean, of cloud forms, and of the uplands (Handy and Pukui 1972:30). Her many roles are reflected in her many names, which include *Hi'iaka-noho lani* (-dweller-in-the-sky), *Hi'iaka-i-ka-wai-ola* (-in-the-water-of-life), *Hi'iaka-i-ka-poli-i-Pele* (-in the-bosom-of-Pele), *Hi'iaka-makole-wawahi-wa'a* (-the-red-eyed-who-smashed-canoes), *Hi'iaka-lei-'ia* (-the-beloved-garlanded), and *Hi'iaka-i-ka-pua-'ena'ena* (-in-the-glow-of-the rising-sun). These names and epithets reflect Hi'iaka's duality as a largely benign yet powerful being whose powers possess a destructive potential. I also highlight Hi'iaka as the female actor who personifies the most intimate gendered landscape setting I have encountered on the Hawai'ian Islands or on the North-west Coast.

Besides volcanoes, another category of places associated with females are birthing places. Kamakau describes the famous birth place
Kukaniloko (Figure 8.7) as follows:

> A line of stones was set up on the right hand and another on the left
> hand, facing north. There sat thirty-six chiefs. There was a backrest . . . on
> the upper side, this was the rock Kukaniloko, which was the rock to lean
> against. If a chiefess entered and leaned against Kukaniloko and rested
> on the supports to hold up the thighs in observance of the Liloe *kapu [the
> prescribed regulations for birthing]*, the child born in the presence of the
> chiefs was called an *ali'i*, an *akua*, a *wela*—a chief, a god, a blaze of heat
> (Kamakau 1991:38).

Figure 8.7. Kukaniloko stones. Adapted from Becket and Singer 1999.

Such a distinguished child was attended to by chiefs. The stone Kukaniloko was surrounded by other ritual stations (see also Becket and Singer 1999:61, 64–65). It is fascinating that Kame'eleihiwa also mentions Kukaniloko through her pronounced feminist lens: according to her, the high chiefess Kukaniloko was born at this birthing *heiau* (temple) around A.D. 1375 to become the first *Mo'iwahine* or supreme female ruler of O'ahu. She situates this site on the plains of Wahiawa known for especially violent thunderstorms that brought the *mana* of the heavens down to the chiefly children being born (Kame'eleihiwa 1999:9). Kame'eleihiwa (1999), Linnekin (1990), and others have added fresh feminist perspectives to Hawai'ian ethnography.

The final female actor to be discussed here is the surfing chiefess *Kelea* whose domain was not only rooted in the landscape but in the seascape. More strongly human than a goddess, she is described as a beautiful chiefess from Maui with clear skin and sparkling eyes. Her hair flutters like the wings of the *ka'upu* bird and therefore she is called *Kelea-nui-noho-'ana-'api'api* or Great-Kelea-Who-Flutters. Surfing is her greatest pleasure and she spends much of her time surf riding with all of the chiefs (Kamakau 1991:45–49).

Lo Lale is a chief in the uplands of O'ahu and he is looking for a wife. So he sends a canoe expedition to the other islands. When his men come to Maui, they hear about Kelea and decide to obtain her as the wife. They find the chiefess surf riding and trick her into boarding their canoe as she does not know that theirs is a "wife-snatching" canoe. The canoe is blown away at sea and lands on O'ahu. Kelea is taken into the uplands where she becomes the wife of Lo Lale. They have three children. After ten years of living in the uplands, Kelea misses the ocean and asks to go sightseeing. Her husband agrees to her request and sends two travel companions to go with her. She greatly enjoys the beautiful views of water and the beaches and is driven to continue on when she hears tales of places where people enjoy surfing. Eventually the party arrives at Waikiki. The local people describe their area as "a place for enjoyment" where one may watch the chiefs surfing (Kamakau 1991:48). Kelea is able to obtain a surfboard from the local people. She joyfully paddles out and demonstrates unsurpassed skills in riding tall waves to shore. The local people are surprised because they have thought that Kelea was born in the uplands and they cheer loudly. The chief Kalamakua is working in his nearby fields and hears the noisy cheering. He remembers the chiefess Kelea of Maui. So he leaves his work and goes to watch himself. When Kelea rides in on a wave, he takes hold of her board and asks if she is indeed Kelea. She confirms and he covers her naked body and takes her to his house. The two marry and have children.

Kelea is perceived as primarily a human being. Her character interweaves her beauty as a woman with the beauty, sun, warmth, and openness of the Hawai'ian natural setting. In the Hawai'ian storyscape, protagonists in mytho-histories easily cross the membrane between their human and supernatural identities as in the Northwest Coast material. Hawai'ians have clearly included more females in their relational networks with the land. However, the Hawai'ian storyscape stands in stark contrast to lived cultural reality as has been indicated above and will be analyzed in the following conclusions.

Conclusions

The Pacific Northwest Coast and the Hawai'ian Islands share two broad geographic and social commonalities: they border or are surrounded by the Pacific Ocean and they have chiefly societies. I am reaffirming here that the great differences in gendered landscape constructions between both societies have their root cause in the natural settings and geography that conditioned their distinct settlement histories. I will frame these differences through origin narratives and notions of wealth production.

As discussed, the natural setting of Kwakwaka'wakw territory is defined by the ocean, a beachfront, and the inland forests. This territory had been occupied by humans as long as people can remember. In this natural setting, humans had to carve out and solidify a human cultivated place for themselves while being surrounded and always encroached upon by the vast, threatening, and mysterious expanses of the sea and the woods. Due to climate and seasonal cycles, food supply had to be pre-planned and storage provisions had to be made. This type of human position called for a closely-knit community unified by strict traditional rules, in which women who ventured outside social norms were described as monsters and men who defied those rules were publicly shamed and quickly reintegrated, such as Hamatsa. I argue that Kwakwala speaking people projected their social organization and ceremonial system back onto their environment—which had conditioned such social and ceremonial systems in the first place—primarily to order and validate land ownership.

My first frame is that origin stories featuring ancestor figures in identifiable spatial settings are pivotal. All of these ancestors are male, and numaym chiefs have traced their authority and property rights back to them for generations. Females appear as daughters and wives who do not own land by themselves; their role is to transfer such rights between families, in much the same way as demonstrated by Duncan and Diaz-Granada (Chapter 3) in this volume. Thus animated landscapes on the Northwest Coast closely reflect, explain, and justify traditional social organization as well as the ceremonial system and function to reinforce each other. During my fieldwork in Alert Bay, I have observed several scenarios in which ceremonial/social standards have been broadened to make them more compatible with present-day lifestyles and thus maintain them. During a potlatch hosted by the Wadhams family in the early 2000s, for example, two young men who had committed criminal offenses were reintegrated into their community by publicly describing what they had done. Trevor Isaac's story about the lady from Village Island who farted a rock into pebbles approaches asocial female behavior with humor. I think ritual humor is an important component in contemporary culture as it relaxes the ceremonial rigidity and reaches out to include the audience, for example, in social dancing during potlatches. These represent some of the recent tactics to foster identity formation among young people within a traditional community context. As the influence of the natural setting decreases in our global world, new strategies have to be invented to reinforce social and ceremonial settings of Kwakwaka'wakw culture.

Turning to the Hawai'ian Islands, their location is first of all much further south at the general latitude of northern Mexico. The geography of the islands is open to all directions and Hawai'ians have maintained continuous contacts among the islands and with the islands of their origin to the south through most of history. The economic and social backbone of traditional Hawai'ian society was the 'ohana community whose members lived in dispersed habitations in differing zones of their 'ili land division. As members from the upland and seashore zones traded and exchanged agricultural products and fish, the 'ohana functioned as largely self-sufficient unit. Agricultural growing seasons continue all year and food supply is steady unlike in the Northwest Coast economy. This type of natural environment fostered the construction of a cultural and social landscape that was based upon fewer constraints and was more open to outside influences than the worldview on the Northwest Coast.

The island geography imposed the psychological need to explore the origin of their people, and Hawai'ians physically experienced and mentally perceived and imagined relational networks with numerous other islands. I present geography as a primary reason for the differences in gendered landscape constructions between the Northwest Coast and Hawai'i. Hawai'ians were newcomers and began to settle open land, probably driven by a "pioneer-mentality" American style. In my first frame, they tried to explain how this island group was created and to make sense of their existence upon it, applying collective memory and imagination. They remember discovery and settlement as human activities involving male and female actors and construct women, such as Papa/Haumea, as supernatural agents instrumental in birthing the Hawai'ian Islands.

When early Hawai'ians established themselves in their new island setting, they had brought with them a social organization rooted in chiefly societies that would be redefined over the following five hundred years. Chiefs grounded their authority and prerogatives in genealogies linking them to the first settlers of the Hawai'ian Islands whom they imagined as semi-supernatural male and female protagonists and heroes. Thus the recording and maintenance of chiefly bloodlines was vitally important; it was performed in oral traditions but not viewed as strict ceremonial properties as on the Northwest Coast.

I argue that the processes of wealth production emerge as a second key frame in distinguishing gendered landscape constructions among the Kwakwaka'wakw and the Hawai'ians. On the Northwest Coast, women in their role as wives were the social key to increasing territories and intangible properties and thus wealth, and therefore had to be carefully guarded within the community. In Hawai'i, women as marriage partners were also vital in maintaining chiefly and royal bloodlines. By A.D. 1500, chiefdoms were changing from a subsistence agricultural economy to one built on wealth production from surplus and tribute. Chiefs began to compete for land and material wealth and some rose in power to form a distinct social class that exempted them from manual labor and elevated them to rule over the large majority of commoners in a state-like system. This new economy based upon material wealth had male-only actors and held no logical or fitting positions for women. I reason that due to these factors gender roles of women became increasingly contradictory as confirmed by the contemporary feminist writers cited in this chapter.

Hawai'ian religion based up kapu/tabu was theoretically speaking very strict but in lived reality held many inconsistencies (Linnekin 1990) and could be bent and adjusted, particularly for chiefesses. I view such contradictions as a reflection of the undeniable presence of powerful female figures in the migration and origin narratives, who participated in creating initial wealth on the islands (thus linking both of my frames). The result was that females had many opportunities to exercise initiatives, step outside of rigidly defined social norms, and make lasting contributions in their land and to their people: Haumea birthed the islands, Pele controls volcanic forces, and Kelea mesmerizes by her surfing skills and simply by her beauty. These women are not "monsterized" as on the Northwest Coast but honored, worshipped, loved, and adored by the Hawai'ian people.

At the same time, as Western scholars we must be very cautious not to instinctively treat female agency in non-Western cultures as synonymous with emancipatory goals. First, let us not forget that the great majority of consultants who have provided Hawai'ian oral narratives were males and that we read their construction of gender. Second, indigenous women may be social "movers and shakers" but in contexts very different from those of Euroamerican female liberation movements; for example, in the realm of social work.[15]

In this sense—and as a surprise to our Western mindset—Kelea willingly gives up her surfing freedom and follows Chief Kalamakua to make a new family. Some writers have argued that the kapu/tabu system including its gender segregation and draconic penalties was indeed healthy for all Hawai'ians because it protected commoners from the dangerous power/mana of chiefs, and from the chief's point of view, it safeguarded his mana and kapu for the common good (Kanahele 1986:38–39). Kame'eleihiwa (1999:9, 11–12) seems to offer the final feminist word to the debate about gender discrimination through kapu/tabu when she interprets the introduction and termination of the 'Aikapu religion as scenarios in which females had to agree to a male proposal and later abolished the system when it no longer served their people's best interests. In her view, women held the ultimate say over Hawai'ian traditional religion.

In sum, among the Kwakwaka'wakw, the natural environment and origin narratives cross-fertilized each other to construct and maintain an inward and community-oriented social organization and ceremonial system controlled by male chiefs. The authority of chiefs rested upon wealth defined as land granted by ancestral figures and as tangible and intangible ceremonial properties acquired through marriage from their wives' families. Any digression or abnormality that posed a threat to the social order and wealth distribution had to be denounced as asocial and was imagined and visualized in female gendered storyscapes. Stability of traditional Kwakwaka'wakw society in the 21st century has depended on multiple tactics devised to reinforce oral narratives, Kwakwala language, and the intertwined social and ceremonial system, which are no longer land-based.

On the Hawai'ian Islands, people looked outward, constructing dynamic relational networks with many islands and lineages. Origin stories attempt to explain these networks through collective memory. They retell events of exploration and discovery in which male and female mytho-historical heroes played complimentary parts and contributed to initial accumulation of wealth. Over the course of five hundred years, the roles of some chiefs changed from being anchored in lineage and subsistence to new elevated leadership positions grounded in material wealth. Women were needed to maintain chiefly genealogies but were given outsider positions in the official ceremonial system, which freed them to assume vital and active roles mirrored in the Hawai'ian storyscape.

This comparison demonstrates that in the dynamic relational networks between people and land the experiences of geography and natural environment had primacy in social perceptions and imagination. In both regions, people perceived their natural and social worlds as divided and ordered by chiefs. The crucial difference emerges in spatial imagination as both societies construct gendered landscapes performed in storyscapes in which women play very different parts. My analysis also adds vivid examples to the ongoing debate over the precise definition and internal variations of chiefdoms.

NOTES

1. In the older literature, the non-indigenous term *Kwakiutl* was common. In the wake of postcolonial efforts of indigenous language revitalization and scholars practicing respect for their consultants, the indigenous term *Kwakwaka'wakw* is now used.

2. For example, on the Hawai'ian Islands, the archaeological record prior to ca. A.D. 1400 provides very limited evidence about forms of political economy (Bayman and Dye 2013:94).

3. Lefebvre (1991:73–77) juxtaposes the notions of a work of art and product to show that all "works" and created objects as well as spaces are ultimately the outcome of complex social relations of production and product exchange. He reasons that "social space contains a great diversity of objects, both natural and social, including the networks and pathways which facilitate the exchange of material things and information. Such 'objects' are thus not only things but also relations. . . . Social labour transforms them, rearranging their positions within spatio-temporal configurations without necessarily affecting their materiality, their natural state (as in the case, for instance, of an island, gulf, river or mountain)" (Lefebvre 1991:77). While the rigor with which Lefebvre dissects the layered production dynamics of social space inspires my study, his secular focus and grounding in the

economic sector following Marx leaves out religious factors and mythic geography that are surely part of social processes in most societies and particularly on the Northwest Coast and the Hawai'ian Islands.

4. Franz Boas was a German-American anthropologist who has shaped the way that anthropology is taught today. In the U.S., he worked as museum curator at the Smithsonian, and in 1899, he became professor of anthropology at Columbia University. His fieldwork was concentrated in the Pacific Northwest. He left a lasting impact on the field of anthropology by arguing against scientific racism and against social evolution. Boas further foreshadowed late twentieth-century thinking by reasoning that culture does not progress in evolutionary stages toward standards created in the Euroamerican world. Instead different cultures must be studied and understood in their own natural, historical, and social settings.

5. The Kwakwala term "'na'mima" (one kind) was anglicized by Boas (1920; 1921) as "numaym" (Suttles 1991:86). From the gender perspective, it should be noted that the Kwakwala term "'na'mima" or "one kind" seems to simply refer to one particular social group defined by a common ancestor whereas Lévi-Strauss's links to English aristocratic houses implant associations with male-dominated social organizations.

6. Particularly close relationships are established between humans and Thunderbird and Wolf (Boas 2002:252-253 [1895]), who live in houses and social groups parallel to human constructions. Two versions of a narrative about Thunderbird–which Boas recorded among the Comox, a Kwakwaka'wakw tribe, and among the Nutka/Nuu-chah-nulth on the west coast of Vancouver Island–illustrate this intimate human–mythic connection. The structure of the story is very similar while details and the names of the characters differ.

> A man had a beautiful wife who attracts the attention of the Thunderbird. With the help of his friends, Thunderbird abducts the woman from her husband. The latter then councils with his friends and they contrive plans and tricks to get her back. Through various acts of transformation first into a salmonberry and then into multiple fish, the husband's group is able to enter Thunderbird's house. The husband in the guise of a salmon-trout speaks to his wife and tells her not to throw his bones away after she would eat him but to return his bones to the water. So she does and when she wades in the water, the fish come back to life and carry her home.
>
> After their mission is completed successfully, the husband and his friends meet again and council how to take revenge and kill Thunderbird. They manage to borrow Whale's canoe which functions like a canoe but has the shape of a whale. The husband and friends enter the canoe, take a knife, and place a heavy piece of stone into the bottom of the canoe. Then they navigate to the house of the Thunderbirds. Thunderbird is famous for catching whales so when he sees one swimming in front of his house, he calls on his sons to fly out and catch it. The Thunderbirds hunt by clawing onto the back of the whale and lifting it out of the water. But this one is too heavy because of the rock inside the canoe. The husband and friends cut the feet of the Thunderbirds and all of them are pulled into the depth of the sea and drown. In the Comox version, one baby Thunderbird remains to become the next Thunderbird. In the Nuu-chah-nulth version, the canoe and its occupants are transformed into rocks which can still be seen at Whale Point. Whale Point has been identified on the south end of the southernmost Stopper Island in Barklay Sound (Boas 2002:205–207, 253–256 [1895]).

7. A second example of an ancestor narrative with identifiable place names:

> O'meatllEme was the ancestor of another numaym of the Nimpkish people. He lived in the upper portion of the Nimpkish River drainage. Once his four slaves went out to

hunt and pursued a large elk so far to the west that they saw the ocean. They returned to O'meatllEme to tell him what they had found and he wanted to see for himself whether people were living in the beach zones. He started his journey from Woss Lake, climbed up to the top of the mountain ridge and reached the Tahsis River that flows west. As he sat down to rest, he noticed Qoi'nkulatl, one of the ancestors of the Ma'tsatq [Mowachaht] people, approaching. The Ma'tsatq/Mowachaht people led O'meatlEme to their village and they bartered the latter's rings of inner cedar bark for the former's valuable skins. O'meatlEme returned to his home and hid the treasured skins at two mountains which sit close together on Lake Woss at the head of the Nimpkish River. Then he gave a great feast and assumed the name Ma'qolagyilis (Boas 2002:327–328 [1895]).

8. In another Nimpkish narrative, Koa'koaqsanok, a boy who was born and lives in the Nimpkish Valley, plays by the Nimpkish River and hears a horrifying voice calling from the mountain, "o, o, hu, hu, hop." He runs to his mother and asks whose voice it is. She answers that it is the big Tsono'koa who lives in a lake up on the mountain and that she would kill anyone coming near her. So Koa'koaqsanok decides to go up the mountain and see her. His mother begs him not to go fearing he would be killed. Koa'koaqsanok, however, thinks he can succeed and departs to look for Tsono'koa. Eventually he arrives on the mountain summit and finds the big, deep lake. He calls on Tsono'koa to come out of her house. But instead of the rising of the monstrous hairy body of Tsono'koa, the lake drains and refills and several other apparitions occur. One of them is a canoe with three people and a bone arrow. Koa'koaqsanok takes this arrow which turns out to have magical properties and returns home (Boas 2002:314–315 [1895]). There is no direct encounter with Tsono'koa.

9. This conclusion could be interpreted in two ways: from the perspective of a gender-conscious Euroamerican, the negative depiction of "liberated" women might be read as female discrimination and punishment; through the lens of a Kwakwaka'wakw traditionalist, the same negative portrayal might raise awareness about the dangers of venturing outside community norms. I think, though, that in most contemporary eyes this latter view may embrace some humor.

10. For example, consider the case of *Papa*:

> Papa, or Walinu'u, is called Haumea by some people, but Haumea was an entirely different person. She was a goddess, ... and her children were of the family of gods. ... But Papa, or Walinu'u, gave birth to supernatural beings. ... However, although she gave birth to supernatural beings, some humans came forth, and from them came the ancestors of chiefs and people. It is said that Papa went to Kahiki because her parents [were from there]. There Papa would transform her body, ... and she would become a young woman again. Papa was the very first Hawai'ian to travel to Kahiki, it is said in the ancient traditions (Kamakau 1991:91–92).

I can use this example that women could be travelers. We must conclude that imagined boundaries between gods, supernatural beings, ancestors, chiefs, and people were quite permeable.

11. Historians differentiate two waves of migration that populated the Hawai'ian Islands. During the first and second centuries of the Christian era, the Polynesians were slowly but steadily pushed out from the large coast islands of southern Asia to the smaller and more remote islands of the Pacific. Coming from the Fiji group and passing the Samoan and Society Islands, Polynesians first arrived on the Hawai'ian group around A.D. 550. According to oral traditions, Nanaula was the first distinguished chief on the Hawai'ian Islands. He brought with him his gods,

priests, prophets, astrologers, and many retainers. Other chiefs of lesser importance arrived with their families and followers from other islands in the south. It is said that these people populated and cultivated the Hawai'ian Islands without any documented contacts to the outside world until approximately A.D. 1000 (Kalakaua 1888:19–20).

A second migratory group from the southern islands came in the eleventh century under the leadership of Nanamaoa. He established his family on Hawai'i, Maui, and Oahu. Two generations later, the high-priest Paao arrived from Samoa. Since the Hawai'ian people were in transition between two rulers, he brought in P'ili, a distinguished chief from Samoa. P'ili quickly assumed sovereignty of the island of Hawai'i and founded a new dynasty. Paao became his high-priest and priests have claimed descent from him through the nineteenth century (Kalakaua 1888:20–21). Until about A.D. 1200, the Hawai'ian Islands thrived under the new rulers. It was a time of frequent travel between islands, back to the southern islands, and to other more distant islands. Polynesians developed strong navigation skills. Strangely, after A.D. 1200, contacts between the Hawai'ian and southern island groups ceased. For almost six hundred years until the close of the eighteenth century, Hawai'ians lived without documented interactions with the world beyond them.

12. It must be emphasized that our current state of knowledge concerning Hawai'ian history continues to be contested. Archaeologists debate radiocarbon-based estimates and one current range for the settlement event is between A.D. 780–1119, roughly corresponding with the second migration wave discussed above (Bayman and Dye 2013:20–25). A frequently cited source is the writings of Samuel Kamakau that appeared in weekly local newspapers from 1866 to 1871. Since Kamakau's original texts about Hawai'ian history and culture seem highly confusing to outside readers, they have been formatted and revised with commentaries in multiple editions (see Kamakau 1964, 1991).

For example, Kamakau's account of the peopling of the Hawai'ian Islands does not precisely match Kalakaua's version: Kamakau lists a man called Hulihonua and a woman Keakahulilani as the earliest ancestors. For 28 generations from Hulihonua to Wakea, there were no chiefs. It is significant that Kamakau describes this time as a phase without socially instituted hierarchies. From the 25 generations linking Wakea to Kapawa, noted events are remembered. Kapawa became the first ruling chief at Waialua, O'ahu [Kalakaua 1888:20 mentions Kapawa]. From then on, the Hawai'ian Islands were organized as chief-ruled kingdoms. Records and genealogies of the chiefs began to be kept (Kamakau 1964:3).

13. The male association with the sky world versus female connections with the earth can be observed in many world cultures, for example, in the Andes and in Indo-European mythologies. This is one moment in which it could be reasonable to raise the question of an existential human "gendered gaze" of sky as male and earth as female. Exceptions do exist in ancient Egypt where Geb was the earth god and Nut the goddess of the sky. On the Northwest Coast, the vertical sky-earth duality appears less significant than the horizontal axis encompassing ocean-shore-forest, perhaps due to the predominant cloudy and dark weather conditions concealing blue skies for much of the year.

14. There exists a wealth of material which could be added regarding gendered zones of the ocean: female realms are near the shores where women collect shellfish on

the beaches; where female Mo'o lure male fish from the deep ocean into the fish-ponds (see Kame'eleihiwa 1999:5). The male realm is the open ocean where they venture out for deep-sea fishing. European explorers around 1800 remarked that Hawai'ian women who visited their ships felt free to enjoy foods under tabu the sailors offered to them whereas they abided by traditional rigid eating restrictions as soon as they were on land. Linnekin suggests that a sea/land gradient in the force of tabu may well have existed (Linnekin 1990:20–22). Such incidences, of course, were most likely due to the women's curiosity for an alien cultural context rather than to their transition of environmental zones.

15. Leslie Lewis (2014) made such observations in her fieldwork with a group of Egyptian Muslim women in Cairo. These women affirm their segregated gender status as a means of drawing support from each other and investing their energies in self-sacrificing social work.

REFERENCES CITED

Ashmore, Wendy, and A. Bernhard Knapp (editors)
   Archaeologies of Landscape. Contemporary Perspectives. Blackwell, Malden, MA.

Bayman, James, and Thomas Dye
2013   *Hawaii's Past in a World of Pacific Islands.* The SAA Press, Washington, DC.

Becket, Jan, and Joseph Singer (editors)
1999   *Pana O'ahu Sacred Stones, Sacred Land.* University of Hawai'i Press, Honolulu.

Berlo, Janet, and Ruth Phillips
1998   *Native North American Art.* Oxford University Press, Oxford.

Boas, Franz
1920   The Social Organization of the Kwakiutl. *American Anthropologist* 22:111–126.
1921   Ethnology of the Kwakiutl (Based on Data Collected by George Hunt). 2 Pts. In *35th Annual Report of the Bureau of American Ethnology for the Years 1913–1914.* Washington.
1934   *Geographical Names of the Kwakiutl Indians.* Columbia University Press, New York.
1966   *Kwakiutl Ethnography*, H. Codere, editor. University of Chicago Press, Chicago.
2002   *Indian Myths & Legends from the North Pacific Coast of America.*
[1895]   Randy Bouchard and Dorothy Kennedy, editors; Dietrich Bertz, translator. Talonbooks, Vancouver.

Christie, Jessica (editor)
2009   *Landscapes of Origin in the Americas: Creation Narratives Linking Ancient Places and Present Communities.* University of Alabama Press, Tuscaloosa.

Codere, Helen
1990   Kwakiutl: Traditional Culture, in Northwest Coast. In *Handbook of North American Indians*, Vol. 7, William C. Sturtevant, editor.. Smithsonian Institution, Washington, DC.

Cosgrove, Denis, and Stephen Daniels (editors)
1988   *The Iconography of Landscape.* Cambridge University Press, Cambridge.

Gulliford, Andrew

2000   *Sacred Objects and Sacred Places: Preserving Tribal Traditions.* University
         Press of Colorado, Boulder.

Handy, Craighill

1971   *Polynesian Religion.* Bernice P. Bishop Museum Bulletin 34; Bayard Dominick
[1927]   Expedition Publication, No. 12. Bishop Museum, Honolulu; Kraus Reprint
         Co., New York.

Handy, Craighill, and Mary Kawena Pukui

1972   *The Polynesian Family System in Kaa'u, Hawai'i.* Charles E. Tuttle Company,
         Rutland, Vermont.

Janowski, Monica, and Tim Ingold (editors)

2012   *Imagining Landscapes: Past, Present and Future.* Ashgate, Farnham, Surrey,
         England.

Joseph, Robert

1998   Behind the Mask. In *Down from the Shimmering Sky. Masks of the
         Northwest Coast*, Peter MacNair, Robert Joseph, and Bruce Grenville,
         editors, pp. 18–35. University of Washington Press, Seattle.

Kalakaua, David

1888   *The Legends and Myths of Hawai'i. The Fables and Folk-lore of a Strange
         People.* Charles L. Webster & Company, New York.

Kamakau, Samuel Manaiakalani

1964   *Ka Po'e Kahiko: The People of Old.* Dorothy Barrere, editor; Mary Kawena
         Pukui, translator; . Bernice P. Bishop Museum Special Publication 51, Bishop
         Museum Press, Honolulu.

1991   *Tales and Traditions of the People of Old.* Bishop Museum Press, Honolulu.

1992   *Ruling Chiefs of Hawai'i.* The Kamehameha Schools Press, Honolulu.

Kame'eleihiwa, Lilikala

1999   *Na Wahine Kapu Divine Hawaiian Women.* Ai Pohaku Press, Honolulu.

Kanahele, George Hu'eu Sanford

1986   *Ku Kanaka Stand Tall A Search for Hawaiian Values.* University of Hawaii
         Press and Waiaha Foundation, Honolulu.

Kirch, Patrick Vinton

2012   *A Shark Going Inland is My Chief: The Island Civilization of Ancient
         Hawai'i.* University of California Press, Berkeley.

Lefebvre, Henri

1991   *The Production of Space.* Donald Nicholson-Smith, translator. Blackwell,
         Malden, MA.

Lévi-Strauss, Claude

1982   *The Way of the Masks.* University of Washington Press, Seattle. Translation
         of *La Voie des Masques* (1975) by Sylvia Modelski.

Lewis, Leslie

2014   When the Apolitical Is Political. *Anthropology News* 55(1–2): 7, 13.

Linnekin, Jocelyn

1990   *Sacred Queens and Women of Consequence. Rank, Gender, and Colonialism
         in the Hawaiian Islands.* University of Michigan Press, Ann Arbor.

Moore, Jerry

2005   *Cultural Landscapes in the Ancient Andes: Archaeologies of Place.* University
         Press of Florida, Gainesville.

Nabakov, Peter, and Robert Eaton
1989   *Native American Architecture*. Oxford University Press, New York.
Smith, Adam T.
2003   *The Political Landscape. Constellations of Authority in Early Complex Polities*. University of California Press, Berkeley.
Suttles, Wayne (editor)
1990   Northwest Coast, *Handbook of North American Indians*, Vol. 7, William C. Sturtevant, editor. Smithsonian Institution, Washington, DC.
Suttles, Wayne
1991   Streams of Property, Armor of Wealth: The Traditional Kwakiutl Potlatch. In *Chiefly Feasts: The Enduring Kwakiutl Potlatch*, Aldona Jonaitis, editor, pp. 71–134. American Museum of Natural History, University of Washington Press, Seattle.
Tilley, Christopher
1994   *A Phenomenology of Landscape Places, Paths and Monuments*. Berg Publishers, Oxford.
Wickwire, Wendy
2001   The Grizzly Gave Them the Song: James Teit and Frans Boas Interpret Twin Ritual in Aboriginal British Columbia, 1897–1920. *American Indian Quarterly* 25(3): 431–452.
Wyatt, Gary
1999   *Mythic Beings: Spirit Art of the Northwest Coast*. University of Washington Press, Seattle.

9

WOMEN PILGRIMS, LANDSCAPE, AND POLITICS IN POSTCLASSIC MESOAMERICA

Shankari Patel

It is a central tenant of this volume that women traveled extensively through the landscapes that they could see. They discovered places, they named places, and they personified places. In these landscapes, they conducted tasks, performed rites, and taught stories. One way that women traveled and learned of distant places—such as the Medicine Lake Boulder (Chapter 5), Arnold Research Cave sandal shelter (Chapter 1), Kilauea volcano (Chapter 8), or numerous places in Mexico—was through participating in pilgrimages.

Pilgrimages were not simple acts. Archaeologists should examine pilgrimage as an explicitly political act within the construction and maintenance of societies, their ideologies and their social interactions, and movements across the landscape. Although symbols related to fertility and womanhood are a common component at many of these places—such as in the Zuni boy's salt pilgrimage (Stoffle et al. 2009) or modern rain-calling pilgrimages described by Claassen (2013)—we continue to exclude gendered examinations of pilgrimage. Why is this? Perhaps, if women were deemed important social actors in this process then we might be forced to consider how women were also significant political actors, let alone recognize their extensive travel and landscape knowledge documented in the Introduction.

Gender, Landscape, and the Public/Private Divide

When discussing landscapes it is important to disentangle traditional Western assumptions of gender from our interpretations of the past.

The study of landscapes has a particular history in the West and exists in a system of power relations that affect the production of gendered identities. It is a product of the rise of industrialization and capitalism and is associated with hierarchal gender relations. Landscapes were originally tied to paintings commissioned by wealthy male landowners who wished to show off their landholdings. Landscapes were possessions and feminized through traditional western gender roles. Men were defined as the active producers of such images and women, like the landscape paintings themselves, were depicted as passive objects of visual pleasure (Ashmore 2006:200).

Landscapes became a medium in which gender stereotypes were constructed and perpetuated in the context of colonialism. Landscapes came to be gendered through the use of descriptive metaphors that equated indigenous femaleness with a disordered wilderness in contrast to the ordered pastoral paradise of Western womanhood (Westling 1996; Dowler et al. 2005). Native American women were portrayed as untamed, uncivilized, and un-pure—whose bodily integrity did not matter (Smith 2009). Racial descriptions of gender roles paralleled a civilized–native dichotomy where the public spaces of religion, politics, and power were deemed masculine and the private spaces, such as the household, were designated as feminine (Lamphere 2005). Such conceptions of space became naturalized in anthropological and archaeological descriptions of landscape.

Rosaldo's (1974:18) paradigm of the gendered public/private divide sought to explain the universal subordination of women by charting the recurrent psychological and cultural aspects of social organization that led to the domestic orientation of women and the inclination of men to occupy the public world. As feminism evolved over the years the public/private model was largely discredited. Critiqued for its universalizing elements, the public/private dichotomy grew out of the industrial revolution when the home became separated from the workplace and was therefore not very useful for investigating ancient or historical societies where economic production occurred in the home (Leacock 1978: 253).

Colonialism and industrialization naturalized contemporary descriptions of gender roles and women's status in past societies through landscape imagery that portrayed the divide between nature and culture in gendered terms. We often think nature is separate from culture but in reality it is a social construction with political ramifications. One of the justifications for political domination has often followed arguments regarding the union of the political institution and the physiological or natural environment. The ancient Greeks used elaborate organic images of human society in order to depict the citizen, the city, and the cosmos as comprised of the same material. The political body is sometimes illustrated as an organism, which is alive and part of a larger cosmic form. Equating the structure of human groups with forms found in nature is a powerful metaphoric tool used to depict domination based on difference as natural, given, and therefore inescapable and even moral (Haraway 1991). When social facts are equated with natural facts, the social realm is given the same immutability that is often associated with nature (McLellan 1995:56).

Motherhood as defining the primary role of woman's existence was central to nineteenth- and early twentieth-century scientific accounts of gender. Scientific theories of difference between men and women defined natural difference through empirical studies of bodies and brain sizes that assumed the white male to be the norm on which all others were measured. Women deviated from the norm in ways which made them fit for domesticity or motherhood and justified a range of social policies that excluded them from suffrage, higher education, equal pay, and public life (Gailey 1988, Weedon 1999:5–16).

The modern link between gender and landscape is most apparent in archaeological narratives that link the fertility of the earth (i.e., Mother Earth) with female bodies (Ashmore 2006:202). When nineteenth-century researchers looked at women's ritual through the lens of fertility, they reified Western gender stereotypes. As Hackett (1989) argues, fertility rites, particularly in the way they are described in the secondary literature of the ancient Near East and Mediterranean religions, are really a euphemism for ritual sex or prostitution that ensures the fertility of the earth. Rituals relating to women were described in terms of nineteenth-century conventions of gender that focused on the "polluting" reproductive attributes of the female body, such as maternity, sexual relations, and menstrual blood. Purity and pollution became the religious metaphors primarily applied to women who must either deny their bodies or bring their dangerous sexuality under control. Women's roles in society and religion (e.g., wife, whore, and nun) were primarily depicted in relation to their sexual function in delineating which patriarchal institution had access to their sexuality (Rosaldo and Lamphere 1974:31). These Western stereotypes inevitably found their way into archaeological interpretations. Scholars exaggerated the connection between fertility and female deities in the religions of the ancient Near East because fertility and mothering were aspects of women that Westerners found comforting and nonthreatening. Putting them into the category of fertility was one way of saying women of different cultures were interchangeable in terms of always fulfilling the same role as mothers and dependent sexual partners. Such misrepresentations reinforce the reduction of all women to the nature side of the nature/culture dichotomy (Hackett 1989:75) and perpetuate the myth that gender is ahistorical.

Within this fertility paradigm, archeologists were quick to equate nude female figurines with fertility rituals particularly when found in household contexts but less willing to explore aspects of menstruation and women's reproduction in public or political contexts. Because these elements of women's experiences were considered "polluting," "dangerous," and "taboo" in Western culture, it was assumed that women in all times and places hid menstruation and pregnancy and that these cultural practices would be invisible in the archaeological record of public spaces (Galloway 1997:66). As archaeologists it is important that when we examine ancient civilizations where fertility is equated with the earth and associated with gender that we look beyond nineteenth-century stereotypes. For instance, in ancient Mesoamerica social metaphors linked earth and water to fertility and applied these associations to both men and women. As Claassen (2013) points out, fertility rites in modern-day Mexico continue to utilize pre-Columbian metaphors regarding landscape and gender that relegate male fertility to celestial water and female fertility to terrestrial water.

Archaeological Discussions of Postclassic Pilgrimage in Mesoamerica

Archaeologists often use ethnohistorical and ethnographic descriptions of women's work to establish archaeological correlates. Given the bias of these sources, women's activities have been linked to the household. Thus women are defined by the artifacts associated with domestic and utilitarian affairs (such as weaving implements including awls and spindle whorls, cooking and storage vessels, food processing equipment, figurines, etc.). While the above markers reflect women's activities in the domestic sphere, they are often interpreted as objects owned by men when found in public, ritual, or even mortuary contexts.[2] Feminist critiques of Mesoamerican archaeology have illustrated that the public/private dichotomy relies on inherently patriarchal viewpoints that reconstruct the past through the lens of modern androcentric social ideologies (Ardren 2002, 2008; Ashmore 2002; Blackmore 2011; Brumfiel 2006;

Brumfiel and Robin 2008; Hendon 2006; Joyce 2006, 2008; Pyburn 2004; Robin 2002), that exclude women. Despite such feminist critiques, Mesoamerican archaeological narratives of pilgrimage continue to employ the public/private dichotomy and thereby validating the very nature of gendered movements within and through space (see Kubler 1985; Smith and Berdan 2003; Vail and Hernandez 2010).

Scholarship regarding pilgrimage in Mesoamerica has tended to reproduce colonial perspectives regarding a woman's place in the domestic sphere. Because pilgrimage is associated with religion and the politics of the state, archaeologists have tended to ignore the role of women in this important activity. Archaeological discussions of pilgrimage started with an attempt to understand a series of material linkages that crossed ethnic and linguistic barriers and connected various sites in Mesoamerica through similar architecture, religious motifs, rituals, and ceramic assemblages in the Epiclassic (A.D. 700–950) and Postclassic (A.D. 950–1519) periods. The first serious discussion of these linkages arose as a result of trying to answer the question of why the Early Postclassic (A.D. 950–1200) cities of Chichén Itzá and Tula were so similar to one another.

Ringle and colleagues (1998) proposed that the reason Chichén Itzá and Tula shared similar architecture and art was because they were part of a network of pan-Mesoamerican pilgrimage sites extending from Morelos and Puebla to the Gulf Coast and into Yucatan. These sites shared a similar art style (the Mixteca-Puebla or International Art Style) that transcended political boundaries and included the pilgrimage sites listed in the colonial documents, such as Cholula, Tula, Cacaxtla, El Tajin, Isla de Sacrificios, Xochicalco, Izamal, Uxmal, Isla Cozumel, and Chichén Itzá (Figure 9.1). The authors further defined the focus of the cult activity as centered on Quetzalcoatl/K'uk'ulkan in his aspect as Feathered Serpent, and as the patron of merchants and leaders. According to Ringle (2004) the main purpose for such sites was to serve as locations for rituals of investiture regarding kingly and elite authority.

One of the major problems with a Feathered Serpent pilgrimage model that uses the colonial "Quetzalcoatl" terminology is that it erases the participation of women in Mesoamerican pilgrimage practices. The colonial documents mention many other gods and goddesses that were consulted at pilgrimages centers and that pilgrims went to these places for a variety of reasons. However, the Spanish friars were fascinated by the Tula accounts of a priest king who proselytized his return, particularly when associations could be made between Quetzalcoatl, bearded white men, Cortes, and the arrival of the Spaniards. Some friars

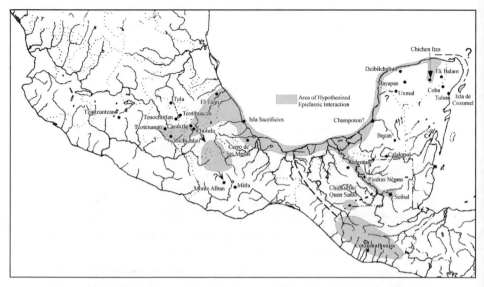

Figure 9.1. Map of Mesoamerican pilgrimage interaction in Epiclassic and Postclassic periods. Map created by Chelsea Blackmore and used courtesy of William Ringle.

promoted the idea that Quetzalcoatl/K'uk'ulkan could be an early apostle of Christ so they took great care to link Christian features to him and note his objections to human sacrifice (Gillespie 2007). In friar accounts Quetzalcoatl is always thought to be an important historical male god personage rather than a deity with many overlapping powers and that colonial assumption has influenced subsequent archaeological arguments regarding Feathered Serpent pilgrimage as the primary (and only form of pilgrimage) pertaining to male priests, kings, and merchants. Many pilgrimage locales had both male and female healers, scribes, and priests; however, when archaeologists use unmarked male gender categories for occupational positions a subtle assumption regarding gender is immediately perpetuated. For example, in a recent Mesoamerican volume, titled *Astronomers, Scribes, and Priests,* (see Vail and Hernandez 2010) that explored the linkages between the religious texts and symbolism found at pilgrimage centers in the Northern Maya Lowlands and at sites in Highland Mexico, it is assumed that the exchange of intellectual information only occurred between elite males.

Ancient pilgrimage traditions were often not part of a single religion but rather a collection of beliefs and practices that could be incorporated into divergent religious viewpoints and varying ritual practices (Coleman and Elsner 1995:29). Thompson (1970) based his Putun Maya theory on the ethnohistoric works of Scholes and Roys (1968 [1948]) who analyzed early Spanish records[3] concerning the homeland of the Chontal (Putun) Maya in Acalan, Tabasco. Thompson downplayed the association of the Putun Maya with a feminine cult whose focus was on a goddess associated with pregnancy and weaving. Scholes and Roys (1968 [1948]:48) stated that the Chontal Maya held a strategic position in the economy of Mesoamerica by facilitating trade between the Gulf and Caribbean coasts and across the Yucatan peninsula by virtue of controlling the river routes along Candelaria and the Usumacinta–San Pedro Martír drainages that flow into Laguna de Terminos. The authors noted that trade was made easier by the similarities in the languages spoken over this large area, which included Yukatecan Maya, the main language of the peninsula, and the Chontal,[4] Chol, and Chorti dialects spoken from Laguna Tupilco in Tabasco down to the Ulua River. The authors relied on the colonial Chontal text that detailed the ancestry of Don Pablo Paxbolon described as the original ancestor of the Acalan ruling family who founded the town after visiting the island of Cozumel off the northeastern coast of Yucatan. From Cozumel, this ancestor came to Tenosique in the Usumacinta basin with a group of followers and took over the government that included establishing four regional temple sanctuaries aligned to the cardinal directions. Each sanctuary had its own "chief" and patron deity, but the principle deity of the region was a goddess also revered on Cozumel (1968 [1948]:57).

At the time of the Spanish conquest, Cozumel Island served as a pilgrimage center associated with Ix Chel–a goddess of divination, medicine, and childbirth. According to Fr. Diego de Landa (in Tozzer 1941) pilgrims came to visit the oracle shrine of Ix Chel. In addition, the island north of Cozumel, Isla de Mujeres, was also thought to have participated in this network because it had received its name from the Spaniards due to numerous feminine idols and sculptures found on it (Tozzer 1941: 9).[5] Scholes and Roys (1968[1948]:57) argued that Ix Chel was a popular deity among the Chontal not only because the site of Tixchel in Tabasco had been named after her but also because many towns on the Usumacinta River and in central Tabasco reflected the presence of a feminine cult. This included Ciuatecpan (palace of the woman) on the Usumacinta; Ciuatan (the place of the woman) in central Tabasco; and Cuyo de las Damas on the Rio Chico, a branch of the Usumacinta River (Scholes and Roys 1968[1948]:57).

However, Thompson's (1970) discussions of women reflected colonial perspectives regarding the inherent impurity of women's bodies
and the need to control women's dangerous sexuality. For example, his
view of women included the following statement (1970:184), "As among
many people, the Maya regarded women as contaminated" (the view
that menstruation is ritually impure is worldwide). When women are
mentioned in Thompson's accounts, they are described as either "wives"
or "virgins" rather than pilgrims or priestesses.

> There was an order of "vestal virgins," who lived under a "mother supe-
> rior" in a building alongside the temples. Their duties included tending
> the sacred fires in the temples. Death by arrows was their punishment for
> loss of chastity. There was a tradition that the building at Uxmal known
> as the Nunnery was their abode, but I much doubt that. Among the deco-
> rative elements of the façade are naked men with prominent genitals, a
> very rare feature in Maya art and hardly what one would expect on a
> building to house dedicated virgins. (Thompson 1970: 169)

Thompson's account refers to the colonial material from Lopez de
Cogolludo's 1688 narrative that relates the story of an exalted pre-
Columbian woman known as Zuhuy Kak. Defined as "virginal fire,"
Zuhuy Kak lived in a convent and was the daughter of a king and
the protector of small girls that were left in her care at Uxmal. However, Landa (Tozzer 1941:153) mentions *Zuhuy Kak* not as a historical
woman but rather as a religious office associated with the New Fire ceremonies and linked with matters regarding warfare and healing. Lopez
de Cogolludo's (as translated in Blom 1983: 308) account states:

> Close to the temple buildings, in some places, there are other buildings
> wherein lived some maidens, who were like nuns somewhat similar to
> the Vestal Virgins of the Romans. They had a Superior or Abbess, whom
> they called Ix Nacan Katun, "She Has Been Raised in War," because she
> guarded her virginity and that of those who were in her charge. If some-
> one forced the chastity of a maiden while she was there, she was killed
> with arrows, though they could leave (the convent) to get married, if they
> had the permission of the high priest. They had a woman door-keeper to
> guard their retreat, and they tended the perpetual fires in the temples. If
> this fire went out, the one who failed to watch it was put to death. In
> Uxmal there is a great Patio with many separate rooms just like a con-
> vent, where maidens lived.

Blom (1983:308) speculates that Lopez de Cogolludo's vestal virgins
may have also been "the beautiful virgin maidens" that other colonial

documents note were cast into the Sacred Cenote at Chichén Itzá. Historian Clendinnen (1982:28) deduced from these accounts that prior to Spanish contact women were excluded from public rituals except for prepubescent girls who were ritually sacrificed and the old women who "were safely past menopause" and therefore allowed to dance before the idols. Hooton (1940: 272–280) who initially examined several of the skeletons from Chichén Itzá's sacred well remarked, "All the individuals involved (or rather immersed) may have been virgins, but the osteological evidence does not permit a determination of this point." Subsequent years of osteological analysis of the human sacrificial remains from the wells and caves of Chichén Itzá demonstrate that contrary to colonial accounts males and children were the actual preferred victims (Beck and Sievert 2005:291, Tiesler 2005:356).

Reevaluating Material Evidence of Women's Roles in Pilgrimage Ritual

In Veracruz in particular, an area identified as an important part of pan-Mesoamerican pilgrimage circuits, the rituals pertaining to women need to be reevaluated. The Aztecs described the women from Veracruz as expert weavers and proficient sorcerers who imported their Tlazolteotl-Ixcuina cult from the Gulf Coast into the Central Plateau of Mexico (Sahagun 1950–1982, Bk. 10:185–186). During the Late Classic and Postclassic periods, the peoples of the Mixtequill–an area in the western lower Papaloapan Basin in south-central Veracruz–produced two commodities vital to interregional exchange: textiles and figurines (Stark and Curet 1994). During the Classic period the production of cotton cloth increased in economic importance in the region. Cloths and garments have common social and functional properties in that they can represent gender, ethnicity, rank, class, or office. Because of the amount of labor that went into elite garments they were presented at life-crisis rituals, rites of passage, and other social negotiations (Stark et al. 1998:9). Another product related to life cycle rituals is the ceramic figurine produced in south-central Veracruz known as the Smiling Face (*caritas sonrientes*) figurines. Distinctive characteristics of these figurines include the upright arms or hands on hips and a smile or enigmatic expression that researchers think may be related to a state of drug induced euphoria associated with *pulque* drinking rituals (Wilkerson 1987). Many of these figurines are dressed in rich textiles distinctive of both the Veracruz and Maya regions.

Postclassic Isla de Sacrificios

Isla de Sacrificios, an island site off the coast of south central Veracruz has been linked to the Feathered Serpent cult ever since Zelia Nuttall (1910) excavated a wall with a mural depicting Quetzalcoatl in 1909. Isla de Sacrificios received further attention by Miguel Angel Fernandez and Wilfrido du Solier (du Solier 1943) whose excavations revealed similar ceramic vessels as those found at Cholula leading them to the hypothesis that Isla de Sacrificios participated in the same pan-Mesoamerican pilgrimage network. They postulated that the island had served as a place of ritual and a necropolis for the elite who lived on the mainland. Alfonso Medellín Zenil (1955) also conducted salvage excavations at Isla de Sacrificios and determined that while a small amount of material could be correlated with the Preclassic and Classic periods, the majority of artifacts from Isla de Sacrificios reflected the Epiclassic/Early Postclassic periods (A.D. 900–1200) with a decline in the deposition of material during the Late Postclassic period (A.D. 1200–1519). Because of the numerous representations of Quetzalcoatl on the funerary ceramics, Medellín Zenil concluded that the introduction of the Postclassic Feathered Serpent cult to the region prompted the increase in mortuary ritual on the island (1955).

However, Nunez Ortega (1885) originally argued that Isla de Sacrificios and the mainland just opposite to it also corresponded to Aztec descriptions of Chalchiuhtlicuecan, the home of the water goddess, "Jades-Her-Skirt," Chalchiuhtlicue. Nuttall (1910:268) disagreed with him on the basis that the Spanish explorers had not described any human sculptures on the island. Also, Quetzalcoatl was a male deity and female sculptures had already been associated with the Huastecs in northern Veracruz. However, more data has come to light since Nunez Ortega and Nuttall first debated this hypothesis.

Nicholson (1971:120) pointed out that in the days preceding the Spanish conquest both the northern and southern Gulf Coasts constituted the primary region for the cult of Tlazolteotl-Ixcuina. The Nahua name, Tlazolteotl, comes from term *tlazolli,* which derives from the verb *izolihui* indicating something that is old or worn out and *teotl* designating divinity. Implicit in this was the concept that in order to be renewed *tlazolli* was required (Burkhart 1989:88). The manure distributed throughout agriculture fields to make them sustainable was called *tlazolli* (Molina 1970:II, 137r). In Postclassic Central Mexico *tlazolli* belonged to the deities Tlazolteotl and Tezcatlipoca following the Mesoamerican tendency to split a single function between male and female deities (Estrada Quevedo 1962:163). Ixcuina comes from the Huastec Mayan language and means "Lady Cotton." Tlazolteotl-Icuina was often depicted with a headband of unspun cotton. The Huastec-Totonac section of the Gulf Coast was a region associated with richly woven textiles from the Early Classic period to the time of contact (Stark 2001). The goddesses of the Gulf Coast were also called by other Central Mexican names, such as Teteo innan, "Mother of the Gods"; Toci, "Our Grandmother"; Temazcalteci, "Grandmother of the Bathhouse"; Yohualiticitl, "Midwife of the Night"; Tonantzin "Our Mother"; Tlalli iyollo, "Heart of the Earth"; Ilamatecuhtil, "Old Woman"; Itzapapalotl, "Obsidian Butterfly"; Xochiquetzal, "Flowery Quetzal Feather"; and Cihuacoatl "Snake Woman" (Sullivan 1982:7–8). In the Codex, Borbonicus Tlazolteotl-Teoteo innan-Toci is portrayed in a jade net overskirt with a triangle *quechquemitl* top and the trapeze ray Mexican Year Sign in her headdress. The *quechquemitl* costume element was worn by Aztec goddesses and their impersonators, but it was also a garment most often associated with women from northeastern Mesoamerica. In the Central Mexican codices most depictions of the *quechquemitl* costume element pertained to representations of Tlazolteotl, Chalchiuhtlicue, and Xochiquetzal (Anawalt 1982:42).

Worship and supplication involved offerings and insignia among other material expressions. What evidence is there of these cults and their shrines?

The Nepean Collection

During the 19th century, the ancient Maya and Gulf Coast peoples became a source of public fascination in the U.S. and Europe. This demand to know more about these culture groups along with the relative geographic proximity of the Yucatan Peninsula's and Veracruz's coasts made coastal and island sites a focus for foreign museum expeditions. As a result, these 19th and early 20th century collections are comprised primarily of ceramic vessels, *incensarios*, figurines, sculptures, and ceramic and stucco fragments taken from ritual shrines and settlements located along the coasts of Veracruz, Campeche, Tabasco, and Yucatan. As part of my dissertation research, I took a closer look at the Nepean collection of artifacts from Isla de Sacrificios in order to recover an unconsidered source of data regarding women and pilgrimage. Research conducted in late 2011 and early 2012 sought to document over two thousand items from the Nepean Collection, the largest group of artifacts from Isla de Sacrificios that the British Museum acquired from a British naval officer Captain Evan Nepean in 1844. While several well-known pieces from this collection had received prior attention, very little information was available regarding the non-ceramic vessel items in the collection.

Acquired in 1844, the Nepean Collection was first described by Nepean and Birch (1843) and also discussed in *Archaeologia, Vol. XXX* (Birch 1844). Nuttall (1910) who first summarized the Spanish documents that recorded the conquistador's impressions on visiting Isla de Sacrificios also analyzed the iconography from 22 Nepean ceramic vessels and two vessels acquired by the British Museum in 1851 from Lt. Forrest and then compared them to similar island vessels found in Mexican and U.S. museums. Thomas Joyce (1912, 1914) published additional photos of the ceramics and provided drawings featuring six of the collection's spindle whorls. Iconographical analysis of the collection's motifs by Strebel (1885–1889) and E. Spinden (1933) situated this island site in relation to Totonac history. In Smith's (1958: 158) ceramic description and an analysis of Fine Orange pottery in Mesoamerica, he stated that the Isla de Sacrificios stood out because of the variety of Fine Orange ceramic ware types and the amount of distinctive fine polychromes from nearby and distant sites. McEwan (1994, 2009) highlighted the importance of the Nepean collection for understanding Mesoamerican pilgrimage offerings. Clara Bezanilla whose work (Dahlin et. al 1998) helped to document the importance of coastal sites in the northwestern Gulf Coast of Yucatan also worked on organizing the collection. I chose to focus on the items indicative of gender in household contexts: figurines and spindle whorls.

Figurines from Isla Sacrificios generally fall into two categories: figurines with hollow bodies and figurines with flat backs. Each type has mold-made characteristics. Most figurines with torsos in the Nepean collection delineate women. Figurines that have flat backs include the Postclassic Cerros de las Mesas II type first documented by Drucker (1943:63–64) at Cerros de las Mesas and later observed by Stark (2001:206) for the Mixtequilla. In these figures the bodies are flat with arms at their sides or across their abdomen. Similar to the Cerros de las Mesas and the Mixtequilla examples, the Isla de Sacrificios figurines depict feminine figures with conical hats and braided headdresses in addition to figurines who wear the *quechquemitl* and a mirror (Figure 9.2) or a unique combination of *quechquemitl* and a version of the Veracruz diving bird headdress. The drilled holes on the sides of several of these

Figure 9.2. Cerro de las Mesas II/Isla de Sacrificios figurines small flat back pendant variety with *quechquemitl*. Photo by S. Patel.

examples suggest they may have been worn as pendants or costume elements. In addition to the small flat back variety, the Nepean collection also has examples of the large flat back type Cerros de las Mesas III reminiscent of the flat back figurines from Postclassic Central Mexico.

Isla de Sacrificios' hollow figurines of the Cerros de las Mesas II type also have their hands at their sides or across their abdomen. Figurines associated with the Isla de Sacrificios type from previous excavations include two hollow figurine-rattle varieties (Medellin Zenil 1955). In the first group, the feminine figure wears a blue and white *quechquemitl* (Figure 9.3), or the hollow figurine body is depicted sitting cross-legged in a blue *quechquemitl*. This particular type of hollow figurine sitting cross-legged and wearing a *quechquemitl* was also found on Cozumel (Phillips 1979:63). The second group of hollow figurines is shaped like a bell or a rattle but also has the *quechquemitl* clearly delineated.

If we follow Drucker's (1943:64) chronology regarding female figurines at Cerro de las Mesas, many of the female figurines in the Nepean collection from the island date to the Middle and Late Postclassic periods. Representations of female figurines in the collection denote changes to ritual practices. First, many of the figurines reflect local coastal traditions and are identical to figurines excavated from Cerro de las Mesas.

Second, according to Garraty and Stark (2002:29) spatial arrangements and ceramic features in the Mixtequilla underwent a significant change from Middle to Late Postclassic times because of the extension of the Aztec empire into south-central Veracruz. It is during the Middle and Late Postclassic period that the region became much more oriented to highland stylistic patterns with subsequent changes to ritual practices reflected by the introduction and use of flat mold-made figurines (Curet et al. 1994:27). Based on his excavations of the island, Medellín Zenil (1955) concluded that there was a pronounced decline in material deposition for the Middle and Late Postclassic periods. As Garraty and Stark (2002:27) note, the Late Postclassic period in the Mixtequilla is defined by a greater gap between the rich and the poor most likely resulting from elevated Aztec tribute demands. The extension of the Aztec empire into Veracruz changed social relations resulting in changes to depositional practices and to material culture.

Figure 9.3. Isla de Sacrificios hollow feminine figure wearing the quechquemitl. Photo by S. Patel.

Spindle Whorls

In what ways does the Nepean collection reflect religious practices dedicated to the cult of Tlazolteotl-Ixcuina? The best evidence for ritual
practices associated with a cotton goddess cult comes from the numerous
incised and decorated spindle whorls found in the collection and the
variety of bone awls, needles, and weaving picks that time constraints
prevented me from documenting. Many of the spindle whorls I examined
exhibited isthmian imagery as well as themes related to the International
Art Style. Spindle whorls were used for the production of textiles, a vital
activity to Postclassic Central Mexico because textiles served as a unit
for tribute payment. In addition to being found in domestic contexts,
spindle whorls often show up in ritual and burial contexts. McCafferty
and McCafferty (1991) noted that incised and decorated spindle whorls
start to appear in Cholula's archaeological record after A.D. 900, with
many examples originating from ritual contexts. Proyecto Cholula excavated over 600 spindle whorls from the ceremonial center surrounding
the Great Pyramid (McCafferty and McCafferty 2000:42).

The presence of spindle whorls in ritual contexts is associated with
certain Feathered Serpent pilgrimage cult centers but was not included
in Ringle and colleagues (1998) inventory of pilgrimage related artifacts.
Seventy-six spindle whorls with incised decorative designs were excavated from Postclassic ritual contexts at Cozumel (Phillips 1979:64).
Archaeologists found over 500 spindle whorls in the Pyramid of the
Flowers at Xochitécatl in Tlaxcala (Serra Puche 2001:268). The Carnegie Institution excavated 106 spindle whorls from Chichén Itzá, many
from ritual contexts, such as the sweathouse east of the Court and the
Temple of the Xtoloc Cenote (Kidder 1943: 96). Kidder delineated two
types of spindle whorls representative of the collection found at Chichén
Itzá. The first type consisted of an incised oval form with decorative
designs characterizing one side. The second type of spindle whorl re-
sembled a steep-sided truncated cone or "cupcake." Decoration commenced through deep incising and possibly the use of a mold-made
ceramic stamp. Two designs seemed consistent: one that denoted geometric shapes and flower-like symbols and the other that depicted more
realistic portraits of animals such as birds and monkeys. The spindle
whorls originated from the near surface layers that indicated to Kidder
that they were most likely deposited after the site's abandonment.

There are over 300 spindle whorls in the Nepean collection from
Isla de Sacrificios. Most of the spindle whorls were made from clay

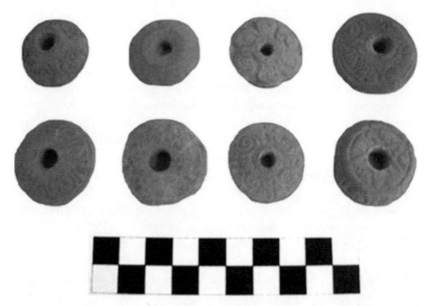

Figure 9.4. Spindle whorls from Isla de Sacrificios in the Nepean Collection. Photo by S. Patel.

or ceramic mold designs although a few examples were crafted from bone and coral. The incised designs on the spindle whorls do reflect Kidder's categories from Chichén Itzá. Such specimens include depictions of birds, monkeys, and geometric flowers (Figure 9.4). However, many of the designs on the Isla de Sacrificios' spindle whorls also depict earlier isthmian specific symbols and motifs.

Isla de Sacrificios was simultaneously a funerary ritual site, a place for human sacrifice, and a location associated with a feminine cult. The Feathered Serpent pilgrimage assemblage of items from Isla de Sacrificios in the Nepean collection included special jars, plates, and vessels involved in feasting or the consumption of ritual alcoholic beverages. Such items could have also been interred with the dead for their possible use in similar activities found in the afterlife. Funerary rituals as rites of passage helped individuals as well as their community to accept changes resulting from the loss of one their members. In many world religions death is a liminal or transitional period prior to a rebirth in a new status (Livingston 2005:90), and funerary rituals served to situate the deceased into this new status in the afterlife (Van Gennep 1960[1909]). Many of the animal effigy vessels and jars in the Nepean collection as well as their iconographic content reflected themes associated with a floral solar paradise where the departed dead were transformed into birds, butterflies, and other animals (Taube 2010, 2011).

As Robles Castellanos (2010:66) has argued, the Feathered Serpent cult lost ground in Central Mexico to the Aztec imperial cult of Huitzilopochtli in the Late Postclassic period. One of the strategies that the Aztecs utilized to bring Feathered Serpent cult activities under imperial control included integrating Quetzalcoatl into their pantheon and the importation of the Gulf Coast goddess cults, including their priestesses, to their capital at Tenochtitlan. Some of these goddesses included Tlazolteotl-Ixcuina, Cihuacoatl "Woman Serpent" and Coatlicue "Serpents Her Skirt," the goddess that gives birth to Huitzilopochtli. Many of the serpent elements that relate to Cihuacoatl and Coatlicue representations, such as the two headed serpent belt (see Boone 1999), have their antecedents at El Zapotal in the Late Classic period.

Discussion: Pilgrimage, Landscape, and Gender

The preconquest books of the Mixtec region and the early colonial codices from Central Mexico depict the importance of pilgrimage for the legitimization of political power (Pohl 1999) and serve as a model for what Postclassic pilgrimage practices may have been like for women in Postclassic Veracruz and Yucatan. Pohl and Byland (1990) delineated the Mixtec landscape in terms of its polities and dynastic interactions including ritual travel to physical landmarks. The codices marked movement across the landscape with foot prints connecting travelers to sacred places and events (Ashmore 2009; Pohl 1999). Women travelled across the landscape to visit women healers and priestesses at pilgrimage shrines. These were sites where the practice of medical knowledge took place and where women could consult female healers about their reproductive options. Travel for healing and consultation are documented elsewhere in this volume for women on the Plains and in California and proposed in the Ozark and Cumberland plateaus (see Claassen, Chapter 1 and Greer and Greer, Chapter 5).

Priestesses and healers used divination for issues related to both health and politics. The proximity of the dead was vital to the acts of divination that affected the living, and mortuary gambling was widespread in the Americas (Ventur 1980 specifically but see also Eyman 1965). In the Mixtec codices, the oracular priestess, Lady Nine Grass's power to commune with the dead or with the spirit world derived from the Chalcatongo cave shrine where prominent Mixtec personages had been buried. In the Yucatan, religious shrines and centers located on the coast increased in importance during the Postclassic period. For many Meso-american groups, the sea was an entrance to the spirit realm. Coastal sites represented geographic and spiritual outposts associated with birth, death, the underworld, and the afterlife (Andrews 1994:162). An island used for the interment of the dead may have given priestesses associated with Isla de Sacrificios the power of oracular divination and the ability to talk with departed ancestors. Sculptures of prominent women were an integral part of the political and public landscape of coastal Veracruz. Many of these statues can be found in museum collections in the U.S. and abroad (see catalog compiled by De La Fuente and Gutierrez Solana 1980:51–134). The British Museum has several such sculptures from coastal Veracruz including a priestess wearing a headdress with solar rays

Figure 9.5. Statue of a Priestess with international style headdress at the British Museum. Photo by S. Patel.

depicted in the International Art Style (Figure 9.5), and a priestess wearing a conical hat associated with the cult of Quetzalcoatl. The small flat back figurine pendants in the Nepean collection may have been costume elements worn by the Ixcuiname priestesses conducting rituals at Isla de Sacrificios. These pendants depict women wearing the *quechquemitl*, a costume element that originated in the Gulf Coast realm (Anawalt 1981) and represented the rank of religious and political office worn by goddesses and elite women in the Mixtec, Aztec, and Maya regions.

Gods and goddesses in Mesoamerica were linked to powers found in the environment, such as the sun, moon, water, and the earth, but they were also associated with occupational specializations. Despite religious equivalencies between women, the moon, maize, and the earth in ancient Mesoamerica, women were not disempowered with respect to their own bodies and reproduction rights. While it is often assumed that priestesses associated with the pregnancy and childbirth goddesses, such as Tlazolteotl and Ix Chel, were primarily patronized in order to become pregnant (Miller 2005), we also know from colonial records that they were consulted in matters relating to a woman's fertility, such as how not to become pregnant or how to end a pregnancy once it commenced, or for their knowledge of midwifery. Elite women travelled to certain oracle shrines for rituals relating to the birth of their children just as women in Central Mexico travel to sacred ahuehuete trees today (Claassen 2013) soliciting fertility and aid in life crises of children. The depiction in the Codex Zouche-Nuttall of Lady Three Flint visiting Lady One Eagle's sweat bath river shrine, just prior to giving birth, the accompanying religious rituals involved in promoting a successful delivery, and the rites of reincorporation involved thereafter is one such example. Another archaeological example that such shrines existed include the shrines on Cozumel whose temples contained sculptured architectural columns depicting women in birthing positions (Patel 2009). The numerous examples of sweat baths on Cozumel (Ríos Meneses 1988) indicate the possible use of such structures in birthing rituals in Yucatan. There is also evidence that oracular priestesses from Cozumel delivered prophesies regarding war and future events. In the National Library of Berlin there is a woodcut made between the years 1521 and 1523 that describes in German the arrival of the Spaniards to a country called Yucatan and the women they found on Cozumel Island. On the upper right angle of the woodcut is an image of two oracle priestesses from Cozumel "beseeched by the Devil" in the midst of prophesizing about upcoming events related to warfare (Figure 9.6).

While most archaeological discussions of the fertility/earth goddesses in Mesoamerica equate women's fertility with the fertility of the earth, they often forget that earth goddess iconography also emphasizes women's roles in economic production in addition to their other important social roles as diviners, curers, and warriors, as has been explained by Duncan and Diaz-Granados (Chapter 3) for the societies in the greater Cahokia area of the midwestern U.S. In the Maya codices there are numerous representations of goddesses engaged in economic production, such as spinning, weaving, and apiculture. Goddess I, although depicted performing rituals involving water (Ciaramella 1994), is primarily shown weaving. Although Goddess O or Chak Chel had water associations, she was also linked to divination, medicine, childbirth, and weaving. These roles and attributes that define Goddess O compare closely to the roles and traits associated with Tlazolteotl (Ciaramella 1994:103). Much like Tlazolteotl, Goddess O is also a weaver, a midwife, and a warrior with specific attributes that link her to the Central Mexican fierce goddesses associated with warfare and sacrifice (Klein 2000). The priestesses of Goddess O were diviners who often carried mirrors used in divination rituals as depicted on the Dresden Codex page 42a where Goddess O holds a mirror containing the face of God C. A similar example from Central Mexico is the sculpture from the Feathered Serpent cult site of Xochicalco in Morelos that denotes a woman holding a mirror while wearing the war serpent headdress (Taube 1992). The Goddess O impersonator as depicted on the mural from structure 16 at Tulum wears the *quechquemitl* designating religious and noble office as well as a serpent and spindles in her headdress denoting the importance of women in priestly offices and their value to the occupation of textile production. These images indicate that in the context of Postclassic religious discourses there is an emphasis on the importance of women in the professional and occupational organizations of Mesoamerican society. The deposition of decorative spindle whorls at sites such as Isla de Sacrificios calls attention to women's roles in economic production particularly during a period of increased tribute and labor extraction resulting from the centralization of Aztec power (Brumfiel 2006; McCafferty and McCafferty 1991:31–32, 2000:47–48).

After the first Franciscan friars arrived to convert the natives in accordance with Christian policy and as a prerequisite for incorporating natives into the hierarchal relations of colonial society, indigenous priestesses were vilified. This process took place through the reorientation of language, social space, the human body, and everyday social conduct

Figure 9.6. Detail of a sixteenth century German woodcarving depicting the witches of Cozumel "beseeched by the Devil" in the midst of prophesizing about future events related to war. Photo by S. Patel.

(Hanks 2010:2). One of the main ways of reorienting language and indigenous society was to describe existing gender relations in terms of the Christian patriarchal good versus evil binary. Fr. Sahagún discusses in great detail the different types of evil women in Aztec society. An Aztec woman who went to a healer for herbs that caused abortions or who had a child outside of marriage was a *tetzauhcihuatl* "an ominous woman" (Burkhart 1989:150). Another evil woman as described in Sahagún's narrative was the "hermaphrodite"–a "detestable woman" who has a penis or who has carnal relations with other women or who went about acting like a man. An additional example was the evil female physician who provided herbs for contraception or abortion and who "has a vulva, a crushed vulva, a friction-loving vulva. [She is] a doer of evil. She bewitches—a sorceress, a person of sorcery, a possessed one" (Sahagún 1958–70:10, 53). Fr. Sahagún probably had the Ixcuiname priestesses in mind when he described the Aztec harlots in Book 10 of the Florentine Codex.

The Spanish friars were not too fond of the Tlazolteotl-Ixcuina cult or the Huastec priestesses, the Ixcuiname, who had brought the cult to

Central Mexico. The friars linked this cult with vice and sexual licentiousness. Because Haustec and Gulf Coast women were often linked to this deity, they became, from the friars' point of view, deviant women defined in terms of European views of sexuality not under patriarchal control: the adulterers, the exhibitionists and the promiscuous women sorcerers who drank too much *pulque* in their worship of the "Filth Deity" (Burkhart 1989:94; Klein 2000).

When the friars encountered indigenous women in Mesoamerica who controlled their own fertility and the decisions affecting their own bodies, the friars could not help but to think that such women had been swayed by the Devil and thus feverishly worked to reorient them into more acceptable views of sexuality, gender relations, and physical movement that reflected European Christian policies. This reworking included the destruction of shrines and of medicine women. The colonial process would eventually change women's taskscape, ritescape, and storyscape.

As archaeologists reconstructing ancient Mesoamerican societies, when we perpetuate colonialism by only focusing on images of women as broad tropes of fertility we literally remove women from pre-Columbian landscapes. Furthermore, we incorrectly assume that only men had access to public and political power through land ownership and their knowledge of land among other things, all contradicted by articles in Schroeder et al (1997) and the codices. We willingly relegate women to goddess status but not to roles of active historical figures, rulers, priestesses, or pilgrims, an idea that allows archaeologists to ignore and essentialize not only women's participation but their central role in pilgrimage practices and international politics. Women's bodies, contrary to the evidence, are erased from the landscape.

REFERENCES CITED

Anawalt, Patricia

1981   Indian Clothing before Cortes: Mesoamerican Costumes from the Codices. University of Oklahoma Press, Norman.

1982   Analysis of the Aztec Quechquemitl: An Exercise in Inference. In *The Art and Iconography of Late Post-Classic Central Mexico*, Elizabeth Hill Boone, editor, pp. 37–72. Dumbarton Oaks, Trustees for Harvard University, Washington DC.

Andrews, Anthony P.

1984   Political Geography of the Sixteenth Century Yucatan Maya: Comments and Revisions. *Journal of Anthropological Research* 40:589–596.

1994   The Role of Trading Ports in Maya Civilization. In *Vision and Revision in Maya Studies*, Flora S. Clancy and Peter D. Harrison, editors, pp. 159–168. University of New Mexico, Albuquerque.

Ardren, Traci

2002   Women and Gender in the Ancient Maya World. In *Ancient Maya Women*, Traci Ardren, editor, pp. 1–11. Altamira Press, Walnut Creek, CA.

2008   Studies of Gender in Prehispanic Americas. *Journal of Archaeological Research* 16:1–35.

Arvey, Margaret C.

1988   Women of Ill-Repute in the Florentine Codex. In *The Role of Gender in Precolumbian Art and Architecture*, Virginia E. Miller, editor, pp. 179–204. University Press of America, Lanham, MD.

Ashmore, Wendy

2002   Encountering Maya Women. In *Ancient Maya Women*, Traci Ardren, editor, pp. 229–245. Altamira Press, Walnut Creek, CA.

2006   Gender and Landscapes. In *Handbook of Gender in Archaeology*, Sarah Milledge Nelson, editor, pp. 199–218. Altamira Press, Walnut Creek, CA.

2009   Mesoamerican Landscape Archaeologies. *Ancient Mesoamerica* 20(2):183–187.

Beck, Lane A. and Sievert, April K.

2005   Mortuary Pathways Leading to the Cenote at Chichén Itzá. In *Interacting with the Dead: Perspectives on Mortuary Archaeology for the New Millennium*, Gordon Rakita, Jane Buikstra, L. Beck, and S. Williams, editors, pp. 290–304. University Press of Florida, Gainesville.

Birch, Samuel

1844   *Archaeologia or Miscellaneous Tracts Relating to Antiquity* 30:139–143.

Blackmore, Chelsea

2011   How to Queer the Past without Sex: Queer Theory, Feminisms, and the Archaeology of Identity. *Archaeologies: Journal of the World Archaeological Congress* 7(1):75–96.

Blom, Frans

1983   Cherchez La Femme Maya or Woman's Place among the Ancient Maya. In *Antropología e historia de la Mixe-Zoques y Maya: homenaje a Frans Blom*, Lorenza Ochoa y Thomas A. Lee Jr., editors, pp. 309–320. Universidad Nacional Autónoma-BYU, México.

Boone, Elizabeth H.

1999   The "Coatlicues" at the Templo Mayor. *Ancient Mesoamerica* 10:189–206.

Brumfiel, Elizabeth

2006   Methods in Feminist and Gender Archaeology: A Feeling of Difference—and Likeness. In *Handbook of Gender Archaeology*, Sarah Milledge Nelson, editor, pp. 31–58. Altamira Press, Walnut Creek, CA.

Brumfiel, Elizabeth, and Cynthia Robin

2008   Gender, Households, and Society. *Archaeological Papers of the American Anthropological Association* 18(1):1–16.

Burkhart, Louise M.

1989   *The Slippery Earth: Nahua–Christian Moral Dialogue in Sixteenth-Century Mexico*. University of Arizona Press, Tucson.

Ciaramella, Mary A.

1994   The Lady with the Snake Headdress. In *Seventh Palenque Round Table 1989*, Virginia M. Fields, editor, pp. 201–210. The Pre-Columbian Art Research Institute, San Francisco.

Clendinnen, Inga

1982   Yucatec Maya Women and the Spanish Conquest: Role and Ritual in
        Historical Reconstruction. *Journal of Social History* 15(3):427–442.

Coleman Simon, and John Elsner

1995   *Pilgrimage: Past and Present in the World Religions.* Harvard University
        Press, Cambridge, MA.

Curet, Antonio L., Barbara L. Stark, and Sergio Vasquez Z.

1994   Postclassic Change in South-Central Veracruz, Mexico. *Ancient Mesoamerica*
        5:13–32.

Dahlin, Bruce H., Anthony P. Andrews, Timothy Beach, Clara Bezanilla, Patrice Farrell,
Sheryl Luzzadder-Beach, and Valerie McCormick

1998   Punta Canbalam in Context: A Peripatetic Coastal Site in Northwest
        Campeche, Mexico. *Ancient Mesoamerica* 9:1–15.

De La Fuente, Beatriz, and Nelly Gutiérrez Solana

1980   *Escultura Huasteca en Piedra Catalogo.* Instituto de Investigaciones Estéticas
        Universidad Nacional Autónoma de México, Ciudad Universitaria, México
        D.F.

Dowler, Lorraine, Josephine Carubia, and Bonj Szczygiel

2005   Introduction: Gender and Landscape: Renegotiating Morality and Space.
        In *Gender and Landscape*, Lorraine Dowler, Josephine Carubia and Bonj
        Szczygiel, editors, pp. 1–16. Routledge, New York.

Drucker, Philip

1943   *Ceramic Stratigraphy a Cerro de Las Mesas Veracruz, Mexico.* Bureau of
        American Ethnology Bulletin 141.

Du Solier, Wilfrido

1943   A Reconnaissance on Isla de Sacrificios, Veracruz, Mexico. *Notes on Middle
        American Archaeology and Ethnology* 14:63–80. Carnegie Institution of
        Washington, Washington, DC.

Ehrenreich, Barbara, and Deirdre English

2010   *Witches, Midwives, and Nurses: A History of Women Healers.* The Feminist
(1973) Press, New York.

Estrada Quevedo, Alberrto

1962   Neyolmelahualiztli—acción de enderezar los corazones. *Estudios de Cultura
        Náhuatl* 2:163–175.

Eyman, Frances

1965   American Indian Gaming Arrows and Stick Dice. *Expedition* 7(4):39–47.

Gailey, Christine W.

1988   State Formation and Uneven Development. In *State and Society:
        the Emergence and Development of Social Hierarchy and Political
        Centralization*, John Gledhill, Barbara Bender, and Mogens Trolle Larsen,
        editors, pp. 77–90. Unwin Hyman, London.

Galloway, Patricia

1997   Where Have All the Menstrual Huts Gone? The Invisibility of Menstrual
        Seclusion in the Late Prehistoric Southeast. In *Women in Prehistory: North
        American and Mesoamerica*, Cheryl Claassen and Rosemary A. Joyce,
        editors, pp. 47–64. University of Pennsylvania Press, Philadelphia.

Garraty, Christopher P., and Barbara L. Stark

2002   Imperial and Social Relations in Postclassic South-Central Veracruz, Mexico. *Latin American Antiquity* 13(1):3–33.

Gillespie, Susan D.

2007   Toltecs, Tula, and Chichen Itza: The Development of an Archaeological Myth. In *Twin Tollans: Chichen Itza, Tula, and the Epiclassic to Early Postclassic Mesoamerican World*, C. Kristan-Graham and J. K. Kowalski, editors, pp. 84–127. Dumbarton Oaks, Washington, DC.

Gutiérrez Solana, Nelly, and Susan K. Hamilton

1977   *Las esculturas en terracota de El Zapotal, Veracruz.* Universidad Nacional Autónoma de México, México.

Hackett, Jo Ann

1989   Can a Sexist Model Liberate Us?: Ancient Near Eastern "Fertility" Goddesses. *Journal of Feminist Studies in Religion* 5(1):65–76.

Hanks, William

2010   *Converting Words: Maya in the Age of the Cross.* University of California Press, Berkeley.

Haraway, Donna J.

1991   *Simians, Cyborgs, and Women. The Reinvention of Nature.* Routledge, London.

Hendon, Julia A.

2006   The Engendered Household. In *Handbook of Gender in Archaeology*, Sarah Miledge Nelson, editor, pp. 171–199. Altamira Press, Walnut Creek, CA.

Hooton, Earnest

1940   Skeletons from the Cenote of Sacrifice at Chichén Itzá. In *The Maya and Their Neighbors: Essays on Middle American Anthropology and Archaeology*, C. L. Hay, R. Linton, S. K. Lothrop, H. Shapiro, and G. C. Vaillant, editors, pp. 272–280. Apple Century, New York.

Joyce, Rosemary A.

2006   Gender and Mesoamerican Archaeology. In *Handbook of Gender Archaeology*, Sarah Miledge Nelson, pp. 785–811. Altamira Press, Walnut Creek, CA.

2008   *Ancient Bodies, Ancient Lives: Sex, Gender and Archaeology.* Thames and Hudson, New York.

Joyce, Thomas A.

1912   *A Short Guide to the American Antiquities in the British Museum.* Oxford University Press, Oxford.

1970   *Mexican Archaeology.* Hacker Art Books, New York.
[1914]

Kidder, Alfred

1943   *Spindle Whorls from Chichén Itzá, Yucatan.* Notes on Middle American Archaeology and Ethnology, No. 16. Carnegie Institution of Washington, Washington DC.

Klein, Cecilia

2000   The Devil and the Skirt: An Iconographic Inquiry into the Pre-Hispanic Nature of the Tzitzimime. *Ancient Mesoamerica* 11:1–26.

Kubler, George

1985   Pre-Columbian Pilgrimages in Mesoamerica. In *Fourth Palenque Round Table, 1980*, Elizabeth P. Benson, editor, pp. 313–316. Pre-Columbian Art Research Institute, San Francisco.

Lamphere, Louise

2005   The Domestic Sphere of Women and the Public World of Men: The Strengths and Limitations of an Anthropology Dichotomy. In *Gender in Cross-Cultural Perspective*, Caroline B. Brettell and Carolyn F. Sargent, editors, pp. 86–94. Pearson, Upper Saddle River, NJ.

Leacock, Eleanor

1978   Women's Status in Egalitarian Society. Implications for Social Evolution. *Current Anthropology* 19(2):247–275.

Livingston, James C.

2005   *Anatomy of the Sacred. An Introduction to Religious Studies.* 5th Edition. Pearson, Prentice Hall, Upper Saddle River, NJ.

McCafferty, Geoffrey G., and Sharisse D. McCafferty

1991   Spinning and Weaving as Female Gender Identity in Post-Classic Mexico. In *Textile Traditions of Mesoamerica and the Andes: an Anthology*, Margot Blum Schevill, Janet Catherine Berlo, and Edward B. Dwyer, editors, pp. 19–44. Garland, New York.

1999   The Metamorphosis of Xochiquetzal: A Window on Womanhood in Pre- and Post-conquest Mexico. In *Manifesting Power: Gender and the Interpretation of Power in Archaeology*, Tracy L. Sweely, editor, pp. 103–126. Routledge, NY.

2000   Textile Production in Postclassic Cholula, Mexico. *Ancient Mesoamerica* 11:39–54.

McEwan, Colin

1994   *Ancient Mexico in the British Museum.* The British Museum Press, London.

2009   *Ancient American Art in Detail.* The British Museum Press, London.

McLellan, David

1995   *Ideology.* 2nd Edition. University of Minnesota, Minneapolis.

Medellín Zenil, Alfonso

1955   *Exploraciones en La Isla de Sacrificios. Informe.* Gobierno del Estado de Veracruz, Jalapa, Veracruz.

Miller, Mary E.

2005   Rethinking Jaina: Goddesses, Skirts, and the Jolly Roger. *Record of the Art Museum* 64:63–70.

Molina, Fray Alonso de

1970   Vocabulario en lengua castellana y mexicana y mexicana y castellana. Facsimile of 1571 edition. Introduction by Miguel Leon-Portilla. Editorial Porrúa, Mexico.

Neilsen, Jesper

2006   The Queen's Mirrors: Interpreting the Iconography of Two Teotihuacan Style Mirrors from the Early Classic Margarita Tomb at Copan. *PARI Journal* Vol. XI (4). http://www.precolumbia.org/pari/index.html. Accessed March 4, 2012.

Nepean, Evan, and Samuel Birch

1843   *Mexican Antiquities from the Island of Sacrificios, from excavations made in the year 1840, by Captain Evan Nepean, whilst in command of H.M. Ship Comus.* J. B. Nicholas and Son, London.

Nicholson, H. B.
1971   Religion in Pre-Hispanic Central Mexico. In *Handbook of Middle American Indians*, Robert Wauchope, Gordon F. Ekholm, and Ignacio Bernal, editors, 92–134. University of Texas Press, Austin.

Nunez Ortega, Angel
1885   Varios Papeles sobre Cosas de Mexico. In *Apuntes históricos sobre la rodela azteca: conservada en el Museo nacional de Mexico*. Bruselas. Gustavo Mayolez, editor.

Nuttall, Zelia
1910   The Island of Sacrificios. *American Anthropologist* 12(2):257–295.

Patel, Shankari U.
2009   Religious Resistance and Persistence at Cozumel. In *Maya Worldview at Conquest*, Timothy W. Pugh and Leslie G. Cecil, editors, pp. 205–218. University Press of Colorado, Boulder.

Phillips, David A.
1979   Material Culture and Trade of the Postclassic Maya. Doctoral dissertation. Department of Anthropology, University of Arizona, Tucson.

Pohl, John M. D.
1999   The Lintel Paintings of Mitla and the Function of the Mitla Palaces. In *Mesoamerican Architecture as a Cultural Symbol*, Jeff Karl Kowalski, editor. Oxford University Press, Oxford.

Pohl, John M. D., and Bruce E. Byland
1990   Mixtec Landscape Perception and Archaeological Settlement Patterns. *Ancient Mesoamerica* 1(1):113–131.

Pyburn, K. Anne
2004   Rethinking Complex Society. In *Ungendering Civilization*, K. A. Pyburn, editor, pp. 1–46. Routledge, NY.

Ringle, William
2004   On the Political Organization of Chichen Itza. *Ancient Mesoamerica* 15(2):167–218.

Ringle, William, Tomás Gallareta Negrón, and George J. Bey
1998   The Return of Quetzalcoatl: Evidence for the Spread of a World Religion during the Epiclassic Period. *Ancient Mesoamerica* 9:183–232.

Ríos Meneses, Miriam Beatriz
1988   Centro Prehispánico, Religioso y Comercial de los Mayas. In *Cozumel: Un Encuentro en Historia*. Eva Saavedra Silva, y Jorge Sobrino Sierra, coordinadores, pp. 62–67. Fondo de Publicaciones y Ediciones de Quintana Roo.

Robin, Cynthia
2002   Gender and Farming at Chan Noohol, Belize. In *Ancient Maya Women*, Traci Ardren, editor, pp. 12–30. Altamira Press, Walnut Creek, CA.

Robles Castellanos, Fernando
2010   Interaction between Central and Eastern Mesoamerica before and during the Culhua Mexica Expansion. In *Astronomers, Scribes, and Priests: Intellectual Interchange between the Northern Maya Lowlands and Highland Mexico in the Late Postclassic Period*, Gabrielle Vail and Christine Hernandez, editor, pp. 37–76. Dumbarton Oaks, Washington DC.

Rosaldo, Michelle Z.

1974   Theoretical Overview. In *Woman, Culture, and Society*, edited by Michelle Z.
          Rosaldo and Louise Lamphere, pp. 17–43. Stanford University Press, Stanford.

Rosaldo, Michelle Z., and Louise Lamphere

1974   *Woman, Culture and Society*. Stanford University Press, Stanford, CA.

Sahagun, Fray Bernardino

1958   *Florentine Codex: General History of the Things of New Spain*, Arthur J. O.
  –1982   Anderson and Charles E. Dibble, translators. School of American Research,
          Santa Fe, NM.

Scholes, France V., and E. B. Adams

1938   *Don Diego Quijada, Alcalde Mayor de Yucatan*, 1561-65, 2 vols. Biblioteca
          Histórica Mexicana Vols. 14–15, Mexico.

Scholes, France V., and Ralph L. Roys

1968   *The Maya Chontal Indians of Acalan-Tixchel: A Contribution to the History*
  [1948]   *and Ethnography of the Yucatan Peninsula*. University of Oklahoma Press,
          Norman.

Schroeder, Susan, Stephanie Wood, and Robert Haskett (editors)

1997   *Indian Women of Early Mexico*. University of Oklahoma Press, Norman.

Serra Puche, Mari Carmen

2001   The Concept of Feminine Places in Mesoamerica: The Case of Xochitécatl,
          Tlaxcala, Mexico. In *Gender in Pre-Hispanic America*, Cecilia Klein, editor.
          Dumbarton Oaks, Washington, DC.

Smith, Andrea

2009   Rape and War against Native Women. In *Gender, Sex, and Sexuality*, Abby L.
          Ferber, Kimberly Holcomb, and Tre Wentling, editors, pp. 363—371. Oxford
          University Press, Oxford.

Smith, Michael E., and Frances F. Berdan (editors)

2003   *The Postclassic Mesoamerican World*. University of Utah Press, Salt Lake City.

Spinden, Ellen S.

1933   The Place of Tajin in Totanac Archaeology. *American Anthropologist*
          35(2):225–270.

Stark, Barbara L.

2001   *Classic Period Mixtequilla, Veracruz, Mexico: Diachronic Inferences from
          Residential Investigations*. Institute for Mesoamerican Studies Monograph
          12, University of Albany, Albany, NY.

Stark, Barbara L., and L. Antonio Curet

1994   The Development of the Classic Period Mixtequilla in South-Central
          Veracruz, Mexico. *Ancient Mesoamerica* 5:267–287.

Stark, Barbara L., Lynette Heller, Michael A. Ohnersorgen

1998   Mesoamerican Economic Change from the Perspective of Cotton in South-
          Central Veracruz. *Latin American Antiquity* 9(1):7–36.

Strebel, Hermann

1885–89 *Alt-Mexico. Archaologische Beitrage zur Kulturgeschichte seiner Beiwohner*,
          2 vols. Hamburg u Leipzig, Leopold Voss.

Sullivan, Thelma D.

1982   Tlazolteotl-Ixcuina: The Great Spinner and Weaver. In *The Art and
          Iconography of Late Post-Classic Central Mexico*, Elizabeth Hill Boone,

editor, pp. 7–36. Dumbarton Oaks, Trustees for Harvard University, Washington DC.

Taube, Karl A.

1992 *The Major Gods of Ancient Yucatan.* Studies in Pre-Columbian Art and Archaeology 32. Dumbarton Oaks Research Library and Collection, Washington DC.

2010 At Dawn's Edge: Tulum, Santa Rita and Floral Symbolism of Late Postclassic Yucatan. In *Astronomers, Scribes, and Priests: Intellectual Interchange between the Northern Maya Lowlands and Highland Mexico in the Late Postclassic Period,* Gabrielle Vail and Christine Hernandez, editors, pp. 145–191. Dumbarton Oaks, Washington, DC.

2011 In Search of Paradise: Religion and Cultural Exchange in Early Postclassic Mesoamerica. Paper presented at the Tercero Congreso Internacional de Cultural Maya, Merida, Yucatan.

Thompson, J. Eric S.

1970 *Maya History and Religion.* University of Oklahoma Press, Norman.

Tiesler, Vera

2005 What Can the Bones Really Tell Us? The Study of Human Skeletal Remains from Cenotes. In *Stone Houses and Earth Lords. Maya Religion in a Cave Context,* Keith M. Prufer and James E. Brady, editors, pp. 341–363. University of Colorado Press, Boulder.

Torquemada, Fray Juan de

1975 *De los veinte y un libros rituales y monarquía Indiana, con el origen y*
–1983 *guerras de los indios occidentales, de sus poblazones, descubrimiento, conquista, conversión y otras cosas maravillosas de la mesma tierra.* 7 vols. Universidad Nacional Autónoma de Mexico, México.

Tozzer, Alfred M.

1941 *Landa's Relación de la Cosas de Yucatán, a Translation.* Papers of the Peabody Museum of Archaeology and Ethnology 33. Harvard University, Cambridge, MA.

Vail, Gabrielle, and Christine Hernandez

2010 Astronomers, Scribes, and Priests: An Introduction. In *Astronomers, Scribes, and Priests: Intellectual Interchange between the Northern Maya Lowlands and Highland Mexico in the Late Postclassic Period,* Gabrielle Vail and Christine Hernandez, editors, pp. 17–36. Dumbarton Oaks, Washington DC.

Van Gennep, Arnold

1960 *The Rites of Passage.* University of Chicago Press, Chicago.
[1909]

Ventur, Pierre

1980 A Comparative Perspective on Native American Mortuary Games of the Eastern Woodlands. *Man in the Northeast* 20:77–100.

Weedon, Chris

1999 *Feminism, Theory and the Politics of Difference.* Blackwell, Oxford.

Westling, L. H.

1996 *The Green Beast of the New World: Landscape, Gender, and American Fiction.* University of Georgia Press, Athens.

Wilkerson, Jeffrey K.

1987   Cultural Time and Space in Ancient Veracruz. In *Ceremonial Sculpture of Ancient Veracruz*, Marilyn M. Goldstein, editor, pp. 7–17. Long Island University, New York.

INDEX